Readings in International Economics

Selected Writings of Prof. Kishore G. Kulkarni

Readings in International Economics

Selected Writings of Prof. Kishore G. Kulkarni

PROF. KISHORE G. KULKARNI
Professor of Economics
Metropolitan State College of Denver
Denver, Colorado, USA
Editor: Indian Journal of Economics and Business
(visit: www.ijeb.com)

2011

SERIALS PUBLICATIONS
New Delhi (INDIA)

First Published-2004, Second Edition 2007, Third Edition 2011

ISBN: 978-81-8387-499-1

SERIALS PUBLICATIONS
4830/24, Prahlad Street, Ansari Road
Darya Ganj, New Delhi-110002 (India)
Phone : 23245225. Fax : 91-11-23272135
E-mail: serials@sify.com

This Edition is dedicated, for his 25 years of cheerful professional co-operation, to Prof. John P. Cochran, Dean, School of Business, Metropolitan State College of Denver.

CONTENTS

PREFACE

Over the last 30 years, I am fortunate to have published more than 100 journal articles, many of them on Indian Economics and most of them on International Economics. In numerous classes I taught on International Economics, we used several of these articles and referenced to numerous others. In 2002 Mr. S.K. Jha of Serials Publications, Delhi, suggested that we publish some selected articles in a book form. I think the present book includes some of the most applied and relevant pieces of my work which can be used in all types of International Economics courses, including, but not limited to B.A., B. Com., M.A., M.Com and Ph.D. courses in Indian universities and B.A., M.A. and Ph.D. courses in universities abroad.

The book is arranged with a wide ranging subject areas such as the International Monetary Flows, International trade and Economic Development, Twin Deficits, Dutch Disease, Purchasing Power Parity Theory, J-Curve Hypothesis, Monetary Approach to BOP and Gold Standard Analysis. Students will find the applied part most encouraging and quite adaptable for their own research. While the theoretical principles are well summarized in each of these chapters, there is an application to the real world situations in most of these studies. Hopefully there will be new chapters added in the future editions. I would love to hear from the readers with their suggestions for improvement in this collection at my e-mail address *kulkarnk@mscd.edu.*

I thank Serials Publication for the timely publication of this book and all the help they have offered for my other ventures such as the publication of the Indian Journal of Economics and Business (IJEB)

(*Visit: www.ijeb.com*). My sincere thanks to Ms. Meg Hendricks, Mr. Jeremy Gilmore, Ms. Tressie Weide, Mr. Timothy Gerrells, Mr. Matt Bates and Mr. William Warfel for the help in reading proofs of this document. I am truly obliged to all the co-authors who not only agreed to do a project with me but also have been of a great help in getting these articles published. I have acknowledged the help for each chapter, but if someone is inadvertently missed, I apologize. I thank my family members for their patience, especially my wonderful wife of 30 years, Jayashree, and our outstanding student athlete daughters, Dr. Lina (orthodontics) and Aditi.

Kishore G. Kulkarni
Denver, Colorado, USA

1

EARLY DAYS

SECTION - 1

MERCANTILISTS AND PARTIAL VIEW OF INERNATIONAL TRADE

In this chapter we discuss the early trade theories, basically of the 16th and 17th centuries, as well as the Ricardian model of comparative advantage. In the early days, thoughts about trade were presented in disorganized, scattered pamphlets and booklets that were published by a group of economists popularly called mercantilists. Since mercantilists did not have their arguments systematically assembled, their exact ideas about international trade are at times unique and varied (if not illogical), however, there are several common concepts usually associated with the writings of the mercantilists which we will address here. Mercantilists viewed international trade in terms of economic nationalism. The benefits of trade were to be enjoyed by the country that exported more and imported less because being a net exporter meant that gold was flowing into the country. The pursuit of gold was deemed imperative as the general belief was that survival of a kingdom depended on the ability to spend increasingly on defense. Because a King (or any other ruler) could increase the money supply only through exports, increasing defense expenditures required that a country exports more than it imported.

Mercantilist economics may have made sense for specific countries' economic growth during the period that it was popular. However, it is easy to see why the fundamental principles of mercantilism cannot be applied to a majority of countries. From an international perspective, when one country is forcing improvement in its exports, there has to be another country (or countries) that is (are) accepting increases in its (their) level of imports. Naturally, policies of increasing exports while decreasing imports cannot be successfully pursued by all. Mercantilists failed to understand this, partly because they were more concerned with one country's economic growth rather than the international community's welfare change resulting from trade. The first significant criticism of mercantilist theory was put forward by David Hume in 1752. According to Hume, mercantilists were wrong to emphasize exports alone and ignore the use of the exports, namely financing imports. Hume insisted that economic growth is dependent on international trade and that international trade should concern itself with imports as well as exports of goods and services.

SECTION - II

ADAM SMITH AND ABSOLUTE ADVANTAGE THEORY

Naturally, mercantilist's emphasis on exports is a problematic nationalistic and also erroneous economic argument. In the later part of the 18th century, Adam Smith would pioneer a new age of economics, formulating the foundations of the argument for free trade. According to Smith, international trade is beneficial because countries have an absolute advantage in the production of certain commodities. For instance, when a country has a vast endowment of labor, there is a good possibility that labor intensive productions, like agriculture, are produced more efficiently in that country than any other commodities. If a labor abundant country producing agricultural commodities, produces more than is sufficient for the needs of the domestic population, then this country can benefit by exporting the surplus production to other countries. In this case, the exporting country has an absolute advantage in the production of agricultural goods relative to the importing country.

Smith's theory of absolute advantage further demonstrated that there can be a mutual benefit of international trade when a country has an absolute advantage in a commodity. He argued that in a two-countries, two-good world, one country may have higher efficiency in the production of one good while another country may have higher efficiency in the production of the other good. In this case, international trade would be mutually beneficial. A country should export that commodity in which labor has the higher absolute efficiency (and import the one in the production of which her labor has lower absolute efficiency). For example, if Mexico can produce coconuts with a lower labor cost than the U.S., and if the U.S. can produce wheat at a lower labor cost than Mexico, then the U.S. should export wheat to Mexico and import coconuts from Mexico. This exchange would benefit both countries and increase overall global welfare.

Another way to visualize the concept of absolute advantage is shown in Table 1. Assume that there are two countries, A and B, and two goods, X and Y, which are both produced in each country. Table 1 shows us that in country A, one unit of labor produces 10 units of good X and 20 units of good Y while in country B, one unit of labor can produce 15 units of good X and 10 units of good Y. In this case, the labor in country A has an absolute advantage in the production of good Y and in country B labor has an absolute advantage in the production of good X. Therefore, both countries would benefit if country A's labor produces more of good Y and exports it to country B and country B's labor produces more of good X and exports it to country A.

Table 1
One Unit of Labor Produces

	Country A	*Country B*
Good X	10	15
Good Y	20	10

By understanding the cost structure of certain products and recognizing disparate labor efficiencies between countries, Adam Smith was the first to propose the mutual benefits of "free-trade" between countries. Smith paved the way for a more systematic approach to the analysis of the benefits of trade which would be developed in the early 19th century by the great economist, David Ricardo. Adam Smith failed to address the consequences of international trade when cost structures are such that one country has absolute advantage (or lower absolute cost) in the production of multiple goods relative to another country. Absolute advantage theory examines exclusively the trade implications when the cost of production is higher for one good and lower for another good between countries. It does not address a situation where one country has lower absolute costs in both productions than the costs of another country in the same productions. Ricardo, however, was able to show that trade can benefit both countries even when one country's labor has absolute advantage in the production of both goods considered.

SECTION - III

DAVID RICARDO AND THE COMPARATIVE ADVANTAGE THEORY

David Ricardo has made several important contributions to economics such as the important idea of rent. Here we will examine his analysis of the benefits of international trade when one country has an absolute advantage in the production of both goods traded. In 1817, Ricardo published "Principles of Political Economy and Taxation". In it, he argued that international trade is almost always beneficial for all countries involved; even countries that do not have an absolute advantage in the production of a good can have a comparative advantage in that production, relative to other countries. In order to fully examine the comparative advantage theory, we must first look at the assumptions upon which the theory is built.

- First, the theory assumes a world of only two goods; good X and good Y, two countries; country A and country B, and only one factor of production, labor. Because only one factor of production was assumed, the cost of production was equivalent to the wage offered in those countries. This assumption made sense in Ricardo's era as most production was primarily labor intensive, land was abundant, capital was not scaree and technological innovations were not yet evident.
- Secondly, the theory assumes that there was perfect competition in the product market, meaning that the prices of the goods were assumed to be constant. Under perfect competition, since there are numerous suppliers and free entry/exit for firms into the industry, the price of a product is not only constant but also equal to its cost of production.
- The third assumption Ricardo made was that labor productivity for specific goods was different in different countries. Therefore, the labor suppliers decided the wage rate, which in turn decided the cost of production, and the cost of production decided the prices of the specific outputs.
- The fourth assumption was that between the two countries, free trade of goods was permitted. There were no transportation costs, no other barriers to free trade and the labor in both countries was homogeneous in nature (one labor unit is the same in both countries).
- The fifth assumption was constant cost conditions. This means that an increase in input, of a certain percentage increase output by the same percentage at all levels of outputs. Due to this simplifying assumption, the marginal productivity of labor, at all levels of its employment, is the same. As a consequence of a constant marginal product, the production possibility curve (PPC) of a country becomes a straight line.

You may recall that the production possibility curve is the locus of combinations of two goods the economy can produce by using all its resources. When all resources are used up, the increase in the production of one good has to be made through a sacrifice in the production of another good. The reduction in the production of the other good is called an opportunity cost. By assuming constant cost conditions, the opportunity cost is assumed to be constant at all levels of production. This is reflected into the PPCs of Figures 1 and 2.

Due to constant costs, with an increase in labor employment in either good's production, the marginal productivity of labor stays the same. Therefore, in order to

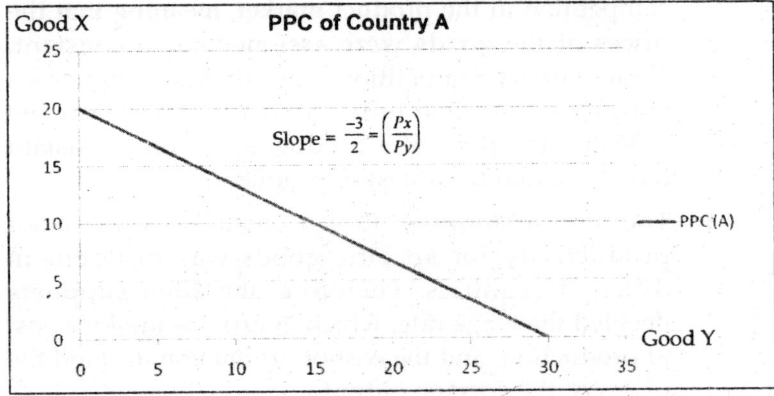

Figure 1

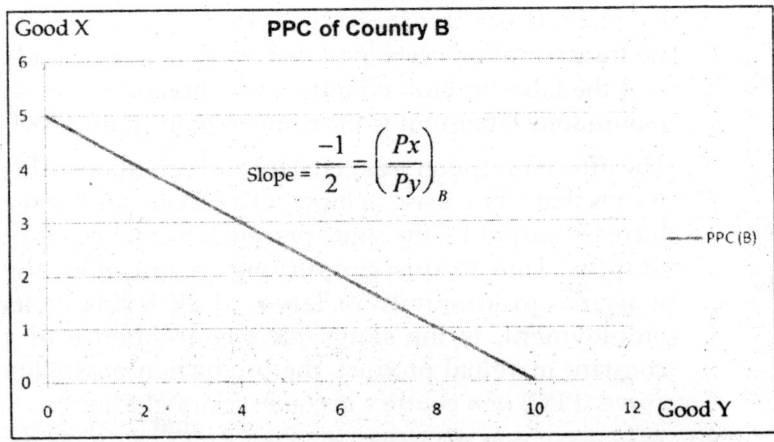

Figure 2

increase the production of one good, the "price" (or opportunity cost) the country pays in terms of the reduction in the production of the other good is constant at all times. If the opportunity cost is constant, then the slope of the PPC has to be constant and the PPC will be a straight line. More information about concavity of PPCs is given in Chapter 3.

With these assumptions, let us examine a theoretical situation outlined in Table 2. In country A, one unit of labor can produce 20 units of good X or 30 units of good Y. While one unit of labor in country B can produce 10 units of good X or 5 units of good Y.

Table 2
One Unit of Labor Produces

	Country A	*Country B*
Good X	20	10
Good Y	30	5

Observe that country A has an absolute advantage in the production of both goods X and Y. Therefore, Adam Smith's theory of absolute advantage would have suggested that trade between A and B would be impossible and non-beneficial to either party. Adam Smith would have thought that country A was more efficient in both goods; therefore, no need for trade between A and B.

David Ricardo however, was able to show that even country A could benefit from international trade in goods it had absolute advantage. According to the law of comparative advantage, even if one nation is more efficient in the production of both commodities, there is still a basis for mutually beneficial trade. The argument is as follows: Country A will find out that its labor is comparatively more efficient in the production of good Y than in the production of good X. This is because country A has a lower comparative cost of production for good Y than for good X. To demonstrate, observe that the cost of good X is equal to $3/2$ of good Y in country A (which is the same as saying the cost of one unit of good Y is equal to $\frac{2}{3}$ units of good X in country A). However, in country B the cost of one unit of good X is equal to one-half unit of good Y, while one unit of good Y is equal to two units of good X. Therefore, the cost of good X is comparatively less in country A than in country B. As a result, country A will be happy to trade good Y for good X from country B (country A will export good Y and import good X).

Now we must decide the exact exchange rate between good X and good Y in these countries. To determine this, we need to calculate the relative labor costs in country A and country B. To do this, observe the following:

Suppose, L(A) = Total labor units available in country A

L(B) = Total labor units available in country B

a(XA) = Labor necessary to produce one unit of good X in country A

a(YA) = Labor necessary to produce one unit of good Y in country A

Similarly we can define a(XB) and a(YB) for country B. Under full employment conditions,

$$L(A) = a(XA) \bullet X(0) + a(YA) \bullet Y(0) \tag{1}$$

Where X(0) and Y(0) are quantities of good X and good Y respectively.

Equation 1 specifies the production possibilities curve (PPC) of country A. If we solve it for the amount Y, then we get

$$Y(0) = \frac{a(XA)}{a(YA)} * X(0).$$

In this equation, notice that the Y axis intercept of this straight line PPC is the first term on the right hand side and the slope of this PPC is the ration of $a(XA)/a(YA)$. We can show that this slope is the same as the ratio of prices in the economy $P(X)/P(Y)$. With a constant stock of labor (L(A) = constant total labor supply), the total differentiation of equation 1 yields:

$$a(XA) * dX(0) + a(YA) * dY(0) = 0$$

$$\text{Or } \frac{a(XA)}{a(YA)} = \frac{dY(0)}{dX(0)}$$

In competitive conditions, prices are determined by marginal costs of products, hence we get:

$$P(XA) = a(XA) * W(A) \qquad (2)$$

$$\text{And } P(YA) = a(YA) * W(A) \qquad (3)$$

where P(XA) and P(YA) are prices of good X and good Y respectively in country A. A constant and identical wage rate in both productions is assumed to be W(A) in country A. (In similar terms P(XB) and P(YB) and W(B) can also be expressed.)

Dividing equation 2 by equation 3 we get,

$$\frac{P(XA)}{P(YA)} = \frac{a(XA)}{a(YA)} \qquad (4)$$

This is an important result because it expresses the ratio of prices of products determined by the labor requirements in the production of goods X and Y. In symmetrical fashion, price ratio in country B is expressed as:

$$\frac{P(XB)}{P(YB)} = \frac{a(XB)}{a(YB)}$$

Since the labor supplies in both countries (L(A) and L(B)) are different, the comparative labor requirements in the production of same goods in the two countries is different. Therefore, as long as

$$\frac{a(XB)}{a(YB)} \neq \frac{a(XA)}{a(YA)}$$

then trade is beneficial to both countries. The equilibrium price ratio is decided by the demand conditions. If demand conditions are such that the trade (or equilibrium) price ratio is close to the domestic price ratio of country A, the trade is less beneficial to country A. Figure 3 shows the relative importance of trade to country A and B.

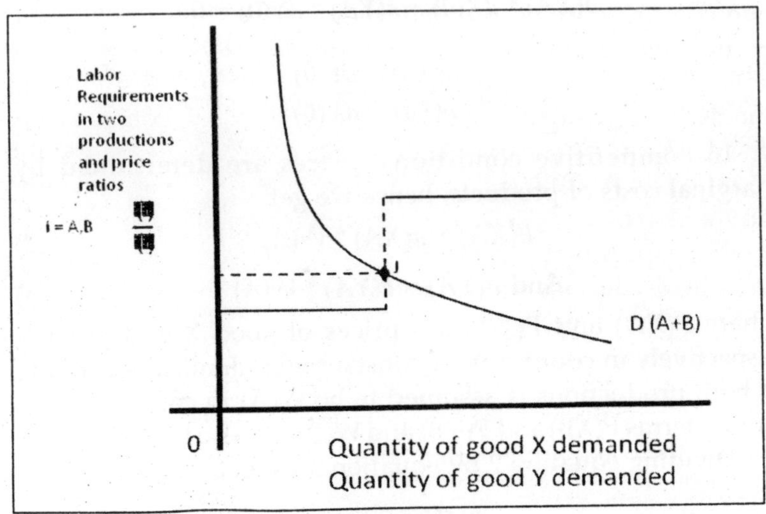

Figure 3

D(A+B) shows the combined demand curves of good X in relation to both countries. Point J determines the equilibrium trade price ratio. The closer this price ratio is to the domestic price ratio, the fewer gains from the trade for the country. This is because the trade does not offer any significantly different price or cost ratio so that the country is not much better off by engaging in trade.

Further developments in comparative advantage theory have concentrated in evaluating the necessity of the rigid assumptions made by Ricardo. It can be easily argued that all of the assumptions of Ricardian theory are not needed to conclude that international trade is dictated by comparative advantage. Consider, for example, the assumption of only two goods. It is easily illustrated that even if a country has more than two goods, then the Ricardian theory needs only a small modification. The theory of comparative advantage in the case of goods would dictate that the country would export all goods in the production of which it has the lower comparative cost and import all those in production of which it has higher comparative cost. Hence the assumption of only two goods is unnecessary for the conclusion of comparative advantage theory.

The second assumption of only two countries is not very necessary for the Ricardian conclusion either. When more than two countries are considered, they can be divided into two groups: one group of those countries that have comparative advantage in the production of one good over the other and the second group of the countries that have comparative disadvantage in the production of that good. Obviously the countries in the first group would export and specialize in the production of that good, and the countries in the second group would import that good.

Third, the assumption of labor as the only factor of production can easily be seen as a non-crucial assumption for the Ricardian conclusion of trade direction. When there are other factors of production present, the Ricardian argument can be transferred into the statement of average total comparative costs. Haberler (1936) has aptly concluded that the Ricardian principle can be stated as "a country would specialize in the production of a good that has lower comparative cost and would export the good to the rest of the world". The Ricardian conclusion remains unchanged even when we consider other factors of production besides labor.

The only assumption that needs a correction (and the one that leads to improvement of the Ricardian argument once corrected) is the assumption of constant costs. Because of this assumption, it becomes a natural conclusion in the faulty Ricardian argument that countries would completely specialize in the production in which they have comparative advantage. When constant costs are assumed, it is imperative that the increase in employment of the factors of production keeps on increasing the output proportionately and there is no stopping mechanism until complete specialization occurs. Hence a complete specialization is an unwanted and false conclusion of Ricardian argument because of the constant cost assumption. When this assumption is modified and replaced by a more realistic increasing cost (or diminishing marginal productivity) then the incomplete specialization can occur after trade. A country can therefore still produce both goods in the post trade period. As mentioned before, the modern trade theory recognizes this fact. The shape of the PPC in Ricardian theory is a straight line (because of the constant cost) while in the case of modern trade theory, it is concave to the origin (because of the increasing cost assumption).

Thus the Ricardian theoretical argument is so well structured and so conclusive that even when its assumptions are modified, it holds its conclusion. It is natural that several economic studies have used the comparative advantage argument to test its empirical evidence. One of the foremost studies of comparative advantage is the one carried out by MacDougall (1951). MacDougall used the data of 1937 and 26 industries in the U.S. and the U.K. He observed that the wages in the U.S. were twice as high as wages in the U.K. at the time, which meant that the costs would be lower in American industries in which the labor productivity is at least twice as great as the labor productivity in the U.K. In the industries where the U.S. labor productivity was greater than twice the labor productivity in the U.K., it is expected by the Ricardian theory that the export share of the U.S. would be higher than the export share of the U.K. for that product to the rest of the world. MacDougall observed that 22 out of 26 industries fulfilled the expectations of the Ricardian theory. Moreover, the Ricardian argument is logically so consistent that a country would naturally export the product in which it has a lower comparative cost. There is no other empirical evidence needed for such a strong conclusion.

Nonetheless, the Ricardian theory leaves one question unanswered, why do countries have comparative advantage in the first place? This means that Ricardo does an excellent job of explaining which commodity would be exported and imported by a country once it realizes its comparative advantage. In the next chapter our main interest is in the use of refined microeconomic tools to show the gains from international trade in Neo-classical theory.

2

NEOCLASSICAL MODEL OF FREE TRADE AND GAINS FROM TRADE

GAINS FROM INTERNATIONAL TRADE

For any modern economy, the need for international trade cannot be overemphasized. As technological improvements take place, the national demand for certain goods is completely satisfied at its competitive prices and there is still leftover quantity supplied. As the international demand for the good produced domestically grows faster than its overall supply, and as countries for political reasons or otherwise get interested each other's economic growth, the international trade is a logical result.

Common sense tells us that the very fact international trade and financial transactions have grown so fast in recent years is result of gains from such trades. If a free, voluntary trade is permitted, then two entities would not engage in trade unless both feel they have benefited from it. Hence, one does not need a very theoretical explanation of gains from trade. Nonetheless, a sound explanation for the gains from international trade, and the plausible identification of the increased welfare due to trade, can be made by observing standard microeconomic concepts.

SECTION-I

We shall use the basic principles of microeconomics to show gains from trade. However, before one understands the mechanism in which the international trade enhances the economic welfare, a clear understanding of internal general equilibrium of an economy must be reviewed.

For internal equilibrium, consider that an economy consists of only two major sectors, the consumer sector and the producer sector, and produces only two goods X and Y. For economic efficiency of the consumer sector, we need to have information about the community indifference curve (CIC hereafter) of that economy. Recall the typical definition of an indifference curve is the locus of combinations of two goods that yield the same satisfaction to the consumer. Also recall that the way there is a separate indifference curve for each level of satisfaction. This satisfaction from consumption is defined as utility. Hence for every indifference curve, there is a level of utility the community gets by consuming different combinations of those goods.

One of the important characteristics of CIC is that it is convex to the origin as shown in Figure 1. Convexity of the shape of CIC is observed because, as can be observed from Figure 1, the slope of this curve is negative, and the slope's value in absolute terms is declining as a movement from left to right on that curve. This slope of the CIC is called the marginal rate of substitution (MRS) between two goods, X and Y.

A good question to ask is, why is it the slope of CIC, namely MRS, as declining from left to right? An economic reason for this is given as Law of Dimishing Marginal Utility. This law, initially stated in the early nineteen hundreds, is summarized as: When a higher quantity of any normal good is consumed, then the utility derived from the last unit of its consumption, popularly called the marginal utility, declines. Hence for a normal good, with an increase in its consumption at any given time, the marginal utility decreases. Observe that the ratio of change in good Y to change in good X, that the slope of CIC is same as the ratio of the marginal utilities of good Y and X respectively. In an overall perspective, the slope of CIC is the ratio of marginal utility for good Y to marginal utility for good X, and also the Marginal rate of substitution (MRS).

The law of diminishing marginal utility has a worldwide application, and a very simple, logical justification. Apply the law of diminishing marginal utility to the consumption of a good, say apples. When a rational consumer consumes higher and higher quantity of apples, the marginal utility from the consumption of apple declines. This is because from every extra apple consumed, the consumer would receive lower and lower satisfaction, irrespective of how hungry he/she was at the beginning.

Let us see how the law of diminishing marginal utility is applied to explain the declining slope of CIC. Remember on the CIC, the total utility is constant. Hence, point A in Figure 1 "where the consumers have already consumed higher quantity of good Y, the marginal utility for good Yis low and the marginal utility for good Xis high. Therefore, to get any additional unit of good X for good Y, and to keep the same level of total utility, the consumers would like to have a higher quantity of good Y for a smaller quantity of good X. Hence MRS is, in absolute terms, large at point A. However, consider the situation at point C. The units consumed of good X are more than the units consumed of good Y at point C. Hence the

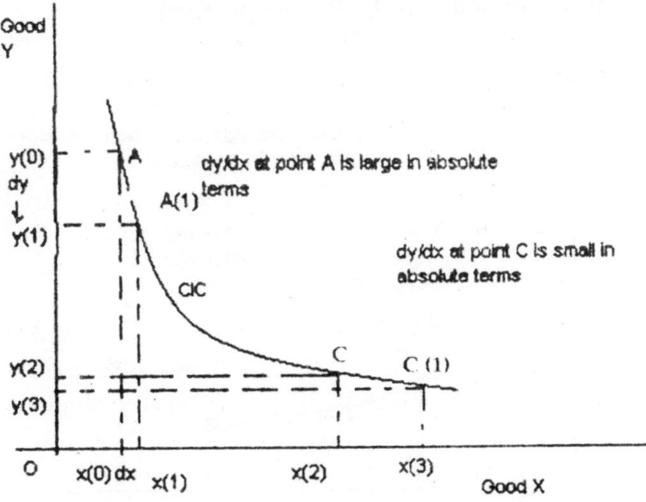

Figure 1: Community Indifference Cure (CICl

marginal utility for good X consumption is low and that of good Y is high. Therefore to trade one unit of good Y, we need several units of good X, to keep the same level of total satisfaction. Hence the absolute value of MRS is small at point C. Thus, as we consider a movement from point A to C on CIC in Figure 1, the absolute value of MRS declines.

Another characteristic of CICs is that the higher level of CIC shows a higher level of satisfaction and vice versa. This can be easily proved. Consider two CICs in Figure 2. Compare now two combinations of goods X and Y, one or each CIC. Clearly, point A on CIC1 shows a combination of two goods that has both quantities smaller than the combination of same two goods shown by point B on CIC2. Then it is obvious that combination of point B is preferable to combination of point A. Hence, CIC2 shows a higher level of satisfaction than CICl. (Notice that all other combinations on CIC1 show the same level of satisfaction as the combination of point A, and all other combinations on CIC2 show the same level of satisfaction as the combination of point B. Therefore, if we prove that point B's combinations shows a higher level of satisfaction than point A's combinations, then we do not have to prove it for any other combinations on CICI and CIC2 respectively.

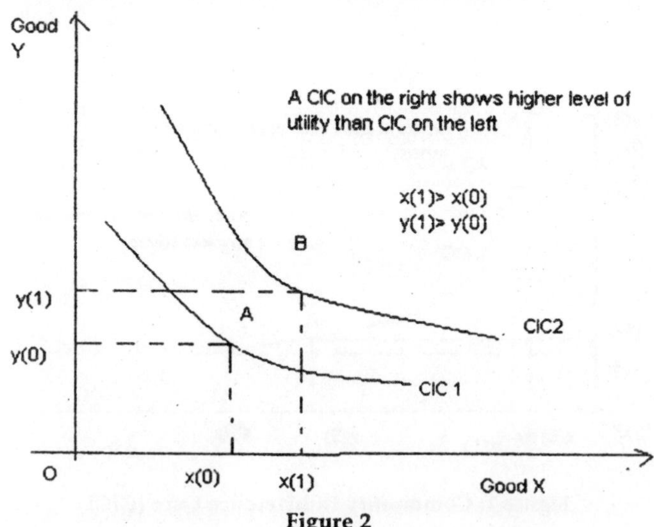

Figure 2

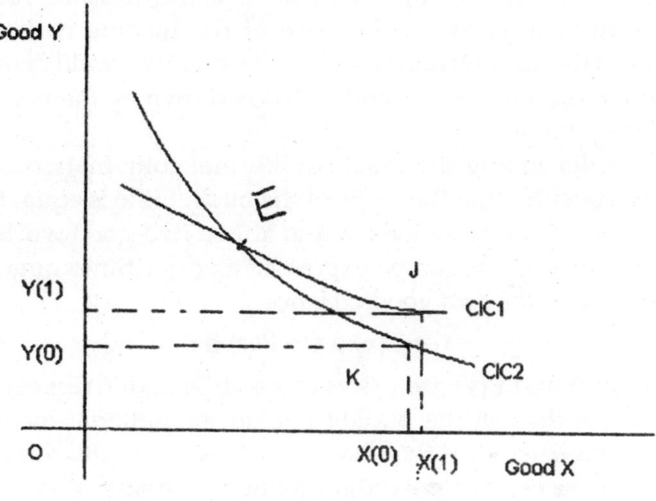

Figure 3

The third characteristic of CICs is that two CICs never intersect each other, or to put it differently, two CICs are always parallel to each other. This is not very hard to prove either. Consider for a moment the case of two CICs which intersect each other as in Figure 3. Consider also the combinations shown by the intersection point E and two other points J and K on each CIC. Since point and E are on the same CIC, they show combinations of goods X and Y that yield the same level of satisfaction. Similarly, since points K and E are on the same CIC, they also yield the same level of satisfaction. Hence we can conclude that combinations shown by points J and K also show the same level of satisfaction. However, this is clearly impossible, because point J shows higher quantities of both goods. Therefore it is safe to argue that two CICs are parallel to each other.

Consider now the fact that the total national income that can be consumed by consumers, is constant. The income line, popularly called, "the budget line" is given by the straight line Z in Figure 4. All the combinations of goods X and Y inside the budget line are plausible for the community to consume, but there is some income left after such consumption. All the points outside the budget line are impossible for the community to consume because of the income constraint. Hence in the equilibrium case, the community would consume a combination of good X and Y that is shown by the points on the budget line.

In order to find the exact equilibrium combination of two goods, consider that the slope of the budget line is equal to the ratio of prices of two goods, X and Y. In a two-good world, the national income, Y, can be expressed as price times quantities consumed of the two goods. Hence

$$Y = P(x).dX + P(y).dY \quad (1)$$

where P(x) and P(y) are prices of goods X and Y respectively. Observing that on the budget line all the national income is consumed, therefore the change in Y is zero, and assuming constant prices, the total differentiation of equation (1) is given as

$$P(x)dx + P(y)dy \quad (2)$$

Hence on the budget line, the ratio of change in good Y to change in good X is given as the ratio of price of good X to price of good Y. In equilibrium, the community would consume a combination of goods X and Y as given by point E in Figure 4.

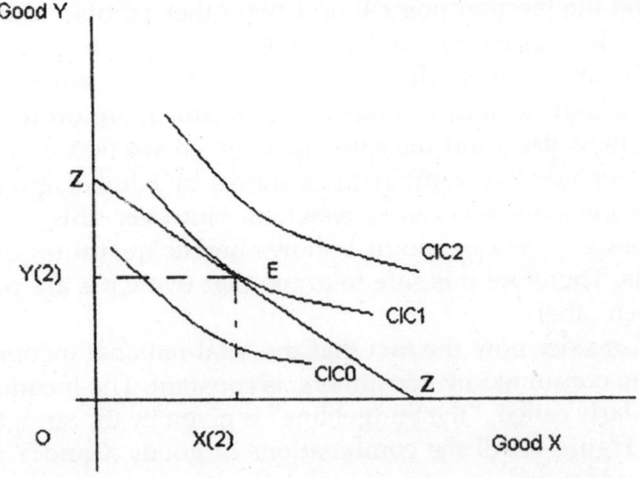

Figure 4: Consumer Equilibrium = CICs and Budget Line

At point E, the budget line is tangent to the CIC, or to put it differently, the slope of the budget line is equal to the slope of the CIC. But the slope of the budget line is the ratio of prices of goods X and Y, and the slope of CIC is the ratio of marginal utilities for goods X and Y respectively. Hence at point E the MRS, or the ratio of marginal utilities, is equal to the price ratio.

SECTION-II

EQUILIBRIUM ON THE PRODUCTION SIDE

To consider the equilibrium of the producer sector in an economy we need more information about the Production Possibilities Curve (PPC hereafter). Recall that the PPC is defined as the locus of combinations of goods X and Y that the economy would be able to produce by using all of its resources. All points inside the PPC are possible for an economy to produce, but they leave some resources unused, and the combinations shown by all points outside the PPC are impossible for the economy to produce by using the available resources. A typical PPC of an economy is shown in Figure 5. The shape of a non-linear PPC is concave to the origin which means that its slope is shown by the change in good X quantity required to have any change in good Y quantity produced. The PPC increases as we move from left to right. The slope of PPC is called marginal rate of transformation (MRT) between good X and Y on production side.

One good question is, why the slope of PPC increases as a movement on the PPC, from left to right, is considered? The economic answer to this question is hidden in the famous law of diminishing marginal productivity of a factor of production. Simply stated, this law tells us that when the employment of all factors of production is kept constant, and if the employment of one factor of production is increased, then the addition to the total product due to increased factor of production, popularly called the "marginal product" of that changeable factor of production declines.

An application of this law, is a case of a constant land, like the room you are sitting in, and constant machinery, like ten machines fitted in your room, and a constant knowledge of technology, (say each labores is equally talented, and does not improve or deteriorate his/her knowledge of the production process). Then consider an increase in employment of labor by sending in one labor unit through your room-door. The increase in total production by additional employment of labor (that is marginal product of labor) can be seen as declining, at least after some time. Thus, the law of diminishing marginal productivity has universal application. Now apply this law to two cases on the PPC at points A and B. At point A, a high quantity of good X has already been produced, hence a lot of factors of production units are already employed in it, whereas the marginal productivity in the production in good X is small. Therefore to have additional units of good Y produced, we need to release a lot of good X units. Remember that all resources are completely employed at all points on PPC, hence the additional production of good Y can occur only if a large quantity of good X is traded off, with small quantity of good Y at point A.

However, at point B a lot of units of good Y are already produced. Therefore the marginal productivity in production of good Y is low, and that of good X is high. Hence the large quantities of good Y have to be traded off to increase the production of good X at point B. Thus the slope of PPC increases in absolute terms when we consider a movement from left to right on it.

Our next interest is in finding out the equilibrium point of production for which we need information about the prices of the products, or their price ratio. This is given by the information of the budget line on the production side. This is a straight line that shows the combinations of good X and Y that can be produced by using the available income of the economy. This straight line is called the transformation line or budget line of producers. The slope of such a straight line on the graph represents the price ratio of goods X and Y. Given any price ratio, the economy in equilibrium would produce a combination of two goods shown by a point on PPC at which the price ratio line is tangent to the PPC. As can be seen in Figure 5, that point is point J, where slope of the tangent, namely price ratio, and the slope of the PPC, namely the marginal rate of transformation (MRT), are equal. Hence the production sector equilibrium requires that the MRT = prize ratio, and the consumption sector requires that MRS = price ratio. Therefore the overall equilibrium of the economy needs the condition of MRS = MRT = price ratio, to be fulfilled. This is done in Figure 5 at point J. This equilibrium stage is called the autarky equilibrium, or equilibrium without international trade.

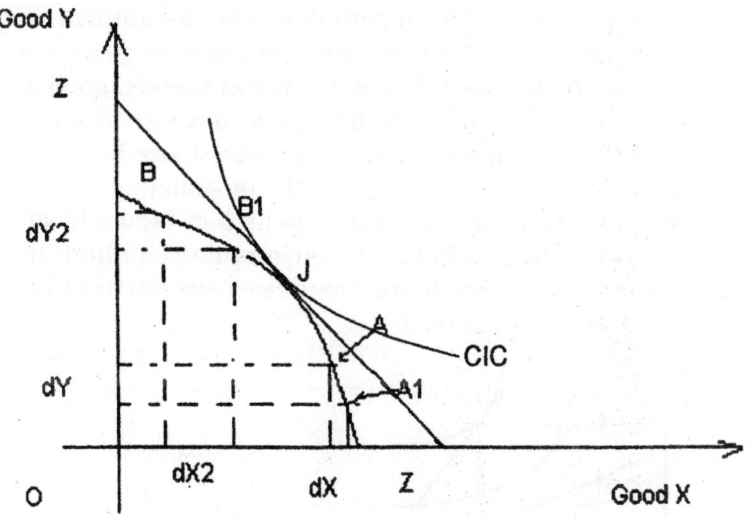

Figure 5: Production Possibility Curve (PPO and Budget Line

SECTION-III

OPEN ECONOMY AND THE GENERAL EQUILIBRIUM COMBINATION

When the economy is ready to be open (which means it is ready to deal with other economies via international trade) the equilibrium point of production and consumption would change. This is because the rest of the world would offer another price ratio of two goods, to the domestic economy.

With another price ratio that is different from the domestic price ratio, the economy would start producing and consuming different combinations than before. This would always happen unless the world price is exactly the same as the domestic price ratio, which is a very special case.

To find out the combination of two goods the economy would produce after trade, consider another price ratio line, (Px/Py)2, that is the world price ratio. In Figure 6, with this new price ratio the economy's production equilibrium is achieved at point K2. This happens due to our assumption that the world price ratio is steeper than the domestic price ratio. This is the same as saying that, in the world market, good X is more expensive than in the domestic market. Point K2 represents the production equilibrium after trade Recall that for production equilibrium we need the tangency of PPC and the price ratio line. The occurs at point K2 in Figure 6. With the new price ratio (Px/Py)2, the consumption equilibrium is achieved at point KI, where the new price ratio line is tangent to another CIC namely CIC3.

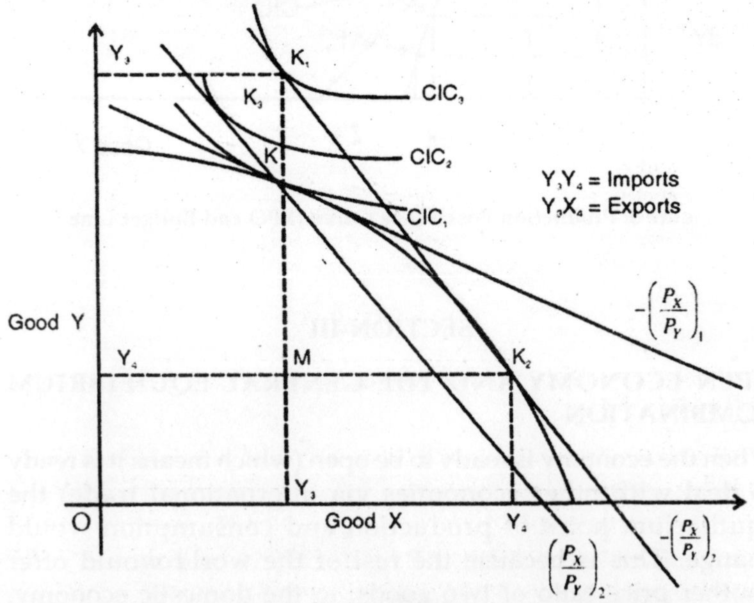

Figure 6: Gains from Trade: Exchange and Specialization

Hence the economy produces X4 and Y4 quantities of goods X and Y respectively, and consumes X3 and Y3 combination of goods X and Y respectively. The difference between production and consumption of these quantities would be the amount of export and imports of this economy. The next question is to find out whether there is any gain from this openness of the economy. Observe that with the consumption of higher quantity of one good and less quantity of the other, the economy has enhanced its welfare. It has started consuming the combination on a higher CIC, which shows an increase in its utility, therefore higher welfare. The movement from CIC1 to CIC3 is an increase in welfare for the economy, due to its readiness to enter into the international trade.

For convenience sake, on a conceptual basis, this total gain from trade is further divided into gains from exchange and gains from specialization. The gain from exchange is said to have occured when the economy is forced to produce the same production combination as before trade, and is allowed only to exchange goods with the rest of the world. In that case the economy would produce at point K, as under autarky and consume at point K3, where with the new price ratio CIC2 is tangent to the price ratio line. The gain from exchange is realized by observing an improvement in the welfare which is shown by the movement from CIC1 to CIC2 in Figure 6. The gain from specialization is observed by allowing the economy to change the production combination to one that maximizes its economic efficiency with the new price ratio. This is done at the point of tangency between the PPC and the new price ratio line at point K2 in Figure 6. With the production combination of K2, however, the consumption equilibrium is achieved at point KI, where the new price ratio line is tangent to another CIC namely CIC3. Hence the movement of welfare from CIC2 to CIC3 is called the gain from specialization. Overall, it is safely argued that due to trade the economy gains an increased welfare. In order to locate the exact quantities of consumption, production, and export and import of the commodities, consider the production and consumption equilibrium points.

To summarize, recall that after trade, the economy has its consumption equilibrium at the point where its budget line is tangent to CIC, and has its production equilibrium at a point where budget line is tangent to PPC. This occurs at points K1 and K2 respectively. At point K1, (X3, Y3) combination of good X and good Y is consumed and at point K2 (X4, Y4) combination of good X and good Y is produced. Hence the difference in higher production than consumption is exported while the difference between higher consumption than production is imported. In our case, the country exports X3X4 quantity of good X, and imports Y3Y4 quantity of good Y. The triangle KIMK2 is popularly called "Trade Triangle" for this country. Second, it is possible to determine which country would export which commodity, given the shape of its PPC. When the country has a PPC that has a larger value of an X axis intercept than the value of Y axis intercept, then that country would export good X and import good Y.

SECTION -IV

EQUILIBRIUM PRICE OF A COMMODITY IN INTERNATIONAL TRADE

Under free trade, it is possible to see that the excess supply of a commodity is equivalent to the export of it, and the excess demand for a commodity can be taken as the import of that commodity from the international market. For a given good, say good X, the price in the domestic market is Px and the price in the foreign market is Px*. Also suppose that Px* > Px as shown in Figure 7. At any price higher than Px, the domestic producers would supply the commodity in terms of exports to the rest of the world. Moreover, the price from Px, would be the quantity supplied by the domestic producers in the international market. Hence the export supply curve is upward sloping from left to right in Figure 7.

Similarly at any price lower than Px*, the foreign customers would demand-the good X in the international market in terms of their imports. Moreover, the price from Px*, would be the quantity imported. Thus, the import demand curve is downward sloping from left to right. At the point of

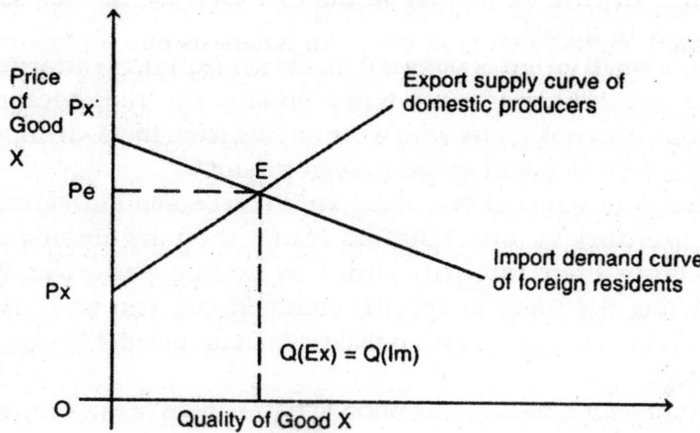

Figure 7: Equilibrium in International Trade: One Commodity Case

intersection of these two curves, the equilibrium price, Pe, and quantity of good X is defined. It is obvious that the location of point E depends clearly on the shapes and location of import demand and export supply curves. Nonetheless the simple demand and supply analysis can be used to show the equilibrium price and quantity of a good in the international market.

One good question about this analysis of gains from international trade is: "What are, if any, exceptions to them?" The second question is that: "Are there any sections of the domestic population that would feel (or actually be) worse off by opening the international trade with other economies?" One can always find a group of individuals (we call them supporters of protectionist policies) that complains about the bad effects from the foreign competition. There are some rational complaints on the basis of the welfare depletion of a specific group, even though it is very hard to prove theoretically, that the whole economy is worse off due to international trade. Given the fact that in international trade, the lower priced commodity is imported and the higher priced is exported, we can see that there are individuals who are net suppliers who find that the demand for their products is lower in case of free trade than in the case of a closed economy or autarky.

As a small group of population, the net suppliers can argue that their condition is much worse off after the trade because the domestic consumers who were buying from them, are now shifting their demand to the foreign products.

If it is recognized that there are in fact some individuals who are hurt by international trade, then arguments of protecting their interest, either by compensation or by restricting the trade in specific commodities, can be made. However the protectionist's policies we shall consider in future chapters.

Another interesting exception to the analysis of this chapter is seen in a special case when two countries export and import the same commodity, to and from each other, like the case of automobiles for the United States and Germany. It is easily observed that these two countries buy and sell each others cars that are made by both. This is called the case of intra-industry trade. For intra-industry trade to take place, three things are important: (1) There has to be enough excess supply of the commodity in both the countries: (2) There have to be two groups of individuals who would like to buy the products of each other: And (3) The product is slightly differentiated when produced in another country, so that it satisfies the needs of specific individuals. Given these conditions and the free trade, intra-industry trade is observed in several instances. However, these special issues will be discussed in the future chapters. In the next chapter our main interest is to concentrate on the early theories of international trade with special attention to Ricardian theory of comparative advantage.

3

HECKSCHER-OHLIN-SAMUELSON (H-O-S) THEOREM AND THE CASE OF THAILAND'S ECONOMIC CRISIS

INTRODUCTION

Over the years, Thailand has made great progress in instituting outward-oriented policies focusing more on export promotion (than on import restriction or substitution). A further opening of the economy, by increasing exposure of industry to international markets has made Thailand one of the world's fastest growing economies since the mid-1980's to 1996. The average real GDP growth of Thailand accounted for over 11.5% in 1986-1990 and moderated to 8% annual rate over 1990-1994. International trade has played an important role in the success of expanding Thailand's exports, making the growth rates between 14-28 percent, per year from 1990 until 1998.

However, in 1997 Thailand's economic growth was obstructed by an economic crisis due to a combination of a severe slowdown in export growth, followed by the appreciation of the US dollar against Baht, and a rising import bill and corruption in certain Thai banks. After 1999 the Thai economy slowly recovered as exports continued to grow, led rapidly by a significant growth of intra-industry trade with ASEAN countries.

This chapter is based on a co-authored paper with Mr. Jiraporn Wajawuth in Indian Journal of Social and Economic Policy (2004).

The focus of this chapter is to explore the effect of trade on the Thai economy by concentrating on the case of how the international trade partly caused a slowdown in the export sector and became a trigger of the crisis in 1997. In the first part, this paper presents a model conforming to the H-O theorem, and discusses the Samuelson Theorem of factor price equalization. In the second section, we describe the application of this model to the case of the economic crisis in Thailand. Further, this paper discusses the recovery of the economy after the crisis including the future of trade in Thailand.

SECTION - I

HECKSCHER-OHLIN-SAMUELSON THEOREM

Unlike the Ricardian model of comparative advantage, which assumes only one factor of production-labour, the H-O theorem emphasizes a two-factor economy. Developed by two Swedish economists, Eli Heckscher and Bertil Ohlin, the theorem argued that while trade is partly explained by differences in labour productivity, it also can be a reflection of differences in countries' resources. In realistic terms, trade involves with not only labor, but also other factors of production such as land, capital, and natural resources. As Krugman and Obstfeld (2000) demonstrate, this model illustrates that comparative advantage is influenced by the interaction between nations' resources, abundance of factors of production, and the technology of production which influences the relative intensity with which different factors of production are used in the production of different goods.

THAILAND
"The Land of Smile"

Population: 62 million
Land Area: 513,115 sq. km.
GDP: $379,640 million
GDP growth rate: 4.31%
GDP Per capita: $6,200
Exports of goods and services: $67.9 million
Major export trading partners: USA 24%, ASEAN 18%, EURG 18%, Japan 14%
Imports of goods and services: $62,4 million
Major import trading partners: Japan 24%, NAFfA 15%, ASEAN 15%, EU 12%
Trade Balance: 5.5 million.

The H-O model is explained by six assumptions as followed:

1. It considers the world can be explained by a 2×2×2 model: two countries (A, B), two goods (x, y), and two factors of production (capital-K and labour-L).
2. All productions occur under increasing cost conditions. This assumption implies that all resources have diminishing marginal productivity, which means that when resources are used in the same production, the last unit of the resource produces less and less. Thus, as output increases, average cost increases, which finally leads to the country's loss of comparative advantage in given production. Under increasing cost conditions, two countries could not completely specialize (in either good x or good y). Therefore, the end result is an incomplete specialization.
3. All productions occur under perfect competition, which means there are large number of producers and large number of consumers. An individual producer has no control over the price of goods. Therefore, the price is constant. Also in an industry, there is a free entry and free exit for the firms. If the industry shows positive profits, then new firms enter into the industry, thereby decreasing profits to zero in the long run. As a consequence of zero profit, price of goods equal to the cost of production.
4. Both countries have free trade. There are no quotas, no tariffs, and no transportation costs.
5. Both countries have similar demand conditions. This means both countries have same tastes and preferences. Therefore, trade direction is determined by the production side rather than by consumption side. However, this assumption has been criticized by today's trade, where there are some goods whose trade direction is determined by the consumption side such as perfumes, cars, diamonds, etc.
6. Technology of production of the same good is the same across countries. In other words, if both countries had

the same quantity of resources, then their output combination would be exactly the same.

The H-O theorem argues that, unlike in the Ricardian case, even if both countries have exactly same technology of production, they can still benefit from trade. The reason is countries can have different factor endowments. There are two ways to define factor endowments, by factor abundance and by factor intensity. In order to define factor abundance, suppose that there are two countries (A and B), and two factors of productions (K and L).

1. One way to define factor abundance by considering capital labour ratio.

   (K/L) A = Capital labour ratio in country A

   (K/L) B = Capital labour ratio in country B

   If (K/L) A > (K/L) B, then country A is said to be capital abundant and country B is said to be labour abundant.

2. Another way to determine factor abundance is by considering "Factor prices". Assumed that price of labour is Wage rate (w) and price of capital is rental rate (r). In this case, capital represents those physical things such as machinery, tools and equipment.

   (w/r)A = Wage rate rental in country A

   (w/r) B = Wage rate rental in country B

If (w/r) A > (w /r) B, then country A is said to be capital abundant, and country B is said to be labour abundant. The low wage rate in given country can be taken as an indication that it is a labour abundant.

To define factor intensity, suppose that two goods are produced such that,

(K/L)X = Capital labour ratio required to produce 1 unit of good X

(K/L)Y = Capital labour ratio required to produce 1 unit of good Y

If (K/L) X > (K/L) Y, then good X is said to be capital intensive, and good Y is labour intensive.

Suppose given these assumptions, if (K/L) A > (K/L) B, then country A is capital abundant and country B is labour abundant. And if (K/L) X > (K/L) Y, then good X is capital intensive and good Y is labour intensive. (The idea is similar for considering factor prices, suppose (w/r) A > (w/r) B, then country A is said to be capital abundant, while country B is said to be labour abundant).

Given the above assumptions, the H-O theorem illustrated that a mutually beneficial trade occurs when country A exports good X (and country B imports good X). Thus the H-O theorem concludes that, "a country will export that commodity whose production uses country's abundant factor more intensively". In other words, a labour-abundant country will export a labor-intensive product to the world, while a capital-abundant country will export capital-intensive product.

This theory can be explicitly applied in the case of less developed countries (LDCs), where mutually beneficial trade occurs when LDCs specialize in a production of a labor-intensive product and export it to developed countries. For example, according to Thailand's trade statistics, a high volume of exports is seen in labor-intensive products such as textile and agricultural products to the United Sates and Japan, two large trading partners of Thailand. The application of the H-O theorem to Thailand's export performance will be discussed more in the next section.

The H-O theorem has been expanded further by Paul Samuelson who considered the H-O theorem and situations after trade. According to H-O theorem, if (w/r) A > (w/r) B, and if (K/L) X > (K/L) Y, then country A should specialize in the production of good X and exports good X to country B. As Country A produces more of good X, under full employment of resources, production of good Y has to decline. However, to produce more of good X, the country needs capital faster than labor, but notice that good X is a capital intensive good. When lower quantity of Y is produced, labour is released faster than capital. Therefore, wage rates in country A will decline and rental rates will increase.

In contrast, country B specializes in the production of good Y and exports to country A. When country B produces more of good Y, production of good X has to be decreased, under the assumption of full employment. Then, capital is released faster than labor. As a result, wage rate in country B will increase and rental rate will decline. The incidence of wage increase can be explicitly seen as one of the factors causing the economic crisis in Thailand. As the wage rates increase in a labor-abundant country, leading to higher cost of production in labor-intensive products. The result is the price of products is higher, which finally reduces the quantity demanded of goods exported to rest of the world.

SECTION-II

APPLICANON OF H-O-S THEOREM TO THAILAND'S EXPORT

Even though the Thai economy is at its weakest in recent years, it still remains one of the most promising in Southeast Asia. One part of the strength of the economy lies in the ability of Thailand to export commodities such as rice, maize, sugar, rubber, tin, etc. History of Thailand's trade is seen in the implementation of commercial banking in the 1800's that gave Thailand an opportunity to set up trade with other countries, like China and Japan. Since then foreign trade has been playing a very important role in the economy of Thailand. Another important characteristic of the Thai economy is that it is called an "export economy," partly because many of Thailand's agricultural commodities are produced not for home consumption, but for the export market. For example, while rubber has been one of the mainstay, of the economy, there was hardly any demand for it within the country. (Sithi & Amnuai, 1964).

Interestingly, over the decades of export economy, Thailand's export composition has changed from specializing in land-and-mineral-intensive products to labor-and-capital-intensive products. With a force of the government policy in changing the country's economy from agriculture to industrial, the government readily promoted the industrial sector, thus changing the composition of exports to more labor-and-capital-intensive. The following section shows the applicable of the H-O Theorem.

THAILAND'S EXPORT PERFORMANCE PRIOR TO THE CRISIS

According to Warr (2000), over the past three decades, Thailand's economic experience has been a classic example of export-led growth. As a share of GDP, exports of goods and factor services grew from 15 percent in 1970 to 42 percent in 1995. GDP growth increased from an average rate of 6.3 percent over the previous decade to an average rate of 9.9 percent over this nine-year period. Exports grew at an average annual rate of 22 percent, expressed in dollars. Until the 1970s, most of Thailand's export industries were agricultural products, such as milled rice, frozen seafood, and canned fruit, which uses agricultural products, such as rnilled rice, frozen seafood, and canned fruit, which uses agricultural products as raw materials (Setboonsarang & Ammar, 1989). From 1980, these exports became more diversified into categories of garments, office machines, rubber, and electrical machinery. In order to illustrate the changing composition of Thailand's exports, Warr (2000) creates the composition of gross exports obtained by classifying exports factor intensity (see appendix 1).

According to the composition of the gross exports table, commodity categories are classified into four groups: land, mineral, labour, and capital-intensive. Explicitly, these numbers show growth in the importance of capital-intensive exports and the relative decline of land-intensive exports. As a consequence, the comparative advantage of the economy was moving in favor of capital-and-Iabour intensive commodities, and away from land-and-mineral-intensive goods.

Clearly, the largest contribution to the growth of gross exports, until 1988, came from land-intensive commodities. After that the highest contribution came from capital-and-Iabour-intensive products. Notice that the classification of gross exports is determined by the factor intensity of the value-adding processes occurring in Thailand, and does not include all processes required to produce the final product. Besides, by looking at the major imports of Thailand, more than three-quarters of them are capital goods, and intermediate products and raw materials (see appendix 2) (Bank of Thailand, 2001). These types of goods and materials are used in expanding industrial capacity and supply inputs into many of Thailand's export industries. This means the country did not completely produce the products but had to import some parts. Part of the major force came from the government policy that planned to expand its production away from agriculture by establishing several manufacturing industries to promote the new industrial sector. Finally, Thailand is considered to be-more labour-abundant country, where having a skilled, but relatively low cost, to produce labor-and-capital-intensive products such as garments, footwear, jewelry integrated circuit boards and other electronic products.

According to the H-O theorem, the growth in labor-and-capital-intensive products exports, means Thailand has a comparative advantage in labour intensive products compared to the United States. When (w/r) US > (w/r) Thailand, then Thailand specialized in producing these labour intensive products such as office machines, electrical machinery, clothing, rubber, crude, fish, and fresh preserves (see appendix 3). The thai economy exports many of these products to the United States, making it the largest export destination.

Further, according to the Samuelson theorem (Samuelson, 1949), which emphasizes that labour abundant country should speciallize in the production of labor-intensive goods and export them to other countries. When that country produces more of those goods, production of other goods has to be decreased. Then capital is released faster than labor. As a result, wage rates in the country will increase and rental rates will decline. Because of significantly increased labor-intensive exports compared to the rest of the world, especially to the United States, the result was a higher demand of labour in Thailand. This led to a wage rate increase in a labor-abundant country, leading higher cost of production in labor-intensive products. Even though trade helped increase the country's welfare, the increase in wage rate also led to a higher cost of future productions of labour intensive goods. This is where trade adversely affected the economy due to wage increases responding to a decline in the world market demand.

FINANCIAL CRISIS

The economic crisis had turned Thai's economy into chaos in 1997, starting with the devaluation of the Thai Baht. Though, it is obvious that there was a serious slowdown of exports in 1996, this is an only factor causing the crisis. Thailand had been showing signs of financial strain for more than a year with a temporary balance of payments problem, requiring the country to borrow abroad to smooth out import capacity until exports recovered. This included the corruption of the government sector.

The export sector was slowed down significantly due to:

- The worldwide demand recession in the electronics and computer industries, which was Significant for Thailand as Thailand's export composition has been changing from agriculture and light industries to more sophisticated industries.
- A major decline is more evidence in textiles industries because of the increased competitiveness of People Republic of China (PRC) products. Besides textiles, there were declines in exports of a few major commodities: garments, shoes and parts, frozen shrimps (Bangkok Post, December 1996). Notice that these are all labor-intensive products.
- An increasing wage rates in labor-intensive after 1990 (see appendix).
- According to the Thailand Development Research Institute, this real wages data provide the single most significant explanation for Thailand's export slowdown specifically in labor-intensive industries. From 1982 to 1994, real wages increased by 70 percent, which increased especially after 1990. A rising real wage was the result of the rising demand from the industry and service sector for labour during the economic growth. Workers moved from agriculture in the rural area, to more productive jobs in the manufacturing and services sectors. This process continued until the cheap rural labour shortages, in both agriculture and non-agriculture, further increased the demand for labour then led to rising wages.

As a result of rising real wages, Thailand's export industries suffered from increasing cost of production, which finally led to a loss of competitiveness in the labor-intensive export-oriented industries that have been the basis of the country's growth over the past decade. Along with a rising wage, exports were threatened by intense competition in the region as a shift in comparative advantage toward China also intensified. Additional pressure was exerted as Yen depreciated by 50 percent against the US dollar in 1995. This made Thai's products less competitive in the Japan and US markets which have been the two largest markets of Thailand. Consequently, these major factors led to the economic crisis in 1997.

There were other factors causing the export slowdown too. When considered a significant increase of imports in response to increasing investment, the amount of imports was in excess, over exports, leading to an account deficit of 8 percent of GDP in 1996. Therefore, foreign borrowing was being used mainly to balance the payments. In addition, the devaluation of Thai's Baht intensified trade deficit problems when-the price of export was lower while the price of import was higher. As a result, the country needed more money to buy capital goods and input parts for further export production, while it received less money from exports of labor-intensive products to the world.

ECONOMIC RECOVERY AFTER CRISIS

After experiencing the crisis, Thais economy in 2000 showed signs of continued recovery from the dramatic downturn of 1997-98, registering 4.3 percent growth that was led largely by continued expansion in exports of almost 20 percent. Since the end of 2000, however, Thailand's economic outlook has become considerably more uncertain due to continued weak domestic demand and investment as well as the slowdown in the global economy, particularly in the United States and Japan, Thailand's two largest export markets.

As the Bank of Thailand's data show, Thailand's total trade climbed nearly 25 percent in 2000. Thailand's exports were $6.79 billion to the US and imports $6.24 billion, yielding a Thai surplus of $5.5 million.

Exports continued to play the crucial role in Thailand's recovery, preventing the Thai economy from contracting. This was because of a substantial volume increase in manufacturing exports using high technology, including electronics and automobiles products, and agricultural exports, such as rice and canned fish (Somsak, 1993). However, total exports value decreased by 6.8 percent, resulting from the slowdown of the world economy and financial crisis in Asian countries. A declining value was a result of intense price competition among Thailand's major competitors, whose currencies also depreciated. Also, an investment incentive and cheap labour in neighboring countries such as China, Vietnam, and Indonesia, led to further stagnation of Thai exports.

An increase in exports volume was partly due to the baht's depreciation, which resulted in lower price of exported commodities. The NAFTA countries, specifically the US, remained the largest export market with the export share of 24 percent in 1998 rising from 21 percent in 1997. The second largest market is the EU, followed by the ASEAN, and the Japanese market (see appendix 5).

In 2001, exports shrank by 7 percent, as a result of global economic recession reducing the trade surplus to about $2.5 billion in 2001 from $5.5 billion in 2000. Additionally, the global slowdown intensified by the September 11 events adversely affected the near-term outlook for Thailand.

FUTURE OF THATLAND'S TRADE

The future of Thailand's trade will shift a focus to export industries, which will have to change their modes of production from labor-intensive to capital-and-skills intensive, in order to have competitive advantage over its neighboring countries, where providing cheaper labour such as China and Vietnam. As wages continue to rise, by adjusting itself from labor-intensive and move into more skills-intensive industries, the education sector must play a key role in supplying skills-intensive labour force required. This sector will be the most important determinant of Thailand's future export performance and of its economic prospects in general.

Thailand's export was expected to grow with a forward looking of the private sector and rising of the upgrading process from a number of firms, especially in the computer industry using cutting-edge production processes. Thailand natural resource advantages will ensure the longevity of the jewelry industry and agricultural sector.

Thailand's exports market will continue to grow with the US, Japan, the EU, and the ASEAN. A recovery of economic growth in the US, the world's largest market, will continue to provide opportunities for Thailand's exports. Similarly, economic growth in the EU provides a positive sign for Thai exporters to that market. In addition, trade liberalization with the regional trading partner such as ASEAN, APEC, and the Greater Mekong region will encourage Thailand's exports in ASEAN countries as a number of Asian countries are recovering from the economic downturn. Further, the China entry to the WTO will significantly impact Thailand's export. In fact, this will increase a number of opportunities for Thai's export to expand overseas, especially in food and agricultural products, textiles and furniture and tourism services where. Thailand is capable of producing sufficiently and efficiently for exports.

TARIFF POLICY

During its 1999 fiscal year, Thailand's average effective tariff rate was 3.81 percent, up from 1998 of 3.28 percent. Import tariffs in the fiscal year accounted for 9.3 percent of government revenues. The simple average tariff on 5,846 dutiable items was 16.97 percent. The lower rates are reflective of Thai government policies to reduce rates in line with ASEAN Free Trade Area *(AFTA)* and World Trade Organization commitments.

Thailand has been revising a tariff structure since 2000, which categorized products into three categories of primary, intermediate, and finished goods. Effective July 2000, the government has approved import tariff reductions on 542 industrial raw materials and 326 capital goods to improve competitiveness of Thai manufacturers.

In terms of tariffs on agricultural products, the government has significantly eased other barriers for a small, select group of agricultural and good products in the past 2 year as to comply with its WTO tariff reduction commitments. The United States has benefited from these measures through increased sales and additional market share.

In addition, the Board of Investment provides for duty-free imports of machinery used in projects that result in the exportation of at least 80 percent of output.

In December 1998, the ASEAN members decided to accelerate the completion of the ASEAN Free-Trade Area. In this regard, the six original founding members, Thailand, Singapore, Malaysia, the Philippines, Indonesia, and Brunei, would advance their tariff reductions to 0-5 percent from 2002-2003.

SECTION-III

SUMMARY AND CONCLUSION

In conclusion, one can safely state that the H-O-S Theorem has a good application to the case of Thailand, specifically to the economic crisis period. The experience of real wage increases, along with the worldwide slowdown in few commodities and a depreciated Baht against dollar are seen clearly to be major factors of declining exports demand in Thailand, which finally led to the crisis in 1997. In this case, trade brought a negative effect to Thai's economy.

Nevertheless, over the decades of Thailand's trade history shows that trade has played a key role in economic development of Thailand. Since Thailand is an export the economy, which concentrates more on the exports market than domestic market. Trade allowed Thailand to specialize in, not only labor-intensive products but also capital-intensive products. Thailand got benefits from trade in terms of boosting economic growth during the period of 1980s-1996. This was similar to the case of India, where it was proved by Kulkarni (1992) that free trade has been favorable to LDCs and not as an undesirable of trade, as argued by some LDCs against free trade.

The future prospect of Thailand's export would remain open to trade and investment and would continue liberalization trends within the regional trading partners such as ASEAN countries as a number of Asian countries are recovering from the economic downturn. Moreover, the export industries will have to shift its mode of production from labor-intensive to more skilled-and-capital-intensive, where it would help improve its competitiveness over other neighbor countries. As a matter of fact the future of Thailand's trade will heavily rely on her ability to supply skilled-labour which requires education to improve its competitiveness and respond to a shift in its mode of production. Education sector will play a significant role in supplying skills-labour to improve export performance and drive its economy into an Asian miracle as experienced in the past.

REFERENCES

Bank Economic Conditions in 2001 and Outlook for 2002. *http://www.bot.or.th/*

Country Commercial Guide (2001), USA.

Krugman, R. P. & Obstfeld M., (2000), International Economics: Theory and Policy, Addison-Wesley Publishers, New York, Sixth Edition, 2003.

Kulkarni, Kishore G., (1992), Has International Trade Benefited LDCs? -India's Case, Margin, April-June 1992, pp. 235-244.

International Economics Policy Briefs March 1998: The Asian Financial Crisis. *http://www.iie.com/policybriefs/news98-1.htm.*

Ministry of Foreign Affairs Business Handbook (2000), *http://www.mfa.go.th.*

Samuelson, P. A., (1949), "International Factor-Price Equalization Once Again", *Economic Journal*, Vol. 59, pp. 181-196.

Setboonsarng, S. & Ammar S., (1989), "Trade Exchange Rate and Agricultural Pricing Policies in Thailand: Comparative Studies on the Agricultural Pricing Policy:" in Peter G. Warr Edited, "The Thai Economy in Transition", Cambridge University Press, Cambridge, UK, 1993.

Somsak, T., (1993), "Manufacturing." In Peter G. Warr, The Thai Economy in Transition, Cambridge University Press, Cambridge, UK, 1993.

Warr, G. P., (2000), Asian Exports, Case Study: Thailand. Oxford University Press, NY. *http://www.usatrade.gov/website/ccg.nsf/CCGurl/CCGTHAI LAND 2002-CH-2:-005ACCC9.*

APPENDICES

APPENDIX-I
COMPOSITION OF GROSS EXPORTS BY FACTOR INTENSITY SELECTED YEARS

Year	*Land Intensive*	*Mineral Intensive*	*Labour Intensive*	*Capital Intensive*	*Total*
1970	77.4	16.6	1.5	1.2	100
1975	76.3	11	7.1	3.4	100
1980	59.5	16.5	11.4	9.7	100
1985	57.1	9.4	18.2	14.6	100
1986	54.5	6.9	20	17.9	100
1987	47.6	6.6	24.9	20.0	100
1988	44.5	6.2	24.8	23.7	100
1989	42.4	5.8	25.3	25.7	100
1990	35.5	6.0	26.6	30.6	100
1991	33.1	5.3	27.5	32.9	100
1992	32.1	4.5	26.3	36.1	100
1993	27.4	4.6	26.9	39.6	100
1994	27.2	4.2	24.6	43.3	100
1995	26.1	4.0	24.1	45.0	100
1996	25.9	4.3	16.0	52.4	100

Source: *Peter G. Warr (Author's calculations) based on IMF,* Direction of Trade Statistics *database.*

APPENDIX-2
THAILAND'S IMPORTS BY ECONOMIC CLASSIFICATION

(Billion baht)

Economic classification	*1996*	*1997*
Capital Goods	832.2	925.8
Machinery and parts	459.2	474.1
Metal manufactures	54.4	62.5
Fertilizers and pesticides	22.6	22
Scientific and optical instruments	47.9	51.6
Construction materials	0.6	0.4
Other	247.5	315.2
Intermediate Products and Raw Materials	530.1	552.5
Chiefly for consumer goods	334.6	349.3
Chiefly for capital goods	195.5	203.2
Consumer Goods	151.1	160.7
Non-durable goods	51.8	58.6
Durable goods	99.3	102.1
Fuels and lubricants	160.6	178.3
Vehicles and parts	123.3	67.3
Other imports'	35.6	39.6
Total	1,832.80	1,924

Source: Bank of Thailand.
Note: Figures may not sum due to rounding.

APPENDIX 3
TOP 10 EXPORTS BY SITC 3-DIGIT CATEGORY, RANKING BASED ON 1996 VALUES

Rank	*SITC Heading*	*1970*	*1975*	*1980*	*1985*	*1998*	*1990*	*1995*	*1996*
1.	Office Machines		376	3,093	52,876	60,152	1,560,287	5,484,114	9,449,768
2.	Electrical Machinery, n.e.s.	189	17,722	11,365	84,959	151,522	1,032,635	3,705,535	4,265,678
3.	Clothing, not of Fur	878	53,500	266,587	572,647	824,747	2,825,598	4,842,561	2,957,660
4.	Rubber, Crude, Synthetic	108,165	170,561	604,158	500,255	573,087	922,925	2,462,008	2,422,204
5.	Fish, Fresh, Simply Preserved	15,956	86,089	214,215	329,828	486,160	1,264,873	2,856,100	2,375,378
6.	Telecommunications Equipment	113	1,918	8,847	4,550	7,443	563,551	2,003,748	2.140,686
7.	Elec. Power Mach., Switchgear	88	2,637	305,884	332,374	526,970	201,421	1,960,965	1,810,169
8.	Machines, n.e.s., Nonelectric	266	2,153	18,623	88,105	96,962	442,843	1,780,626	1,749,484
9.	Rice	120,998	287,177	952,770	829,567	769,097	1,086,122	1,951,536	1,562,223
10.	Fish, etc., Tinned, Prepared	4	9,962	87,313	284,966	4.44,965	993,130	1,590,429	1,434,303

Note: n.e.s. = not elsewhere specified.

Source: Peter G. Warr (Author's calculations) based on IMF, *Direction of Trade Statistics* database.

APPENDIX 4

FIGURE 1: THAILAND'S MAJOR EXPORT MARKETS BY GEOGRAPHIC REGION

(Billion baht)

Region	*Value in 1996*	*Value in 1997*	*Value in 1998*	*Growth 1997*	*Growth 1998*	*Share in 1997*	*Share in 1998*
NAFTA	270.7	379.1	537.4	40%	42%	21%	24%
EU	224.9	290.4	401.4	29%	38%	16%	18%
ASEANI/	296.3	380.8	396.7	29%	4%	21%	18%
Japan	237.5	270.8	308.5	14%	14%	15%	14%
NIEs 2/	143.8	187.7	212.3	31%	13%	10%	9%
Middle East	54.7	62.3	77.5	14%	25%	3%	3%
China	47.4	55.5	72.9	17%	31%	3%	3%
GMS3/	41.1	51	66.2	24%	30%	3%	3%
Former USSR	5.4	4.9	3.6	-9%	-27%	1%	1%
Eastern Europe	12.3	14.6	13.0	18%	-11%	1%	1%
Others	76.9	156.2	159.3	103%	2%	8%	7%
Total	1,411.0	1,806.7	2,248.8	28%	25%	100%	100%

Source: Bank of Thailand.

Notes: 1/ includes Myanmar, Viet Nam, and Lao People's Democratic Republic, 2/includes Taiwan, Hong Kong, and South Korea, 3/ Myanmar, Vietnam, Lao People's Democratic Republic, and Cambodia, excluding Yunnan.

Figures may not sum due to rounding.

FIGURE: THAILAND'S MAJOR IMPORT SUPPLIERS BY GEOGRAPHIC REGION

(Billion baht)

Region	*Value in 1996*	*Value in 1997*	*Value in 1998*	*Growth 1997*	*Growth 1998*	*Share in 1997*	*Share in 1998*
Japan	518.1	492.1	420.3	-5%	-15%	25%	24%
NAFTA	246.7	286.3	265.7	16%	-7%	15%	15%
ASEAN 1/	243.3	245.4	265.6	1%	8%	13%	15%
EU	276.1	268.5	221.8	-3%	-17%	14%	12%
Others	548.6	632.0	600.7	15%	-5%	33%	34%
Total	1,832.8	1,924.3	1,774.1	5%	-8%	100%	100%

Source: Bank of Thailand.

Figures may, not sum due to rounding.

4

APPLICATION OF THE HECKSCHER-OHLIN THEOREM TO TRADE IN CHILE

INTRODUCTION

Since the mid-1970s, Chile has used international trade as its main driver of economic growth. This strategy has increased trade from accounting for 20 percent of GDP in the 1960s to 80 percent of GDP today (Bartók & Onodera, 2007), helping to create one of the most stable and productive economies in Latin America. This paper will use Chile as a case study to test whether the Heckscher-Ohlin Theorem of international trade can be aptly applied today. That is, does Chile continue to gain from international trade by producing and exporting goods that require a factor in which it has a relative abundance of and importing goods in which it does not? In order to answer this question, the nature of Chilean trade, who it trades with and what it trades, will be examined as to its current context. These results will then be compared to what types of trade should occur according to the Heckscher-Ohlin Theorem based on the individual country's factor abundance. Since trade has been such an important factor of economic growth of Chile, we expect to find that the Heckscher-Ohlin Theorem can be aptly applied. Minor deviations from the theorem are certainly possible, but on a whole, the Theorem should hold true.

This Chapter is based on an article, with the same title co-authored with Mr. Kyle Barker

The rest of the chapter will be divided into four sections. The following section, Section 1, will give a brief historical background of Chile's relationship with international trade. The second section will provide a review of the Heckscher-Ohlin Theorem and survey some of the literature produced on the Theorem in the past fifty years along with how it applies to Chile. The third section of the paper will empirically study how the Heckscher-Ohlin Theorem applies to Chile today and whether it is a valid application. The last section will conclude the chapter.

SECTION - 1

HISTORICAL BACKGROUND OF CHILEAN INTERNATIONAL TRADE

From post-World War II until the 1970s, the Chilean economy followed the import substitution industrialization model of economic growth (Bartók & Onodera, 2007). This development strategy calls for the protection of domestic industries through government sponsorship and shelter, from imports. While the Chilean economy experienced moderate growth through this strategy, it essentially closed the Chilean economy to the rest of the world. Salvador Allende's socialist government in 1970 completely shut out the world economy by raising non-tariff barriers to an effective level of over 100 percent (Bartók & Onodera, 2007). As copper prices fell and the Chilean economy experienced inflation in the triple digits, Augusto Pinochet took over power through a coup d'état in 1973 (Bartók & Onodera, 2007).

During Augusto Pinochet's dictatorship, he transformed Chile into a market-oriented economy, following the advice of a group of American economists from the University of Chicago. Pinochet reduced the size and influence of the public sector, liberalized trade, and opened up the financial sector (Bartók & Onodera, 2007). This had an immediate impact on the trade sector, consolidating all non-tariff trade protections into tariffs and negotiating free-trade pacts with other Andean countries. By 1979, tariff levels had dropped from an average of 94 percent to a uniform 10 percent (Bartók & Onodera, 2007).

Although trade increased in the 1970s with the reform measures, a recession in the 1980s slowed economic growth, Fig. 1. Import tariffs were subsequently increased to 35 percent (Bartók & Onodera, 2007). However, as domestic demand for goods such as wood and agriculture products declined, the excess supply was exported. This increase in exports alleviated political pressure to return to the protectionist measures that precluded trade liberalization (Bartók & Onodera, 2007).

(Million current USD)

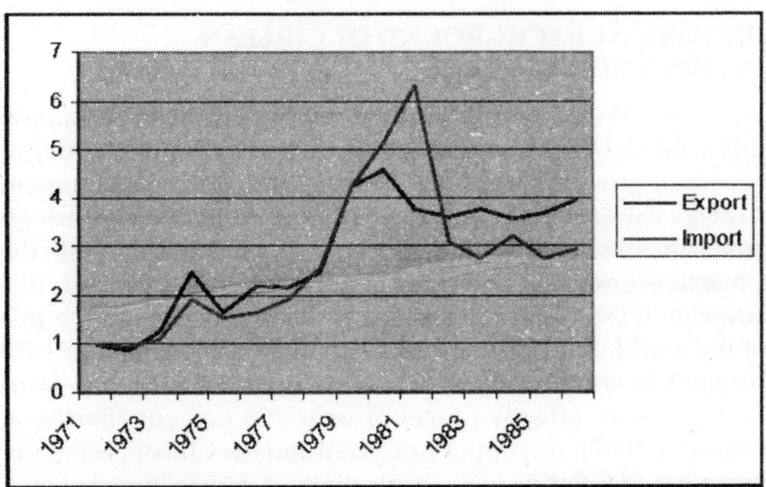

Source: WITS database

Figure 1: Chilean Trade Growth from 1971 to 1987

Once the recession of the 1980s subsided, tariff levels returned to between 10-15 percent, setting the stage for increased economic growth through an export led strategy in the 1990s. By 2003, tariffs were reduced to 6 percent with 70 percent of Chile's exports occurring with countries that have signed bilateral free-trade agreements. In 2005, trade accounted for 70 percent of Chile's GDP, making Chile one of the most open economies of the world.

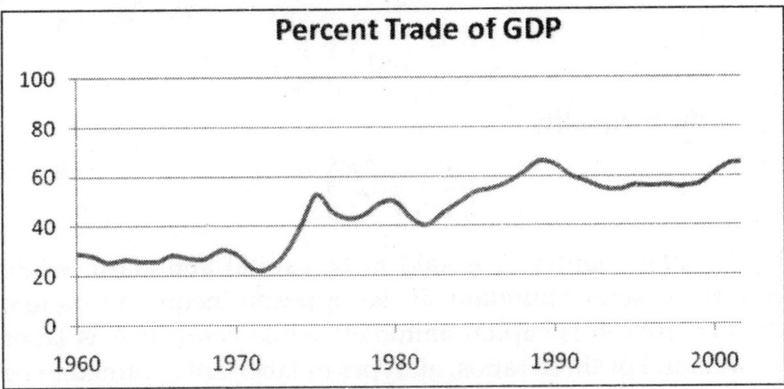

Figure 2: Percent of Trade of GDP growth from 1960 to 2007

SECTION 2

THE HECKSCHER-OHLIN THEOREM AND LITERATURE REVIEW

The Heckscher-Ohlin Theorem of international trade moves beyond the traditional theories of international trade in explaining why trade occurs. Traditional theories believe that the benefits of trade occur because of differences in technology in the production of a good in two countries. The Heckscher-Ohlin Theorem argues that even if two countries share the same technology for producing a good, trade can still be beneficial. This mutually beneficial trade occurs because of the differences in the factor endowments of the two countries.

The determinants of the Heckscher-Ohlin Theorem are the factor abundance of a country and the factor intensity of goods. The factor abundance of a given country is measured in capital (K) and labor (L). Whereas traditional models of international trade assumed that there was only one factor of production, generally this would be labor, the Heckscher-Ohlin Theorem assumed two factors. These factors of any given country can be measured through a capital labor ratio.

$$\left(\frac{K}{L}\right)$$

The ratios of two countries, A and B, are measured as

$$\left(\frac{K}{L}\right)_A \text{ and } \left(\frac{K}{L}\right)_B$$

If the inequality

$$\left(\frac{K}{L}\right)_A > \left(\frac{K}{L}\right)_B$$

holds, then country A is said to be capital abundant, while country B labor abundant. If the opposite inequality occurs, then country B is capital abundant while country A is labor abundant. For these ratios, all types of labor are assumed to be equal. The labor of an engineer is not distinguishable from that of a street sweeper.

Another way to measure the factor abundance of a country is to use the factor price ratio. This ratio assigns a monetary value to both capital and labor. Capital is measured by the cost of rent, (r), and labor is measured in the cost of wages, (w). The wage rent ratios then become

$$\left(\frac{W}{r}\right)_A \text{ and } \left(\frac{W}{r}\right)_B$$

for countries A and B. If the inequality

$$\left(\frac{W}{r}\right)_A > \left(\frac{W}{r}\right)_B$$

holds, then country A is considered to be capital abundant while country B is labor abundant. This is because higher wages are demanded of a lower supply of labor.

The second determinant of the Heckscher-Ohlin Theorem is the factor intensity of goods. This is also measured in capital and labor but refers to the production of goods rather than available resources of a country. The capital labor ratio of two goods, X and Y, are measured as

$$\left(\frac{K}{L}\right)_X \text{ and } \left(\frac{K}{L}\right)_Y$$

These are the required ratios of capital and labor to produce one unit of the given good. If the inequality

$$\left(\frac{K}{L}\right)_X > \left(\frac{K}{L}\right)_Y$$

holds, then good X is capital intensive while good Y is labor intensive. If the opposite inequality holds, then good Y is capital intensive while good X is labor intensive.

To complete the Heckscher-Ohlin Theorem six assumptions are needed. These assumptions are:

1. The world is explained by a 2x2x2 model in that two countries exist (A & B), which produce two goods (X & Y), based on two factors of production (K & L). This model fundamentally differs from that of traditional international trade theories which rely on a 2x2x1 model. The single factor in the traditional theories is usually labor.
2. Technology of production is exactly the same between countries. In other words, the production of a good requires no more or no less capital or labor in one country than in another country to produce a single unit. This assumption is also fundamentally different from traditional trade theories that believe the reason for trade was caused by differences in technology.
3. Perfect competition exists in the production of goods. This means that if there are no barriers to entry or exit, then there can be no long-term profit. Therefore, since profit is zero, the price of the good is equal to the cost of production.
4. The production of goods occurs under increasing cost conditions. Therefore, diminishing marginal productivity is implied so that the average cost increases with an increase in output. This assumption states that complete specialization in either good X or good Y, by either country will not occur. This is also why the production possibilities curve will be concave to the origin.
5. There is no difference between demand preferences between country A and country B. In other words,

consumers in both countries have the same tastes and preferences for goods as well as the same expectations of the future. Therefore, trade is driven by the supply-side, rather than the demand-side of goods.

6. Free trade occurs between countries. There are no tariffs, quotas or any other trade barriers in place. Furthermore, transportation is costless between the two countries.

Given all of these assumptions and the previous definitions of factor abundance and factor intensity, the Heckscher-Ohlin Theorem states that if

$$\left(\frac{K}{L}\right)_A > \left(\frac{K}{L}\right)_B,$$

where country A is capital abundant and

$$\left(\frac{K}{L}\right)_X > \left(\frac{K}{L}\right)_Y,$$

where good X is capital intensive, then for a mutually beneficial trade, country A should specialize in the production of and export good X, while country B should specialize in the production of and export good Y. Or, stated differently, in a mutually beneficial trade, a country should specialize in, and export that good, whose production uses the country's abundant factor intensively.

LITERATURE REVIEW

Since Eli Heckscher and Bertil Ohlin put forth their theorem in 1912, it has been a mainstay of international trade theory. The theorem provides a relatively simple structure, breaking down trade of commodities into bundles of factors (land, labor and capital) (Leamer, 1995). However, the Heckscher-Ohlin Theorem has also been the target of increasing criticisms. From the seminal work of Leontief in 1953, to Trefler's critique (1993), many papers have challenged the empirical validity of Heckscher-Ohlin Theorem. Yet, as Leamer (1995) points out, the Hecksher-Ohlin Theorem continues to be of great use in providing a theoretical framework for the patterns of international trade. The rest of this section will look at critiques and validations of the theorem.

The first major critique of the Heckscher-Ohlin Theorem was a study done by Wassily Leontief and became known as Leontief's Paradox. In 1953, Leontief used data from the US in 1947 to test the Heckscher-Ohlin Theorem. To the surprise of economic community, he found that although the US was a capital abundant country, US exports were 30% more labor intensive than import substitutions. These findings directly contested the Heckscher-Ohlin Theorem. Many subsequent studies tried to rationalize this paradox without success until Stern and Maskus.

In 1981, Robert Stern and Keith Maskus studied US exports of manufacturers from 1958-1976 and found that when using a three-direct-factor model, Leontief's paradox does not hold true for US exports in 1972 (Stern & Maskus, 1981). This three factor model allows for the inclusion of natural resources to explain why countries such as Guatemala or Brazil are able to specialize in and export goods like coffee.

Yet, some economists continue to debate the empirical validity of the Heckscher-Ohlin Theorem. In his 1993 paper, Daniel Trefler simply states, "the Heckscher-Ohlin-Vanek (HOV) theorem constitutes an incomplete description of trade in factor services: its predictions are always rejected empirically" (Trefler, 1993). The largest criticism that Trefler has of the Heckscher-Ohlin-Vanek theorem is the validity of one of the assumptions of the theorem, that trading partners have the same access to technology. In fact, Trefler points out that the transmission of technologies from the US to India is neither costless nor seamless (Trefler, 1993). Trefler also takes exception to the HOV theorem in that its description of trade in factor services is incomplete. However, this exception has more to do with factor price equalization than the pure trade that is the concern of this paper. Trefler concludes that Leontief was right to view the US as labor abundant in 1947 as measured in productivity-equivalent workers (Trefler, 1993).

Maskus defends the empirical validity of the Heckscher-Ohlin Theorem by stating, "The primary reason for the uncertainty regarding the theorem's empirical validity is that it has rarely been subjected to a logically complete test" (Maskus, 1998, p. 201). Maskus further states that the difficulty of these measurements has led to the inference of the factor endowments based on the factor content of the trade rather than a direct measure of the factor endowments themselves (Maskus, 1998).

In 1999 in a paper, a group of academics from Chile looked at the Heckscher-Ohlin Theorem and how it affects wage inequality within Chile (Beyer, Rojas, & Vergara, 1999). Although this paper did not specifically test whether trade in Chile occurred according to the Heckscher-Ohlin Theorem, they did conclude that wage changes within Chile are consistent with the Heckscher-Ohlin-Samuelson model. They found that opening the Chilean economy to trade caused a premium for skilled labor during the period of their analysis (Beyer, Rojas, & Vergara, 1999).

A study commissioned by the Central Bank of Chile (Álvarez & Opazo, 2008), also looks at the Heckscher-Ohlin Theorem in regards to how trade with China will affect wages within Chile. The paper notes that using the basic Heckscher-Ohlin Theorem, wages in Chile for apparel workers should decrease as China is comparatively labor abundant. However, Alvarez and Opazo, cite Leamer's 1987 work using three factors of production to show that natural resource abundant countries, such as Chile, will not compete directly with low-wage countries, such as China, because Chile is producing resource intense goods (Álvarez & Opazo, 2008).

SECTION 3

EMPIRICAL STUDY OF CHILEAN TRADE DATA

As of 2007, the top two trading partners of Chile are the United States and China (CIA, 2009). For exports, China is Chile's top trading partner, accounting for 14.8 percent of all exports while the United States is second, accounting for 12.5 percent of all exports. For imports, the positions are reversed. The United

States is Chile's top importer, providing 16.7 percent of all imports to Chile, while China is second, providing 11.2 percent of all imports. The third largest producer of Chilean imports is Brazil, accounting for 10.3 percent of all imports. Japan is the third largest destination for Chilean exports accounting for 10.5 percent.

To test whether the Heckscher-Ohlin theorem holds true, the factor endowments of the various countries will need to be determined. By doing this, we can determine whether Chile is the capital abundant or labor abundant country compared to the various countries that it trades with. We use the factor price ratio to make this determination. According to the Heckscher-Ohlin Theorem this ratio is

$$\left(\frac{W}{r}\right)_A : \left(\frac{W}{r}\right)_B .$$

For the wages of a given country, we shall use the average wage for teachers of that country. Data on teaching wages is readily available for a wide variety of countries and will give a standard metric of wages to compare. Although there are issues with using teaching wages as a proxy for the cost of labor, such as discrepancies between how much various countries value education, we see this as a relatively complete variable. For the price of rent, we will use the central bank overnight interest rate set by the central bank of the various countries. The figure used is a four year average of this interest rate taken between 2005 and 2008.

After the factor abundance of Chile and its trading partner are determined, we compare this to the factor intensity of the top four imports or exports with the given country. For this paper, we use common assumptions about the given products which are being trade with regards to their factor intensities. While input-output tables can be constructed to determine with certainty the factor intensity of a good, we shall only make broad assumptions. For example, we assume that fish, wood and apparel are labor intensive goods while nuclear reactors, vehicles and electronics are capital intensive.

United States

First, we shall look at the trade relationship between Chile and the United States. The Heckscher-Ohlin Theorem predicts that Chile will export those goods for which it is factor abundant in and import those goods for which it is relatively not. To determine which factor Chile is abundant in and which factor the United States is abundant in the figures in table 1 will be used.

Table 1
Comparison of the Cost of Capital and Labor within Chile and the United States

	Chile	*United States*
Capital (Interest Rates[1])	5.13	3.73
Labor (Average Teacher Salary[2])	10,922	32,703

According to the Heckscher-Ohlin Theorem, the factor abundance of a country can be measured with the factor price ratio:

$$\left(\frac{W}{r}\right)_A : \left(\frac{W}{r}\right)_B$$

For Chile and the United States, using the above data, this ratio is:

$$\left(\frac{32{,}703}{3.73}\right)_{United\ States} : \left(\frac{10{,}922}{5.13}\right)_{Chile} \text{ or } (8{,}768)_{United\ States} > (2{,}129)_{Chile}$$

Since the factor price ratio of the United States is greater than that of Chile, comparatively, the United States is capital abundant while Chile is labor abundant. According to this finding, the products that Chile exports to the United States should therefore be labor intensive while the products that Chile imports from the United States should be capital intensive. Table 2 shows the top four exports to the United States while table 3 shows the top four imports from the United States for Chile.

Table 2
Chilean Exports to the United States[3]

Year	*Ex/Imp*	*Product*	*Dollar Value*
2007	Export	Copper	$3,294,405,094
2007	Export	Edible Fruit and Nuts	$957,488,581
2007	Export	Fish and crustaceans	$909,517,687
2007	Export	Wood and articles of wood	$758,124,236

Table 3
Chilean Imports from the United States

Year	*Ex/Imp*	*Product*	*Dollar Value*
2007	Import	Mineral Fuels, Oils and Products of	$1,776,263,035
2007	Import	Nuclear Reactors and Parts	$1,522,377,590
2007	Import	Vehicles other than railway oriented	$687,143,409
2007	Import	Electrical machinery, recorders, TVs, etc.	$477,613,062

For imports, all of the top four imports from the United States are capital intensive. The production of fuel takes a great amount of capital to be able to refine crude oil to its final product. Nuclear reactors, vehicles and electrical machinery also all take a lot of capital to acquire the resources and knowledge to be able to produce those goods. Again, trade between Chile and the United States is consistent with what would be expected based on the Heckscher-Ohlin Theorem.

China

The second trading partner we will look at is China. Again, the first step is to determine what factor abundance Chile and China comparatively hold. The interest rate and salary will be used for this comparison.

Table 4
Comparison of the Costs of Rent and Wages in Chile and China

	Chile	*China*
Capital (Interest Rates)	5.13	6.29
Labor (Average Teacher Salary)	10,922	1,609[4]

According to the Heckscher-Ohlin Theorem, the factor abundance of a country can be measured with the factor price ratio:

$$\left(\frac{W}{r}\right)_A : \left(\frac{W}{r}\right)_B$$

For Chile and the China, using the above data, this ratio looks like:

$$\left(\frac{1{,}609}{6.29}\right)_{China} : \left(\frac{10{,}922}{5.13}\right)_{Chile} \text{ or } (256)_{China} < (2{,}129)_{Chile}$$

Based on these figures, Chile should be comparatively capital abundant while China is labor abundant. Therefore, the Heckscher-Ohlin Theorem predicts that for mutually beneficial trade to occur, China will specialize in and export labor intensive goods to Chile, while Chile will specialize in and export capital intensive goods to China. The top four goods traded between Chile and China in 2007 are in tables 5 and 6.

Table 5
The Top Four Exports from Chile to China

Year	*Ex/Imp*	*Product*	*Dollar Value*
2007	Export	Copper	$5,418,026,419
2007	Export	Ores, slag and ash	$3,328,947,070
2007	Export	Pulp of Wood	$698,506,448
2007	Export	Residuals and waste from food industry, animal fodder	$206,087,538

Table 6
The Top for Imports from China to Chile

Year	*Ex/Imp*	*Product*	*Dollar Value*
2007	Import	Electrical machinery, recorders, TVs, etc	$924,718,718
2007	Import	Nuclear Reactors and Parts	$695,754,538
2007	Import	Articles of apparel, not knitted	$487,878,435
2007	Import	Articles of apparel, knitted	$421,576,621

For imports, Table 6, the third and fourth largest Chilean imports from China, non-knitted articles of apparel and knitted articles of apparel respectively, are accurately predicted by the Heckscher-Ohlin model. Both of these goods are labor intensive, so that China, a labor abundant country, would produce these goods and export them to Chile. However, the top two Chilean imports from China do not fit well into this model.

Electrical machinery and nuclear reactors are both capital intensive goods; however, both of these goods are exported by the labor abundant China. For the exporting of electrical machinery, an argument can be made that the production of electrical machinery in some countries, such as the US, is in fact capital intensive, while the production of electrical machinery in China is actually labor intensive. This argument is based on the Factor Intensity Reversal (FIR) theory. This theory is based on the assumption that the production of goods can have various factor intensities based on the location in which they are being produced. For instance, since the US is a capital abundant nation, the production of electrical machinery will be done using automated factories that require little or no human interaction but require large amounts of capital. This process is taking advantage of the US's relative capital abundance. Whereas in China, because it is a relatively labor abundant nation, electrical machinery will be produced in factories by hand. The end result of electrical machinery is the same, but the factors to produce it are different.

The second largest import from China in 2007, nuclear reactors and parts, is a unique case that does not fit the Heckscher-Ohlin Theorem. Nuclear technology is highly capital intensive and a highly regulated good throughout the world. The nature of the nuclear industry, and its potential to be weaponized, has restricted its free trade due to national security concerns. In 2007, the Chilean President, Michelle Bachelet, instructed the Chile National Energy Commission to begin work on acquiring the capacity to produce nuclear energy (Comision Nacional de Energia, 2009). In order to acquire the technology to do so, Chile needed to import this very specific knowledge and goods. Therefore, because nuclear technology is not freely traded, the sixth assumption of the Heckscher-Ohlin Theorem is violated. Furthermore, because China had previously obtained the technology to produce nuclear goods and energy but Chile had not, the second assumption of the Heckscher-Ohlin Theorem is violated. Not only is there an uneven distribution of technology between Chile and China regarding the production of nuclear goods, the technology simply doesn't exist in Chile. Therefore, Chile does not even have the option to redirect resources to the production of nuclear goods. They have no other option but to import the technology from those countries which already obtain the technology.

Strictly applying the Heckscher-Ohlin Theorem to Chile's exports to China does not work either. The production of copper and ores could be argued to be capital intensive, but the production of wood pulp and food waste is certainly labor intensive, thus not complying with the Heckscher-Ohlin Theorem. However, when the Stern-Maskus three-factor caveat to the Heckscher-Ohlin Theorem is applied, the export of all four of these goods is compliant with the Heckscher-Ohlin Theorem. Chile is relatively naturally abundant in copper, ores, wood and residual food waste compared to China. Therefore, Chile will produce and export these goods, which is what the data from 2007 supports.

Japan

The third country that we shall look at is Japan, which is the third largest consumer of Chilean exports. Since Chile is not a large importer of Japanese goods, only exports will be examined. As with the other analysis, first the factor abundance relationship between Chile and Japan needs to be determined.

Table 7
Comparison of the Costs of Rent and Wages in Chile and Japan

	Chile	*Japan*
Capital Rent (Interest Rates)	5.13	0.35
Labor Wage (Average Teacher Salary)	10,922	24,469

According to the Heckscher-Ohlin Theorem, the factor abundance of a country can be measured with the factor price ratio:

$$\left(\frac{W}{r}\right)_A : \left(\frac{W}{r}\right)_B$$

For Chile and the China, using the above data, this ratio looks like:

$$\left(\frac{24,269}{0.35}\right)_{Japan} : \left(\frac{10,922}{5.13}\right)_{Chile} \quad \text{or } (69,911)_{Japan} > (2,129)_{Chile}$$

Based on these figures, under the Heckscher-Ohlin Theorem, Japan is capital abundant while it is assumed that Chile is labor abundant. It is expected than, that the products Chile produces and exports to Japan will be labor intensive.

Table 8
Top Four Exports from Chile to Japan

Year	*Ex/Imp*	*Product*	*Dollar Value*
2007	Export	Ores, slag and ash	$4,896,256,918
2007	Export	Fish and crustaceans	$724,456,995
2007	Export	Copper	$422,381,586
2007	Export	Wood and articles of wood	$305,837,595

According to the figures in table 8, the products exported from Chile to Japan are in fact labor intensive. Or, applying the Stern-Maskus caveat to the Heckscher-Ohlin theorem, it can also be argued that Chile is naturally abundant in three of the four goods relative to Japan. Chile certainly has more reserves of ores, copper and wood than Japan does.

As for fish and crustaceans, although Japan is an island nation with 29,751 kilometers of coastline compared to Chile's 6,435 kilometers (CIA, 2009), because they are relatively capital abundant, their energies are more productive in producing electronics and automobiles than it is spent producing fish for export. Furthermore, the question of fish imports to Japan, a country which is naturally abundant in fish, satisfies the Linder

Hypothesis. In 1961, Stefan Linder proposed that modern international trade is often determined more by tastes and preferences for goods, i.e. the demand side, rather than the supply side proposed by the Heckscher-Ohlin Theorem (Kulkarni K. , Alernative Explinations for International Trade, 2009). In this case, Japan's preference for fish, which is consumed at the rate of 70 kilograms of fish a year per capita (Wright, 2009), dictates that it needs to import fish to satisfy its demand.

Brazil

The last country examined is Brazil. Brazil is the third largest country from which Chile imports goods. Although Chile does export goods to Brazil, it is not in the top three consumers of Chilean goods, so we will only look at imports from Brazil. As with the other analysis, first the factor abundance relationship between Chile and Brazil needs to be determined.

Table 9
Comparison of the Cost of Rent and Wages for Chile and Brazil

	Chile	*Brazil*
Capital Rent (Interest Rates)	5.13	14.59
Labor Wage (Average Teacher Salary)	10,922	745[5]

According to the Heckscher-Ohlin Theorem, the factor abundance of a country can be measured with the factor price ratio:

$$\left(\frac{W}{r}\right)_A = \left(\frac{W}{r}\right)_B$$

For Chile and the China, using the above data, this ratio looks like:

$$\left(\frac{745}{14.59}\right)_{Brazil} : \left(\frac{10,922}{5.13}\right)_{Chile} \text{ or } (51)_{Brazil} < (2,129)_{Chile}$$

Based on these figures, under the Heckscher-Ohlin Theorem, Chile is relatively capital abundant while Brazil is labor abundant. The Heckscher-Ohlin Theorem predicts that the products Chile imports from Brazil will be labor intensive goods. However, as can be seen in table 10, this is not the case. The top four imports from Brazil are fuels, vehicles, nuclear reactors and electronics. All of these goods are capital intensive, not labor intensive. Thus, strictly apply the Heckscher-Ohlin Theorem to imports from Brazil does not hold true.

Table 10
Top Four Imports from Brazil to Chile

Year	*Ex/Imp*	*Product*	*Dollar Value*
2007	Import	Mineral Fuels, Oils and Products of	$1,397,444,844
2007	Import	Vehicles other than railway oriented	$762,699,412
2007	Import	Nuclear Reactors and Parts	$372,899,019
2007	Import	Electrical machinery, recorders, TVs, etc	$297,493,143

As with China, the import of nuclear reactors and parts is a special case due to the nature of nuclear products. Mineral fuels and oils are a capital intensive good, however, Brazil is respectively more naturally abundant in fuels and oils than is Chile. Therefore, based on Stern and Maskus's addition to the Heckscher-Ohlin Theorem, Chile should import such goods from Brazil (Stern & Maskus, 1981).

The importation of electrical machinery from a relatively labor abundant Brazil can be explained using the FIR theory, much the same as it was applied to imports from China. Even though electrical machinery is generally a capital intensive good, these products maybe produced by using labor to a much greater degree. The last of the top four goods imported from Brazil are vehicles. While this does not fit the Heckscher-Ohlin theorem, even with the addition of Stern and Maskus, it can be explained by Linder's Hypothesis, much the way that the exporting of fish to Japan was. Although Chile is capital abundant and may produce cars, the demands of the Chilean market may dictate the importation of cars from Brazil. Again, this is another violation of the basic assumptions of the Heckscher-Ohlin Theorem.

CONCLUSION

Using Chile as a case study, the Heckscher-Ohlin Theorem does not accurately predict all trade that Chile participates in. As a general framework, the Heckscher-Ohlin Theorem is still applicable to give a general idea of how trade will occur but it cannot be exhaustively applied. The largest discrepancy between the Heckscher-Ohlin Theorem and Chilean trade in 2007 occurs when trying to fit goods into the two-factor model of Heckscher-Ohlin. As was stated in the empirical analysis, assuming that the production of copper is labor intensive, the Heckscher-Ohlin Theorem is applicable to trade between Chile and the US. However, applying this model to Chile's other major trading partner, China, the Theorem is not applicable to trade without further explanation. This issue is resolved, however, with the addition of the three-factor model of Stern and Maskus. Once the production of copper is assumed to be natural resource intensive, not labor or capital intensive, then trade between Chile and China can be explained by the Heckscher-Ohlin Theorem.

This three-factor model is a necessary caveat to the original Heckscher-Ohlin Theorem when studying Chilean trade. Since the country has an abundance of natural resources, the majority of its exports are resource intensive. This applies to all three of Chile's major exporting countries examined in this paper; the US, China and Japan. Conversely, Chile imports goods that are labor intensive from countries which are labor abundant and goods that are capital intensive from countries which are capital intensive.

However, even with the addition of the three-factor model, anomalies occur within Chile's trade model that are not applicable to the extend Heckscher-Ohlin Theorem. For this study, the largest anomaly was the importation of nuclear reactors and parts. Importing this good from the US is understandable since the US is a capital abundant country. However, Chile also imports nuclear reactors and parts from China and Brazil, two countries which are labor abundant. The specific nature of nuclear goods allows for this discrepancy. The second assumption of the Heckscher-Ohlin Theorem states that technology between the two countries is the same. Nuclear technology, however, is not freely traded nor shared. Therefore, to acquire the knowledge and goods of nuclear energy, Chile must import it from elsewhere, regardless of whether the other country is labor or capital abundant.

Even though the Heckscher-Ohlin Theorem cannot be strictly applied to all aspects of Chilean trade, it does provide a fundamental framework for explaining trade patterns concerning Chile. Chile's export led growth since the 1970s has been dependent on the production and exporting of goods in which it has a comparative advantage and the importing of goods in which it does not. As Chile's economy continues to mature and industrialize, it will export fewer labor intensive goods and begin exporting more capital intensive goods. However, for now, since Chile is such a natural resource abundant nation, resource intensive goods will continue to be the mainstay of Chilean exports. It is conservable, however, that the extraction of these natural resource goods will rely more heavily on capital intensive methods in the future rather than traditional labor intensive methods.

Appendix A
Exports/Imports from the Top Trading Partners with Chile, 2007

USA - Exports/Imports

2007	Export	Chile	USA	Copper	$3,294,405,094
2007	Export	Chile	USA	Edible Fruit and Nuts	$957,488,581
2007	Export	Chile	USA	Fish and crustaceans	$909,517,687
2007	Export	Chile	USA	Wood and articles of wood	$758,124,236
2007	Import	Chile	USA	Mineral Fuels, Oils and Products of	$1,776,263,035
2007	Import	Chile	USA	Nuclear Reactors and Parts	$1,522,377,590
2007	Import	Chile	USA	Vehicles other than railway oriented	$687,143,409
2007	Import	Chile	USA	Electrical machinery, recorders, TVs, etc	$477,613,062

China – Exports/Imports

2007	Export	Chile	China	Copper	$5,418,026,419
2007	Export	Chile	China	Ores, slag and ash	$3,328,947,070
2007	Export	Chile	China	Pulp of Wood	$698,506,448
2007	Export	Chile	China	Residuals and waste from food industry, animal fodder	$206,087,538
2007	Import	Chile	China	Electrical machinery, recorders, TVs, etc	$924,718,718
2007	Import	Chile	China	Nuclear Reactors and Parts	$695,754,538
2007	Import	Chile	China	Articles of apparel, not knitted	$487,878,435
2007	Import	Chile	China	Articles of apparel, knitted	$421,576,621

Brazil – Imports from

2007	Import	Chile	Brazil	Mineral Fuels, Oils and Products of	$1,397,444,844
2007	Import	Chile	Brazil	Vehicles other than railway oriented	$762,699,412
2007	Import	Chile	Brazil	Nuclear Reactors and Parts	$372,899,019
2007	Import	Chile	Brazil	Electrical machinery, recorders, TVs, etc	$297,493,143

Japan – Exports to

2007	Export	Chile	Japan	Ores, slag and ash	$4,896,256,918
2007	Export	Chile	Japan	Fish and crustaceans	$724,456,995
2007	Export	Chile	Japan	Copper	$422,381,586
2007	Export	Chile	Japan	Wood and articles of wood	$305,837,595

NOTES

1. The interest rates used in all comparison are taken from Trading Economics – Global Economic Research. The interest rates are based on a four year average of the central bank overnight rate reported by the given country's central bank.

2. The average teacher salary for Chile and the US are based on a OECD report of education. The figures are for the year 2004 and for Chile, they were converted into USD using PPPs for 2004. The figures are based on the average starting salary for a primary education teacher with a minimum of training.
3. All data for Chilean imports and exports is taken from the United Nations Commodity Trade Statistics Database website, *http://comtrade.un.org/db/*
4. The average teacher salary for China comes from a news report based on information from the Chinese Ministry of Education in 2003, it was 13,300 Yuan. This figure was converted into US Dollars using historical exchange rate data for the year 2003 from *Oanda.com.*
5. This figure is based on estimates from World Salaries, *http://www.worldsalaries.org/brazil.shtml.* It is in constant 2005 USD PPP.

REFERENCES

Álvarez, R., & Opazo, L. (2008), Chinese Penetration and Importer Country Wages: Microevidence from Chile. *Central Bank of Chile Working Papers.*

Banco Central De Chile (2009), *Money, Credit and Interest Rates.* Retrieved May 2009, from Banco Central De Chile: *http://www.bcentral.cl/eng/economic-statistics/series-indicators/index_ms.htm*

Bartók, C., & Onodera, O. (2007), Facilitating Trade and Structural Adjustment: Experiences in Non-member Countries. *OECD Trade Policy Working Paper.*

Beyer, H., Rojas, P., & Vergara, R. (1999), Trade Liberalization and Wage Inequality. *Journal of Development Economics*, 103-123.

CIA. (2009), *The World Factbook.* Retrieved May 2009, from Central Intelligence Agency: *https://www.cia.gov/library/publications/the-world-factbook/geos/ci.html*

Comision Nacional de Energia (2009), *Grupo Consultivo Nuclea.* Retrieved May 2009, from Comision Nacional de Energia: *http://www.cne.cl/cnewww/opencms/12_Utiles/banners/grupo_consultivo_nuclear.html*

Federal Reserve (2009). *Selected Interest Rates.* Retrieved May 2009, from Federal Reserve: *http://www.federalreserve.gov/releases/h15/data/Annual/H15_FCP_M3.txt*

Krugman, P., & Obstfeld, M. (2009), *International Economics: Theory and Policy.* Boston: Pearson Addison Wesley.

Kulkarni, K. G. (2007), *Readings in International Economics: Selected Writings of Prof. Kishore G. Kulkarni,* New Delhi: Serials Publications, pp. 1-347.

Leamer, E. E. (1995), The Heckscher-Ohlin Model in Theory and Practice. *Princeton Studies in International Finance, No 77.*

Maskus, K. (1998), A Test of the Heckscher-Ohlin-Vaneck Theorem: The Leontief Commonplace. *Journal of International Economics*, 201-212.

People's Daily Online. (2009), *Average Salary of Chinese Teachers Grows 14 times in 20 years.* Retrieved May 2009, from People's Daily Online: *http://english.peopledaily.com.cn/200409/07/eng20040907_156221.html*

Stern, R., & Maskus, K. (1981), Determinants of the Structure of US Trade 1958-76. *Journal of International Economics*, 207-224.

Trading Economics (2009), *Country Profile.* Retrieved May 2009, from Trading Economics: *http://www.tradingeconomics.com/default.aspx*

Trefler, D. (1993), International Factor Price Differences: Leontief was Right! *The Journal of Political Economy*, Vol. 101, No. 6, 961-987.

UN Comtrade (2009), Retrieved May 2009, from United Nations Commodity Trade Statistics Database: *http://comtrade.un.org/db/*

Wright, H. (2009), *What future for Fish as Japan's Daily Fare?* Retrieved May 2009, from The Japanese Times Online: *http://search.japantimes.co.jp/cgi-bin/fl20090125x1.html*

5

TESTING THE APPLICATION OF HECKSCHER-OHLIN THEOREM TO CONTEMPORARY TRADE BETWEEN MALAYSIA AND SINGAPORE

INTRODUCTION

Since members of the Association of Southeast Asian Nations (ASEAN) signed the ASEAN Free Trade Area agreement in 1992, trade between Singapore and Malaysia has continued to grow. Historically, the economies of these two countries have had different characteristics, however, with Singapore known as a capital abundant country and a world financial center, while Malaysia has traditionally been relatively labor abundant and capital scarce. Because of this sharp contrast in their economies, one would expect that testing the Heckscher-Ohlin Theorem using trade data between Singapore and Malaysia would provide stark evidence of the H-O Theorem. That is to say that rather than find an exceptional case, as some past studies have done, this paper has attempted to find a country pair that seems to most closely resemble an idealized trade environment for the H-O Theorem. Thus, should a test find that the key hypotheses of the theory – namely that capital abundant countries export capital intensive goods, and labor

This Chapter is based on an article, with the same title co-authored with Mr. Andy Clarke

abundant countries export labor intensive goods—are not evidenced in the data, then a serious re-evaluation of the theory may be necessary.

This chapter will first review past tests of the Heckscher-Ohlin Theorem to determine what relevant studies have been done to date. Following that, export data will be reviewed for several different sectors, dividing them up as either capital intensive or labor intensive. What we would expect is that Singapore is exporting capital intensive goods to Malaysia, and Malaysia is exporting labor intensive goods to Singapore. Further, labor intensive exports will be analyzed as a proportion of capital intensive exports to determine how the labor/capital export ratio compares to the labor/capital abundance ratio for each country. Based on our findings, some conclusions will be able to be made as to whether the Heckscher-Ohlin Theorem stands up to the test with respect to Malaysia and Singapore over time. We will also analyze theoretically what differences in export proportions imply about trade between the two countries.

SECTION - 1

LITERATURE REVIEW

In the introduction of his influential article, "The Case of the Missing Trade and Other Mysteries," Daniel Trefler writes about the Heckscher-Ohlin Theorem that, "empirically, the theory has been repeatedly rejected over the years and rightfully so: it performs horribly." (pg. 1029) He goes on to say that factor endowments correctly predict the direction of factor service trade about 50 percent of the time, "a success rate that is matched by a coin toss." (pg. 1029) Nevertheless, H-O continues to be tested because deviations from the theory have proven fruitful in expanding upon it, and thereby expanding upon our knowledge of the factors that drive trade.

The first noteworthy test of the H-O Theorem was published in 1953 by Wassily Leontief, a Harvard professor who had analyzed 1947 data of U.S. trade in order to determine if the U.S., the most capital abundant country in the world at the time, was exporting capital intensive goods and importing labor intensive goods as the theory would presume. Using input/output tables of U.S. exports and import substitutes, Leontief examined 200 industries broken down into 50 sectors to analyze the factor intensity of each manufacture based on the factor intensity of its component parts. He found that exports in 1947 were 30% more labor intensive than import substitutes, leading him to conclude that "America's participation in the international division of labor is based on its specialization on labor intensive, rather than capital intensive, lines of production." (pg. 343). Because it was contrary to the H-O Theorem, the finding became known as the Leontief Paradox.

Several theories as to why the H-O Theorem didn't hold up to Leontief's test were put forward in the years following. Leontief himself argued that because labor productivity in the U.S. was three times higher than the rest of the world, the U.S. was actually a labor abundant country. When other economists pointed out that capital was also more productive in the U.S., Leontief withdrew his argument. Others argued that the data may have been skewed in 1947 due to World War II having just ended, and Europe unable to compete. Tests on later years showed that the Leontief Paradox diminished, but did not disappear.

Swedish economist Stefan Linder proposed what came to be known as Linder's Hypothesis (Linder, 1961), which noted the preeminence of consumer preference as a driver of international trade. The greater the similarity of tastes, Linder argued, the more likely it is that trade will emerge. Because U.S. consumers had a high preference for capital intensive goods in 1947, imports of capital intensive goods were necessary to meet demand. As a corollary, rest of world did not have high demand for such goods, capital intensive goods were largely consumed by the U.S. and not exported as much as labor intensive goods, which were in high demand in rest of world. This explanation of the Leontief Paradox was found to be insufficient, however, because it wasn't able to be tested quantitatively.

In fact it was not until a 1981 article by Robert Stern and Keith Maskus (Robert Stern, 1981) that the Leontief Paradox was finally put to rest. The article showed that when adding a third factor of production, namely natural resources, the Leontief Paradox disappears because many of the goods Leontief considered to be labor intensive were actually natural resource intensive.

In 1987 (Harry P. Bowen, 1987), a team of economists conducted what they humbly referred to as "the first systematic and complete evaluation of the relationships implied by the H-O-V Hypothesis among these three sets of variables." The three variables referred to are trade, factor endowments, and factor input requirements. The study analyzed 12 factors of production for 27 countries, and expanded the H-O Theorem to allow for technological differences. The authors then calculated the ratio of each country's endowment of each factor to total world supply, and compared the ratios to each country's share of world income. The expectation under the H-O Theorem would be that a country would export those goods for which its factor share exceeded the income share. The study found that for two-thirds of the factors of production, trade occurred in the direction expected by the H-O Theorem less than 70 percent of the time, leading the authors to conclude that the H-O proposition that trade reveals factor abundance is "not supported by these data" (pg. 791).

Regarding this finding, Krugman points out that "this result confirms the Leontief paradox on a broader level: Trade often does not run in the direction that the Heckscher-Ohlin theory predicts." (Paul R. Krugman, 2000) Still, the authors note that although "the Heckscher Ohlin model does poorly, we do not have anything that does better. It is easy to find hypotheses that do as well or better in a statistical sense, but these alternatives yield economically unsatisfying parameter estimates." (pg. 805).

While the studies mentioned all seem to conclude that the Heckscher-Ohlin Theorem is an insufficient model of international trade, some two-country studies similar to the focus of this study find support for H-O.

In a 1993 study (Richard A. Brecher, 1993), Richard A. Brecher and Ehsan U. Choudrhi analyzed bilateral trade data between the U.S. and Canada, using three variations of the H-O model that each account for factor price differences in a unique way. They find that the most robust results come from the third model, which interpreted factor-price differences between industries as consequences of imperfect factor mobility. Thus the authors conclude that "the empirical evidence supports the H-O production model after modifications to account for interindustry differences in factor prices." (pg. 283).

An earlier study (David Clifton, 1984) by two American economists tested the Heckscher-Ohlin Theorem using a different formulation for determining factor abundance than in other studies. Citing that past studies had inadequately measured abundance, the authors used the ratio of gross domestic product per worker versus gross world product per worker to compare the nine countries they examined with the rest of the world in order to determine factor abundance. After examining the GDP/laborer ratios for the United States, Ireland, Australia, New Zealand, the United Kingdom, Israel, Korea, Kenya, and Japan, the authors determined that Kenya and Korea were labor abundant, and the other countries were capital abundant. An analysis of each country's trade data showed that all but three exhibited trade flows congruent with H-O theory. The United Kingdom, Israel, and Kenya were the countries that did not follow suit, however the authors were unable to discern a pattern that would give any indication as to why these countries failed to conform to the expected trade flow.

Two other studies reviewed also seem more willing to give the Heckscher-Ohlin Theorem a chance. One is appropriately titled "Give Heckscher and Ohlin a Chance!" (Wood, 194) and like the Clifton study, criticizes past critiques of the H-O Theorem as inadequate because they have "mis-specified the theory by treating capital as similar to land." Wood concludes that because capital is internationally mobile, it doesn't actually influence the flow of trade, and finds that when capital is excluded, "[the H-O Theorem] often seems to perform rather well." Instead of labor/capital, Wood compared trade between pairs of developed and developing countries based on the skill of manufactures traded, finding that more sophisticated goods are exported by developed countries.

Krugman notes that these findings do not "contradict the observation that overall the Heckscher-Ohlin model does not seem to work very well, because North-South trade in manufactures accounts for only about 10 percent of total world trade." I would add that it seems hard to understand how one can change a core assumption of the H-O Theorem, that the world has two factors—labor and capital, and conclude that the theorem stands up to scrutiny.

And a 2003 paper by Peter K. Schott (Schott, 2003) takes into account factor intensity reversal when analyzing cross sectional trade data. Factor intensity reversal describes the way in which a single good can be considered capital intensive in a developed country because the mode of production is highly automated and computerized, whereas production of the same good in a developing country can be considered labor intensive because it is largely performed by human labor. After analyzing a range of industrial sectors and countries, Schott concludes that by analyzing countries' exports in terms of not only sector, but also the country-specific factor intensity of production, produces a richer set of findings. Ultimately, Schott's findings are in line with the H-O Theorem, though slightly modified, indicating that "countries specialize in *subsets*[1] of goods depending upon their relative factor endowments." (pg. 704).

Though results from the myriad tests of the Heckscher Ohlin Theorem vary, they tell us some important things about the theory. First, we see that despite all efforts to discredit it, H-O Theory remains relevant, with papers and studies ongoing to determine whether Heckscher and Ohlin were wrong, or if we're just missing something. Second, this survey makes apparent the challenges in applying theory to real data. As many studies noted, measuring a country's factor abundance ratio remains a challenge because there remains no generally accepted approach to measuring "capital" for a country. Another difficulty that the studies demonstrate is in measuring factor intensity, since it is difficult to measure exactly labor and capital levels within a certain good, and harder still when one considers more factors of production, as some of the studies did. Some quarrel with H-O's basic assumptions, arguing that the model is too simplified because it assumes that there are no technological differences between countries. But even Trefler, whose criticisms were noted at the outset of this section, concluded in his 1995 test of Heckscher-Ohlin that "the model that performed best combined Armington home bias with neutral international technology differences." (Trefler, 1995).

Though there seems to be an insistence on the part of some scholars to discredit the H-O Theorem, no doubt prompting the exclamation mark at the end of Wood's title, attempts at doing so have remained inconclusive. Leontief himself disagreed with his paradox, and in the end it was proven to be flawed because he was missing something: natural resources as a factor of production. Even the Bowen study confesses that though H-O didn't stand up to scrutiny, their team was unable to come up with something better.

So, what is the relevance of the Heckscher-Ohlin Theorem? Krugman concludes that, "the growth of North-South trade in manufactures—a trade in which the factor intensity of the North's imports is very different from that of its exports—has brought the factor proportions approach into the center of practical debates over international trade policy" (pg. 85).

It is hard to think of a more distinct North-South pair of countries that are more politically, economically, and geographically linked than Singapore and Malaysia. Singapore is the second largest destination for Malaysian exports, and fourth among sources for Malaysian imports. Malaysia, meanwhile, is the largest destination for Singaporean exports, and the largest among sources of Singaporean imports. Thus, the following section will conduct a test of the Heckscher-Ohlin Theorem on trade between these two countries in order to determine whether their trade patterns conform to the model, or if not, determine the cause of the divergence.

SECTION - 2

EMPIRICAL REVIEW OF MALAYSIA/SINGAPORE ECONOMIES

Malaysia: 2007

Like many other developing Asian nations, Malaysia has pursued a policy of state-led development for at least three decades. Though the state has been highly interventionist in markets, it has maintained a bias toward promoting growth in the private sector, particularly since the 1991 Privatization Master Plan, which made the private sector the major engine of economic growth. This domestic initiative coincided with the January 1992 signing of the ASEAN Free Trade Area, which was entered into by six of the ASEAN members, including Malaysia and Singapore. By 2007, Malaysia had complied almost fully with the tariff goals of the AFTA, bringing import tariffs on signatory nations' goods down to 0-5% for 97% of all goods, (Economist Intelligence Unit, 2008) with some notable exceptions like vehicles and rice. This broad reduction of import tariffs from ASEAN partners has led to a growth in regional imports as a proportion of rest of world imports, going from 10% in 1991 to 22% in 2001 (Madani, 2001).

This economic growth strategy has paid dividends, as the Malaysian economy continued its strong growth trajectory in 2007, with 6.3% GDP growth, driven in large part by an increase in private domestic consumption of 11.7%, and a 12.3% increase in private expansion, particularly in the oil and gas, manufacturing, services, and construction sectors. This growth pattern has been steady since the ASEAN Free Trade Agreement of 1992 (see graph[2]). Part of the strength in Malaysia's economy has been its ability to export manufactured goods, particularly labor-intensive electronics, as well as agricultural products such as rubber, palm oil, cocoa, and minerals and oil (Economist Intelligence Unit, 2008). Still, manufactured goods stood out with 70.9% of total exports, followed by minerals and oil at 15% of total exports, and agricultural products with 11% of total exports (WTO, 2009).

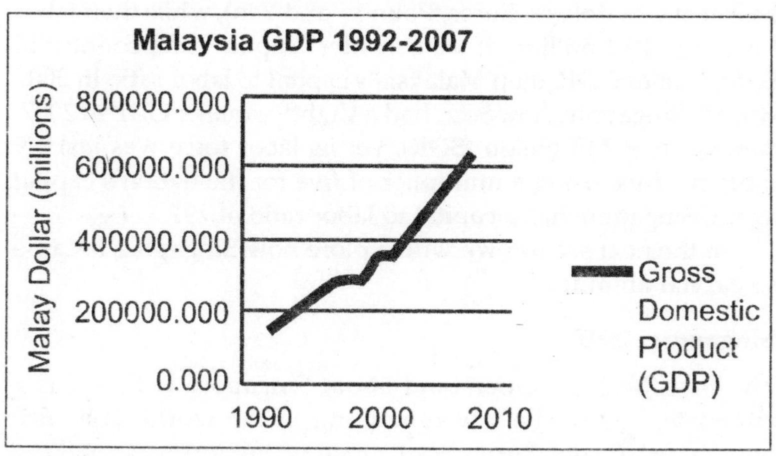

As it continues to develop, however, Malaysia has made diversification of its economy a priority. In the Ninth Malaysia Plan from the central government, announced in 2006, there were five "thrusts" cited as priorities for the future of Malaysia economic growth:

1. Move the economy up the value chain;
2. Enhancing education and training;
3. Reducing poverty and economic inequalities;
4. Improving quality of life;
5. And strengthening institutions.

This demonstrates Malaysia's commitment to shifting into more value-added, knowledge-based production. Further evidence of this commitment came in March of 2007, when plans for the Iskander Development Region (IDR) were announced. The IDR is Malaysia's answer to high-end business in Singapore. Bordering Singapore, the IDR offers special incentives for six sectors: creative industries, education services, financial advisory and consulting services, health care services, logistics services, and tourism activities.

Still, as of 2007 Malaysia remained a relatively labor abundant country when compared with Singapore. Consider that Malaysia's GDP in 2007 was approximately 123 billion (in terms of the IMF special drawing rights, which represent a basket of U.S. dollars, Euros, Pounds, and Yen), while their labor force was 10.4 million. If we consider "capital" of a country to be five times GDP, then Malaysia's capital to labor ratio in 2007 was 59. Singapore, however, had a slightly smaller GDP in 2007, coming in at 113 billion (SDR), yet its labor force was just 1.9 million. Thus, using a multiplier of five for the nation's capital again, Singapore has a capital to labor ratio of 297.

In the next section we will explore how Singapore became so capital abundant.

Singapore: 2007

The first thing to understand about Singapore is that it is a city-state, one of the few remaining in the world. It is also heavily urbanized throughout much of the territory, making for a scarcity of natural resources and land. Thus, Singapore has been forced to maximize a strategy of value-added manufacturing in order to be competitive. Economic reform began in earnest in 1968 when Singapore began to import raw materials and export finished goods. This strategy was aided by the fact that Singapore has a geographically favorable location, with a large port situated in a major shipping route. That location, coupled with favorable tax policies for foreign investors and heavy government investment in infrastructure and education, helped Singapore to develop. Consider Singapore's role in the oil trade. Though it has little of its own domestically produced oil, Singapore was able to attract some of the majors like RoyalDutchShell and Esso to set up refineries, becoming the third largest refining center in the world by the 1970s, (Loeper, 1989) and remains a major refining hub, with the ExxonMobil refinery there the fifth largest in the world. This strategy has helped Singapore become one of the wealthiest countries in the world, with a GDP per capita (PPP) ratio of $51,142 in 2008, far greater than Malaysia's $14,071 in the same year.

Singapore's economy is heavily trade dependent, with a trade to GDP ratio of 447[3] for 2005-2007, and trade per capita of $140,848. Though Malaysia is also trade dependent, it is relatively much less so with a trade to GDP ratio of 209, and a trade per capita of $12, 683 for the same period. Singapore has also become more region-dependent since the signing of the AFTA, with its regional to world export ratio rising from 10% in 1991 to 35% in 2001, far surpassing even Malaysia's heavy region dependency.

Yet as Malaysia seeks to move its way up the economic food chain-from agriculture, labor intensive manufacturing, and extraction to more value-added production as discussed in the previous section-Singapore too is working to move up the ladder from value-added manufacturing and efficient, capital-intensive production to a more innovation driven economy. "Traditionally, Singapore has billed itself as an efficient business city," says a World Bank report. (Song-Tan, 2005) "The ability to provide quality infrastructure services more efficiently than neighboring countries has long given the city-state a comparative advantage in the manufacturing sector."

Still, as we shall see, in its commodities exports to Malaysia, while Singapore has a unique mix of exports, it nevertheless remains strongest in traditional products like electronics, refined petroleum, and machinery.

SECTION - 3

TESTING THE H-O THEOREM

What this chapter will attempt to do in the next section is to find out the nature of the exports from Malaysia to Singapore

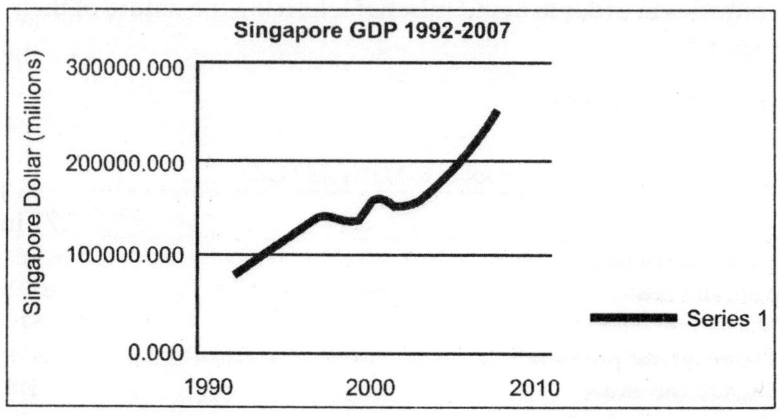

and Singapore to Malaysia to determine whether they are as one would expect based on the Heckscher-Ohlin Theorem, or not. Based on the above description of the two economies, the H-O Theorem says that Malaysia as the relatively labor abundant country should export labor intensive goods to Singapore, and conversely, Singapore as the relatively capital abundant country should export capital intensive goods to Malaysia. Due to a scarcity of data, on bilateral trade by sector, the data to be examined will be from United Nations Comtrade, a database of commodities traded between countries. Because the sectoral breakdown in this database isn't particularly refined, we will use the data in conjunction with other information about the nature of the sectors in each country in order to determine whether the goods being exported are, on the whole, capital intensive or labor intensive. Take for example the category of "mineral fuels," which ranks number two on the commodities exports list for both countries. Though a major export for both countries, Malaysia, as the 25th largest petroleum producer in the world with 750,000 barrels per day of production[4], exports primarily crude oil to Singapore for refining, which Singapore then exports back to Malaysia as gasoline or heating oil. Therefore, Malaysia's export of mineral fuels is largely labor intensive, whereas Singapore's export of mineral fuel is largely capital intensive. This type of analysis will be done when comparing exports between the two countries in order to avoid mischaracterizing the nature of their exports.

Applying the Test

Singapore to Malaysia Trade

Good	*2007 Amount*[5]
Electrical Machinery	16,920
Mineral Fuels	6392
Machinery	5825
Plastic/plastic products	1433
Organic chemicals	808
Optical/photographic	639

iron/steel	588
copper	361
pearls/precious stones	349
vehicles	296
Chemical products	264
Aluminum	255
Clocks	232
Paper	230
Cutlery	175
Perfumes/cosmetics	174
Dyeing extracts	165
Beverages	150
Inorganic chemicals	128
Rubber	118

Malaysia to Singapore Trade

Good	*2007 Amount*
Electrical machinery	9450
Mineral Fuels	7040
Machinery	4170
Iron/steel	737
Plastics/plastic products	720
Fats and oils	564
Aluminum	536
Optical/photographic	441
Pearls/precious stones	283
Aircraft/spacecraft & parts	258
Organic chemicals	249
Copper	228
Paper	220
Chemicals	218
Furniture	200
Live animals	169
Clocks	168
Dairy	152
Wood	151
Salt	150

Amounts for both tables are in millions of US Dollars.

In looking at the data, we can make some qualitative observations with regard to factor intensity of the exported goods. Electrical machinery is first on both lists of exports, and based on the readings we know that electronics production in Singapore is more efficient, using fewer units of labor for a unit of output, making it possible for the much less labor endowed Singapore to export nearly double the electronics to Malaysia than Malaysia exports to it. This high exchange of electronics does lend some credence to Krugman's intra-industry argument. However, because of the relative factor proportions of production in each country, with electronics production much more labor intensive in Malaysia than Singapore, we see that factor intensity reversal has occurred, and that in fact both countries are exporting as one would expect based on the Heckscher-Ohlin Theory.

We can also analyze the relative factor intensities quantitatively, however due to a lack of relevant data, we will have to assume that electronics manufacturing makes up the same proportion of the whole manufacturing sector in both countries. If we make that assumption, which is not a great stretch given that both countries have a high volume of electronics production, we can then consider the proportion of exports to total manufacturing labor in each country (for which data is available). In Malaysia in 2007, there were 1.977 million people working in the manufacturing sector, whereas in Singapore in the same year, there were 103,000 people working in manufacturing. Recall, factor intensity is defined as (k/l)x, then the factor intensity ratio for manufacturing in Malaysia in 2007 was $4,780 per laborer, and in Singapore was $16,427 per laborer[6]. Thus, while the factor intensity of manufactured exports from Singapore to Malaysia was approximately 3.5 times as capital intensive, and thus demonstrates the H-O conclusion to hold up, we would expect the factor intensity of Singaporean exports to be five times as capital intensive based on the relative factor abundance (recall, Singapore's capital/labor ratio was 297, while Malaysia's was 59).

Another sector for which labor statistics were able to be obtained is categorized as "mining, fishing, and agriculture."

In looking at the export tables, we can consider several of the commodities as part of this category, including: iron/steel, copper, aluminum, fats and oils, live animals, salt, and dairy. In this sector, Malaysian exports to Singapore accounted for roughly $2.5 billion with 1.6 laborers, or a capital to labor ratio of $1,585 of output per laborer. Meanwhile, Singaporean exports to Malaysia accounted for roughly $1.2 billion with 313,000 laborers or a capital to labor ratio of $3,846 of output per laborer. Again we see in mining, fishing and agricultural exports that though intra-industry trade is occurring, the factor intensity of Singaporean exports is relatively capital intensive, while Malaysian exports are relatively labor intensive.

The remaining labor categories with available data unfortunately don't include industry sectors that would involve exported goods, such as real estate or construction, or are found in the commodity trade tables, like financial services. Still, we can look at some of the remaining commodity exports from the tables to identify some general qualitative patterns. The Singaporean exports include a much higher ratio of finished goods, high-tech goods, and/or luxury items. These goods include plastic products, optical and photographic equipment, organic chemicals, vehicles, jewelry, perfumes, etc. Together these type of goods, which can be considered capital intensive in terms of their production, account for $4.8 billion of exports to Malaysia, or 13.5% of total exported commodities (among the top 20 export sectors). Malaysian export, however

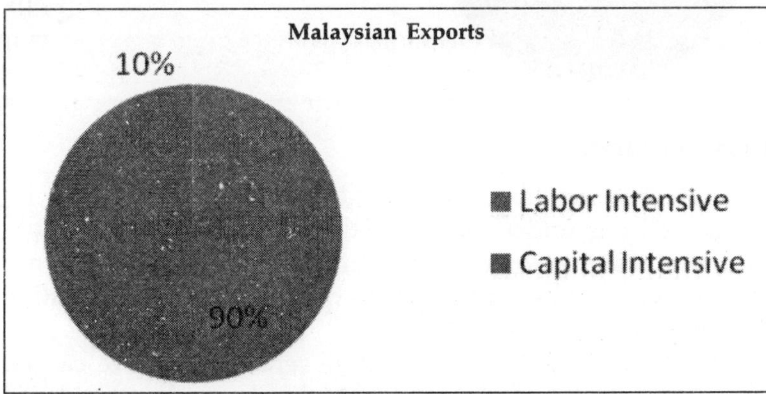

include some of these same capital intensive product categories, however as a smaller proportion to the whole. Consider, capital intensive Malaysian commodity exports to Singapore[7] totaled $2.3 billion, or 8.9% of the total export mix.

Considered another way, if the commodity groups are divided into two categories, labor intensive and capital intensive, we can compare the ratio of exports in each category from each country. Malaysian exports were found to be almost exclusively labor intensive, or 90% of the total (see graph). Singaporean exports, meanwhile, were much more capital intensive. It is important to note that although Singapore's exports were majority labor intensive in this finding, recall that the data used is only for commodities' exports, so one would imagine that much of that production would involve labor. Still, Singapore's commodities exports were 32% capital intensive and just 68% labor intensive.[8]

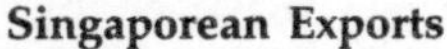
Singaporean Exports

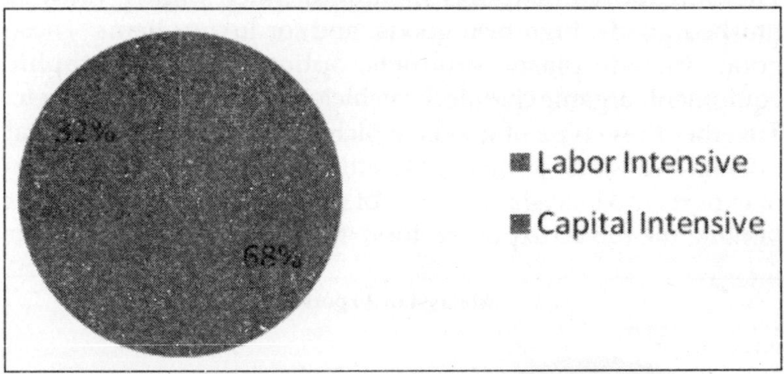

CONCLUSION

Though any conclusions reached from these tests must be tempered by an understanding of the inherent flaws of the data, and the assumptions for reaching determinations, some observations can be made from the quantitative and qualitative findings in the previous section.

First, we find that in a relative sense, Singapore can be considered capital abundant and Malaysia can be considered labor abundant. We also find that the two countries are closely linked economically, politically, and geographically, giving them high relative proportions of bilateral trade, and thus making them a worthwhile country pair to compare when testing the Heckscher-Ohlin Theorem. When comparing the relative factor intensities of sectors for which data was available, a questionable yet not entirely unreasonable method of comparing the export category with the corresponding labor category, and finding the capital output for each unit of labor employed. When applying this method to the two available sectors—manufacturing and agriculture/mining—Singapore's exports were found to be relatively capital intensive and Malaysia's exports were found to be relatively labor intensive. This meets the hypothesis of the H-O Theory. However, when looking at the factor intensity ratios of these two sectors in comparison with the factor abundance ratio, we found that Singapore's exports were relatively lower in terms of capital intensity than would be expected by H-O. Recall, Singapore's capital/labor abundance ratio was found to be 297, while Malaysia's was 59. Therefore Singapore can be considered approximately five times more capital abundant. However, for manufactured goods exports, Singapore's exports were only 3.5 times as capital abundant as Malaysia's; and for agriculture/mining exports, Singapore's exports were only 2.5 times as capital abundant. Therefore, this finding suggests that Malaysia is exporting more than their expected share of capital intensive goods to Singapore.

Likewise, the other assessment conducted on the export data, dividing it up between labor and capital intensive sectors, found that 90% of Malaysian commodity exports were labor intensive, while 68% of Singaporean commodity exports were labor intensive. With the caveat of this data only considering commodities trade, and not other critical sectors like financial services, or other professional services, which Singapore is known to be a world leader in, we can see just from the commodity data that Singapore exports are significantly more biased toward capital intensive production, even in commodities.

Thus we can conclude that with respect to Singapore/ Malaysia trade in 2007, the general thesis of the Heckscher-Ohlin Theorem is found to be accurate, with capital abundant Singapore exporting capital intensive goods to Malaysia, and labor abundant Malaysia exporting labor intensive goods to Singapore, though the factor intensity of the exports were not consistent with the factor abundance of the countries.

NOTES

1. Emphasis added.
2. Data source: International Monetary Fund, International Financial Statistics Database.
3. WTO Data.
4. Source: CIA World Factbook.
5. Amounts for both tables are in millions of US Dollars.
6. Note: Labor statistics obtained from the International Labor Organization labor statistics database.
7. Considered as: plastic products, spacecraft, pearls, chemical products, organic chemicals, clocks, optical/photographic.
8. Note that, as outlined in the previous section, mineral fuels can be considered capital intensive production in Singapore and labor intensive production in Malaysia. The other export categories considered to be capital intensive for Singapore were: plastic products, organic chemicals, optical/photographic, jewelry, vehicles, chemical products, clocks, cutlery, perfume, dyeing extracts, beverages, and inorganic chemicals. The export categories considered to be capital intensive for Malaysia were: plastic products, optical/photographic, precious stones, aircraft/ spacecraft parts, organic chemicals, chemicals, furniture, and clocks.

REFERENCES

David Clifton, W. M. (1984), An Empirical Investigation of the Heckscher Ohlin Theorem. *The Canadian Journal of Economics* , 32-38.

Economist Intelligence Unit (2008), *Country Commerce: Malaysia.* New York: Economist Intelligence Unit.

Harry P. Bowen, E. E. (1987), Multicountry, Multifactor Tests of the Factor Abundance Theory. *The American Economic Review* , 791-801.

Linder, S. (1961), *An Essay on Trade and Transformation.* New York: John Wiley.

Loeper, B. (1989), *U.S. Library of Congress Country Studies*. Retrieved May 14, 2009, from U.S. Library of Congress: *http://countrystudies.us/singapore/11.htm*

Madani, D. (2001), *Regional Integration and Industrial Growth Among Developing Countries: The Case of Three ASEAN Members.* New York: World Bank.

Paul R. Krugman, M. O. (2000), *International Economics.* New York: Addison Wesley.

Richard A. Brecher, E. U. (1993), Some Empirical Support for the Heckscher-Ohlin Model of Production. *The Canadian Journal of Economics*, 272-285.

Robert Stern, K. M. (1981), Determinants of the Structure of U.S. Foreign Trade. *Journal of International Economics*, 207-224.

Schott, P. K. (2003), One Size Fits All? Heckscher-Ohlin Specialization in Global Production. *American Economic Review*, 686-708.

Song-Tan, K. (2005), *From Efficiency Driven to Innovation Driven Economic Growth: Perspectives from Singapore.* Singapore: World Bank.

Trefler, D. (1995). The Case of the Missing Trade and Other Mysteries. *American Economic Review*, 1029-1046.

Wood, A. (1994), Give Heckscher and Ohlin a Chance. *Weltwirtschaftliches Archiv*, 20-49.

WTO. (2009), *World Trade Organization Statistics Database*. Retrieved May 14, 2009, from World Trade Organization: *http://www.wto.org/english/res_e/statis_e/statis_e.htm*

6

A TEST OF PURCHASING POWER PARITY (PPP) THEORY AND THE INTERNATIONAL FISHER EFFECT A CASE OF THE U.S. DOLLAR AND THE JAPANESE YEN

INTRODUCTION

A simple but enduring explanation of exchange rate determination is found in Gustov Cassels' Purchasing Power Parity (PPP) theory, laid down first by Cassel (1922), in the aftermath of the first World War. Over the years, the view that PPP holds in the long-run has not been seriously challenged. It needs to be mentioned, however, that the tests of the theory have been generally carried out for the years around 1930 only.

The present chapter conducts an empirical test of Purchasing Power Parity (PPP hereafter) for the recent time trend 1980-1981, of the Dollar-Yen exchange rate. Ever since the advent of the flexible exchange rate system in 1973, various tests have been carried out for the theories of exchange rate determinants including the portfolio balance approach and the monetary approach, which has been coincided by some to be the "sharpest" formulation.

This chapter is based on an article published in "The Journal of Applied Business Research".

However, even the monetary approach in the simplest form is eventually an evaluation of the price and most relevant only under fixed exchange rates. In general, there are other theories including the expectations-augmented approaches that address the short-run fluctuations and do not really compete with the PPP theory as long-run explanations. Indeed PPP may or may not coincide in the long-run tendency in these models.

In this chapter, we also test another theory of exchange rate determination based on the International Fisher effect, which was also put forth in the early 1900s. At the domestic level, the International Fisher effect concerns the relationship between nominal and real interest rates. When applied internationally, it implies that differences in national interest rates will affect the exchange rate, given the free arbitrage activities. This effect may be tested either directly or serve as the underpinning of a model to test for deviations from PPP. We adopt the former approach.

The chapter is organised as follows: Section 1 reviews briefly the relevant research on PPP and the International Fisher Effect in recent years; Section 2 formulates a simple model of exchange rate determination based on Cassel's absolute and relative PPP specifications, also formulating a testable equation for the International Fisher-Effect; and Section 3 uses monthly and quarterly data of the U.S. Dollar Yen exchange rate to examine the validity of the models specified in the earlier section. There is a final concluding and summary section.

SECTION I

A REVIEW OF RELEVANT RESEARCH ON THE PPP THEORY AND THE INTERNATIONAL FISHER EFFECT

One of the most extensive reviews of earlier studies related to PPP was undertaken by Officer (1977). Hence, in this paper we will concentrate only on recent studies. As can be seen in Broadberry (1987), the arguments for and against flexible exchange rates can be reconciled by appealing to PPP. Using data for the dollar/pound exchange rate, he shows that although exchange rates moved to preserve purchasing power parity in the long run, there were significant deviations from it in the short run. The source of the major deviation from PPP between 1931 to 1933 appears to lie in the asymmetric response of foreign exchange markets to fluctuations in economic variables in the U.K. and the U.S., while the latter adhered to the gold standard.[1] (1) The study is useful for our purposes to make a point, that even in controversies concerning fluctuations in exchange rates as early as the 1930s, the PPP theory figured prominently.

In Taylor and McMahon (1988) one finds the use of the PPP theory in providing explanations for the exchange rate fluctuations of the 1920s. Their results are strongly supportive of the PPP hypothesis as a long-run equilibrium condition on which actual exchange rates tend to converge over the period. However, the main focus of the paper is on the econometric techniques that are used by Frenkel (1980) and Edison (1985). A more recent study of PPP is carried out by Edison (1987), who tested the dollar/pound exchange rate for a very long period (between 1890 to 1978). It uses the "error correction mechanism" that was made popular and was used for consumption and demand for money by Davidson *et al.*, (1978) and Rose (1985), respectively. It concludes that a naive version of the PPP relationship does not adequately represent the dollar/pound exchange rate. This result was reinforced when the sample was divided into two sub-samples and the fixed exchange rate assumption was exploited. The conclusion supports the qualified interpretation of the PPP doctrine: the proportionality between the exchange rates and relative price level emerges in the long run, after taking into account the effects of changes in structural factors. In general, the consensus among economists is that the PPP explanation does not provide a guide for short-run movements of exchange rate. However, one of the major reason for deterioration in the explanatory power of PPP in the 1970s, was the barrage of real shocks to economies in that period that resulted in relative price changes.

Dryden, Reut and Slater (1987) use the U.S. and Canadian dollars to test the importance of PPP doctrine. They formulate in that conventional hypothesis and test it for data spanning 1960 to 1987. Considering specific consumption patterns in the U.S. and Canada they conclude that PPP theory is justified in its argument that, the price ratios approximately equal the real exchange rate. David Binman (1983) summarizes the main theoretical points of PPP theory in comparison to the related theoretical arguments like the monetary models. Similarly the International Fisher Effect has become the primary focus of study for some researchers. Giddy and Dufey (1975) showed that interest differentials have the ability to properly anticipate currency changes. Essentially what the International Fisher Effect advocates is, that arbitrage between financial markets, in the form of capital inflows and outflows, ensuring that the interest rate differential between two countries is an unbiased predictor of the future change in spot-exchange rate. In other words, currencies with low interest rates are expected to devalue relative to the currencies with high interest rates.

In the next section we lay down the models to be used in testing the PPP hypothesis and the International Fisher Effect on exchange rates, after briefly noting the theoretical arguments.

SECTION II

EXCHANGE RATE DETERMINATION WITH THE PPP THEORY AND THE INTERNATIONAL FISHER EFFECT

Essentially, PPP theory postulates that exchange rates adjust over time to offset divergent movements in national price levels. In its absolute version, the exchange rate between two currencies is approximately equal to absolute purchasing power parity given by the ratio of price levels in the two countries. This is because adherents to the theory of the 'law of one price' hold goods produced in the two countries are perfect substitutes, and market arbitrage will bring about price equality in freely interacting markets. The efficient function of the gold standard rested on such arbitrage. However, one does not have to subscribe to the extreme view of the 'law of one price' to establish PPP. Even with product differentiation, substitution in demand would work to bring about uniformity in price levels, but then the process would take longer and would entitle deviations from PPP for extended time periods.

At any rate, in the absolute version of the PPP theory, the exchange rate in time period t, e_t is defined as the ratio of the price level in the home country, for time period t, $P_h(t)$, the price level in the foreign country in time period t, $P_f(t)$. This will hold with the additional assumption of no transportation costs, tariffs, quotas, or other restrictions. In general,

$$e_t = PPP_{\text{absolute}} = P_h(t)/P_f(t) \tag{1}$$

The relationship in (1) is consistent with intuition. The value of a currency is based on the purchasing power of a unit, which may be defined as the inverse of the general price level. Hence, the rates of the value of the two currencies or the equilibrium exchange rate is given by absolute PPP, i.e. the rates of the two price levels in its relative version, the PPP theory relates the absolute version at time period t + 1 to that at base period 0. Then the relative version of PPP status that,

$$e(t) = PPP_{\text{relative}} = \frac{P_h(t-1)/P_h(0)}{P_f(t-1)/P_f(0)} \tag{2}$$

Now, let us define the inflation rate in the home country,

as the $\dfrac{P_h(t-1)/P_h(t)}{P_h(t)}$, so that $P_h(t+1)/P_h(t) = 1 + i_h$.

Expressing the inflation rate, i_f, in the foreign country in a similar fashion and substituting in equation 2, we get

$$\frac{e(t+1)}{e(t)} = \frac{1+i_h}{1+i_f} \tag{3}$$

It is further possible to express a percentage change in exchange rate from time period t to t + 1 as approximately equal to the difference between two inflation rates divided by $(1 + i_f)$. Thus the determination, as well as the forecasting of exchange rates, is possible by using the PPP arguments. Nonetheless, if we consider that PPP expresses the exchange rate, as a price ratio, it is perfectly possible that exchange rate's real value is unchanged, even though nominal value changes. For example, consider a case of increase in domestic inflation that is more than the foreign inflation. This would, according to PPP, devalue the local currency in relation to foreign currency. Still from the perspective of the local firm, it is possible that its competitive position in the world market is unchanged because the devaluation and domestic inflation can have offsetting effects. This is a case of having a change in the nominal exchange rates without a change in the real exchange rate. Therefore, with concern about currency changes affecting relative competitiveness, the focus must be on the changes in the real rather than the nominal exchange rate. For the sake of generality, the real exchange rate is defined as follows:

$$e_{rt} = e_t \frac{(1+i_{ft})}{(1+i_{ht})} \tag{4}$$

For estimation purposes a modified version of equation (4) that uses prior (lagged) values of dependent and independent variables can be specified as follows:

$$\log e_t = bo + b1 \log e_{t-1} + b2 \log (P^*/P)t + b3 \log (P^*/P)t-2 + b4 [\log e_{t-1} - \log (P^*/P)t-1] \tag{5}$$

Equation (5) is similar to the equation used for testing PPP by Broadberry (1987). E_t is the exchange rate defined in the European way meaning the number of units of foreign currency per unit of the home currency. When the change in the domestic inflation rate relative to the foreign inflation rate is substantial, so that even the real exchange rate is changed, there is a deviation from PPP. As can be seen in equation (5), deviations from the PPP is the main reason for the change in the exchange rate between the currencies. An increase in the foreign inflation rate relative to the domestic (P^*/P), creates appreciation of domestic currency (and depreciation of foreign currency) and vice versa; hence, the expected sign of (P^*/P) is negative. As mentioned in the last section, it is not likely that a change in the real exchange rate can occur in the short-run. Therefore, the studies that use short-run data (say monthly, ranging from only 5 to 10 years) generally do not testify the validity of the PPP theory. Our belief is that since exchange rates in the Bretton Woods system were not truly flexible the circumstances have not been satisfactory enough to test the PPP theory either for the short-run or long-run data. It is, therefore, important to test the PPP relatively in the form of equation (5) by using data from recent years, when exchange rates are relatively more flexible.

The International Fisher Effect is another simple concept that is very relevant in international finance. It relates the real interest rates of two economies and claims that the exchange rate between the two currencies would be determined by the difference between two interest rates. In equation form, a test of the International Fisher Effect is represented by,

$$\log e(t) = d_0 + d_1 (r-r^*) + d_2 (r_{t-1}-r^*_{t-i}) + d_3 e_{t-1} \qquad (6)$$

Since the exchange rate is defined as the number of foreign currency units per unit of domestic currency, a higher domestic interest rate creates higher capital inflows, which leads to appreciation of domestic currency, and an increase in exchange rate value as it is defined here. Hence, the expected sign of dl is positive according to the International Fisher Effect.

The next section is devoted to an empirical evaluation of equation (5) and (6) for the dollar-yen rate, using time series data from very recent years.

SECTION - III

TESTING THEORIES: A CASE OF THE DOLLAR/YEN EXCHANGE RATE

To test the PPP theory and the International Fisher Effect, we decided to initially use monthly data of the U.S. and Japanese economies for the time period between 1980 to 1988. The data points were collected from data disk series for the U.S. economy and from the International Financial Statistics (IFS) series of the International Monetary Fund. The exchange rate is defined as the number of yens available per dollar so that the exchange rate is the ratio of foreign currency per domestic currency unit. Consumer 'price index series serves as a proxy for general price levels. The U.S. economy is located as the home country, hence, number of yens per dollar is the exchange. (The estimated results of equation (5) were as follows):

$$\log e_t = .114 + .326 \log e_{t-1} - .9905 \log (P^*/P) +$$
$$\qquad (1.800) \qquad (3.488) \qquad\qquad (-2.2903)$$

$$305 \log (P^*/P)_{t-2} -.02442 [\log e_{t-1} - \log (P^*/P)_{t-1}]$$
$$(.7156) \qquad (-1.8196)$$

R^2 = .2155, Standard Error of Regression = .02246, Durbin-Watson Statistic = 2.008, F Statistic = 6.3197.

Figures within parenthesis under the estimated coefficients represent the t statistic values.

As can be observed, the R^2 value is small (.2155), but the standard error of the regression is satisfactory. The Durbin-Watson statistic is excellent, and altogether the regression form works as expected by theory. The satisfactory Durbin-Watson statistic may be primarily because of the lagged value of dependent variable on the right-hand side. The relative price ratio shows a significant negative (as expected by PPP theory) coefficient. The lagged relative price ratio has a positive non-significant coefficient. In general, except for the small value of R^2, the regression results are not very disappointing. All the results are tested with 95% confidence interval by using the estimated t statistic. For the estimate of the International Fisher Effect, using the same time period and monthly data, we received the following results:

$$e_t = -1.1644+.7842(r_t - r^*_t)-.4728 (r_t -r^*_t)-.0045e_{t-1}$$
$$(-.6279) \qquad (2.771) \qquad (-1.68) \qquad (-.3122)$$

R^2 = .1475, Standard Error of Regression = 2.7897, Durbin Watson Statistic = 1.552, F Statistic = 5.4813.

The results of the International Fisher Effect are more encouraging than the ones for PPP, even though the R^2 value is smaller for the latter. The higher interest rates differential without lag depreciates the exchange rate (as expected from the International Fisher Effect). Moreover, the lagged values of the independent variable are not as significant as the current period values. Also the lagged value of the dependent variable is not significant, as tested by the t statistic.

Nonetheless, to test whether quarterly data could yield any better R^2, we decided to run the PPP regression one more time. Our results for the quarterly data are as follows:

$$\log e_t = .292+.525 \log e_{t-1}-.258 \log(P^*/P)_t\ 1.273$$
$$(1.21) \quad (3.483) \qquad (-.203) \qquad (-1.049)$$

$\log(P^*/P)_{t-2} - .0635\ [\log e_{t-1} - \log(P^*/P)_{t-1}]$
(-1.184)

R^2 = .4261, Standard Error of Regression = .0404, Durbin Watson Statistic = 1.9974, F Statistic = 4.6408.

The above results show a significant improvement in R^2 value without changing the sign of any estimated coefficient. All the estimated coefficients are more or less as significant as in the earlier estimates. As explained in Kennedy (1985) or any other econometrics textbook, a higher R^2 does not necessarily mean a better specification (or estimation) of the relationship. However, compared to monthly, the quarterly data estimation shows: (1) a higher R^2, (2) a low but small increase in Standard Error of Regression, and (3) an equally satisfactory Durbin-Watson Statistic. Hence, we conclude that 'ceteris paribus', relative PPP theory explains quarterly fluctuations in exchange rates better than it explains the monthly fluctuations in exchange rates. Similarly, we used the quarterly data to test the International Fisher Effect to get the following results:

$$et = -6.5908 + 1.1482(r_t - r^*_{t-1}) - .02712(r_{t-1} - r^*_{t-1})$$
(-.9989) (2.1904) (-.0544) (.0479)

R^2 =.3199, Standard Error of Regression = 5.0413, Durbin Watson Statistic = 1.172, F Statistic = 4.3903.

From the results above, the quarterly data estimation once again shows the following facts when compared to monthly data estimation: (1) R^2 value is much more improved, (2) F Statistic is lower than in the case of monthly data, (3) Standard Error of Regression is higher, but by a very small increase, and (4) the Durbin-Watson Statistics is comparable. Thus, there is some evidence that the International Fisher Effect is more applicable to the quarterly data than to the monthly data, as far as the U.S. dollar and Japanese yen are concerned. It seems that both theories can be used to effectively forecast the behaviour of the exchange rate. The R^2 value for both estimations are better for the quarterly data. The expected signs of all coefficients are observed, and, in general, the results are quite satisfactory and seem to validate the theoretical postures.

SECTION IV

SUMMARY AND CONCLUSIONS

The present chapter discusses the theories of Purchasing Power Parity (PPP) and the International Fisher Effect dating back to the early years of the twentieth century, and tests their evidence for the recent time period data for the U.S. dollar-Yen exchange rate. The results show that both these theories provide a satisfactory explanation of the behaviour of exchange rates. One of the main reason why these theories lost their explanatory power in recent years was the inflexibility of exchange rates in the Bretton Woods System. However, as the exchange rates became flexible again in recent years, the theories have become more applicable. It is further observed that the quarterly data are more relevant for these theories than the monthly data.

I am indebted to Mr. Lam for the helpful research assistance on this paper, Mrs. Dianna Dovenmuehle for efficient typing, to Dr. Nandakumar, and an anonymous reference of this journal for valuable comments on the earlier version.

NOTE

1. Frenkel, J.A., (1978), Purchasing Power Parity: Doctrinal Perspective and Evidence from the 1920s', JIE 8, 169-81.

REFERENCES

Brranson, William H. (1981), "Comment: The Collapse of Purchasing Power Parity During the 1970s", *European Economic Review*, Vol. 16, pp. 167-171.

Broadberry, S. N. (1987), "Purchasing Power Parity and the Pound--Dollar Rate in the 1930s", *Economics*, Vol. 54, pp. 69-78.

Cassel, Gustav (1922), *Money and Foreign Exchange Rate After* 1914, New York: Constable and Company Ltd.

Davidson, James E. H., Hendry, David F., Srba, Frank and Yeo, Stephen (1978), "Econometric Modelling of the Aggregate Time Series Relationship Between Consumers' Expenditures and Income in the U.K.", *Economic Journal*, Vol. 88, pp. 661-692.

Dryden, John, Reut, Katrina, and Slater, Barbara (1987), "Comparison of Purchasing Power Parity Between the U.S. and Canada", *Monthly Labour Review*, pp. 7-24.

Edison, Hali J. (1987), "Purchasing Power Parity in the Long-run: A Test of the Dollar/Pound Exchange Rate (1890-1978)", *Journal of Money, Credit and Banking*, Vol. 19, No. 3, pp. 376-387.

Frenkel, J. A. (1981), "The Collapse of Purchasing Power Parity During the 1970s", *European Economic Review*, Vol. 16, pp. 146-165.

Kennedy, Peter (1985), *A Guide to Econometrics, Second Edition*, The MIT Press, Cambridge, MA.

Officer, Lawrence H. (1976), "The Purchasing Power Parity Theory of Exchange Rates: A Review Article", *International Monetary Fund (IMF) Staff Papers*, Vol. 83, pp. 1-60.

Rose, Andrew K. (1985), "An Alternative Approach to the American Demand for Money", *Journal of Money, Credit and Banking*, Vol. 17, pp. 439-455, Nov. 1985.

Taylor, Mark and McMahon Patrick C. (1988), "Long-run Purchasing Power Parity in the 1920s", *European Economic Review*, Vol. 32, pp. 179-197.

7

SHORT-RUN DEVIATIONS FROM PURCHASING POWER PARITY (PPP)
A Case of Expectational Changes

INTRODUCTION

As is well known, the Purchasing Power Parity (PPP) theory states that exchange rates adjust over time, so as to offset divergent movements in national price levels. This implies that a country that runs an inflation higher than its trading partner(s) will see its currency depreciating. Originally put forth by Cassel (1918), this theory was proved to be capable of explaining exchange rate movements. Officer (1976) provides a detailed description of the development of the PPP theory over the years and the empirical work undertaken to test the theory.

In general, there is a consensus that the PPP theory is valid when a sufficiently long-time interval is considered. But at the same time, it is stressed that the concept is relevant only in the long-run, so that deviations from Parity may be what rules in the short-run. While fundamental economic variables and behavior such as substitution in demand would ensure the "law of one price" in the long-run, at any given point in time, other factors such as speculative activity could cause such deviations from PPP. The presence of non-traded goods and services have also pointed out a cause of deviations from PPP. Efforts have also been made to establish that deviations from

PPP form a random walk, with no tendency for reversion to parity.

This chapter is devoted to two tasks, both undertaken for the Canadian Dollar-US Dollar exchange rate, the Deutsche Mark (DM)-US Dollar rate and the US Dollar-Pound rate, with quarterly data for the period from 1974-1988.

First, deviations from PPP in the short-run are modeled as forming a dynamic adjustment mechanism towards a long-run equilibrium. To do this, the error-correction approach popularized in the study of consumption behaviour by Davidson, Hendry, Srba, and Yeo (1978) is adopted.[2] It is also examined whether short-term PPP exists at all. Second, a possible cause for deviations from PPP in the short-run is put forward and examined for applicability to the exchange rates under consideration. The argument tested here is whether PPP holds with respect to *expected,* rather than *actual,* current prices, in which case short-run PPP, in the conventional sense, will not hold.[3]

The rest of the chapter is organized as follows. Section II derives equations incorporating an error-correction mechanism for adjustment to long-run PPP and estimates them. Section III is devoted to the examination of the expected PPP theory. Section IV gathers together the conclusions in a concise fashion.

SHORT-RUN ADJUSTMENT AND LONG-RUN EQUILIBRIUM

Several earlier attempts to test the evidence of PPP have been undertaken. Broadberry (1987) uses the data of 1930s to test the Pound-Dollar fluctuations. As mentioned before, Officer (1976) carries out an extensive survey of numerous studies of PPP. However a clear-cut distinction between absolute and relative versions of PPP is rarely witnessed. Further the present study uses three different exchange rates and concentrates on the 1980s data.

We construct the theoretical model in the following fashion; Let E_t, represent the relevant exchange rate at period t and RP_t the relevant relative price at period t. Starting with the relation:

$$E_t = a_o + a_1 E_{t-1} + a_2 PR_I + a_3 PR_{t-1}, \quad (1)$$

Rewrite (1) as

$$DE_t = a_o\ DPR_t - (l - a_1)\ E_{t-1} + (a_2 + a_3)\ PR_{t-1}, \quad (2)$$

Where $DE_t = E_t - E_{t-1}$ etc.

(2) may be further transformed to get

$$DE_t = a_o + a_2\ DPR_t - (l - a_1)\ (E_{t-1} - PR_{t-l}) + (a_2 + a_3 + a_1 - 1)\ PR_{t-1} \quad (3)$$

Then we get the error correction formulation assuming that $a_j + a_2 + a_3 = 1$, so that the last term in (3) disappears, which implies that the difference between E and PR, in the log form is constant in the long-run. So the error correction formulation which we use is:

$$DE_t = a_o + a_2\ DPR_t - (1 - a_1)\ (E_{t-2} - PR_{t-2}) \quad (4)$$

As can be seen in (4), the previous errors influence the movement towards the long-run equilibrium, which is given by putting DE = DPR = O. This means in the steady state, E and PR are unchanged.

$$E = PR_t^*\ a_o / (l - a) \quad (5)$$

(we could derive the error correction form of equation (4) by starting from the long-run solution of equation (5), and assuming a general lag structure.)

Based on equation (4), the following equations were estimated, but by using the log form (t–statistics are presented in parentheses):

Canadian Dollar–US Dollar rate:

D log CANDOL = 1.145 * D log USCWP (6)
(-3.87)

-0.048 [Log CANDOL (–1) –Log USCWP (–1)] + 0.0062
(-2.42) (1.27)

$R^2 = 0.36$ F =20.0

Where "D" refers to difference, CANDOL is the Canadian Dollar-US Dollar exchange rate, and USCWP is the ratio of the U.S. wholesale price index to the Canadian wholesale price index. The data used in our analysis are compiled from the various issues of *International Financial Statistic* published by the International Monetary Fund. We concentrated on quarterly data alone.

Deutsche Mark -Dollar rate:

D Log DMDOL = –1.4661 D Log USGWP (7)
(-1.183)

–0.0755 (Log DMDOL (–1) –Log USGWP (–1)] + 0.0615
(-1.44) (1.43)

R^2 = 0.02 f =1.2J

Where DMDOL is the Deutsche Mark-Dollar rate and USGWP is the ratio of the U.S. to the German wholesale price index.

D Log DMDOL = -2.198 D Log USGWP (8)
(-1.57)

–0.623 [Log DMDOL (–1) + Log USGWP (–1)] + 0.509 D Log
(-2.52) (2.098)

DMDOL (-1) + 0.137T –0.180
(2.02) (-1.12)

R^2 = 0.294 F = 3.29

Pound-Dollar rate:

D Log PODOL = –0.4525 D Log KSWP (9)
(-0.48)

–0.0783 (Log PODOL (–1) -Log KSWP (–1)] + 0.041
(-2.2) (1.65)

R^2 = 0.08 F= 2.4

Where PDDOL is the Dollar-Pound rate and KSWP is the ratio of the UK to the US wholesale price index.

D Log PODOL = –0.189 DLog KSWP (10)
(–0.12)

–0.5298 [Log PODOL (–1) –Log KSWP (–1) J+0.576 0 Log PODOL (1)
(-2.67) (2.649)

–0.0212T + 1.459
(–2.475) (2.49)

R^2 = 0.11 F =2.38

When looking at the estimates in (6) – (11), we are concerned mainly with the short-run adjustment mechanism and (or) the possibility of short-run homogeneity of the exchange rate with respect to relative prices. By assumption, there is homogeneity in the long-run; the assumption that $a_1 + a_2 + a = 1$ in equation (3) amounts to that.[4] Also, for instance, if Log USCWP (–1), the lagged relative price is added, that independent variable is not significant, which supports the assumption of long-run homogeneity.

For short-run homogeneity of the exchange rule with respect to the relative price, the coefficient of the change (difference) in relative price should be –1. In equation (6) for the Canadian Dollar-US Dollar rate, the coefficient of D Log USCWP is close to -1, and significant, so that the hypothesis of short-run homogeneity cannot be clearly rejected. The coefficient of the error-correction is also significant. The long-run solution is obtained by putting the "difference" terms equal to zero; and we get:

$$\text{Log (CANDOL / USCWP)} = 0.002/0.048 \qquad (11)$$

$$\text{i.e., CANDOL} = 1.347\ \text{USCWP.}$$

Equations (7) and (8) refer to the DM-Dollar rate. In both equations, the coefficient of D Log USGV\'P, the relative price change term, is not close to negative unity. The general fit for the estimated coefficients are a little better in equation (8), after the addition of a lagged exchange rate change term and the time trend (T). In any case, there is no short-run homogeneity with respect to the change in relative price levels. The short-run adjustment, or error correction term, is significant at the 5% level in equation (8). The results of estimation for equations (9) and (10) for the Dollar-Pound rate are quite poor, but the error correction terms are significant at the 5% level. The coefficients of Log KSWP are quite different from -1, so that short-run homogeneity of the exchange rate with respect to relative prices cannot be maintained (though the insignificance of these coefficients make any such hypothesis irrelevant).

Equations (6)-(10) were also re-run with consumer price indices instead of wholesale price indices. The results were, in general, considerably weaker therefore those results are not reported here.

EXPECTED PURCHASING POWER PARITY

In this section, the contention that PPP holds with respect to expected, rather than actual, price levels (which also constitutes an explanation for deviations from PPP in the conventional sense) is examined. An implicit assumption is, as in the currency substitution literature,[5] that domestic currency and foreign currency are not perfect substitutes. Hence, when expected rates of inflation differ between countries, holders of real balances will make change in their composition of real balance (which includes domestic as well as foreign currency), influencing the exchange rate.

To carry out the estimation, forecasts were made for wholesale and consumer price indices for the period 1974-1988. The method of distributed lags was used; in most cases a log of three quarters was seen to give the best forecasts.[6]

Tests were carried out for absolute, as well as relative (expected) PPP for the period 1976-1988 and 1980-1988. The estimated equations are presented below.

Canadian Dollar-US Dollar rate:

$$\text{Log CANDOL} = \underset{(-6.77)}{-0.7437}\ \text{Log USCWPF} + \underset{(36.2)}{0.2602} \qquad (13)$$

$R^2 = 0.562$ $\quad F = 45.8$ $\quad$ Period 1980-88

Where USCWPF is the forecast for the ratio US wholesale price/ Canadian wholesale price.

$$\text{Log CANDOL} = \underset{(-2.97)}{-0.966}\ \text{LogUSCWPF} + \underset{(14.8)}{1.038} \qquad (14)$$

$$\text{Log CANDOL (-1)} \underset{(3.6)}{+1.096}\ \text{Log USCWPF (-1)} \underset{(-0.83)}{-0.016}$$

$R^2 = 0.949$ $\quad F = 212.9$ $\quad$ Period 1980-88

$$\text{Log CANDOL} = \underset{(-13.41)}{-1.2545}\ \text{Log USCWPF} + \underset{(07.95)}{0.2637} \qquad (15)$$

$R^2 = 0.762$ $\quad F = 179.84$ $\quad$ Period 1974-88

$$\text{Log CANDOL} = \underset{(-5.72)}{-0.9816} \text{ Log USCWPF} + \underset{(34.1)}{0.2512} \qquad (16)$$

$R^2 = 0.471$ F =32.72 Period 1980-88

Where USCCPF is the ratio of the forecast for the US consumer price index to the forecast of the Canadian consumer price index.

Deutsche Marx -US Dollar rate:

$$\text{Log DMDOL} = \underset{(-5.92)}{-6.256} \text{ Log USGWPF} + \underset{(25.59)}{0.9941} \qquad (17)$$

$R^2 = 0.494$ F = 35.16 Period 1980-88

Where USGWPF is the forecast of the US wholesale price index divided by the forecast for the German wholesale price index.

Pound-LTS Dollar rate:

$$\text{Log PDDOL} = \underset{(-3.64)}{-0.901} \text{ Log KSWPF} + \underset{(15.27)}{0.4585} \qquad (18)$$

$R^2 = 0.26$ F = 13.2 Period 1980-88

Where KSWPF is the forecast for UK wholesale index divided by the forecast for the US wholesale price index.

$$\text{Log PDDOL} = \underset{(-6.26)}{-0.699} \text{ Log KSWPF} + \underset{(18.51)}{0.464} \qquad (19)$$

$R^2 = 0.406$ F = 39.2 Period 1976-88

Relarive PPP versions:

$$\text{D Log CANDOL} = \underset{(-3.35)}{-0.925} \text{ D Log USCWPF} \qquad (20)$$

R2 = 0.27 F = 12.57 Period 1980-88

$$\text{D Log CANDOL} = \underset{(-4.13)}{-1.1032} \text{ D Log USCWPF} \qquad (21)$$

R2 = 0.20 F = 13.79 Period 1976-88

Of these equations, (13)-(19) test the relative version of (expected) PPP while the last two deal with the absolute version. For expected PPP to prevail, the coefficient of the expected relative price term in these equations should be-1.

In equation (13), which is for the Canadian Dollar-US dollar rate for 1980-1988, the coefficient of Log USCWPF is not close to negative unity. On adding lagged terms for the dependent and independent variables, this coefficient becomes nearly -1. The overall explanatory power of the equation also improves considerably. So the hypothesis of expected absolute PPP for the Canadian Dollar-US Dollar rate, during the eighties cannot be rejected (the t-statistics within the parentheses are also significant at the 5% level). Re-running the equation for the period 1976-1988 hikes up the coefficient of the expected relative price term away from negative unity [see equation (15)]. Equations (13)-(15) were run using forecasts for wholesale prices. Equation (16) is an equation using forecasts for consumer prices. Again, the coefficient of two "expected" relative consumer price terms is almost -1, implying the validity of expected PPP.

For the DM-Dollar rate, the coefficient of the expected relative price term in (17) is far from -1, so that expected PPP is rejected firmly for the 1980s. The test failed even more disastrously when using forecasts for consumer prices, and also for the period 1976-1988. Those results are not presented here.

For the Dollar-Pound rate, the coefficient of the expected relative wholesale price term is close to –1 in equation (18) for 1980-1988. So the hypothesis of expected PPP may be maintained for the eighties. It is less evident in (19) for the period 1976-1988. The tests with forecasted consumer prices were not satisfactory.

The equations for relative PPP are presented only for the Canadian Dollar-US Dollar rate; the tests were singularly unsuccessful for the DM-Dollar and Dollar-Pound rate. Also, only results using forecasted wholesale prices are presented since the equations obtained using forecasted consumer prices were unsatisfactory. However, in both equations (20) and (21), the coefficient or the (change in) expected relative price term is fairly close to negative one, and significant. So expected PPP cannot be rejected as far as the Canadian Dollar-US Dollar exchange rate in the eighties is concerned.

CONCLUSION

While there is no objection raised in the profession against the importance of the notion of Purchasing Power Parity as an equilibrium theory, there is much less consensus regarding the time horizon in which it is relevant. There is a view that as a long-run equilibrium theory, PPP would be irrelevant during a short time interval. One way to get over this difficulty with defining the time interval is to delineate a path or adjustment process towards a long-run equilibrium with PPP. This is done in this chapter by specifying an error correction mechanism where adjustment towards the long-run equilibrium, depends on past discrepancies in PPP. The analysis is undertaken for three Dollar exchange rates for the eighties. The specification allows us to test for short-run homogeneity of the exchange rate with respect to relative prices (short-run PPP) and also to solve the long-run static equilibrium solution. The analysis was conducted using wholesale prices as well as consumer price indices.

It was found that short-run PPP, in the eighties, is a defendable proposition only for the Canadian Dollar-US Dollar exchange rate, and that too, with respect to wholesale prices. No short-run homogeneity with respect to relative prices was exhibited by the DM-Dollar and Dollar-Pound exchange rates. However, in all cases, the coefficients of the dynamic adjustment, or error correction terms, were significant.

The present chapter also turns a searchlight on a possible cause for deviations from PPP; namely that PPP holds with respect to expected, rather than actual, current prices. The argument is that when possibilities for currency substitution exist, there will be re-grouping of currency portfolios and exchange rate adjustment, when expected rates of inflation differ between countries; so there will be no purchasing power parity with respect to current prices.

To conduct tests for expected PPP, first forecasts were made for (quarterly) wholesale price and consumer price indices for USA, UK, Germany, and Canada for the time period 1976-1988. The forecasts were made by the method of distributed lags, adhering to a lag of 3 quarters most of the time. Using these forecasts of expected prices, both absolute and relative versions of (expected) PPP was tested. It was seen that expected PPP holds, and so it can be put forth as an explanation of deviations from current or actual PPP, for the Canadian Dollar-US Dollar rate. This was true for both the absolute and the relative versions, and for experiments with forecasted wholesale as well as consumer price indices. Expected PPP seems to be plausible for the DM-Dollar rate as well, with reference to wholesale prices. The tests fail for the Dollar-Pound rate. The final conclusion must be that expected purchasing power parity is a tenable proposition worth further attention and research.

NOTES

1. See Adler and Lehmann (1983) and Shapiro (1983).
2. Broadberry (1987) has also consider..ed the short-run adjustment towards a long-run PPP equilibrium for the Pound Sterling exchange rates in the 1930s.
3. The only paper concerned with such a test seeins to be Fortune (1986), who is concerned with the Pound-Dollar rate for the period 1973-80. He includes that expected PPP is a tenable position.
4. For long-run homogeneity, the coefficients of the lagged exchange rate and relative price terms should be equal, but of opposite sign.
5. See for instance, Calvo (1986).
6. i.e., expectations formed 3 quarters ahead provided the best forecasts.
7. See Officer (1976) for a detailed discussion of absolute, as well as relative, Purchasing Power Parity and their measurement.

BIBLIOGRAPHY

Adler, Michael, and Lehmann, Bruce, "Deviations from Purchasing Power Parity in the Long Rtm", *Journal of Finance,* Vol. 38, December 1983, pp. 1471-1487.

Broadberry, S. N., "Purchasing Power Parity and the Pound-Dollar Rate in the *1930", Economica,* Vol. 54, February 1987, pp. 69-78.

Calvo, Guillermo, "Currency Substitution and the Real Exchange Rate: The Utility Maximization Approach", *Journal of International Money and Finance,* Vol. 4, June 1985, pp. 175-188.

Davidson, James E.H, Hendry, David F., Srba, Frank, and Yeo, Stephen, "Economic Modeling of the Aggregate Time Series Relationship Between Consumers' Expenditures and Income in the U.K., *Economic Journal,* Vol. 88, December 1978, pp. 661-692.

Forttme, Neill, J., "Expected Purchasing Power Parity" *Weltwirtschaftliclles Archiv,* Band 121, 1985, pp. 97-104.

Frenkel, Jacob A., "Purchasing Power Parity, Doctrinal Perspective and EVidence" from the 1920s", *Journal oflnternational Economics,* Vol. 8, May 1978, pp. 169-191.

MacDonald, Ronald, "Are Deviations from Purchasing Power Parity Efficient" Some Further Answers, *Welthwirtshaftliches Archieve,* Vol. 121, April 1985, pp. 638-645.

Makrowsky, Aleksander, "Modeling Philosophy: The Error Correction Approach", *Mimeo, National Institute of Economic Research,* Stockholm, June 1988.

Officer, Lawrence H, "The Purchasing Power Parity Theory of Exchange Rates: A Review Article", *International Monetary Fund (IMF) Staff Papers,* Vol. 83, March 1976, pp. 1-60.

Shapiro, Alan C., "What Does Purchasing Power Mean?", *Journal of International Money and Finance,* Vol. 2, March 1983, pp. 295-318.

8

THE EXTENSION OF THE J-CURVE HYPOTHESIS, KULKARNI HYPOTHESIS AND MULTIPLE CURRENCY DEVALUATIONS IN CASES OF EGYPT AND GHANA

INTRODUCTION

A question like, what "what is the effect of an exchange rate devaluation on BOP?" is answered by the traditional international trade literature in terms of the elasticity approach. The basic thrust of the answer to this question implies that everything depends upon the values of the elasticities of demand for the imports and exports of an economy. In fact the Marshall-Lerner condition created by Alfred Marshall and Abba Lerner in the early fifties states specifically that the initial balance of trade is zero and if supply elasticities are infinite, then the absolute values of export and import demand elasticities have to be at least large enough to add up to unity to have an exchange rate devaluation bring about the surplus in BOP.

It is easy to prove that since the elasticities values are quite dependent upon the time period, in the short run, when the elasticities are small, the Marshall-Lerner condition is less likely to be satisfied, and the devaluation of a currency leads to a

---

This Chapter is based on an article published in Journal of Applied Business and Economic Research, 1994.

further Balance of Trade (BOT hereafter) deficit. This is popularly called "the perverse reaction" of the BOT to the exchange rate change.

In the long run however, as the elasticities values are high, the Marshall-Lerner condition is satisfied and the devaluation leads to the surplus in BOT. When one plots the relationship between the time period and the BOT behavior, one sees that it is shown by a tilted J-shaped curve. Hence the J-curve hypothesis became popular tool of showing the effect of devaluation on balance of trade in early sixties.

Nonetheless, the time period until 1973 was not a very appropriate time period to test the validity of the J-curve phenomenon because in those days the exchange rates were fixed. In the post-1973 era the relevance of the J-curve is greater but the problem is that exchange rates are too volatile for the BOT to adjust to one exchange rate change.

One of the main theoretical aims of this chapter is to recognize the dynamic events of the devaluation of some currencies and, as a consequence, rationalize them by shifts of the curve to the right. In fact, when the J-curve is shifted to the right after every devaluation and when the correctly assigned points are observed in this case, then the persistent BOT deficit that exists for some economies can efficiently be explained. We use the data of Ghana and Egypt to show the possibility of persistent deficit in BOT after several devaluations.

The chapter is divided into three sections. Section one serves as an introduction and sets the the tone of the problem to be solved. Section two surveys the literature for the J-curve studies and makes a review. It also mathematically shows the Marshall-Lerner condition and makes the theoretical contribution of the shifting J-curve hypothesis. In section three the data of Ghana and Egypt are analyzed and their experiences of devaluating currency are tested in the light of new theory. In Ghana the consistent devaluation of may be make see people know what cedi is has become an excellent case of shifting J-curve. In the case of Egypt the traditional J curve hypothesis is able to show the evidence quite satisfactorily since the devaluation of the Egyptian pound was a one time phenomenon. The paper makes the mathematical derivation of the Marshall-Lerner condition in the simplest form possible, and shows that the real world phenomenon of the devaluating currency in the cases of Ghana and Egypt.

THEORETICAL EXTENSION TO J-CURVE PHENOMENON AND SURVEY OF LITERATURE

When the exchange rate is defined as the number of domestic currency units per unit of foreign currency, (American way of defining exchange as against as opposed to the European way, which is the inverse) then an increase in exchange rate defines the depreciation of the domestic currency.

When this depreciation is carried out by a policy action we call it "devaluation". The devaluation of any currency has to be undertaken when the exchange rate is controlled by the government, as it is clearly obvious that a free exchange rate only depreciates or appreciates the currency. Thus a free exchange rate system exists when exchange rates are decided by demand for foreign exchange and the supply of foreign exchange. In order to conceptualize more clearly the difference between fixed (controlled) and free exchange rate systems, it is useful to think in terms of Figure 1 that has the demand for foreign exchange curve and supply of foreign exchange curve intersecting at point J where the equilibrium exchange rate of e* is determined.

Clearly the demand for foreign exchange curve is sloping downward because as the exchange rate increases and the domestic currency loses value, the imports go down and domestic residents demand lower amounts of foreign exchange. Similarly with an increase in exchange rate, domestic exports increase, and foreign residents supply lower quantities of foreign exchange. Hence the supply of foreign exchange curve is sloping upwards from left to right.

Now in a freely floating exchange rate system, the exchange rate will always be at equilibrium rate e* because of the "Paradox of Flexibility". The Paradox of Flexibility is summarized as saying that if a price (exchange rate in this case) is free to move up and down then it will stay at one level namely at the equilibrium. For a long time economists recognized that

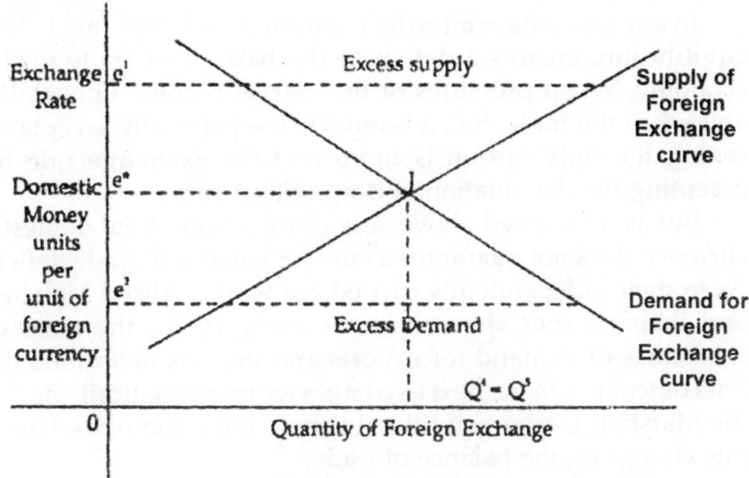

Figure 1: Demand and Supply Curves of Foreign Exchange

at any exchange rate above equilibrium, there is an excess have supply of foreign exchange that will drive down the exchange rate, and at any exchange rate below equilibrium the excess demand for foreign exchange will push it back up towards equilibrium.

But when governments try to control the value of exchange rate they forcefully keep the exchange rate either above or below the equilibrium, because as we just saw, no control is needed to keep it at the equilibrium.

In all of the underdeveloped countries the controlled exchange rate is necessarily below equilibrium. This is because these countries usually like to subsidize imports to help the "importers" which many times are the governments themselves. But as shown in Figure 1 at any exchange rate below e* there is excess demand for foreign exchange by the private sector and to cure that excess demand governments put controls over private imports. To control imports the government also needs to control the free exchange of domestic currency to other currencies as well. Hence controls over imports necessitate controls over foreign exchange transactions. But his leads to illegal transactions of goods and currencies bringing in more administrative problems.

In any case, the arbitrarily controlled exchange rate below equilibrium, creates a deficit in the balance of trade of the economy. When pressures of the market become unbearable and when the trade deficit is outside the politically acceptable realm, the only option is to correct the exchange rate by accepting the devaluation of domestic currency.

But as mentioned above, any devaluation of the domestic currency does not guarantee a cure for balance of trade deficit. As in their independently carried out works. Alfred Marshall and Abba Lerner showed in the early 1950s, the sizes of elasticities of demand for exports and imports determine the final outcome. On the next two pages we mathematically derive the Marshall-Lerner condition to show the effect of exchange rate change on the balance of trade.

Now the J-curve hypothesis argues that in the short-run (meaning immediately after the devaluation of the domestic currency), the elasticities are so small that the Marshall-Lerner condition is not fulfilled and the balance of trade experiences further deficit. As shown in Figure 2 it is only after some time when the elasticity values become large enough to add up to unity, that the balance of trade starts showing surplus. In practice however, it is quite possible that one devaluation is followed by another devaluation in a short time.

An important point here to recognize is that while the J-Curve hypothesis is a comparative static analysis, in reality

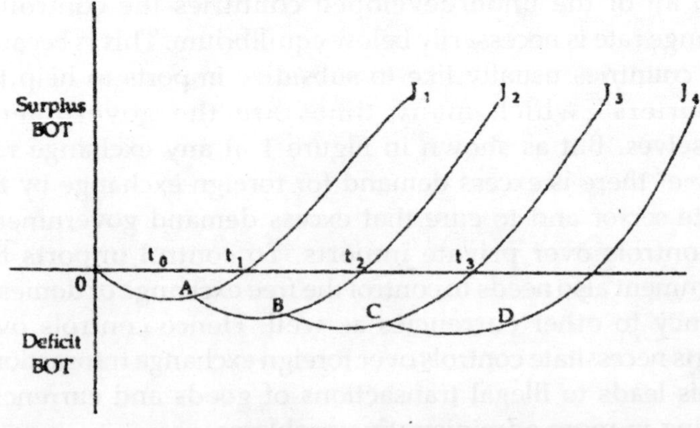

Figure 2: Shifts in The J-Curve due to Continuous Devaluations

we have dynamic events of the J-Curve occurring after every devaluation. In that case, the shift of the J-Curve as shown in Figure 2 is the only way to explain the dynamic effects of currency devaluations.

Observe that in these cases the devaluating currency is leading to further deficits in balance of trade as observed in many developing countries the case of Ghana with the rapid devaluations of Cedi. As we shall see in Sections 3 the devaluation of the Egyptian pound was a one time phenomenon hence the traditional explanation of one J-Curve (without shifts) applies to it. But when devaluations are witnessed in a series of changes in domestic currency values, then the shifts of J-Curves become more relevant. And her important point to notice here is that when a country allows its currency to devalue several times, then a persistent balance of trade deficit is a very likely outcome. In terms of Figure 2 on the next page, four devaluations take place at time periods, t1, t2, and t3. This shifts the J-Curve further to right and there are four J-Curves observed in terms of J1, J2, J3, and J4. It is possible that in reality one observes only the path traced by points A, B, C, and D which shows a continuous BOT deficit.

In terms of a survey of prior J-Curve studies, Artus (1975) uses the data of the U.K. pound devaluation of 1967 to test the validity of the J-Curve hypothesis. Gylfason (1978) uses the data of ten industrial countries to test the effect of exchange rate change on balance of trade. However the J-Curve hypothesis is also questioned on a theoretical level. There is much suspicion regarding the terms of the assumptions of the theory namely the high supply elasticities and the initial balance of payments being equal to zero. Rose (1991) questions the validity of the Marshall-Lerner condition. Gylfason-Risager (1984) ask the basic question of change in balance of trade made by exchange rate change.

TEST OF J-CURVE IN THE CASE OF EGYPT AND GHANA

Case of Egypt

The socialist revolution of 1952 was the starting point for the regulatory controls in Egypt that were further intensified by the governments of Gamal Abdel Nasser and Anwar Sadat. In the decolonization process and the Non-Alignment Movement (NAM) that was started by the Nasser-Tito-Nehru trio, who accepted "self sufficiency" as the main motto in their economic policies that basically involved keeping away the foreign influences by protecting the domestic production by heavy tariff policies. Other countries such as Sudan, Algeria, Nigeria and Kenya also followed their footsteps. In the case of Egypt, the foreign influence on domestic economy was not evident until the Camp David peace agreement signed in 1979. It was only in 1979 with the U.S. initiative that the foreign companies were actively invited into the country. However, there were several reasons why Egypt should have been internationally active in trade in earlier years.

Egypt was blessed with a wide stock of natural sources, Suez canal itself being responsible for six billion Egyptian pounds of revenue per year. Besides oil, the country is also endowed with gold and copper mines. Nonetheless, the heavy imports were consistently higher than the exports of the Egyptian economy.

When the loan of 1986 was negotiated with the IMF, Egypt was supposed to devalue her currency, reduce import tariffs and intensify the liberalization process. It took two years but the Egyptian government devalued the pound by a big margin in 1988. Further the currency was devalued by 200% between 1988 and 1991 and the balance of payment reached a surplus. Only when the devaluation process stopped after 1991 did the balance of payment show a continuous surplus as evidenced in Table 1 of the next page. Figure 3 also shows the well-fitted J-curve for the Egyptian case. This is clearly a result of an abrupt change in the value of the domestic currency rather than continuous series of devaluations.

It is also worth noticing that the stock of foreign reserve went up to $ 1.2 billion in 1993. This meant that Egypt could finance her imports for 10 months in 1993. With the devaluated currency, the governmental authorities no longer needed to support the currency with strict foreign exchange controls, imports became quite expensive and the rest of the world found

Table 1
Egypt's Exchange Rate and Balance of Payment: 1988-1994

Year	*Exchange Rate S/E*	*Balance of Payments in millions of $*
1988	0.7	-1048
1989	1.1	-1309
1990	2.0	184
1991	3.33	1903
1992	3.3303	2812
1993	3.37	2203
1994	3.42	2102

that importing from Egypt was much cheaper. After further developments, the foreign exchange controls are almost completely lifted.

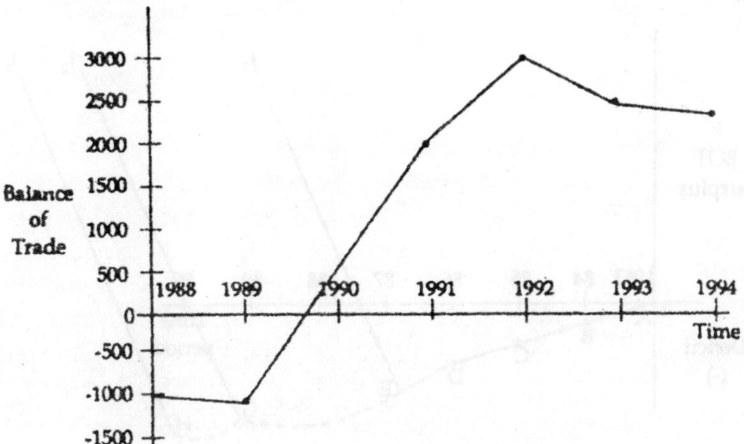

Figure 3: J-Curve Phenomenon: A Case of Egypt

Case of Ghana

The Economic Recovery Program of the early 1980s in Ghana revealed that the main aim of devaluation of Cedi was to turn the BOT movement around. Devaluation was, therefore, a crucial component of the structural adjustment reforms required to influence production decisions in a new economic environment. In initial years, the goal of boosting exports was successful as the main export of Ghana, cocoa, which accounts for 60% of the total export bill, increased in production from 159,000 tons in 1983 to 300,000 tons in 1989. Production also increased in the logging industry and in timber that saw an increase in production to 413,000 cubic meters in 1987. It seemed that the main objective of economic growth and reversal of economic stagnation of years were achieved.

The Ghanian economy registered growth for six consecutive years after 1984. Manufacturing output increased with an annual average rate of 9.2% while mining increased by 7.1% and the agriculture sector grew by 2.2%. Nonetheless, in all these years the import bill kept on increasing even faster than earnings as the purchasing power of consumers increased. The behavior of balance of trade followed an interesting path as shown in Figure 4.

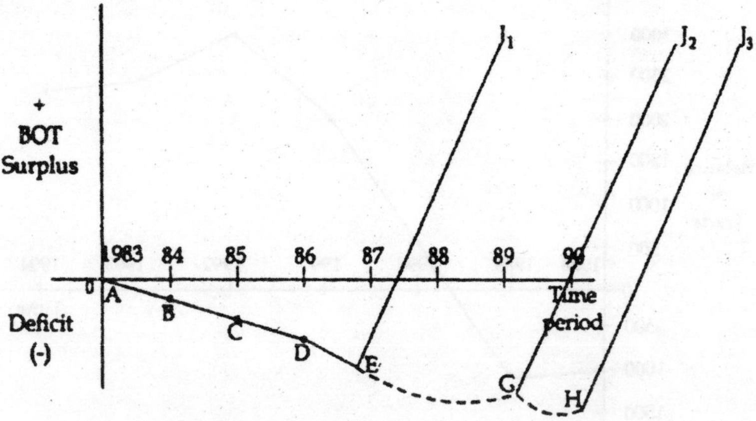

Figure 4: Shift in The J-Curve of Ghana: 1983-1989

As can be seen, even if the devaluation of Cedi was an important step in this adjustment, the benefits were somewhat eroded by the worsening of balance of trade. Table 2 provides data of Ghanian economy. As can be observed in it, with exception of 1988 in all years the balance of trade deficit was increasing despite the tremendous decline in value of Ghanian Cedi.

As mentioned before, one of the reasons for continuous deficits in balance of trade is the series of devaluations in case of Ghana. As a consequence, Ghanian experience suggests that changing real prices must go hand in hand with other policies that make structural adjustment. The structural adjustment that is needed is in the form of changing the export composition. As the export structure is very concentrated in only some goods, cocoa being the main one, the changes in its volume are dependent upon only one market.

Table 2
Balance of Trade and Exchange Rate Changes:
Ghana: 1983-1990

Year	*Exports*	*Imports*	*BOT*	*Market Exchange Rate*
1983	10.22	10.31	.09	30.00
1984	19.39	20.47	1.08	50.00
1985	33.49	44.11	10.62	59.99
1986	78.00	87.00	9.00	90.01
1987	143.00	163.00	20.00	176.06
1988	206.00	174.00	-12.00	229.89
1989	275.00	325.00	50.00	303.03
1990	298.00	375.00	77.00	344.83

Columns 2, 3, and 4 are measured in billions of Ghanaian Cedis. Calculations of column 4 figures are author's. Source: International Financial statistics, International Monetary Fund Publications, Yearbook, 1994.

As mentioned before, one of the reasons for continuous deficits in the balance of trade is the series of devaluations in the case of Ghana. As a consequence, the Ghanian experience suggests that changing real prices must go hand in hand with other policies that make structural adjustment. The structural adjustment that is needed is in the form of changing the export composition. As the export structure is very concentrated in only some goods, cocoa being the main one, the changes in its volume are dependent upon only one market.

SUMMARY AND CONCLUSIONS

This chapter had the aim of revising the J-Curve hypothesis to determine the effect of exchange rate change on the balance of trade. A theoretical explanation in terms of the shifts of J-curves is also put forward to solve the dynamic but realistic situation of continuous series of devaluations. In this case, it is concluded that the existence of a dynamic, persistent balance of trade deficit is possible. The cases of Egypt for a one time devaluation in 1984 and of Ghana, for a series of devaluations between 1983 and 1989 are studied.

SUGGESTIONS FOR FUTURE RESEARCH

Clearly this chapter has added a new dimension to the theory of J-Curve in terms of shifts in the J-Curve that occur when there are several episodes of currency devaluation. It also leads the to unprecedented conclusion that a continuously devaluating currency may lead to further deficits in the balance of trade. Hence devaluation is not an answer to the deficit in the balance of trade of any country. It is obvious that more research is needed to justify this argument in terms of more studies of countries that are experiencing this phenomenon. The author is willing to entertain any correspondence about studies dealing with this evidence.

REFERENCES

Adotey Bing (1991), "Devaluation Brings Little Gain", *Africa Recovery,* Vol. 5.

Artus, Jacques (1975), "The 1967 Devaluation of Pound Sterling", *IMF Staff Papers,* pp. 595-640.

Gylfason T. (1978), "The Effects of Exchange Rate Change on The Balance of Trade in Ten Industrial Countries", *IMF Staff Papers,* pp. 375-390.

Gylfason, T. and Ole Risager, "Does Devaluation Improve the Current Account?", *European Economic Review,* Vol. 25, pp. 37-63.

International Financial Statistics Yearbook, International Monetary Fund Publications, Washington D.C. 1994.

Kulkarni, Kishore (1993), "The J-Curve Hypothesis, Balance of Payment and the Recent Devaluation of Indian Rupee", *Asian Economic Review,* Vol. 30, No. 4, pp. 407-422.

Newman, K. Kusi (1991), "Ghana: Can the Adjustment Reforms be Sustained? *Africa Development,* Vol. XVI, No. 3-4.

Sarpong, Samuel (1993), "Ghana's Economic Recovery: An IMF/World Bank Showcase?", *Politics and Economics Monthly,* Vol. 6, No. 8.

Rose Andrew (1991), "The Role of Exchange Rates in a Popular Model of International Trade: Does the Marshall-Lerner Condition Hold", *Journal of International Economics,* Vol. 30, pp. 301-316.

9

TESTING THE J-CURVE AND KULKARNI HYPOTHESES: CASE STUDIES FROM AROUND THE WORLD

INTRODUCTION

The J-Curve Effect is the term used to describe the impact of currency devaluation on a country's balance of trade. The theoretical basis of the J-Curve Effect comes in part from Alfred Marshall and Abba Lerner, whose "Marshall-Lerner Condition" states that if initially the balance of trade is zero, and if supply elasticities are infinite, then the absolute values of export and import demand elasticities have to be at least large enough to add up to unity to have an exchange rate devaluation bring about the surplus in balance of payments (Kulkarni, 2007) This theory can be proven by looking at the changes in elasticity over time. In the short run, elasticities are small, making the Marshall-Lerner Condition less likely to be satisfied. However, as time goes by, elasticities become larger, ultimately crossing the threshold point described by Marshall and Lerner, thus creating the condition for an improvement in BOP.

Applying this theory, and using simple observation of the effects of currency devaluations over time, economists have developed the J-Curve Hypothesis, which says that in the short

---

This Chapter is based on an article o-authored with Mr. Andy Clarke and presented in IJEB International Conference in New Delhi.

term period following a currency devaluation, the balance of trade for that country will decline, but then as elasticities grow, the balance of trade will begin to improve. The graph showing this trend often looks like a "J", thus prompting economists to refer to it as the "J-Curve." This improvement in the balance of trade occurs as a result of the competitiveness effect of currency devaluation, whereby the devalued currency's home country's products become cheaper in foreign markets relative to foreign goods, and foreign goods become more expensive in domestic markets relative to domestically produced goods. This hypothesis became particularly relevant following the 1973 breakdown of exchange rate controls imposed by the Bretton-Woods System, and the introduction of a largely flexible, market-based pricing mechanism for currencies.

This paper hopes to observe two aspects of the J-Curve Effect. The first is how well it actually characterizes the experiences of several specific cases we observe in this report. To do this, we will look at different countries that have experienced a significant devaluation or depreciation of domestic currency, chart the changes in trade balance, observe the extent to which it followed the course expected by the J-Curve Hypothesis, and try to find explanations for any outliers in the data. The second aspect of the J-Curve Effect we will examine is the extent to which there is any distinction between the long-run effects on trade balance in the cases of government controlled devaluation versus market-based depreciation. This will be done through case studies, primarily looking at a six to eight year time window.

Our hypothesis at the outset of this project was that the J-Curve Effect would be more orderly in the case of devaluation because the currency value is more reliably set at a certain lower value, whereas in the case of depreciation, we expect to find a jagged J-Curve, as currency volatility diminishes the trade effects. We further presume to find a decline in the balance of trade and an appreciation of currency value in the out years in the case of currency depreciation. We will use case studies of four countries—Zambia, Nigeria, Latvia, and Thailand—in order to draw our conclusions.

SECTION - 1

THEORETICAL DESCRIPTION

Literature Review

In discussing the theoretical background for the J-Curve Hypothesis, let us first define exchange rate. Exchange rate is the value of a given currency expressed as a proportion of another currency. There are two ways to express exchange rate. One is as the number of foreign currency units per unit of domestic currency, for example, 105 ¥/$1. The other is the number of domestic currency units per unit of foreign currency, for example, $1.40/€1. The latter expression is the American style, and will be used for the purposes of this work.

When the exchange rate is changed (say, increased), the domestic currency loses value, causing exports to become cheaper for the rest of the world because foreign currency simultaneously gains value. Exports are therefore expected to go up. Likewise, imports are expected to decline as the rest of the world's goods and services become more expensive for domestic residents. Thus, the balance of trade (BOT) should increase.

However, Alfred Marshall and Abba Lerner argued that an increase in exchange rate can lead to a BOT surplus only if the elasticity of demand for exports by the rest of the world, and similarly demand for imports by domestic residents, are strong enough. They created the following test to determine whether the elasticities are strong enough:

Define: elasticity of imports (with respect to exchange rate) $= E_M^{ER}$

Note that *elasticity* is the responsiveness of a dependent variable to the change in an independent variable. Thus:

$$E_M^{ER} = \frac{\%\,change\,in\,quantity\,of\,imports}{\%\,change\,in\,exchange\,rate} \frac{\frac{\Delta M}{M}}{\frac{\Delta ER}{ER}} = \frac{\Delta M}{\Delta ER} \times \frac{ER}{M}$$

For example, if gasoline prices increase from $3 to $4, the percentage increase in price is 33%, which is determined by:

$$\frac{\Delta P}{P} \times 100 = \frac{1}{3} \times 100 = .33$$

Thus,

$$E_M^{ER} = \frac{\Delta M}{\Delta ER} \times \frac{ER}{M}$$

Define: elasticity of exports (with respect to exchange rate)

$$= E_X^{ER} = \frac{\%\, change\, in\, exports}{\%\, change\, in\, exchange\, rate} = \frac{\frac{\Delta X}{X}}{\frac{\Delta ER}{ER}} = \frac{\Delta X}{\Delta ER} \times \frac{ER}{X} = E_X^{ER}$$

Thus, when elasticity is small, the quantity of exports increases by a small amount.

Recall: Export Revenue = Price of Exports × Quantity of Exports

Therefore, if the quantity of exports increases only a little and the price of exports decreases by more (as a result of the lower currency value) then the export revenue goes down. If the elasticity of imports is small, then a 10% increase in the exchange rate makes imports more expensive by 10%. However, if the elasticity of imports is very small, then an increase in exchange rate of 10% will reduce imports by *less than* 10%, causing the import bill to go up. Then, with small elasticity values, an increase in the exchange rate can lead to a balance of trade deficit.

Thus, for an increase in the exchange rate to lead to a balance of trade surplus, we must have strong enough elasticities with respect to imports and exports $\left(E_M^{ER} \text{ and } E_X^{ER}\right)$ that they add up to at least 1, or in equation form: $E_M^{ER} + E_X^{ER} \geq 1$. This is known as the Marshall-Lerner Condition.

The two major determinants of elasticity values are:

1. The number of substitutes for the good. If there are a large number of substitutes available, the elasticity will be high, whereas the elasticity will be low if there are a small number of substitutes available.

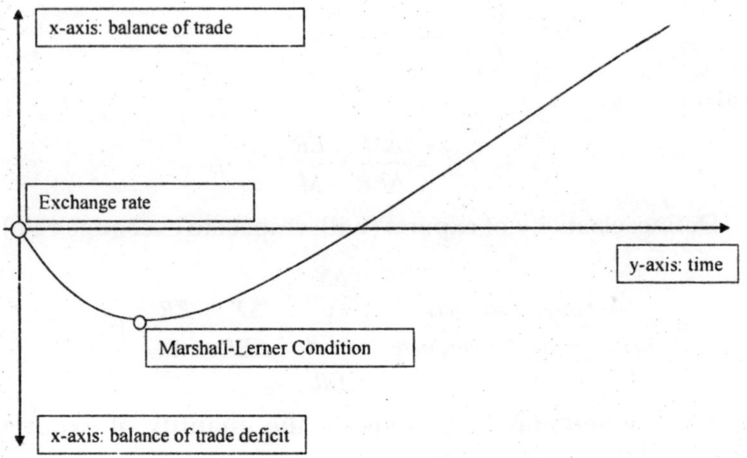

2. Time passed after the change in exchange rate. The longer the time passed after the change in exchange rate, the higher the elasticity.

Consider the graphical representation of a balance of trade curve over time as hypothesized by the J-Curve Theory (see previous page). Notice that initially the elasticities don't satisfy the Marshall-Lerner Condition, and thus the balance of trade goes down. Over time, however, the elasticities increase, ultimately turning the balance of trade positive. The resulting balance of trade curve looks like a lopsided letter "J", hence the name "J-Curve."

The J-Curve Hypothesis was later expanded by Professor Kishore Kulkarni, who demonstrated in a 1994 article that in the case of a series of currency devaluations, the existence of "dynamic, persistent balance of trade deficits is a possibility." This phenomenon is known as the Kulkarni Hypothesis, and accounts for the real world possibility that currencies may be devalued multiple times over a relatively short time period.

In the graph above, there are four devaluations at times t0, t1, t2, and t3, creating four consecutive J-Curves, with consecutively lower lows in balance of trade, as shown at points A, B, C, and D. This occurs because the J-Curve Hypothesis says, as mentioned above, that in the short run, elasticities of

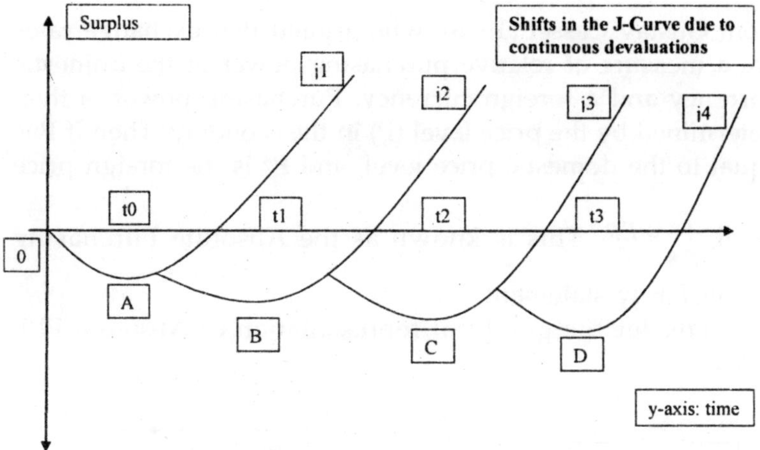

imports and exports are too small to meet the Marshall-Lerner Condition. Thus, if a second devaluation occurs before the Marshall-Lerner Condition is met, the J-Curve is shifted to the right as export/import elasticities again realign.

The J-Curve Hypothesis has gained relevance since the end of the Bretton Woods System in 1973. Prior to that, from 1944-1971, most of the world was under the BWS, in which the U.S. Dollar was the key currency, and all other currencies were pegged to it. This essentially forced all countries that participated in this monetary system, which was all but a few countries in the world, to keep their money supply consistent with U.S. money supply growth. This put the U.S. in what became known as the Triffin Dilemma, where on one hand the U.S. had to satisfy demand for the dollar, however on the other hand, if the supply of the dollar was raised to meet demand, its value relative to other currencies would decline. To avoid this outcome, the U.S. pressured other countries to increase their money supplies. Ultimately, countries in Western Europe—like Germany, France, and Switzerland—refused to continue increasing their money supply, thus undermining the BWS and ushering in a new era of market-determined exchange rates and free monetary policy.

Now that exchange rates can be determined by market forces, we can consider their determination based on theory from Gustav Cassel (1918), who argued that exchange rates are a measure of relative purchasing power of the domestic currency and a foreign currency. Purchasing power is then determined by the price level (P) in the economy. Then if P is equal to the domestic price level, and P* is the foreign price level, $\frac{p}{p*} = ER$. This is known as the Absolute Purchasing Power Parity statement.

Consider the graphical representation of Absolute PPP below:

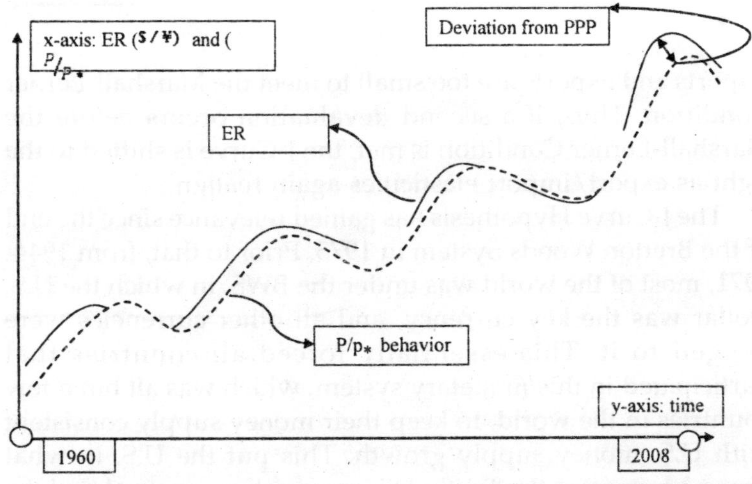

Notice that $P/_{p*}$ generally correlates with ER, though there are some deviations as labeled. The other primary way of determining exchange rates is by considering relative changes in inflation rates.

$(\Delta ER/ER)$ = % change in domestic price level $(\Delta P/P)$ –% change in foreign price level $((\Delta P^*)/(P^*))$

$$\text{Or just: } \left(\frac{\Delta ER}{ER}\right) = \left(\frac{\Delta P}{P}\right) - \left(\frac{\Delta P*}{p*}\right)$$

This is known as the Relative PPP statement, and is graphed in much the same way as the Absolute PPP statement (see next page).

Economists have reached three primary conclusions from studying PPP and its relevance to exchange rates. First, that long-term data show higher validity of both absolute and relative PPP statements than short-term data. Second, that the relative PPP statement has a higher reliability than the absolute. And third, that periods of high inflation rates show smaller deviations and higher reliability of PPP statements than periods with low inflation.

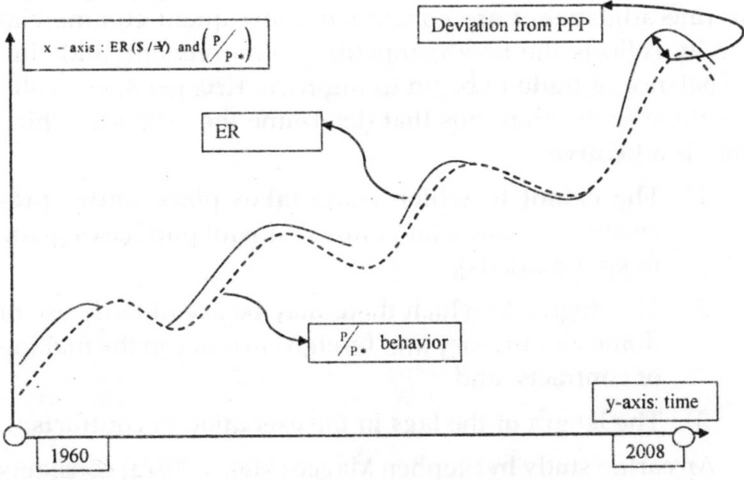

This new era of floating exchange rates dictated by the free market using relationships like PPP to evaluate currency value has allowed governments to increase their money supplies at will, thus creating the opportunity for the tremendously profitable practice of seigniorage, where governments print money for their own use. This has led to currency crises and hyperinflation in some cases, particularly in Latin America and Africa. Perhaps as often, however, a country's money supply has increased as part of a financial sector liberalization package. As we shall see in the empirical section, this can sometimes lead to sharp declines in the value of that country's currency.

We expect to then see a shift in the trade balance as predicted by the J-Curve Hypothesis, however we'll have to test it to find out.

Relevant Academic Work

A relatively early and oft-cited study comes from economist Anne O. Krueger's book Exchange Rate Determination (Krueger, 1983), where she argues that the J-Curve occurs because at the time an exchange rate change occurs, goods already in transit and under contract have been purchased, causing a lag time in the effect of exchange rate changes. Once those transactions that had already been in progress prior to the rate adjustment are concluded, subsequent commercial activity reflects the new competition environment, allowing the balance of trade to begin to improve. Krueger specifically lists three such conditions that determine the extent to which there is a J-Curve:

1. The extent to which trade takes place under pre-existing contracts (as contrasted with purchases made in spot markets);
2. The degree to which there may be asymmetric use of domestic currency and foreign currency in the making of contracts, and
3. The length of the lags in the execution of contracts.[1]

An earlier study by Stephen Magee (Magee, 1973) considers the period between the time of devaluation and the time after adjustment to the new currency value as well, what he terms the "pass-through period," though Magee concludes that "there is no logical necessity for a country's trade balance to deteriorate, any more than for it to improve or remain constant." Krueger seems to agree with Magee's conclusion in theory, but notes that the short-run decline in trade balance following a currency devaluation has become part of the J-Curve Hypothesis more as a result of actual observation than theory.

Another 1973 study by Helen Junz and Rudolf Rhomberg theorized that the dip in trade balance following currency devaluation may be caused by five lags: 1. Lag in recognition of the new currency conditions by producers and consumers. 2. A lag in the decision by producers and consumers to change. 3. A lag in delivery time. 4. A lag in the replacement of inventory and material on the part of producers. 5. A lag in production due to the production cycle.

Regardless of why the J-Curve Effect occurs, we can look to tests of the hypothesis to determine how robust it is in real world situations.

A 1985 test (Bahmani-Oskooee, 1985) of the J-Curve Effect used a set of 12 possible lags that could cause a short-run decline in the trade balance following currency devaluation. The study looked at Thailand, Greece, Korea and India in the 1970s, and found that all the countries except Thailand followed the pattern predicted by the J-Curve Hypothesis, with the only variation being the duration of decline before the trade balance began to increase. Greece took just two quarters, while India and Korea took three quarters, and Thailand took five quarters to begin improving its trade balance. Thus the paper concluded that for most of the cases studied, "the empirical evidence appeared to support the pattern of movement described by the J-curve."

A more recent study (Kulkarni, 2007) seeking to find empirical evidence of the existence of the J-Curve examined seven case studies of countries that had experienced significant changes in their currency value. The effect on the trade balance was analyzed in time spans ranging from five to ten years. The study concluded that in six of the seven countries—the Philippines, Kenya, Japan, Indonesia, Mexico, and Spain—"dramatic change in the exchange rate leads to a J-Curve on the balance of payments." (pg. 62) This finding included an inverted J-Curve in Japan, where a revaluation of the currency had taken place in 1985. The only outlier in the study was China, which was explained by the authors as possibly resulting from regulated import and export flows. Thus, the authors conclude that "if a country's currency is not valued according to market forces, the government is forced to readjust the currency value sooner or later." (pg. 63).

Some studies focused on exchange rates and trade on a bilateral basis, including a 2001 test (Wilson, 2001) of the J-Curve Hypothesis that examined the relationship between the real trade balance and the real exchange rate for bilateral trade in merchandise goods between Singapore, Korea, and Malaysia, and the USA and Japan on a quarterly basis from 1970 to 1996. This study found that the real exchange rate does not have a significant impact on real trade balance. Korean trade with the USA and Japan was the only exception, however the authors explained this by noting that for Korea, it is possible that the J-Curve effects were being muted by small country pricing of exports in foreign currency. This study is unique from the one being conducted by this paper, however, in that it examined the relationship between currency value and trade balance over a long period of time, regardless of what was occurring with the given currency. The study being attempted by this paper, however, looks at specific currency events in order to determine whether they show evidence of the J-Curve Effect.

A 2008 test of the J-Curve Effect looked at bilateral trade effects between Turkey and its 13 biggest trading partners from 1985 to 2005. Ferda Halicioglu used a cointegration statistical model with six different lags to account for the pass-through period, and tested to determine whether currency fluctuation was a statistically relevant causal variable for trade balance. It was determined that in all 13 cases, exchange rate had no effect on bilateral trade balance in the short run, and only some limited effect in the long run with two of the countries—the U.S. and UK.

Another study (Rose, 1990) from 1990 takes a similar approach of looking at the relationship of currency and trade balance over time. This study, by UC Berkeley Professor Andrew K. Rose, examined data from 30 developing countries over 18 years (1970-1988) to determine this relationship. Rose uses a statistical analysis to determine whether exchange rate has a statistically significant effect on trade balance at the .05 level, finding that for 28 of the 30 countries the hypothesis that it does not cannot be rejected. It should be noted that he used a 12-month lag period for trade balance to account for the decline during the pass-through period.

Another similar study (Hacker, 2003) looked at small northern European countries in order to determine if they experienced the J-Curve Effect. This test—which looked at Belgium, Denmark, the Netherlands, Norway, and Sweden—shows that after a depreciation there will be about a six-month period of decline in the trade balance, followed by an increase in the trade balance. The authors further conclude that in these cases, sustainable higher long-term export-import equilibrium was achieved following currency depreciation.

The case of the U.S. seems a vexing one for several authors because of the stubbornness of trade deficits in the U.S. in several periods in spite of a declining currency. One notable study on this topic was done by Oregon State University Professor Michael H. Moffett in 1989 titled: "The J-Curve Revisited: An Empirical Examination for the United States." (Moffett, 1989) Moffett finds that expenditures on imports have typically increased following dollar depreciations, which he explains results from the inelasticity of import volumes in the U.S. Export earnings, meanwhile, are shown to increase only modestly following these currency declines. Moffett concludes that the curve of U.S. trade balance with respect to currency value is better characterized as a sine wave than a J-Curve.

In my opinion, the reason behind the strange behavior of the U.S. trade balance is a result of the fact that essentially all global commodities are denominated in U.S. dollars. Thus, when the dollar declines, the price of imported commodities for U.S. consumers goes up. Moffett talks about the inelasticity of imports, which I agree with, though he simply fails to take the next step of noting that the imports that are inelastic tend to be commodities, and the price of those commodities has a special relationship with the U.S. dollar that could cause this unusual trade balance action.

Halicioglu characterizes the literature on the J-Curve Effect as coming in two basic varieties. The first, he says, employ an aggregate trade balance approach and compare two countries (home country and rest of world). The second group utilizes bilateral trade balance equations to analyze the exchange rate/ trade balance dynamic. Based on my review of relevant literature related to the J-Curve Effect, I would add that the tests conducted seem to be able to be differentiated by the length of time observed. One type of test looks at some period (generally five to ten years) immediately following a significant change in a country's currency value, whereas other studies, often statistically oriented, look at a much longer time horizon that is often arbitrary in the sense that the timing of the period observed is not anchored by the timing of a substantial change in currency value.

For the purposes of this paper, the timing of all case studies will be roughly five to eight years immediately following a dramatic change in currency value. This approach has been chosen primarily because it seems to be more in the spirit of the J-Curve Hypothesis, and also because it seems that any findings that come out of exceptional scenarios will be necessarily laden with caveats, whereas findings in a more idealized case study will be robust, particularly if it is determined that the J-Curve Effect is not observed.

SECTION - 2

EMPIRICAL DATA

Case Study: Zambia

In 1991 Zambia held its first multiparty democratic elections. For 17 years prior to that, the Zambian government had been ruled by the United National Independence Party, who favored a largely state-run approach to economic development. Though a series of stability measures and structural adjustment programs had been put forward in Zambia between 1973 and 1990, in cooperation with the IMF and World Bank, these reforms found little success because they failed to address the underlying structural problems of the Zambian economy that centered around the large, wasteful state sector. Reforming that began in earnest following the 1991 election of the Movement for Multiparty Democracy (MMD), which was given a strong mandate for reform by the public.

Political reforms were relatively marginal during the period from 1991-1996, however economic reforms were profound. For one thing, the MMD launched an ambitious privatization program soon after taking office, which resulted in the 1992 Zambia Privatization Agency. The process began slowly, with only three companies privatized by early 1995. But by the end of 1995, 27 had been privatized, and by the end of 1997, that number jumped to 200. Importantly, however, the massive Zambia Consolidated Copper Mines (ZCCM) company was delayed in its privatization for several years until 1999, as were some utility companies.

For this paper, however, the monetary reforms of the early 1990s are more germane. With inflation of 167% annually in 1992, the government of Zambia saw price stability as a primary precondition for economic growth. The government tightened monetary policy significantly, cutting deficits and restricting growth in the money supply. A key, yet controversial, step toward spending reduction was the step taken in 1991 to end subsidies on maize, a staple of the Zambian diet. A year later the price of maize had increased 700%. Still, the Zambian government pressed on with budgetary reform, instituting a cash budget system in 1993, which meant that government could not spend money it didn't have. This made it impossible for the government to monetize debt, in other words, to print money to pay for deficit spending. (Rakner, 2003).

The MMD also sought to improve the climate for foreign direct investment by beginning a process of lifting currency controls in 1992. By December of 1992, the official exchange rate was unified with the market rate, making the exchange rate fully market determined. By 1994 non-citizens were allowed to open foreign currency accounts in Zambia. The last big currency control was finally lifted in 1996, when the Bank of Zambia allowed Zambian Consolidated Copper Mines, which was by far the largest company in Zambia at the time though it was still largely state controlled, to retain 100 percent of its foreign exchange receipts to supply the market directly. Since the nationalization of the mines in the 1960s, ZCCM's lack of access to foreign exchange prevented it from significant reinvestment into its business. Another key reform occurred in 1993, when the Bank of Zambia (the Zambian Central Bank) removed all restrictions on bank lending and deposit rates. This opened the door for the entry of several new commercial banks and non-bank financial institutions. (Rakner, 2003).

Trade was also reformed in the early '90s, and by 1997 all licensing and quantitative restrictions on imports and exports were eliminated. The tariff structure was also streamlined and simplified, reducing the number of tariff bands from 11 to four, and lowering tariff rates from 0 to 100 percent to a lower range of 0 to 25 percent.

Following the 1996 elections, things began to change for the worse. Levy Mwanawasa, the previous vice president and a founding member of the MMD was sworn into office as president, though with only 29 percent of the vote. The vote was considered by many to be fraught with fairness violations as well, further undermining Mwanawasa's mandate. Early in the new administration, things began to change. Public sector reform efforts which were key conditions of IMF funding had been discontinued, causing the IMF to withdraw funding commitments. Also, the government's commitment to the cash budget system began to drift, as a loophole began to be exploited, allowing the government to run deficits of 14-18 percent of GDP from 1995 to 1997. (Taylor, 2002) Also, the privatization of ZCCM still lingered for the first three years of Mwanawasa's presidency, running up substantial additional government deficits to keep the company afloat until it could be sold. Years of mismanagement, lack of investment, and falling world copper prices caused ZCCM to lose $200-$300 million in 1998 alone, or between 6-9% of Zambian GDP.

Taking growing debt and political instability together, the Zambian currency, the kwacha, began a series of steep declines in 1997, as evidenced by the graph below [2 3].

The results on the Zambian balance of trade offer a further demonstration of the Kulkarni Hypothesis, as one can observe the series of mini J-Curves as the kwacha continued to lose value over a period of years from 1997 to 2003, and not actually leading to surplus in the balance of trade until 2004-2006, when

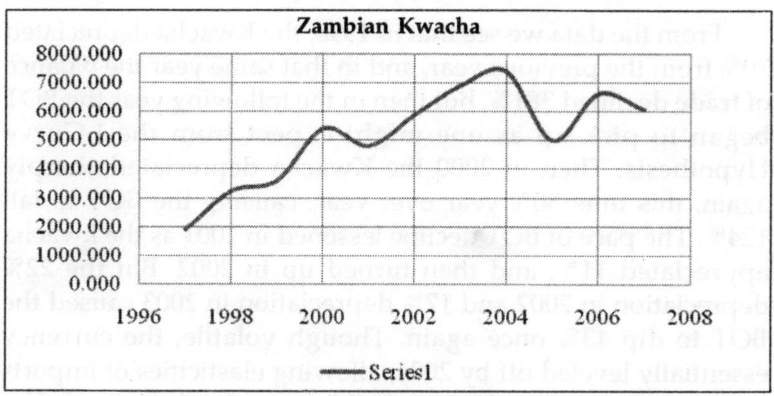

the currency depreciation leveled off and then turned toward appreciation.

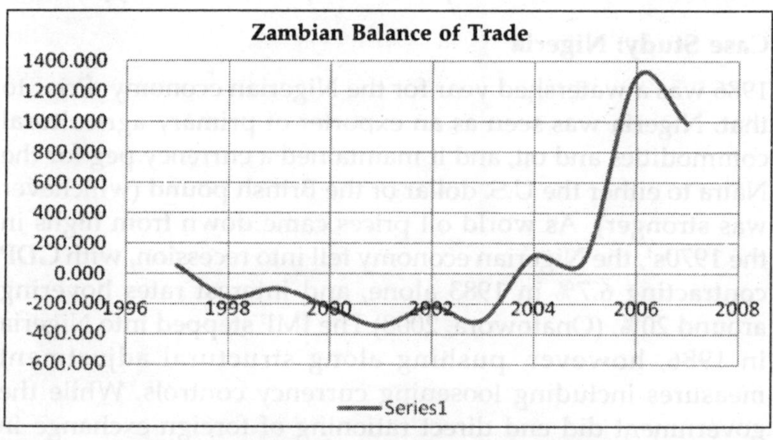

Year	*BOT*	*% Change*	*Year*	*Kwacha/SDR*	*% Change*
1997	54.4		1997	1908	
1998	-153	-381	1998	3236	70
1999	-98	36	1999	3612	12
2000	-220	-124	2000	5417	50
2001	-342	-55	2001	4813	-11
2002	-214	37	2002	5892	22
2003	-306	-43	2003	6903	17
2004	117	138	2004	7409	07
2005	86	-26	2005	5015	-32
2006	1293	1403	2006	6629	32
2007	983	-24	2007	6075	-8

From the data we see that in 1998, the Kwacha depreciated 70% from the previous year, and in that same year the balance of trade declined 381%, but then in the following year the BOT began to pick up as one might expect from the J-Curve Hypothesis. Then in 2000 the Kwacha depreciated sharply again, this time 50% year over year, causing the BOT to fall 124%. The pace of BOT decline lessened in 2001 as the kwacha appreciated 11%, and then turned up in 2002. But the 22% depreciation in 2002 and 17% depreciation in 2003 caused the BOT to dip 43% once again. Though volatile, the currency essentially leveled off by 2004, allowing elasticities of imports and exports to meet the Marshall-Lerner Condition and thus allowing the currency depreciation of 262% from 1997-2003 to effect the trade balance as predicted by the J-Curve Hypothesis.

Case Study: Nigeria

1986 was a watershed year for the Nigerian economy. Prior to that, Nigeria was seen as an exporter of primary agricultural commodities and oil, and it maintained a currency peg for the Naira to either the U.S. dollar or the British pound (whichever was stronger). As world oil prices came down from highs in the 1970s[1], the Nigerian economy fell into recession, with GDP contracting 6.7% in 1983 alone, and interest rates hovering around 20%. (Onafowora, 2008) The IMF stepped into Nigeria in 1986, however, pushing along structural adjustment measures including loosening currency controls. While the government did end direct rationing of foreign exchange in 1986 as part of the program, it instead set up a multiple exchange rate regime, giving preferred institutions access to more favorable exchange rates than everyone else. (Beck, 2005) This opened the door to the incredibly lucrative practice of currency arbitrage by privileged financial institutions, and sparked a boom in the financial sector.

The number of banks tripled in the following six years, from 40 to 120, and the financial sector's contribution to GDP also tripled during that time, as banks were making 300% returns on investment. GDP increased an average of 5% per year during this period as well. Much of this was financial engineering, however, as evidenced by the declines in both deposits and lending to the private sector from 1986 to 1992. By 1990, the amount of non-performing loans began to increase sharply, and by 1991 the Nigerian Central Bank issued a moratorium on licenses for new banks. In 1993, political uncertainty triggered a run on the banks, paralyzing the financial system. By 1994 a military regime had taken power and re-instituted exchange rate controls on the naira.

However by 1998, a civilian government had taken power again, and took several actions on the economy, including floating the naira. This step led to a sharp depreciation of the currency, which jumped from 30.8 naira/SDR in 1998 to 134.4 naira/SDR in 1999[5] [6], or 332%. Notice the leg up in the chart below.

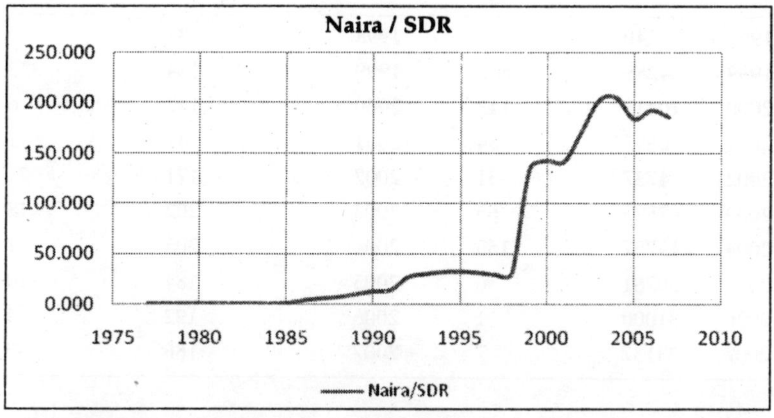

Nigeria's trade balance reacted to this sharp depreciation a bit strangely, however, given the J-Curve Hypothesis. While we would have expected the trade balance to go down in 1999, instead it soared 1800%, and continued its ascent in 2000, growing by 143%. In fact, it was not until the period from 2000-2005 that we saw the J-Curve Effect play out. Also, we don't see evidence of the Kulkarni Hypothesis as a result of the second wave of depreciation in 2002-2003, when the currency fell almost 43%. Notice in the chart on the following page how Nigeria's balance of trade goes up unimpeded during the period 2002-2007.

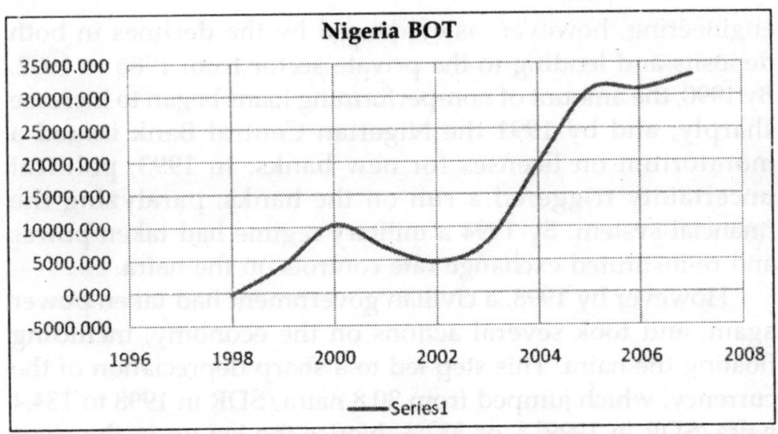

Year	*BOT*	*% Change*	*Year*	*Naira/SDR*	*% Change*
1998	-240		1998	31	
1999	4288	1887	1999	134	332
2000	10415	143	2000	142	6
2001	6895	-34	2001	141	-1
2002	4737	-31	2002	171	21
2003	7823	65	2003	202	18
2004	19757	153	2004	205	1
2005	30781	56	2005	184	-10
2006	31000	1	2006	192	4
2007	33137	7	2007	186	-3

This delayed J-Curve effect was likely due to more to political economy than economics itself. During the military regime, trade had been restricted and trade laws became much more protectionist. Thus, the surge in exports following the fall of the military leadership was a product more of pent up demand for Nigerian exports, particularly oil, than monetary policy. However, it may be that following that initial surge due to the liberalization of the economy, then the elasticities of imports and exports began to draw the BOT lower initially, then up over time as the elasticities grew. As for why the Kulkarni Hypothesis didn't fit with this data, perhaps the depreciation (21% and 18% respectively) wasn't enough to move the needle on trade, or perhaps again, political issues trumped monetary policy on trade. Crude oil prices could also be behind these findings, considering that the price nearly tripled from January 2002 ($18.68/bbl.) to December 2005 ($51.66/bbl.)[7], and therefore allowing the Nigerian economy to shrug off the expected short-term dip in trade balance from the currency depreciation.

Case Study: Latvia

Latvia officially declared independence from the Soviet Union on May 4, 1990, and on September 3, 1991 the Latvian congress passed a resolution to restore the Bank of Latvia as the central bank of the country, giving it the right to issue national currency. After their independence from the Soviet Union in 1991, all three Baltic countries moved to a monetary policy framework within the context of a fixed exchange rate regime. This swift shift from a socialist monetary system allowed them to stabilize their economies much more quickly than other former Soviet republics. Estonia was the first former Soviet republic to issue its own currency, the kroon, in mid-1992, when they adopted a currency board style arrangement where the central bank is strictly prohibited from lending to government or state enterprises, and government reserves are backed by foreign reserves. This approach allowed the Estonian government to insulate monetary policy from political policy so the Kroon could become a stable currency.

In early 1992, Latvia was still using the Russian Ruble, which began to have adverse effects on its economy, as the ruble deteriorated, foreign imbalances grew, and the inability to issue cash domestically began to squeeze money supply. Because Latvia didn't have as much cash on reserve as Estonia, it initially adopted a money-based stabilization strategy, which involved the use of an interim currency—the Latvian ruble—that was circulated along with the Russian ruble until a national currency could be introduced in 1993. In mid-1993, the Latvian Lat was introduced as the new national currency, and its value was pegged in early 1994 to the IMF's SDR. (Blejer, 1999) Based on IMF data, however, the lat was valued 29% higher than the previous currency regime in Latvia, and this data makes for an interesting case study because it is one of the few examples that could be found where a currency was revalued by a significant amount and then remained unchanged for a long period of time. Such data offers a fairly well controlled test for the J-Curve Hypothesis.

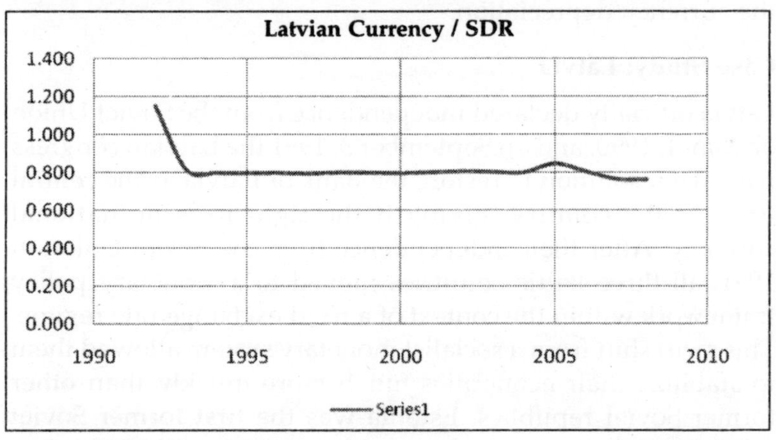

Notice the spike down from 1992 to 1993 in the chart above, which shows the period of introduction of the new currency, and subsequent revaluation. Notice, too, that the exchange rate remained constant for more than a decade following its introduction. Consider then the effects on balance of trade following the currency revaluation seen in the chart below.

We see that the balance of trade continued a protracted slide for the seven years following the currency revaluation. These deficits would be predicted by a common understanding of currency valuations and trade, which, as described in the theory section of this paper, suggest that as currency value goes up exports become more expensive for the rest of world, and thus decline, while imports become cheaper in the domestic market, and thus increase. What is not evident from the BOT chart is the inverse J-Curve Effect, however, where the BOT experiences a slight bump up following a revaluation before legging down in subsequent years.

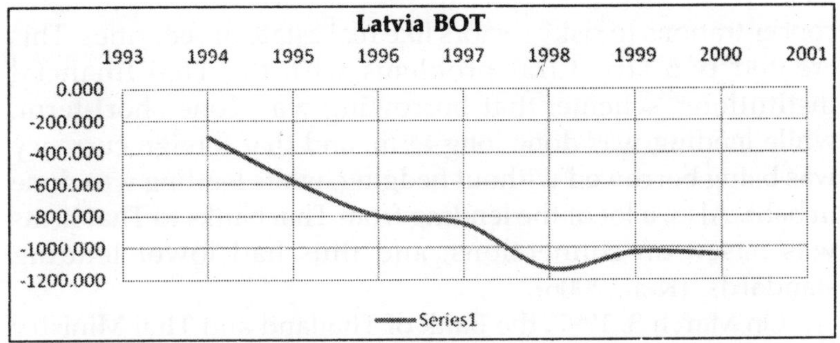

Latvia's trade deficits in the '90s may not be all currency driven, however. The other part of the BOT story is that Latvia is a relatively resource scarce country that has had to import primary materials from abroad to rebuild following independence. Also, with its manufacturing sector below Western standards and with new trade relations with the European Union in the mid-'90s, consumer demand for foreign goods was out of balance with foreign demand for Latvian goods. It will be interesting to see what happens with Latvia's trade balance following the switch to the Euro, which is currently scheduled for 2012.

Case Study: Thailand

In 1992, Thailand completed IMF Article 8 obligations, opening up the foreign exchange market for current account transactions. This allowed Thai financial institutions to get more favorable lending terms from foreign and domestic sources, however financial regulatory bodies were not sophisticated enough to ensure prudential standards were met. This caused a drastic increase in foreign borrowing from 1992-1996 by Thai commercial banks, who borrowed large sums of short-term funds from abroad. (Charoenseang, 2007) What made this borrowing spree even more problematic was that almost none of the borrowing was hedged for currency fluctuations because the Thai baht was pegged to a basket of currencies heavily weighted to the dollar. Thai financial institutions were then taking these short-term loans from foreign lenders, and lending domestically in high concentrations to risky sectors like real estate or securities. This created two structural problems with the Thai financial institutions' scheme: that borrowing was done short-term, while lending was done long-term; and that foreign currency was being borrowed without hedging, while lending was done in baht. Also, a lot of the lending from Thai banks to Thai firms was based on connections, and thus had lower lending standards. (Kali, 2006).

On March 3, 1997, the Bank of Thailand and Thai Ministry of Finance announced that ten banks needed to raise capital due to liquidity and asset quality problems. The Bank of Thailand provided capital to the banks, and took over some of their troubled real estate assets through the newly established Property Loan Management Organization. These actions changed foreign perception of Thailand, and capital started flowing out as quickly as it had flowed in, putting pressure on the Bank of Thailand to defend the currency peg, particularly during the speculative attack in May 1997. The operations of 58 of the largest financial institutions were suspended from June to August by the government who ordered them to restructure their balance sheets and management. By July 2, 1997, Thailand could no longer defend the currency peg, and allowed the baht to float, causing a sharp depreciation.

By the end of 1997, the baht had fallen 73% below its 1996 levels, as illustrated in the chart below.

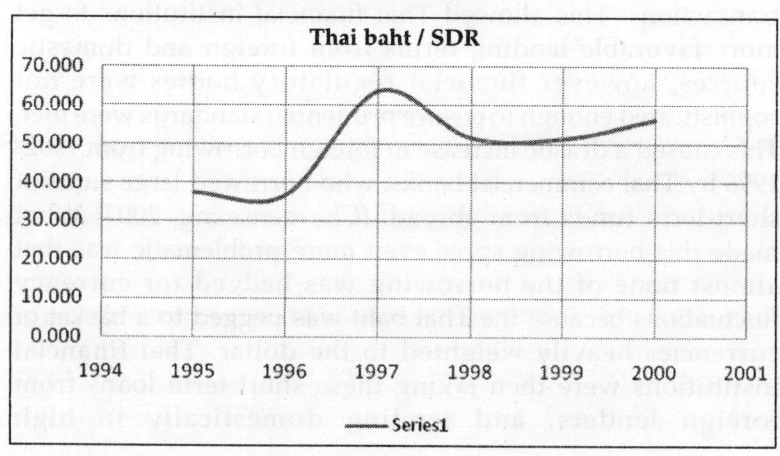

The financial crisis that resulted, and ultimately spread to several other Asian countries, caused a severe recession, with GDP falling 1.5% in 1997 and 11% in 1998. The Thai trade balance reacted opposite of how the J-Curve Hypothesis would anticipate, as seen in the chart below.

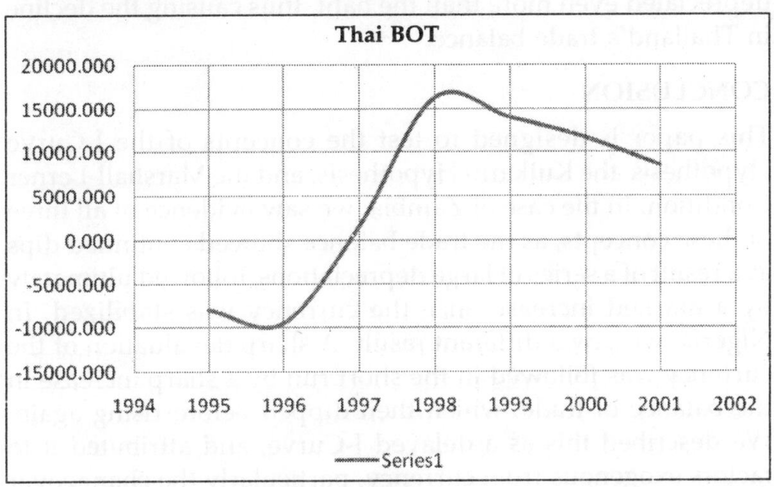

Year	*BOT*	*% Change*	*Year2*	*baht/SDR*	*% Change3*
1995	-7968	-115	1995	38	2
1996	-9488	-19	1996	37	-1.6
1997	1571	117	1997	64	73
1998	16237	933	1998	51	-19
1999	14013	-14	1999	51	0.5
2000	11700	-17	2000	56	9.6
2001	8543	-27	2001	55	-1.4

Notice that in 1998, the year following the 73% devaluation of the baht, the Thai trade balance actually increased, contrary to what one would expect based on the J-Curve Hypothesis. Then in the following years, the trade balance proceeded to steadily decline by 14%, 17%, and 27% in 1999, 2000, and 2001 respectively. Notice too that, although there was a modest appreciation of the baht in 1998, it didn't come close to returning to its prior levels, which suggests that the trade balance should have increased in the out years.

One possible explanation for this phenomenon is that Thailand's key trading partners are other countries in Asia, and thus, although the SDR component currencies remained relatively stable throughout the Asian financial crisis, the currencies of Thailand's key trading partners may have depreciated even more than the baht, thus causing the decline in Thailand's trade balance.

CONCLUSION

This paper is designed to test the concepts of the J-Curve Hypothesis, the Kulkarni Hypothesis, and the Marshall-Lerner Condition. In the case of Zambia, we saw evidence of all three of these concepts, as the trade balance showed continued dips as a result of a series of large depreciations, followed ultimately by a marked increase once the currency was stabilized. In Nigeria, we saw a different result. A sharp devaluation of the currency was followed in the short run by a sharp increase in the balance of trade, which then dipped before rising again. We described this as a delayed J-Curve, and attributed it to factors exogenous from currency, particularly the changeover of government from a protectionist military leadership to a more open civilian government that coincided with the change in currency valuation. More testing would have to be done to determine whether there is such a phenomenon as a delayed J-Curve effect that can occur in such a case, or if the appearance of a J-Curve in the case of Nigeria was simply due to other unobserved factors unique to that case.

In the case of Latvia, the J-Curve Effect did not show up in the data. Though the currency was revalued, which we would predict would result in an inverted J-Curve based on the theory, the balance of trade went straight down following the revaluation. We may be able to attribute this several factors that make Latvia, and perhaps other post-Soviet economies during their transition, poor examples for testing the J-Curve Hypothesis. First, the currency that was shown as being revalued from the data was actually a new currency, so it may be presumptuous to compare the two currencies as if they were the same. Second, the Latvian economy as a whole underwent a complete transition from being centrally planned—both in terms of monetary policy and production—from Moscow to being market-based, with monetary policy coming from the new Latvian central bank. These fundamental economic changes are likely to cause all sorts of changes in trade policy, trade relations, and domestic demand that could have as much or more influence over trade flows as monetary policy, at least in the short-run during the transition, which was the period observed.

Finally, we looked at the case of Thailand, where a financial crisis caused a steep drop in the value of the domestic currency in 1997. Contrary to the J-Curve Hypothesis, however, what followed was a short-term rise in the balance of trade, followed by a decline in the out years, which looked like an inverted J-Curve. Further study could be done on this topic to determine whether this occurred, as theorized in the section above, as a result of steeper currency declines in other Asian countries at the same time, or due to some other unknown factor.

Nevertheless, while the results of these cases are mixed with respect to the J-Curve Hypothesis, we conclude that those cases that did not show evidence of the Marshall-Lerner Condition and the J-Curve Effect did so for external reasons, however in the one example where external factors did not impact the balance of trade—that is, the case of Zambia[8]—we did see clear evidence of the J-Curve Effect and the Kulkarni Hypothesis. Thus we conclude that the concept of the Marshall-Lerner Condition is a relevant one, and is applicable in real world cases. From this study, however, we recognize that the balance of trade is more than just a function of monetary policy, and in many cases external factors can have stronger effects than currency valuation.

NOTES

1. Exchange Rate Determination, pg. 40.
2. Source: IMF International Financial Statistics online.
3. Exchange rate here expressed in terms of kwacha per IMF SDR.
4. Incidentally, oil accounted for roughly 80% of government revenues and 40% of GDP in the early '80s.

5. Source: IMF International Financial Statistics online.
6. Note: SDR, or Special Drawing Rights, are a basket of currencies consisting of the US Dollar, British Pound, Japanese Yen, and Swiss Franc. The weighting of this basket is determined by the International Monetary Fund.
7. Source: U.S. Energy Information Administration official statistics online. *http://tonto.eia.doe.gov/dnav/pet/hist/wtotworldw.htm*
8. Note: Zambia also demonstrated the effect hypothesized in the introduction of this paper, that in the out years following a sharp depreciation, that currency would begin to appreciate and trade balance would begin to decline, as occurred in 2006-2007. This effect was not seen in the data from the three other cases, however.

REFERENCES

Bahmani-Oskooee, M. (1985), Devaluation and the J-Curve: Some Evidence from LDCs. *The Review of Economics and Statistics* , 500-504.

Beck, T. (2005), Bank Privatization and Performance: Empirical Evidence from Nigeria. *Journal of Banking and Finance*, 2355-2379.

Blejer, M. (1999), *Financial Sector Transformation.* Cambridge: Cambridge University Press.

Charoenseang, J. (2007), *Economic Dynamism of Asia in the New Millenium.* New York: World Scientific.

Hacker, S. (2003), Is the J-Curve Effect Observable for Small Northern European Countries? *Open Economies Review*, 119-134.

Kali, R. (2006), Connected Lending: Thailand Before the Financial Crisis. *The Journal of Business*, 21-39.

Krueger, A. (1983), *Exchange Rate Determination.* Cambridge: Cambridge University Press.

Kulkarni, K. (2007), *Readings in International Economics.* New Delhi: Serials Publications Chapter 5.

Magee, S. (1973), Currency Contracts, Pass-Through, and Devaluation. *Brookings Papers on Economic Activity* , 303-325.

Moffett, M. (1989), The J-Curve Revisited: An Empirical Examination for the United States. *Journal of International Money and Finance* , 425-444.

Onafowora, O. (2008), Exchange Rate Volatility and Export Growth in Nigeria. *Applied Economics*, 1547-1556.

Rakner, L. (2003), *Political and Economic Liberalization in Zambia 1991-2001.* Stockholm: The Nordic Africa Institute.

Rose, A. K. (1990), Exchange Rates and the Trade Balance: Some Evidence from Developing Countries. *Economics Letters*, 271-275.

Taylor, M. (2002), *Confidence, Investment, and Growth: Economic Developments and the 2001 Elections in Zambia.* Lusaka: University of Zambia.

Wilson, P. (2001), Exchange Rates and the Trade Balance for Dynamic Asian Economies. *Open Economies Review*, 389-413.

10

EVIDENCE OF EXCHANGE RATE EFFECT ON THE TRADE BALANCE OF 5 COUNTRIES CASES OF MULTIPLE DEVALUATIONS

INTRODUCTION

The question on how to solve a country's balance of trade deficit has plagued policy makers for many years. One theory on how to improve the balance of trade of a country whose imports outnumber exports is to raise the exchange rate. When the exchange rate is raised, the domestic currency is devalued. When this happens prices of exports fall in foreign currency while the prices of imports in domestic currency increase. As this happens the demand for imports is expected to fall and the demand for exports is expected to rise creating a surplus balance of trade (Moosa 2005). In theory, this argument for increasing the exchange rate makes sense. The Marshall-Lerner condition backed this theory up a showing that in the short run the elasticity of demand for imports and exports are not large enough for there to be an increase in balance of trade, but in the long run elasticities will grow creating an increase in the balance of trade.

Numerous papers have been written on the topic of the Marshall-Lerner condition and the J-curve that comes from it.

This Chapter is based on an article with the same title co-authored with Mr. Adam Spencer

These studies have conflicting results based on which countries were studied, what methods were used and the time period that was covered. This paper intends to show that increasing the exchange rate multiple times will not lead to an increase in balance of trade because of the shifting J-curve known as the Kulkarni Hypothesis. Creating multiple devaluations in order to increase balance of trade only creates more of a deficit. To show the effect of the shifting J-curve hypothesis this paper will examine five African countries from ten year data.

The next section will be a literature review of previous studies on the J-curve hypothesis to give a foundation for the paper. Following the literature review will be an overview of the theory that was used to set up the analysis. Next will be a short description of the data. Finally there will be a discussion of the results for each of the five African countries followed by a short conclusion.

SECTION - 1

LITERATURE REVIEW

There have been many papers written on whether the J-curve exists or not. There are numerous studies that have been written to show support for the J-curve (Noland 1989, Bahhmani-Oskooee 1985, Brooks 1999, Onafowora 2003, Hacker and Hatemi-J 2003 and Kulkarni 2006) in some countries and not in other countries. Also, there are papers written that show there is no J-curve (Rose and Yellen 1988). Even though there are papers that have been written against the J-curve, the main consensus is that the J-curve does exist in many countries given the correct economic conditions.

There have been studies that have shown that there is no evidence of the J-curve existing in many countries. Rose and Yellen (1988) have found no evidence of the J-curve for the United States using both bilateral data and aggregate data. Further they found no evidence that the balance of trade has a long term relationship with the exchange rate. While no relationship is found, they do bring up a key concern with the traditional theoretical argument, "The theoretical model excludes the possibility of "third-country effects". For instance, in their equation, bilateral trade with Canada is seen as being dependent only on the Canada/US real exchange rate and not on, say, the Japan/U.S. real exchange rate as well. (page 63) Some previous studies could suffer from omitted variable bias without this effect accounted for.

Noland (1989) finds that there are significant effects between the exchange rate and the balance of trade. He found there are short run lags in all of the variables of less than one year, meaning a perverse reaction for the balance of trade. After the initial lags, a decrease in the balance of trade, an improvement was seen for Japan and a long run surplus in balance of trade was observed. While he finds significant J-curve evidence Noland warns that while there could be improvements of the trade balance in the long run, there will be long periods of lags and perverse reactions with the trade balance. Governments should be aware of this and should use an economic activity policy rather than an exchange rate policy (Noland 1989).

Bahmani-Oskooee (1985) shows that there is evidence of the J-curve in many LDC's. This is done by examining the cases of four countries, Greece, India, Korea and Thailand. To see if any of these countries exhibited the J-curve phenomenon Bahmani-Oskooee used a technique that had never been done at the time. Instead of examining only the exchange rate and the balance of trade, many other factors were used to evaluate the J-curve. In addition to the balance of trade and exchange rate, GDP, real world income index, domestic and world high power money indexes were also used. The regression results found that in three of the four countries there was evidence of the J-curve. The exchange rate coefficient was negative and the distribution lag coefficients were initially positive and then became negative, which follows the J-curve path (Bahmani-Oskooee 1985). This paper explains the J-curve differently than the traditional elasticity approach, rationalizing the movement of the trade balance, "it is quite possible that flows of goods respond only with time lags to changes in the exchange rate" (Bahmani-Oskooee, 502). Using a unique approach at the time Bahmani-Oskooee has shown that in some of the less developed countries there is evidence of a J-curve.

Along with Brooks, Bahmani-Oskooee (1999) also found long run evidence of the J-curve with the United States and six of her largest trading partners. They employed the technique of disaggregating the data between the United States and Canada, France, Italy, Germany, Japan and the United Kingdom. When they used the disaggregated data it was found that in the short term there was no sign of the J-curve, but in the long term the J-curve did exist. Thus they conclude that a depreciation of the U.S. dollar can have favorable long run effects on the balance of trade (Bahmani-Oskooee, Brooks).

Onafowora (2003) presents another case in which currency devaluation could lead to a favorable increase in Balance of trade. Onafowora studied Indonesia, Malaysia and Thailand to find the effects of the exchange rate and the balance of trade. Using a cointigration analysis Onafowora found that there was a relationship between real exchange rate, real domestic income, real trade balance and real foreign income. Also the Marshall-Lerner condition held true in the long run (2003). This paper found short run J-curve effects for bilateral trade with U.S. and Japan between Malaysia and Indonesia and between Thailand and the U.S. For Malaysia and Indonesia there was an initial decline in balance of trade but then over time balance of trade improved.

Another study that confirms the J-curve hypothesis was written by Hacker and Hatemi (2003) when they studied north European countries. In this study they examined the monthly and quarterly trade statistics for Belgium, Denmark, Netherlands, Norway, and Sweden. To analyze the effect of exchange rate on balance of trade they used a export import ratio instead of the commonly used export minus import. Also, because of the other factors that influence trade balances, both domestic and foreign inputs such as GDP were used as variables in the regression as well. Using the trade ratio, Hatemi and Hacker found that these countries do exhibit the J-curve phenomenon (2003). In nine of the ten cases that were studied a decline in the trade balance was found to happen after the initial devaluation of the currency. After the initial trade balance declined seven of the ten countries were found to have an increased trade balance in the long run (2003), which is not as convincing of an argument.

Innovative work by Kulkarni (2006, Chapter 10) forms the basis of this paper. In the case of Ghana, he shows that there are several devaluations in the currency accompanied by a worsening balance of payment deficit. From this he concludes that, "a continuously devaluating currency may lead to further deficits in balance of trade" (49). Based on the case of Ghana, devaluating a currency multiple times creates shifts in the J-curve and an ever increasing deficit in balance of trade.

This paper studies the effects of five African countries in a way that previous literature has not. We will look at the long run relationship of exchange rate and balance of trade in periods of multiple devaluations using comparative analysis. This paper examines the effects of multiple devaluations that are not seen before in previous papers besides Kulkarni (2006) and address the policy implications of such devaluations.

I. J-Curve Hypothesis and Marshall-Lerner Condition

The J-curve hypothesis explains the relationship between changes in exchange rates and balance of trade. Conventional arguments have shown that an increase in exchange rate, or depreciation of currency, leads to a reduction in imports and an increase in exports and a balance of trade surplus. The J-curve hypothesis by Marshall and Lerner shows that the conventional argument might not be the case. Increasing the exchange rate would only lead to a surplus in the balance of payments if the absolute value of demand elasticity of exports and imports is greater than or equal to one. This statement is proven by the derivation of the Marshall-Lerner condition. If the Marshall-Lerner condition is not satisfied, there is a perverse reaction, a increase in exchange rate will lead to a decrease in balance of trade.

The J-curve hypothesis incorporates the Marshall-Lerner condition and the time determinant of elasticity demand. As time progresses, the elasticity demand of both imports and exports will increase. So, initially after the devaluation the elasticity demand of imports and exports should be relatively small. As time goes by the elasticity demand for imports and exports will increase and the Marshall-Lerner condition is met when the elasticity demand for imports plus exports will be greater than or equal to one.

$$\left(Nx + Nm > 1 \ for \ \frac{\partial BOT}{\partial J} > 0\right)$$

Once the Marshall-Lerner condition is met, there will be a balance of payment surplus. When graphing the balance of trade over time there will be a J-shape to the curve that balance of trade takes. Here is the simplistic derivation of the Marshall-Lerner Condition.

There are three definitions that are required for the Marshall-Lerner Condition:

(1) $\left(real\ Exchange\ Range\,(j)\frac{ep*}{p}\right)$

Where

e = Nominal Exchange rate

p*= Foreign general price level

p= Domestic general price level

(2) Elasticity Demand for imports with respect to real exchange rate (N_m)

$$\left(Nm = \frac{\Delta M}{\Delta J} \times \frac{J}{M}\right)$$

(3) Elasticity Demand for exports with respect to real exchange rate (N_x)

$$\left(Nx = \frac{\Delta X}{\Delta J} \times \frac{J}{X}\right)$$

To derive the Marshall-Lerner Condition there are three assumptions that must be followed:

(1) The supply elasticity's of exports and imports are infinite.

(2) Balance of Payment is defined as balance by only balance of trade.

(3) At the time of devaluation, the balance of trade is balanced.

(1) $(BOT = x - JM = 0)\ so\ x = JM\ or\ M = \dfrac{X}{J}$

(2) Derive the BOT equation with respect to J

$$\frac{\partial BOT}{\partial J} = \frac{\partial X}{\partial J} - \frac{\partial X * M}{\partial J} - \frac{\partial M * J}{\partial J}$$

(3) $\dfrac{\partial BOT}{\partial J} = \dfrac{\partial X}{\partial J} \times \dfrac{J}{X} \times \dfrac{X}{J} - \dfrac{X}{J} - \dfrac{\partial M}{\partial J} \times \dfrac{J}{M} \times M$

$\rightarrow$ So $\partial\ BOT = M(Nx - 1 - Nm)$

For an increasing real exchange rate (J) to lead to a surplus in BOT, we must have absolute value of demand elasticity of X and M to be at least one. When Marshall-Lerner condition is not satisfied the devaluation of currency leads to a balance of payment deficit. To have a surplus in the BOT after a devaluation $\dfrac{\partial BOT}{\partial J} > 0$

Because both X and M are positive by definition $\left(Nx + Nm > 1\ for\ \dfrac{\partial BOT}{\partial J} > 0 \right)$

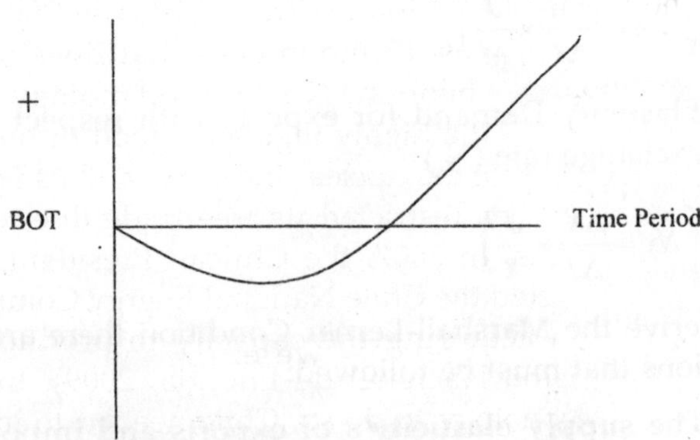

Figure 1: Traditional J-Curve Hypothesis

Shifting J-curve/ Kulkarni Hypothesis

The extended J-curve Hypothesis put forward by Kulkarni addresses the issue of a country whose currency continuously devaluates. This theory states that when currencies are continuously devaluated, a continuous deficit in the balance of trade can result (Kulkarni 2006). This happens because when there are multiple devaluations, there will be a shift of the J-curve every time the currency devaluates. The series of rightward shifts will cause the balance of trade to decrease and the effect will continue to be perverse.

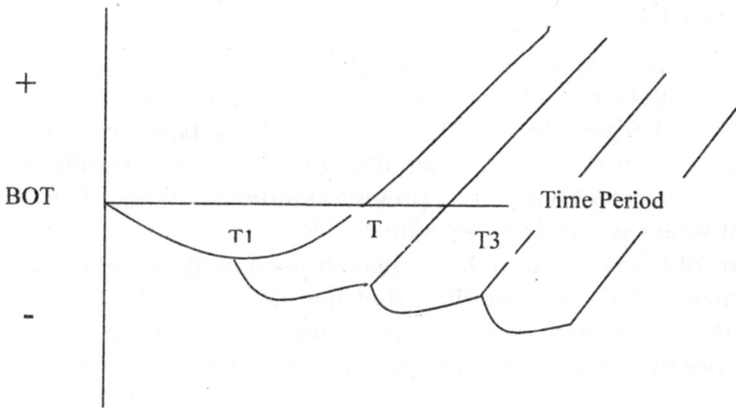

Figure 2: Multiple Devaluations and Shifts in J-Curve

In this paper we will use the extended J-curve hypothesis to see if the constant devaluations of currencies in Africa lead to a drop in balance of trade and whether the path of balance of trade resembles the shifting J-curve model seen in figure 2.

SECTION - 2

DATA

This study examined the effect of exchange rate on the balance of trade to find if there was evidence of the J-curve and the extended J-curve. To do this we examined five African countries, Kenya, Tanzania, Morocco, Mozambique and Uganda from 1994 to 2004. To find the existence of the extended J-curve data were collected for both exchange rate and balance of trade. The exchange rate for all countries was in the form of domestic currency per US dollar, for example Kenyan shillings per US dollar. The balance of trade is computed by subtracting exports from imports. The balance of trade data were aggregate for each year's end starting in 1994 and ending in 2004. The figures for exchange rates for each country were also found at the year's end beginning in 1994 and ending in 2004. Figures on both exchange rate and balance of trade were collected from the International Financial Statistics Yearbook by the International Monetary Fund 2006.

RESULTS

This paper examined the possibility of the shifting J-curve hypothesis put forward by Kulkarni (2006). Using data collected from 1994 to 2004, we plotted the balance of trade across the time period. When doing this we found results that were consistent with many previous studies showing a J-curve. But when we looked at multiple devaluations we found that four of the five countries studied showed evidence of shifting J-curves. This is something that has not been shown before and has economic policy implications for countries to consider before devaluating their currency.

KENYA

Kenya is a country which has had a short independence with many different exchange rate regimes (State Dept.). Kenya has had a policy of devaluating their currency multiple times, and has also had an increasing balance of trade deficit. After a devaluation in 1992 and 1993, there is evidence of the J-curve by the increasing trade deficit for the year 1994 followed by a decrease in trade deficit for one year following. This is a perfect example of the J-curve. But following other currency devaluations from 1996 to 2004 there are a number of other J-curve taking place. The result of multiple currency devaluations is the shift of the J-curve to the right when currencies devaluate. Because of this, Kenya experienced an increasing trade deficit for all of the years the currency devaluated.

Year	*Balance of Trade*	*Exchange Rate (Against US dollar)*
1994	-504.00	56.05
1995	-1,112.00	51.43
1996	-881.00	57.11
1997	-1,225.00	58.73
1998	-1,189.00	60.37
1999	-1,085.00	70.33
2000	-1,371.00	76.18
2001	-1,248.00	78.56
2002	-1,129.00	78.75
2003	-1,314.00	75.94
2004	-1,869.00	79.17

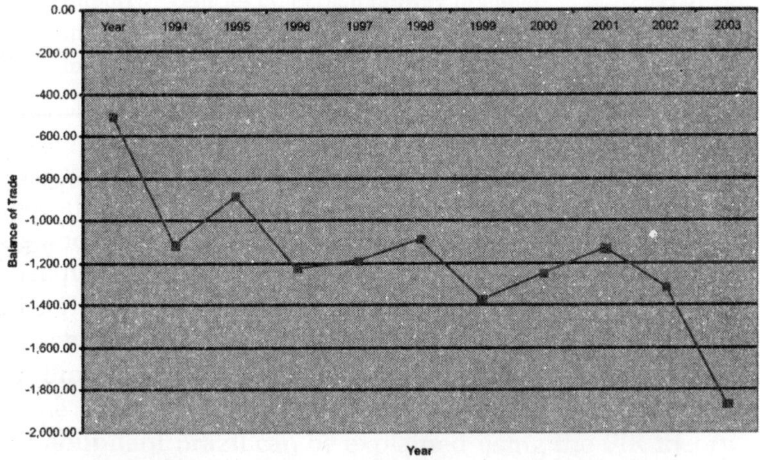

TANZANIA

Tanzania is a country who has had very few exports in the past decade due to the decline in clove production which is one of the countries few exports. The Tanzanian government has recently turned to a floating exchange rate which has created more foreign investment, but has created large increases in the exchange rate and a devaluating currency (State Dept.). During the time period we observed Tanzania's currency had devaluated every year, and in some instances, by a large amount. From 1994 to 1997 the balance of trade actually increased, which was not expected. Following 1997 there was a sharp decline in the trade balance, a perverse reaction to the increase in the exchange rate. Following the sharp decline, there was an increase in the balance of trade for one year, and then the deficit began to increase again. This is another perfect form of the J-curve. The constant increase in exchange rate has again caused the balance of payment to decrease almost every year, brought about by the shifting of the J-curve.

Year	*Balance of Trade*	*Exchange Rate (Against US dollar)*
1994	-789.90	523.45
1995	-657.50	550.36
1996	-449.00	595.64
1997	-449.10	624.57
1998	-775.90	681.00
1999	-872.10	797.33
2000	-704.30	803.26
2001	-819.60	916.30
2002	-614.90	976.30
2003	-823.70	1,063.62
2004	-906.00	1,042.96

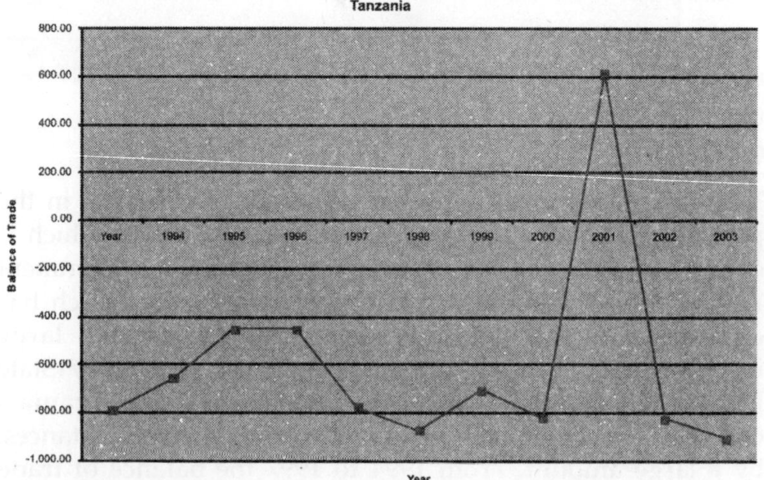

UGANDA

Uganda is a country whose economy focuses around agriculture. Their main exports are coffee and fish products. Being focused on agricultural production and having almost no manufacturing, their exports are nearly half that of their imports, which are capital equipment, vehicles and petroleum (State Dept.). From the beginning time period of the study Uganda has had an increasing exchange rate every year. Because of this there is a sharp decline on the balance of trade. This balance of trade decline can be seen to go along with the devaluation of their currency. There is about a one year period when the balance of trade actually increases, just as the J-curve hypothesis would predict. But because of the shifting J-curve the balance of trade continues to worsen.

Year	*Balance of Trade*	*Exchange Rate (Against US dollar)*
1994	-251.20	926.80
1995	-366.50	1009.5
1996	-347.60	1029.6
1997	-449.90	1,140.10
1998	-656.10	1,362.70
1999	-505.60	1,506.00
2000	-499.80	1,766.70
2001	-499.90	1,727.70
2002	-571.30	1,852.60
2003	-681.90	1,935.30
2004	-757.30	1,738.60

MOZAMBIQUE

Mozambique is known as one of the poorest countries in the world with a GDP per capita of around $320 US dollars in 2006. This, however, is an improvement from the 1980's where it was around $120. Their main exports are agricultural and natural gas(State Dept.). Mozambique's exchange rate with the US dollar has increased substantially over the period 1994-

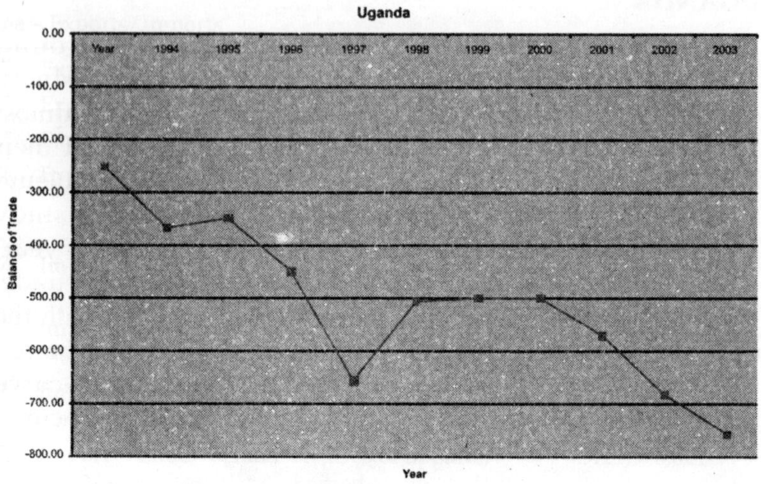

2004, by an amazing 2700%. This constant devaluation has almost cut the balance of trade deficit in half over ten years. There can be two J-curves observed during this time period, but they do not show the shifting J-curve hypothesis. Rather, they show the perverse reaction and then the increase in the balance of trade.

Year	*Balance of Trade*	*Exchange Rate (Against US dollar)*
1994	-767.20	6,651.00
1995	-536.30	10890.00
1996	-478.30	11377.00
1997	-454.00	11,543.00
1998	-491.00	12,366.00
1999	-806.20	13,300.00
2000	-682.00	17,140.50
2001	-271.30	23,320.40
2002	-666.60	23,854.30
2003	-604.20	23,856.70
2004	-345.80	188,899.30

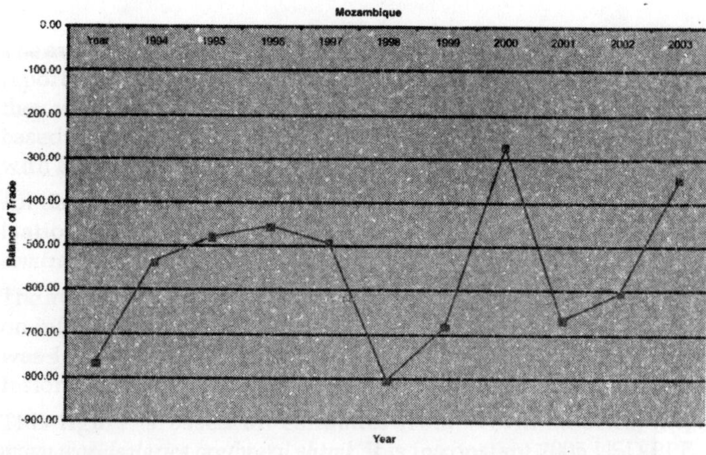

MOROCCO

Morocco has seen a time period of low inflation and slow economic growth over the past decade. Morocco is extremely dependent upon agriculture for their economic growth, which has slowed dramatically. Morocco has had several exchange rate increases during the ten years of interest. Along with the exchange rate increases the balance of trade continued to worsen. Morocco shows several J-curves following the devaluations occurring in 1994, 1996 and 1991-2001. Following these devaluations are decreases in the balance of trade, and a small increase afterward. But, these small increases last only for one year because of the constant devaluations and the shifting J-curve effect.

Year	*Balance of Trade*	*Exchange Rate (Against US dollar)*
1994	-2,107.00	8.69
1995	-2,482.00	8.469
1996	-2,193.00	8.8
1997	-1,864.00	9.71
1998	-2,319.00	9.25
1999	-2,448.00	10.09
2000	-3,235.00	10.62
2001	-3,022.00	11.56
2002	-3,061.00	10.17
2003	-4,345.00	8.75
2004	-6,487.00	8.22

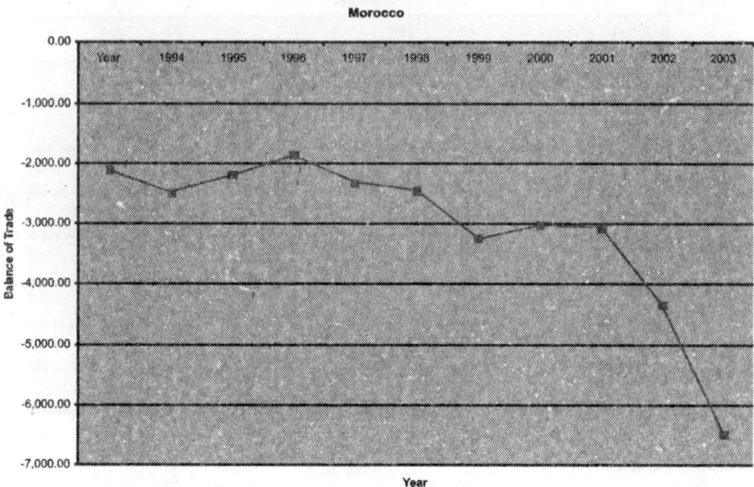

CONCLUSION

After analyzing five African countries, Kenya, Tanzania, Morocco, Mozambique and Uganda it is clear that the extended J-curve hypothesis holds true. When a country is experiencing a balance of trade deficit and devaluates their currency multiple times, the extended J-curve takes effect. When there is a devaluation there is a perverse reaction until demand elasticity grows for imports and exports and the Marshall-Lerner condition is satisfied. When this happens, there is an increase in the balance of trade. But when there are multiple devaluations, the J-curve shifts to the right with the devaluations and the balance of payment can never increase. When a country is experiencing a balance of trade deficit, it must realize that increasing the exchange rate may not be the answer. Devaluating the currency many times will actually make the problem worse and should not be considered an economic policy for improving the balance of trade.

REFERENCES

Bahmani-Oskooee, Mohsen, and Taggert Brooks. "Bilateral J-Curve between U.S. and her trading ." *Review of World Economics* 135 (1999): 156-165. In Springerlink [database online]. (accessed Mar. 5, 2008).

"Countries." U.S. Department of State-Home Page. *http://www.state.gov/countries/ (accessed Apr. 10, 2008).*

Hacker, Scott and Abdulnasser Hatemi-J. "Is the J-Curve Effect Observable for Small North European Economies? ." *Open Economies Review* 14 (2003): 119-134. In Springerlink[database online]. (accessed Mar. 25, 2008).

Husted, Steven, and Michael Melvin. *International Economics (7th Edition).* Toronto: Addison Wesley, 2006.

Kulkarni, Kishore G.. *Reading in International Economics: Selected Writings of Prof. Kishore G. Kulkarni.* New Delhi, India: Serials Publications, Third Edition, 2007, Chapter 5, pp. 41-52.

Moosa, Imad A. *Exchange Rate Regimes: Fixed, Flexible or Something in Between.* New York: Palgrave Macmillan, 2005.

Noland, Marcus. "Japanese Trade Elasticities and the J-Curve." *The Review of Economics and Statistics* 71 (1989): 175-179. In JSTOR[database online]. (accessed Mar. 5, 2008).

Onafowora, Olugbenga. "Exchange rate and trade balance in east asia: is there a." *Economics Bulletin* 5 (2003): 1-13, *http://www.economicsbulletin.uiuc.edu/2003/volume5/EB-03E00003A.pdf.*

Rose, Andrew, and Janet Yellen. "Is there a J-curve?." *Journal of Monetary Economics* 24 (1989): 53-68. In Science Direct[database online]. (accessed May 25, 2008).

International Financial Statistics 2006 (International Financial Statistics Yearbook English Edition). Washington: International Monetary Fund, 2006.

11

APPLICATION OF THE J-CURVE TO SELECT CFA ZONE COUNTRIES 1990-PRESENT

INTRODUCTION

Many governments will allow their currency to depreciate, or devalue their currency by manipulating the fixed exchange rate, because it is believed this will create a surplus in the balance of trade obviously relieving or improving a trade deficit. But is this the case in reality? The J-Curve hypothesis attempts to explain what happens to a country's balance of trade upon, and subsequent to, devaluation of the country's currency. The purpose of this paper is to discuss the effects of currency devaluation on the balance of trade in select African countries, specifically the CFA Zone countries of Benin, Cameroon, Côte d'Ivoire, Mali, Niger, and Senegal.

The first section of this paper will discuss the basic concepts of exchange rates and the determination of fixed exchange rates. The next section will discuss further fixed exchange rates and the balance of trade along with the Marshall-Lerner Condition. This section is followed by a discussion of the J-Curve hypothesis, its background and the underlying assumptions thereof. The Kulkarni Hypothesis is then discussed, followed by two sections on the background of the

This Chapter is based on an article with same title co-authored with Mr. Jeffrey A. Sasakura

CFA Zone and the CFA Franc along with its devaluation in 1994. Finally, 6 CFA Zone countries' balances of trade are analyzed along with historical CFA Franc exchange rate data to apply the J-Curve Hypothesis and locate any J-Curves that may appear. Appendix I explains the derivation of the Marshall-Lerner Condition.

SECTION - 1

EXCHANGE RATES UNDER FIXED AND FLOATING SYSTEMS

An exchange rate is the value of a specific currency in terms of another. There are two methods to determining exchange rates. First is the American Method which expresses an exchange rate as the value of domestic currency per unit of foreign currency. The second method is the European Method, which express the exchange rate as the value of a foreign currency per unit of domestic currency. In the interest of clarity and consistency, this paper will utilize only the American Method.

In a floating exchange rate system, the foreign exchange rate is constantly changing due to the forces of supply and demand. There are several determinants of the supply of a currency. These include: exports of goods and services, travel to the country by foreign residents, purchase of domestic real assets by foreigners, and purchase of domestic financial assets by foreigners. The supply of foreign exchange is always created by foreign parties. As the exchange rate increases, the quantity of foreign exchange increases since the demand for all of the above drivers for the supply of foreign exchange increase.

Conversely, the demand for foreign exchange is created by domestic residents, although it is through similar activities, including: travel abroad by domestic residents, purchase of foreign financial assets, purchase of foreign real assets, and the purchase of foreign goods and services. The exchange rate and the quantity of foreign exchange demanded by domestic residents are inversely related. As the exchange rate increases, the quantity of foreign exchange demanded by domestic residents decreases because the drivers of foreign exchange demand become relatively more expensive.

This relationship between the supply of and demand for foreign exchange is shown by Graph 1 (below). As is shown, when the exchange rate increases, the supply of foreign exchange increases while the demand for foreign exchange decreases.

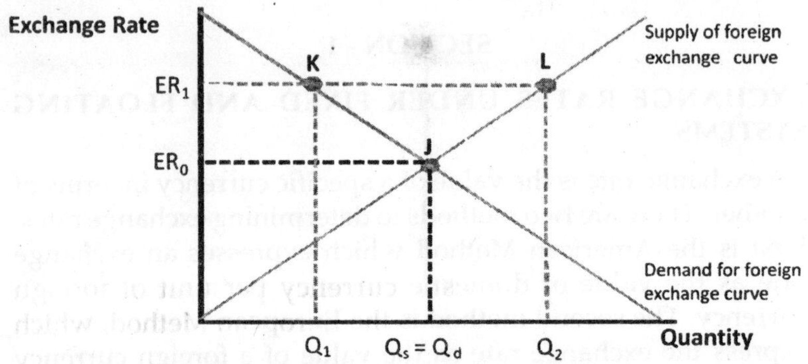

Graph 1: Foreign Exchange Supply and Demand with Excess Supply

Under a floating exchange rates system, it can be shown that the exchange rate will always be at the equilibrium rate ER_0, where the quantity of foreign exchange supplied equals the quantity of foreign exchange demanded. This is called "Paradoxal Flexibility." If the exchange rate were above the equilibrium rate at ER_1, the quantity of foreign exchange supplied (quantity Q_2) would be far greater than the quantity of foreign exchange demanded (quantity Q_1). In other words, there would be a foreign exchange supply surplus of quantity Q_1 Q_2 or K L. This surplus would force the exchange rate back down to ER_0.

Similarly, if the exchange rate were below the equilibrium rate, as shown in Graph 2 (right), there would be a shortage in the quantity of foreign exchange demanded over what would be supplied. This shortage would be equal to quantity Q_3 Q_4 or S H in the graph above. This excess demand for foreign exchange would act to push the exchange rate back up to the equilibrium rate ER_0.

Under fixed exchange rate systems, the government will always fix the exchange rate below the equilibrium point

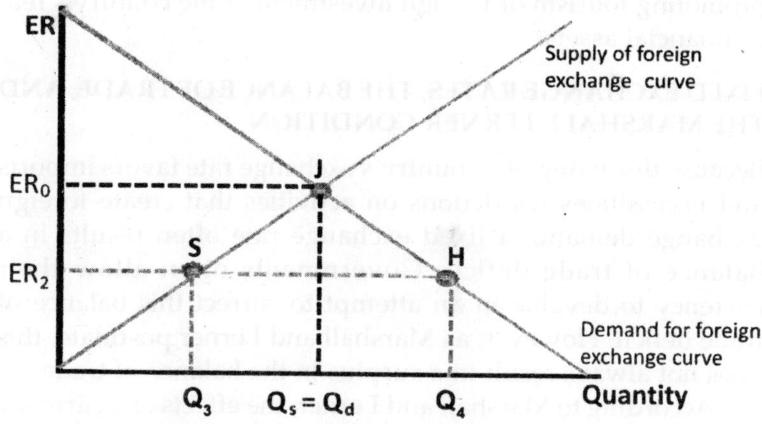

Graph 2: Foreign Exchange Supply and Demand with Excess Demand

creating this excess demand for currency. This can be attributed to the fact that the government wants an environment where imports are less expensive. Under a fixed exchange rate system, the exchange rate will never be the equilibrium rate. If this were the case, the government would let the exchange rate float (they would do nothing to fix the exchange rate).

This excess demand for foreign exchange can be problematic, however. Because there is a shortage of foreign exchange, as the country's economy as a whole demands a higher quantity of foreign exchange than is supplied, the government must either finance this shortage or adopt policies that restrict all activities that create an excess demand for foreign exchange. This restriction on demand drivers may include: restricting the private sector from importing via tariffs or quotas; stopping or limiting domestic residents' ability to travel abroad; and/or limiting domestic residents' investment in foreign real or financial assets. Alternatively, the government can seek to finance this shortage in foreign exchange by borrowing money from the IMF or World Bank. Another alternative governments may seek to counteract this shortage in supply of foreign exchange involves creating policies that encourage activities that increase the supply of foreign exchange. As previously noted, these activities may include promoting tourism or foreign investment in the country's real or financial assets.

FIXED EXCHANGE RATES, THE BALANCE OF TRADE, AND THE MARSHALL-LERNER CONDITION

Because this fixing of a country's exchange rate favors imports and necessitates restrictions on activities that create foreign exchange demand, a fixed exchange rate often results in a balance of trade deficit. Governments often allow their currency to devalue in an attempt to correct this balance of trade deficit. However, as Marshall and Lerner postulate, this does not always result in a surplus in the balance of trade.

According to Marshall and Lerner, the effects of a currency devaluation on the balance of trade is a function of the elasticity of demand for imports $\left(E_M^Q\right)$ with respect to the real exchange rate (Q) and the elasticity of demand for exports $\left(E_X^Q\right)$ with respect to Q. Specifically, unless these elasticities are large enough that the sum of their absolute values is 1, the expected balance of trade surplus will not materialize. In equation form, this relationship, called the Marshall-Lerner Condition, can be expressed as follows:

$$| E_{\downarrow} M^{\uparrow} Q[1+ | E]_{\downarrow} (X)^{\uparrow} Q |\geq 1$$

Utilization of the Marshall-Lerner condition necessitates the outlining of several key assumptions:

1. There is no capital account in the balance of payments. If there is no capital account, this assumes that there are no capital flows into or out of the economy, so the balance of payments is equivalent to the balance of trade.
2. The elasticity of supply for imports and the elasticity of supply for exports are infinite. In other words, there are no supply constraints. This means there is sufficient supply for any quantity of imports or exports demanded.
3. The balance of trade at the time of the increase in exchange rates is zero. In other words, it is assumed

that the current account starts at zero (is balanced) before the currency devaluation. According to Krugman and Obstfeld, "if the current account is not zero initially the [Marshall-Lerner] condition becomes substantially more complex" (Krugman & Obstfeld, 2006).

There are two main determinants of E_M^Q and E_X^Q, and any elasticity for that matter. These are:

1. The number of substitutes available for goods and services. As the number of substitutes increases, so does the elasticity.
2. The time period after the change in the independent variable. As the time since the change in the independent variable (the denominator in the elasticity equation) increases so does the elasticity.

See Appendix I for the derivation of the Marshall-Lerner Condition.

THE J-CURVE HYPOTHESIS

It is often observed that immediately following currency devaluation, in the short term, the Marshall-Lerner Condition is not satisfied, which results in a deficit in the balance of trade. This can be attributed to the fact that, as noted above, the shorter the time period from the change in the independent variable, the smaller the elasticity. In the case of the elasticity of imports and the elasticity of exports with respect to the exchange rate, in the short term, these values are often too small to satisfy the Marshall-Lerner Condition. Specifically, immediately following currency devaluation, the decision to purchase goods and services is often made based on the previous exchange rate, since many import and export orders are made in advance. According to Krugman and Obstfeld:

"In the first few months after the depreciation, export and import volumes therefore may reflect buying decisions that were made on the basis of the old real exchange rate: The primary effect of the depreciation is to raise the value of the precontracted level of imports in terms of domestic products.

Because exports measured in domestic output do not change while imports measured in domestic output rise, there is an initial fall in the current account..." (Krugman & Obstfeld, 2006).

In terms of the Marshall-Lerner Condition, there is often a deficit in the balance of trade until enough time passes that these elasticities increase sufficiently so their sum is greater than or equal to one. Once this occurs, the balance of trade eventually increases to a surplus. This is shown by the J-Curve depicted in Graph 3 (below).

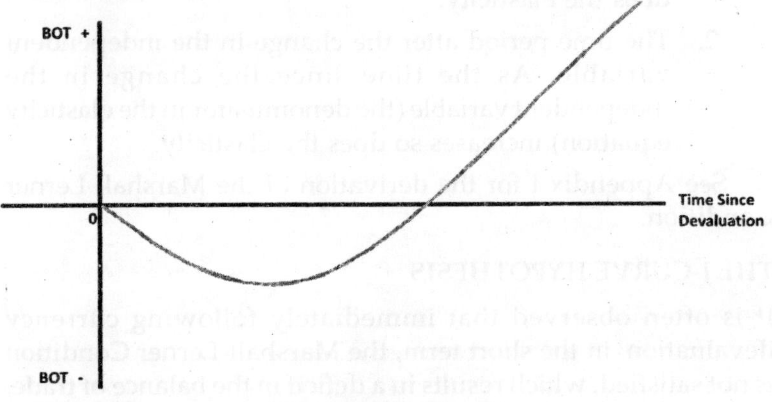

Graph 3: The J-Curve

In the above graph, the X-Axis represents the time since the currency devaluation, and the Y-Axis depicts the balance of trade where values greater than 0 represent a balance of trade surplus and values less than zero represent a balance of trade deficit.

EXTENSION OF THE J-CURVE: THE KULKARNI HYPOTHESIS

Kulkarni suggests that continued devaluations in a currency will have the effect of shifting the J-Curve to the right prolonging and/or worsening the decline in a country's balance of trade. This has been shown with empirical evidence from Ghana, where the currency experienced successive devaluations from 1983 through 1989. Regarding a situation involving continuous currency devaluations, Kulkarni says "it is concluded that the existence of dynamic, persistent balance of trade deficit is a possibility" (Kulkarni, 2007). Graph 4 (below) depicts the effects of continuous currency devaluations on a country's balance of payments. It can be seen that after the initial devaluation at point A, there are two successive currency devaluations at points B and C, resulting in a deepening and prolonging of the deficit in the balance of trade.

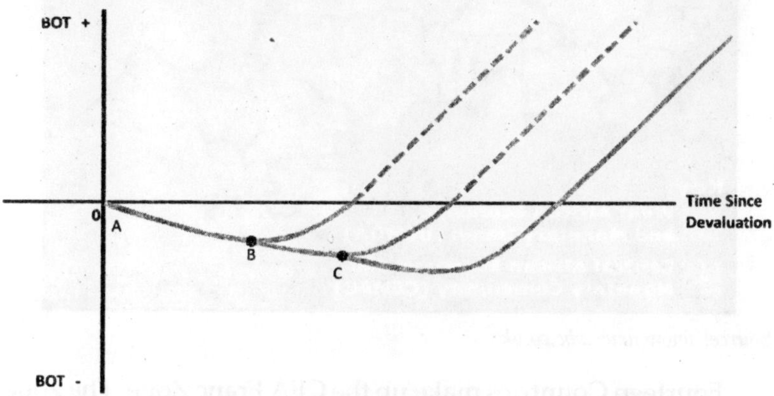

Graph 4: The J-Curve with Successive Currency Devaluations

SECTION - 2

HISTORY OF THE CFA FRANC

Immediately after France ratified the Bretton-Woods Agreement, the French Franc experienced substantial devaluation due to the establishment of a fixed exchange rate between it and the US Dollar. In an effort to shield its Sub-Saharan African Colonies from this devaluation, France created a separate currency known as the Colonies françaises d'Afrique (CFA) Franc for what was termed the CFA Franc Zone. This new currency was pegged to the Metropolitan French Franc at a rate of 1.7 CFA/FF. In January 1948, the CFA Franc was allowed to devalue along with the French Franc, but its value was held constant in October 1948, when the French Franc devalued again. This revaluation would prove to be the last change until the major devaluation of the CFA Franc in 1994 (Stasavage, 2003).

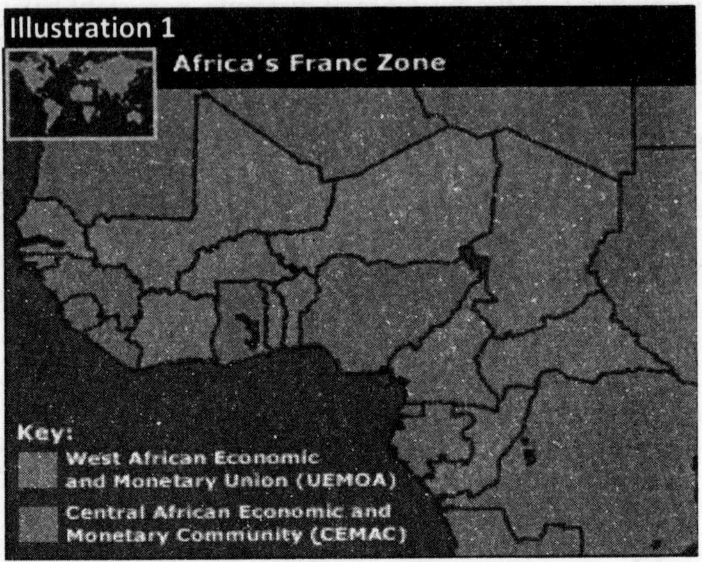

Source: www.news.bbc.co.uk

Fourteen Countries make up the CFA Franc Zone. The zone is comprised of two groups: the West African Economic and Monetary Unions (WAEMU) and the Central African Economic and Monetary Union (CAEMC). The WAEMU consists of: Benin, Burkina Faso, Côte d'Ivoire, Mali, Niger, Senegal and Togo, and the CAEMC is made up of Cameroon, the Central African Republic, Chad, the Congo, Equatorial Guinea, and Gabon (Clement, Mueller, Cosse, & Le Dem, 1996). Illustration 1 (left) shows the CFA Zone Countries.

THE 1994 DEVALUATION OF THE CFA FRANC

In 1994, many economists were arguing that the CFA Franc was overvalued, in part because of inflationary issues that lead to appreciation of the real exchange rate along with severe declines in commodity prices. From the beginning of the 1980s until the devaluation in 1994, the CFA Zone countries experienced extreme balance of payment problems due to the decline in commodity prices. "Given the heavy reliance of all CFA governments on taxes on international trade for revenue, these balance of payment problems also led to large budget deficits" (Stasavage, 2003). Some countries experience double digit leaps in their budget deficits during this time, which lead the World Bank to call for the CFA Franc to be devalued.

After the financial crises became too large to ignore, the CFA zone countries began to move toward devaluation. In the January 13, 1994 issue of the Financial Times, one author called this "the most foretold and least well prepared devaluation in economic history." After a failed attempt by the IMF and the French treasury to force devaluation in 1992, the French Treasury resorted to restricting the conversion of the CFA Franc and convinced the CFA Zone leaders to accept devaluation in the Fall of 1993 (Stasavage, 2003). The historical exchange rate between the CFA Franc and the US Dollar is shown in Chart 1 (below).

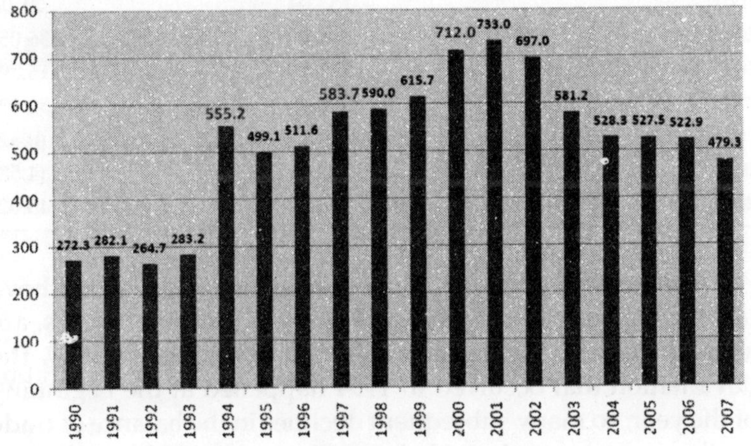

Chart 1: Historical Exchange Rate (CFA Franc / US Dollar), in Annual Averages

Looking at the above data several key devaluations are apparent, in 1994, 1997 and 2000. While the latter two devaluations were not nearly as substantial as the 1994 devaluation, they still had a relevant impact on the currency. These key changes in the exchange rate are shown by the data in Table 1 (next page).

Table 1
Historical CFA Exchange Rates

Year	*Exchange Rate (CFA/USD)*	*Δ From Previous Year*
1990	272.27	
1991	282.11	9.84
1992	264.69	(17.42)
1993	283.16	18.47
1994	555.21	272.04
1995	499.15	(56.06)
1996	511.55	12.40
1997	583.67	72.12
1998	589.95	6.28
1999	615.70	25.75
2000	711.98	96.28
2001	733.04	21.06
2002	696.99	(36.05)
2003	581.20	(115.79)
2004	528.29	(52.92)
2005	527.47	(0.82)
2006	522.89	(4.58)
2007	479.27	(43.62)

It is important to note that the exchange rates in the above table, which are those utilized in the analysis that follows, are annual average exchange rates. As previously noted, the devaluation that occurred in 1994 happened at the beginning of the year; so many subsequent declines in the balance of trade for the countries analyzed below appeared in 1994 as well since the balance of trade numbers are as of the end of the calendar year.

THE J-CURVE AND SELECT CFA ZONE COUNTRIES

Benin

The sharp devaluation of the CFA franc in 1994 had a negative impact on the Benin balance of trade. From 1991 to 1994, the country's balance of trade had been improving. After the devaluation in 1994, the country experienced a sharp decline in its balance of trade by approximately $150 million dollars in 1995 to a deficit of just over $200 million. This decline was not sustained however. In 1996 the country saw an improvement in the balance of trade deficit bringing it to approximately $32 million. Unfortunately, the volatility continued. As the CFA Franc continued to devalue throughout the late 1990s and into the present decade, the country saw its balance of trade deficit continue to grow steadily with the exception of a slight increase in 2000. The country's historical balance of trade from 1990 through 2005 is shown in Graph 5 (below). As is shown, the continual devaluations from 1997 through 1999 are accompanied by continual declines in the balance of trade as the Kulkarni Hypothesis would predict.

Table 2
Benin

Year	*Exchange Rate (CFA/USD)*	*Balance of Trade*
1990	272.27	(85.88)
1991	282.11	(299.84)
1992	264.69	(215.46)
1993	283.16	(167.88)
1994	555.21	(53.60)
1995	499.15	(202.52)
1996	511.55	(32.03)
1997	583.67	(152.90)
1998	589.95	(158.30)
1999	615.70	(213.71)
2000	711.98	(123.73)
2001	733.04	(179.54)
2002	696.99	(231.05)
2003	581.20	(277.90)
2004	528.29	(273.46)
2005	527.47	(287.40)
2006	522.89	n.a.
2007	479.27	n.a.
2008	n.a.	n.a.

Table 2 (above) shows historical data regarding Benin's balance of trade response to the CFA Franc currency devaluations. As is shown by Graph 5 (below), this economy exhibits a reaction consistent with the J-Curve hypothesis. Although the country did experience a significant improvement in the balance of trade deficit in 1995, one year after the substantial devaluation seen in 1994, subsequent currency devaluation continued to push the balance of trade down.

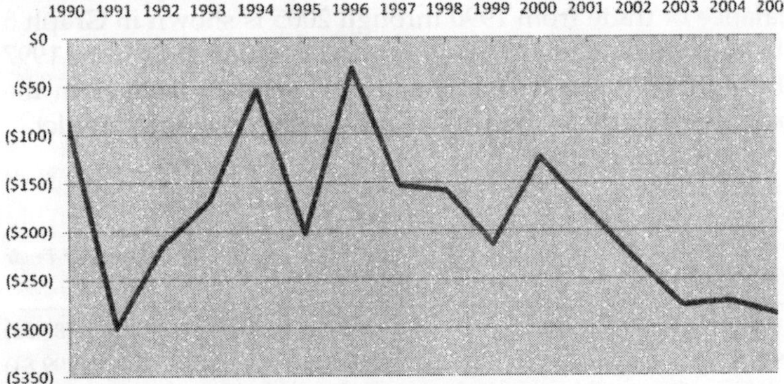

Graph 5: Benin Balance of Trade 1990-2005 (Millions)

Cameroon

Cameroon had a significant balance of trade surplus going into the major currency devaluation of 1994. During 1990 through 1993 as the CFA/USD exchange rate fluctuated +/ – approximately 20 CFA/USD, Cameroon saw an improving balance of trade, at least until 1993 when the country's balance of trade dropped severely by over $390 million. While the currency did devalue in 1993, it was a nominal devaluation of approximately 19 CFA. Considering the previous devaluation 1991 was accompanied by a small improvement in the balance of trade, this substantial decline in the balance of trade what uncharacteristically large. Similarly, the major devaluation in 1994 brought only a small decline in the balance of trade suggesting, that something else was likely at play in this economy.

The Cameroon economy exhibited some behavior consistent with the J-Curve at all three significant devaluations in 1994, 1997, and 2000. First, the 1994 devaluation resulted in a decrease in the country's balance of trade. Further, as the currency appreciated in 1995 and then devalued minimally again in 1996, the country saw a gradual improvement in its balance of trade, at least until 1997 when the CFA devalued again by 72 CFA and Cameroon's balance of trade once again declined substantially.

Table 3
Cameroon

Year	*Exchange Rate (CFA/USD)*	*Balance of Trade*		
1990	272.27	695.32	CURR	BOT
1991	282.11	850.25	9.84	154.93
1992	264.69	892.66	(17.42)	42.42
1993	283.16	502.40	18.47	(390.26)
1994	555.21	401.89	272.04	(100.51)
1995	499.15	626.89	(56.06)	225.00
1996	511.55	761.60	12.40	134.72
1997	583.67	582.24	72.12	(179.36)
1998	589.95	372.46	6.28	(209.78)
1999	615.70	411.39	25.75	38.93
2000	711.98	501.97	96.28	90.58
2001	733.04	94.12	21.06	(407.85)
2002	696.99	152.70	(36.05)	58.58
2003	581.20	269.92	(115.79)	117.22
2004	528.29	235.18	(52.92)	(34.74)

The balance of trade rebounded from 1998 through 2000, while the CFA continued to devalue. However, when the CFA devalued again in 2000 there was a severe drop in the balance of trade to only $100 million. Again the economy of Cameroon exhibited J-Curve behavior as the balance of trade improved slowly through 2004. The country's balance of trade and exchange rate statistics are shown in Table 3 (above), while the its balance of trade is shown in graphical form in Graph 6 (below).

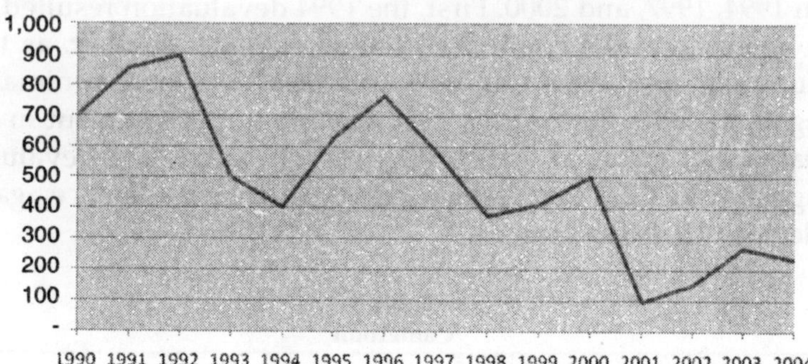

Graph 6: Cameroon Balance of Trade 1990-2004 ($ millions)

Côte d'Ivoire

Côte d'Ivoire was one of the few CFA Zone countries to have a positive balance of trade going into the currency devaluation of 1994. The country's balance of trade increased significantly subsequent to the 1994 devaluation climbing to approximately $1.3 billion in 1994, up from $750 million during 1993. The balance of trade continued to increase until 1997 when another significant devaluation of 72 CFA/USD occurred. At this point, a J-Curve is apparent, as the country's balance of trade decreased for next two years before making a small jump to approximately $1.9billion in 1999. At this point the CFA devalued again, this time by approximately 96 CFA/USD, at which time the balance of trade dropped significantly by $409 million. This is a good example of the J-Curve as well, as this devaluation in 1999 lead to a significant drop in the balance of trade for the year, with a nominal improvement the next year, before an appreciation in the currency in 2002 and a simultaneous leap in the balance of trade by almost $1.3 billion from its 2001 level. Subsequent to 2002, the CFA continued increased in value against the dollar and the country's balance of trade exhibited volatile behavior, moving lower as many would expect. Table 4 (right) shows the relevant data for Côte d'Ivoire from 1990 to 2007. Graph 7 (below) show the value of Côte d'Ivoire's balance of trade from 1990 through 2006.

Table 4
Côte d'Ivoire

Year	*Exchange Rate (CFA/USD)*	*Balance of Trade*	*Change from Prior Year*	
1990	272.27	1,093.79	CURR	BOT
1991	282.11	923.41	9.84	(170.38)
1992	264.69	994.74	(17.42)	71.33
1993	283.16	748.33	18.47	(246.41)
1994	555.21	1,289.07	272.04	540.74
1995	499.15	1,375.54	(56.06)	86.47
1996	511.55	1,823.66	12.40	448.12
1997	583.67	1,792.80	72.12	(30.86)
1998	589.95	1,719.98	6.28	(72.82)
1999	615.70	1,895.48	25.75	175.50
2000	711.98	1,486.23	96.28	(409.25)
2001	733.04	1,528.19	21.06	41.96
2002	696.99	2,819.27	(36.05)	1,291.08
2003	581.20	2,556.78	(115.79)	(262.49)
2004	528.29	2,627.92	(52.92)	71.14
2005	527.47	2,446.31	(0.82)	(181.61)
2006	522.89	3,151.91	(4.58)	705.60
2007	479.27	n.a.		

Graph 7: Côte d'Ivoire Balance of Trade 1990-2006 ($ millions)

Mali

There two distinct J-Curves in the data for Mali's balance of trade, one appears at after the 1994 devaluation and the other appears with the 1997 devaluation. The 1991 devaluation of the currency came with a worsening of the balance of trade deficit. However, after 1992 when the currency appreciated, the balance of trade improved by approximately $42 million. After the 1994 currency devaluation, the balance of trade actually improved nominally during the year, before declining for the ensuing two years after the currency appreciated minimally in 1995 and declined again in 1996, exhibiting a lagging response to the devlauation. Defying conventional theory, as the currency devalued in 1997 by 72 CFA/USD, Mali saw a dramatic improvement in their balance of trade by approximately $134 million, giving them a surplus, albeit small. While this 1997 devaluation brought Benin and Côte d'Ivoire

Table 5
Mali

Year	*Exchange Rate (CFA/USD)*	*Balance of Trade*	*Change from Prior Year*	
1990	272.27	(120.54)	CURR	BOT
1991	282.11	(146.29)	9.84	(25.75)
1992	264.69	(162.76)	(17.42)	(16.46)
1993	283.16	(120.43)	18.47	42.33
1994	555.21	(114.28)	272.04	6.14
1995	499.15	(114.96)	(56.06)	(0.67)
1996	511.55	(118.63)	12.40	(3.68)
1997	583.67	15.74	72.12	134.37
1998	589.95	(2.04)	6.28	(17.79)
1999	615.70	(34.51)	25.75	(32.47)
2000	711.98	(46.92)	96.28	(12.41)
2001	733.04	(9.56)	21.06	37.36
2002	696.99	162.66	(36.05)	172.22
2003	581.20	(60.50)	(115.79)	(223.15)
2004	528.29	(116.44)	(52.92)	(55.95)
2005	527.47	(144.59)	(0.82)	(28.14)

worsening balances of trade, Mali saw definite improvement. This trend did not continue, however, when in 1998 the country saw a decline in their balance of trade to deficit levels, once again showing a lagging response to the devaluation. As the currency continued to devalue through 2000, the country's balance of trade deficit worsened until 2001 when the currency experienced a minimal devaluation and the balance of trade approached surplus levels once again. With the appreciation in the CFA in 2002, the country saw a vast improvement in its balance of trade, which jumped by over $172 million giving the country a substantial surplus. Again, this did not continue. While the CFA Franc appreciated against the dollar through 2005, Mali saw a dramatic fall in its balance of trade to deficit levels. Table 5 (left) shows Mali's balance of trade and the CFA/USD exchange rate from 1990 through 2005. Graph 8 (below) shows Mali's balance of trade during the same time period.

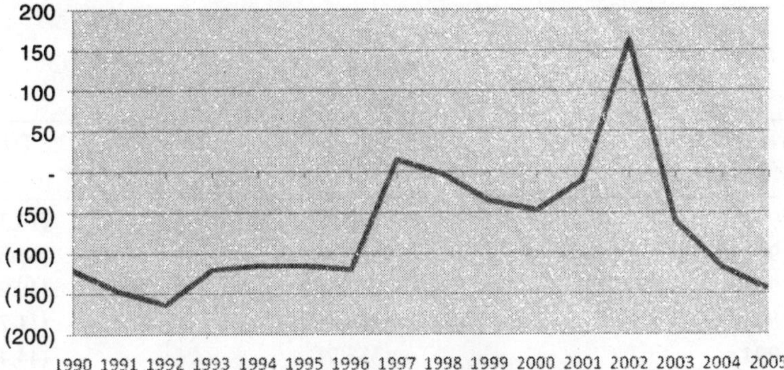

Graph 8: Mali Balance of Trade 1990-2005 ($ millions)

Niger

As with Mali, the devaluation of the CFA Franc from 1990 to 1991 brought Niger a worsening in the balance of trade deficit. However, as the currency appreciated in 1991, then devalued again in 1992 bringing it close to its 1991 level, Niger's balance of trade improved to near surplus levels. Upon significant devaluation in 1994, the country's balance of trade again reverted to a deficit before improving in 1995, showing J-Curve behavior.

The continued CFA devaluations from 1995 through 1999 prolonged Niger's balance of trade deficit, as is predicted by Kulkarni. In 1997, when the CFA dropped by 72 CFA against the dollar, the country saw a substantial decline in its balance of trade by almost $42 million. Following the minimal devaluation in 1998 and devaluations in 1999 and 2000, the country realized unexpected results. As the currency devalued at an increasing rate, the country saw continual improvements in the balance of trade. But in later years, as the CFA Franc continued appreciate against the dollar, the balance of trade deficit grew increasingly worse. In 2005, the country's balance of trade deficit was almost 22 times the level seen in 1990. Historical exchange rate data and Niger's balance of trade are shown in Table 6 (above), while the balance of trade is depicted graphically in Graph 9 (below).

Table 6
Niger

Year Exchange Rate	*Balance of (CFA/USD)*	*Trade*
1990	272.27	(13.34)
1991	282.11	(66.35)
1992	264.69	(49.24)
1993	283.16	(11.72)
1994	555.21	(44.49)
1995	499.15	(17.56)
1996	511.55	(26.33)
1997	583.67	(28.27)
1998	589.95	(69.86)
1999	615.70	(48.61)
2000	711.98	(40.56)
2001	733.04	(58.76)
2002	696.99	(91.72)
2003	581.20	(136.65)
2004	528.29	(153.02)
2005	527.47	(291.89)

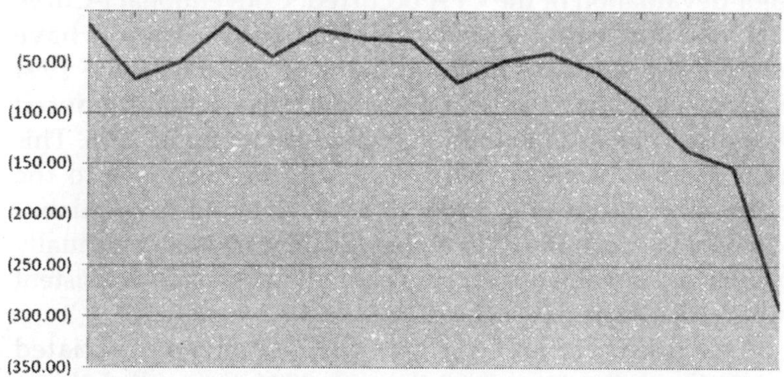

Graph 9: Niger Balance of Trade 1990-2005 ($ millions)

Senegal

While the currency appreciated in 1992, the Senegal's balance of trade deficit worsened and continued to do so through the devaluation in 1993. The unexpected occurs in 1994, when the

Table 7
Sengal

Year	*Exchange Rate (CFA/USD)*	*Balance of Trade*		
1990	272.27	(226.40)	CURR	BOT
1991	282.11	(265.50)	9.84	(39.11)
1992	264.69	(331.14)	(17.42)	(65.64)
1993	283.16	(349.91)	18.47	(18.77)
1994	555.21	(203.20)	272.04	146.70
1995	499.15	(249.57)	(56.06)	(46.36)
1996	511.55	(275.92)	12.40	(26.35)
1997	583.67	(271.48)	72.12	4.44
1998	589.95	(312.87)	6.28	(41.39)
1999	615.70	(345.78)	25.75	(32.91)
2000	711.98	(416.74)	96.28	(70.96)
2001	733.04	(425.29)	21.06	(8.56)
2002	696.99	(537.39)	(36.05)	(112.10)
2003	581.20	(808.54)	(115.79)	(271.15)
2004	528.29	(986.37)	(52.92)	(177.83)

major devaluation of the CFA occurred. Conventional J-Curve theory would suggest that this devaluation should have resulted in a decrease in the balance of trade over the 1994 year, however, the balance of trade deficit was actually reduced by approximately $140 million, before declining in 1995. This suggests that Senegal also had a lagging response to the devaluation. From 1996 through 2001, the country's balance of trade deficit continued to worsen as the currency continually experienced devaluations, again exhibiting behavior consistent with the Kulkarni Hypothesis.

As with Niger and Mali, as the currency appreciated against the dollar from 2002 through 2004, Senegal's balance of trade declined sharply to over 5 times the level seen in 1990. Senegal's balance of trade data are shown in Table 7 (left) and Graph 10 (below).

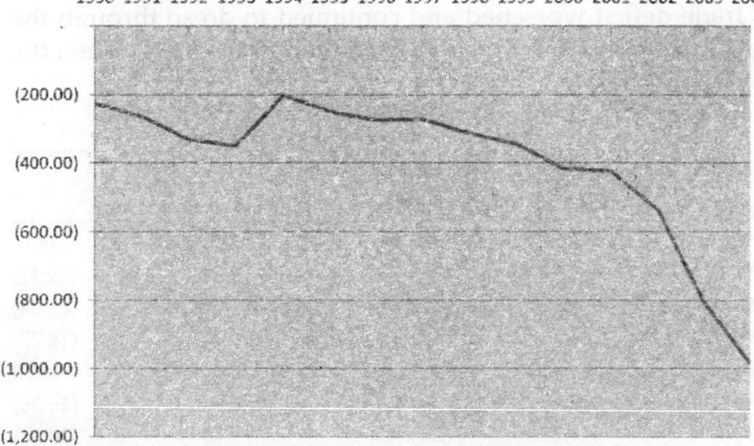

Graph 10: Senegal Balance of Trade 1990-2004 ($ millions)

CONCLUSION

While France's original goal in creating the CFA Zone in 1945 was to shield its Sub-Saharan African Colonies from the substantial currency devaluation associated with fixing the French Franc to the US dollar as required by the Bretton-Woods Agreement, it only effectively postponed the devaluation of the currency. Eventually, because of severe economic difficulties, the CFA Franc too had to be devalued. While some expect that the devaluation of a currency will result in an increase in a country's balance of trade, the data shows that in the overwhelming majority of cases, this increase in the balance of trade is not immediate and is actually preceded by a decline in the balance of trade as explained by the J-Curve Hypothesis. Furthermore, as Kulkarni has hypothesized, continual devaluations in a currency act to prolong and deepen the balance of trade declines often seen with a single devaluation. As is shown in the data for many of the CFA Zone countries contained here, and in other empirical studies as well, there is significant empirical evidence to this effect.

Overall, the J-Curve is apparent at the majority of the major currency devaluations for the countries analyzed herein. In 1994, Benin, Mali and Senegal all experienced increases in their balances of trade, and declines in the balance of trade in the following year(s). These countries seem to have had a lagging response to the devaluation. The economies of Cameroon and Niger seem to have responded more quickly to the devaluation of the currency in 1994, as they saw declines in the balance of trade immediately, and increases in the balance of trade in ensuing year(s). The one exception seen here is Côte d'Ivoire, who saw an increase in the balance of trade in 1994 and in ensuing years, showing that the country was immune from the J-Curve effects seen in the other countries. This may be because its elasticities of demand for imports and exports were large enough to satisfy the Marshall-Lerner Condition.

At the next major devaluation in 1997, the vast majority of countries saw a decline in their balances of trade in 1997; although, Mali saw a sharp increase in its balance of trade. During this time period, Mali seems to have had a lagging J-Curve response to the devaluation, as it saw a decline in the balance of trade in the years following the devaluation. Niger, Côte d'Ivoire, Cameroon and Benin all exhibited J-Curve behavior following the 1997 devaluation. Senegal, on the other hand, saw a further decline in the balance of trade, which continued through the most recent data from 2004. Obviously, there are other factors at play in Senegal's economy that have resulted in this steep decline in its balance of trade.

In 2000, at the last major devaluation, Niger, Cameroon, and Benin saw spikes in their balance of trade before it declined in the following years, exhibiting J-Curve behavior. Here these countries seem to have a lagging response to the 2000 devaluation. Côte d'Ivoire, Mali and Senegal all experienced declines in their balances of trade immediately in 2000. J-Curves are apparent in both Côte d'Ivoire and Mali, as they had a slow increase in their balance of trade subsequent to the 2000 devaluation. Conversely, Senegal saw the decline that began in 1994 continue after the devaluation.

After the 2000 devaluation, Benin, Mali, Niger and Senegal all saw steep declines in their balances of trade as the CFA appreciated continually against the dollar, while Côte d'Ivoire and Cameroon have seen improvements in their balances of trade in recent years. By and large, despite the fact that all of these countries undoubtedly violate some or all of the assumptions underlying the Marshall-Lerner Condition, they all exhibit the J-Curve to some degree or another over the time period analyzed. Undoubtedly there are several micro and macroeconomic factors at play in these economies, however, the devaluation of the currency seems to have had a significant impact on them overall. The data collected and analyzed for the CFA Zone countries shows that a currency devaluation rarely has the effect of increasing a country's balance of trade, in fact it usually decreases the balance of trade for some period of time prior to any improvement.

REFERENCES

Clement, J. A., Mueller, J., Cosse, S., & Le Dem, J. (1996), *Aftermath of the CFA Franc Devaluation.* International Monetary Fund. Washington D.C.: International Monetary Fund.

Hinkle, L. E., & Montiel, P. J. (1999), *Exchange Rate Misalignment: Concepts and Measurement for Developing Countries.* Washington DC, USA: Oxford University Press, Inc.

Krugman, P. R., & Obstfeld, M. (2006), *International Economics: Theory & Policy* (7th Edition ed.). Boston, MA, USA: Pearson Education.

Kulkarni, K. G. (2007), *Readings in International Economics* (Third Edition ed.). Darya Ganj, New Delhi, India: Serials Publications.

Masson, P. R., & Pattillo, C. (2005). *The Monetary Geography of Africa.* Washington D.C.: The Brookings Institution.

Stasavage, D. (2003). *The Political Economy of a Common Currency: The CFA Franc Zone Since 1945.* Aldershot, Hants, England: Ashgate Publishing Limited.

The Interantional Monetary Fund. (n.d.). *IMF Statistical Databases.* Retrieved May 18, 2008, from International Monetary Fund: http://www.imfstatistics.org/imf/

APPENDIX I: THE DERIVATION OF THE MARSHALL-LERNER CONDITION

Before deriving the Marshall-Lerner Condition we need to define some key parameters.

(1) The elasticity of demand for imports with respect to changes in $Q\left(E_M^Q\right)$

is given by: $E_M^Q = \%\Delta M / \%\Delta Q$

Which is equivalent to:

$$E_M^Q = \left(\Delta M / M\right) \Big/ \left(\Delta Q / Q\right)$$

$$E_M^Q = \left(\Delta M / \Delta Q * \left(Q / M\right)\right)$$

(2)The elasticity of demand for exports with respect to changes in $Q\left(E_X^Q\right)$

is given by: $E_M^Q = \%\Delta X / \%\Delta Q$

Which is equivalent to:

$$E_X^Q = \left(\Delta X / X\right) \Big/ \left(\Delta Q / Q\right)$$

$$E_X^Q = \left(\Delta X / \Delta Q * \left(Q / X\right)\right)$$

Now, to derive the Marshall-Lerner Condition there are three key assumptions necessary:

The supply elasticities of exports and imports are infinite.

The balance of trade is equivalent to the balance of payments. This implies that the economy has no capital account and, therefore, or no capital inflows or outflows.

At the time of the devaluation the balance of payments (trade) or BOT is zero. This can be shown in equation form as:

$BOT = X - QM = 0$, so $X = QM$ or $M = X/Q$

Where X = the value of a country's exports, M = the value of a country's imports, and Q = the real exchange rate. Q can be defined as:

Q = Nominal Exchange Rate * (P/p^*)

Where P = the domestic price level, and P* = the foreign price level.

Now to look at the BOT equation above in terms of changes in BOT with respect to changes in Q, we have a new equation:

$$\frac{\Delta BOT}{\Delta Q} = \frac{\Delta X}{\Delta Q}\left[\frac{\Delta Q}{\Delta Q}M + \frac{\Delta M}{\Delta Q}Q\right]$$

Which is equivalent to:

$$\frac{\Delta BOT}{\Delta Q} = \frac{\Delta X}{\Delta Q}M - \frac{\Delta M}{\Delta Q}Q$$

By factoring M out of the above equation we have:

$$(A): \frac{\Delta BOT}{\Delta Q} = M\left[\frac{\Delta X}{\Delta Q} * \frac{Q}{X} - 1 - \frac{\Delta M}{\Delta Q} * \frac{Q}{M}\right]$$

Now if we recall that

$$E_M^Q = \left(\Delta M/_{\Delta Q} * \left(Q/_M\right)\right)$$

and

$$E_X^Q = \left(\Delta X/_{\Delta Q} * \left(Q/_X\right)\right)$$

By substituting the elasticities above in equation (A), we have:

$$\frac{\Delta BOT}{\Delta Q} = M\left[E_X^Q - 1 - E_M^Q\right]$$

Further, because is always negative, we have:

$$\frac{\Delta BOT}{\Delta Q} = M\left[E_X^Q - 1 + E_M^Q\right]$$

In order to have $\frac{\Delta BOT}{\Delta Q} \geq Q$, we need $\left[E_X^Q - 1 + E_M^Q\right] \geq 0$ which is equivalent to $\left[E_X^Q + E_M^Q\right] \geq 1$ which is the Marshall-Lerner Condition.

12

EMPIRICAL EVIDENCE OF THE J-CURVE HYPOTHESIS

INTRODUCTION

When a country's currency depreciates, goods and services from that country become cheaper relative to other countries. This boosts their exports and decreases the volume of their imports. One might expect a corresponding decrease in a country's trade deficit, while in fact, the trade deficit may get worse before it improves. The graph showing this effect is shaped like the letter J, and hence, the name "J-curve effect". Currency depreciation affects the quantity of imports and exports, but the price of exported goods levels in the country. However, there is an increase in dollar price of imports, as the currency now buys less of foreign currencies. The question then arises whether this increase in the price of imports has bigger effect than the decrease in quantity of imports, foretelling a negative impact on the trade balance[1] or is the quantity effect large than the price effect, improving the trade balance? After the breakdown of the Bretton-Woods system in 1973, the exchange rates have become relatively more flexible, making this more relevant to test the J-curve hypothesis.

This Chapter is based on an article published in Indian Economic Journal (April 2002). Co-author: Alpna Bhatia

Our study shows that the negative effect dominates initially all but one of the countries. In Section I, we study the cases of Philippines Kenya and Japan.

In case of Japan, an increase in Yen value is seen an evidence for the case of inverted J-Curve. In Section 2 we use data from Mexico and Indonesia to test the J-curve hypothesis when devaluations of their currencies occurred. Section 3 is used for the cases of the remaining two countries: China and Spain. The experience of these 8 countries, under different monetary regimes and tremendous changes in their exchanges rates is sufficient, we believe, to make a meaningful conclusion about the relevance of the J-curve hypothesis. In Section 4 we summarize these observations and carry out the conclusions regarding trade balances and J-curve effects.

SECTION – I

The Philippines instituted a multiple exchange rate system in 1960 when the government fixed the official exchange rate at $1 = 2 pesos. The market rate at this time was around $ 1=3.2 pesos and further deteriorated to $1= 3.9 pesos by 1969, an event that caused much concern to the governmental authorities. At the same time protectionist policies of the government were causing structural weaknesses in the economy by channeling resources from exportable products to the production of capital-intensive import substitutes. As the balance of payment crisis worsened the government asked for a large loan from the IMF. The IMF conditioned the loan on the government making adjustments to the exchange rate. The Philippines is a country comparatively endowed with more land and labor, rather than capital. Imported goods were high demanded and exported goods were unable to find market destinations because they were not well promoted. Government protection policies thus contributed to slow growth during the 1960s. Without doubt, devaluation was not a favourable decision for the political parties. In the 1969 presidential campaign, President Marcos made a promise of no further devaluation of the peso. However as the IMF conditionality became stronger, President Carlos gave in to the exchange rate reform.

Sicat (1972) maintains that elasticities of import demand and export demand are not very large for the Philippines even though empirical evidence does not support his assertions. The dominant, almost monopoly status that the Philippines enjoys in trade of such commodities as coconut oil, copra and abaca products implies a higher elasticity of demand for these products, especially in the case of declining prices. On the import side, the Philippines is importing mostly importing necessities like oil products, which clearly have high price elasticities. Hence, in the case of Philippines, one can expect that the Marshall-Lerner conditions are satisfied, at least after passage of time, and a corresponding improvement in the balance of payments as the currency is devalued. Table 1 presents the relevant data after the devaluation took place in 1969. As can be seen exchange rates went up substantially in 1970, while the balance of trade deteriorated further after 1970, and the economy experienced a surplus after three years in 1973: As the exchange rate increased further the balance of trade deteriorated substantially in 1974-1976 period. Figure 1 is a graphical representation of the J-curve phenomenon for the Philippines. The period 1973-1975 represents the economics shock of rising oil prices.

Table 1
The Philippines Data

Year	*Exchange Rate*[2]	*Balance of Trade*[3]
1967	3.93	-241
1968	3.93	-290
1969	3.93	-277
1970	6.43	-26
1971	6.987	-49
1972	7.32	-125
1973	8.119	275
1974	8.65	-450
1975	8.778	-1196
1976	8.630	-1116

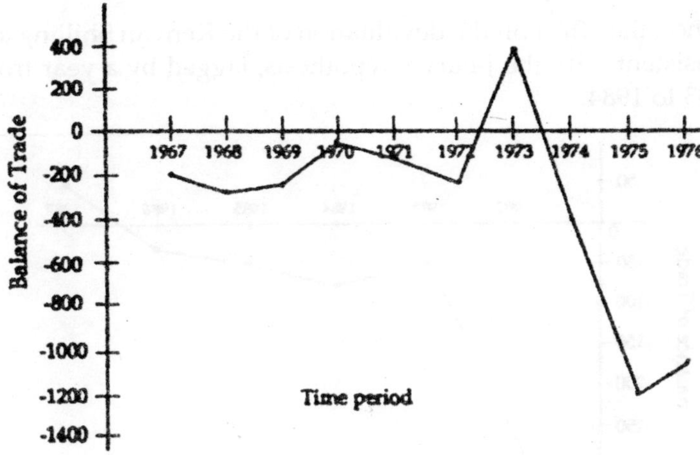

Figure 1: J-Curve for the Phillippines 1967-1976 ($ Millions)

Case of Kenya

After gaining independence, the Kenyan economy showed promise of growth of remarkable recovery, thanks to the tourism industry and the exports of coffee and tea. In fact, compared to the other African nations the Kenyan economic growth seemed to be a miracle. Job prospects and GDP steadily increased until the later 1970s. In the early 1980s, as coffee prices plummeted, earnings from exports declined, which combined with the oil shock of 1979 made the country suffer from a deficit in it's balance of trade. Soon it became clear that the increasing bureaucracy was mismanaging borrowed funds and the corrupt administrators did not allow early high expectations to be completely realized. Thus in the later of 1970s that balance of trade of Kenyan economy was too significant to be ignored. In 1982, when the IMF was approached for loans, the devaluation of the Kenyan shilling by 17% was inevitable.

In the following years, the balance of trade deteriorated further and for 5 years between 1982 and 1986 (both inclusive) the defect in the balance of trade increased steadily.

The J-Curve in the case of Kenya has limited applicability. It is only after 1983 once can see a clear shape of the J-Curve.

Hence, the effect on the devaluation of the Kenyan Shilling are consistent with the J-curve hypothesis, lagged by a year from 1983 to 1984.

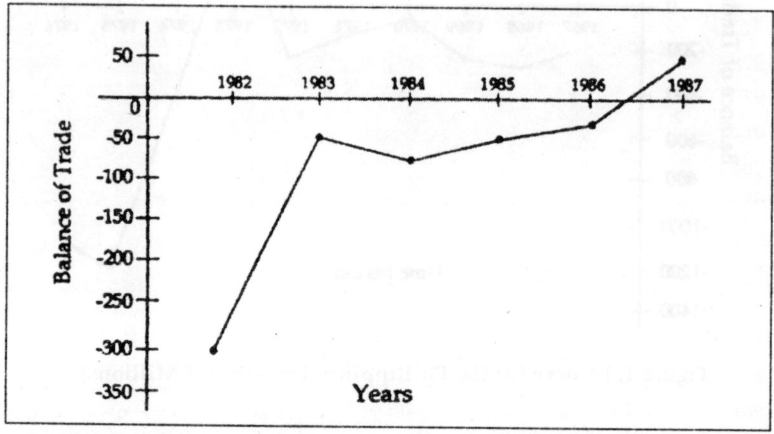

Figure 2: J-Curve: The Kenyan Economy: 1982-1986 ($ Millions)

One can attempt to explain these findings in terms of elasticities that changed over the period of time after devaluation. If the elasticities adjust after a lapse of time then the curve takes the specific shape?

Case of Japan

Over the period of time that we are looking at, the value of the Japanese Yen went steadily up, declining the exchange rate, which was a major concern of the Japanese authorities. At the end of the Bretton Woods system as countries around the world were struggling to keep their exchange rates from going up, Japan was trying to keep her exchange rate from dropping down. As the Yen kept appreciating against other major currencies, the Japanese current account was experiencing a major surplus. After much criticism, in 1977, the Japanese authorities allowed a major appreciation of the Yen which continued through 1978. In the next three years Japan's trade balance showed a trade deficit, partly because of the appreciation and party because of the increase in oil prices.

Table 2
The Data for Japan

Year	*Balance of Trade*[4]	*Exchange Rates*[5]
1976	3.71	292.8
1977	10.91	240
1978	16.54	194.6
1979	-8.74	239.7
1980	-10.75	203
1981	4.77	4.77
1982	6.85	235
1983	20.8	232.2
1984	35	251.1
1985	49.17	200.5
1986	85.83	159.1
1987	87.02	123.5
1988	79.61	125.5
1989	56.99	143.45
1990	35.87	134.4

From 1980 to 1985, the Japanese Yen depreciated steadily and the current account surplus increased. In 1985, the Japanese Yen was a record low of 200 yens per U.S. dollar. The trend of appreciating Yen began right after this low value, appreciating 40 percent in the next two years, although the current surplus continued to grow, and beginning it's decline only after 1988. These numbers are shown in Table 2. Because of the appreciation of the Yen, the J-curve hypothesis should be expected to demonstrate the behaviour of a trade balance in an inverted J-curve. Thus even if the usual J-curve hypothesis is measured for cases of devaluation, its validity can be still be demonstrated. Fig. 3 represents a graphical movement in the balance of trade for the Japanese economy between the periods 1976 to 1990. One can see that the yen appreciated approximately 50 percent from 1976, while the trade surplus grew until the end of 1978, when it turned into a deficit. Thus it seems that the elasticities of demand for export and import, in fact do adjust over time as all elasticities are time sensitive.

Due to imported values of elasticities over the period of time the Marshall-Lerner Condition is satisfied only in the long run. Therefore the balance of trade shows a surplus only some time after a currency's devaluation.

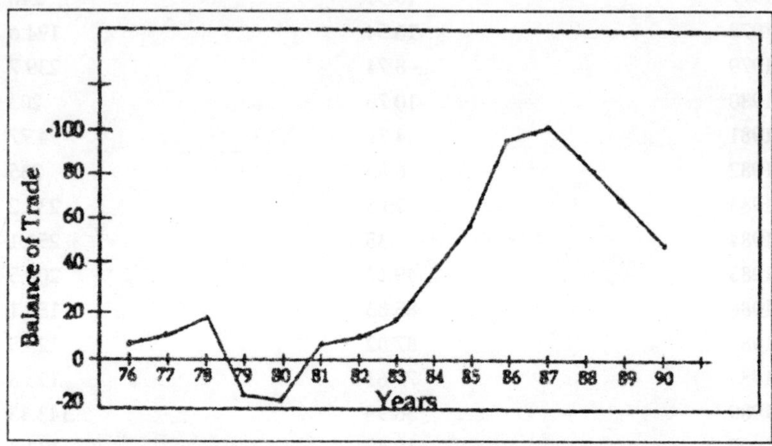

Figure 3: Inverted J-Curve: Japan 1976-1990 ($ Millions)

Case of Indonesia

The Indonesian currency, the Rupiah, went through a major devaluation in 1970. The Indonesian economy like many other developing economies faced a challenging task of economic reoganization. Under the presidency of Sukarno, Indonesia adopted an inward looking policy by the means of heavy protectionism. Sukarno adopted a guided economic policy whose main thrust was to regulate the markets, have an emotional attachment to self-reliance, manifestation of national pride and distrust of anything foreign. Not surprisingly the Indonesian economy gradually deteriorated to the point of an economic crisis. The expansionary monetary and fiscal policies led to heavy inflation and unemployment steadily increased. But 1965 both the budget and trade deficits were enormous, foreign reserves were used up. The government's international credit rating was dismal, with $2.1 billion in external debt.

In 1966, newly elected President, Suharto, adopted outward looking policies of trade, market openness, and liberalization.

His administration, renegotiated aid, arranged for a settlement of the country's foreign aid, and devalued the Indonesian Rupiah in 1970. Two successive devaluation, in April 1970 by 14% and in August 1971 by 9% brought the Rupiah closer to the it's market determined parity. These devaluations were followed by further adjustment of the Rupiah value in 1978. Consequences of these devaluations were immediately evident in terms of (a) revived foreign exchange reserves, building the confidence of potential aid donors, and (b) a substantial improvement in country's exports. Table 3 enlists the export, import, and balance of trade statistics of the Indonesian economy, from 1970 to 1993. Figure 4 shows the changes in the balance of trade over the period of time and the evidence of J-curve hypothesis in case of Indonesia, as can be seen the devaluations of Rupiah coupled with a policy of devaluation of the Rupiah coupled with the liberalization policy has shown positive results for Indonesia.

Table 3
The Data of Indonesia

Year	*Balance of Trade*[6]	*Total Imports*	*(% growth)*	*Total Exports*	*(% growth)*
1970	3.71	1001.50		1152.3	
1971	10.91	1102.8	(9.19%)	1246.7	(7.6%)
1972	16.54	1561.7	(29.38%)	1534.0	(18.7%)
1973	-8.74	2729	(42.77%)	3061	(49.9%)
1974	-10.75	3841.9	(28.97%)	7444	(58.9%)
1975	4.77	4769.8	(19.45%)	7103	(–4.8%)
1976	6.85	5673	(15.92%)	8546.5	(16.9%)
1977	20.8	6230	(8.94%)	10853	(21.3%)
1978	35	6690	(6.88%)	11643	(6.8%)
1979	49.17	7202	(7.11%)	15590	(25.3%)
1980	85.83	10834	(33.52%)	21909	(28.8%)

Case in Mexico

In Mexico, the peso devaluation was most evident in 1976. Through out the 1950s, Mexico had pursued an import

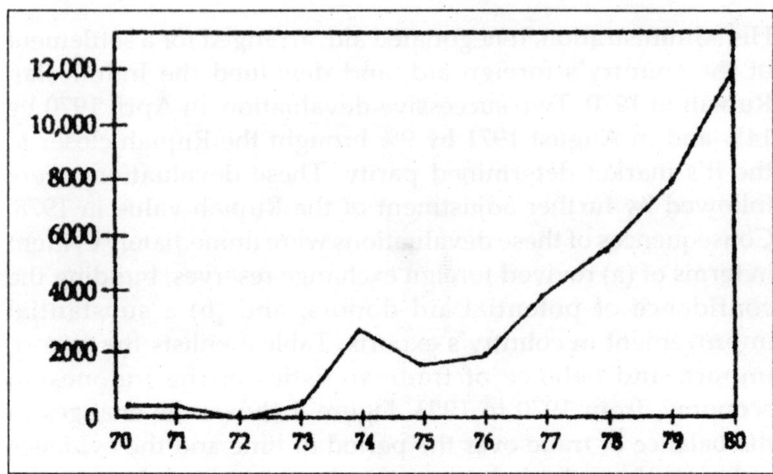

Figure 4: J-Curve: for Indonesia 1970-1980 ($ Millions)

substitution policy that kept the Mexican market relatively closed to foreign competition, restricted foreign direct investment, and tightly regulated domestic financial markets. Nonetheless, the Mexican economy performed relatively well from 1950 to 1970. Thanks mostly to increased oil findings and heavy economic inefficiencies and corrupt bureaucracy that slowed real per capita GDP growth to about 3%. By the mid 1970s the peso had become increasingly overvalued and a balance of payment crisis arose, in response to which the government increased the import tariff and expanded the protectionist policies.

Fueled by the expansionary fiscal and monetary policies, in the absence of real structural reforms the Mexican economy needed a devaluation of the peso by about 60% against the US dollar. The devaluation made the Mexican oil cheaper for the rest of the world and out became the main exported commodity reaching to about 78% of total Mexican imports in 1982. Following the devaluation however the huge discover of oil further expanded the total export earnings, which led to further import liberalization through the 1977-1979 period.

In the Mexican system of fixed exchange rates, excess public spending, and import liberalization, caused overvaluation of the peso which made non-oil export almost impossible. As US real interest rates increased and oil prices began to fall, the Mexican economic worries multiplied. In light of another chronic economic situation in 1982, the peso was devalued 260%. Towards the end as 1982, the crisis worsened, and the Mexican government adopted tighter economic measures regulating all trade and instituting full exchange rate controls on capital.

Table 4
The Data for Mexico

Year	*Balance of Trade*[7]	*Balance of Trade (less oil exports)*	*Exchange Rate*
1973	-1551	-1551	12.5
1974	-3066	-3066	12.5
1975	-3665	-3806	12.5
1976	-2567	-2773	15.4
1977	-1315	-2126	22.6
1978	-1606	-3135	22.8
1979	-2004	-5759	22.8
1980	-2130	-12600	23
1981	-2552	-16603	24.5
1982	7522	-8936	56.4
1983	14113	-1908	120

Table 4 and Figure 5 show the Mexican case of changes in the balance of payment after 1976 devaluation. Whether the trade balance is measured with or without oil exports, the J-curve is quite evident over time first as the trade balance got worse and then improved through 1982. It is clear however that earlier Mexican imports were dominated by the export of oil and oil related products whose production received a tremendous boost by the increased findings of oil in the country. When one takes the oil exports out of the trade balance, the J-curve is not as evident, but the lack of increased export is due to inflation and expansionary fiscal and monetary policies.

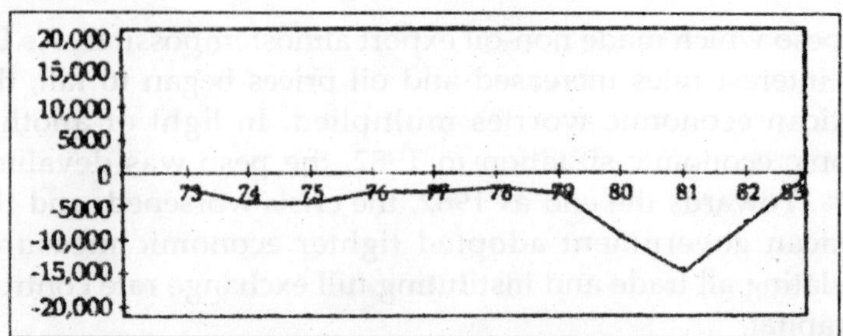

Figure 5: J-Curve and Effect of Peso Devaluation in Mexico 1973-1983 ($ Millions)

Case of China

The official currency, Renminbi, was pegged to a trade--weighted basket of currencies before 1985. In January 1986, the trade-weighted basket was abandoned and official exchange rate was placed on a controlled float based on developments in balance of payments and in costs and exchange rates of China's major competitor's. In November 1986 Foreign Exchange adjustment centers known as swap centers were established. These centers were quasi-official markets where authorized entities could trade for foreign currencies for the Renminbi (or RMB), outside official procedures but still under official supervision. Swap centers were initially open to foreign investment corporations and Chinese enterprises in the four economic zones but were expanded in 1988 to include all domestic entities authorized to retain foreign exchange earnings. Foreign exchange purchases rates in those markets are determined by supply and demand but in practice, calor rate was heavily managed and usually represented about a 50% premium over the official rate.

The official exchange rate was RMB 3.73 per U.S. dollar at the end of 1986 and remained at this level until 1989. On Dec. 1st, 1989, China announced a devaluation of RMB, by 215% making it the largest single cut in 1980s. With debt repayments were peaking and with foreign exchange reserves depleting to $14.3 million in 1989, the Chinese government needed to adjust the exchange rate to RMB 4.72 per US dollar. Devaluation step aided by the liberalization trend in China showed the positive results immediately on the Chinese economy. In 1990, exports increased by 19.2% and imports decreased by 13.3% leading to a surplus in the trade balance of $10.62 billion.

Considering that both export and import activities were heavily regulated by the Chinese governmental authorities the latent demand for imported commodities was very high. This put further pressure on the value of the RMB which by all indications from the black market was still overvalued. Hence from 1990 to 1993, there were further decline in the value of the RMB when the official rate reached to 5.81 per U.S. dollar.

In 1992 and 1993 the Chinese economy received a further setback the inflation rate increased to 21%, due to increases in money supply of almost 54%. The trade balance was again in deficit by $11.52 billion and the new policy steps had to be undertaken. The Chinese policy makers announced that the swap rate and the official rate would be unified on New Year's Day in 1994.

In practice this translated to an abolition of the official rate for the RMB thereby allowing swap markets to become sole arbiters of calor value of the RMB. Officials of the Foreign Exchange Control (SEAC), a unit of the People's Bank of China declared that SEAC would electronically link the 100 + swap centers to create a single rate and they also indicated.

The swap center rate that was accepted in 1994 was RMB 8.71 = $1 US, which meant that there was a devaluation of 33%. One of the direct and immediate consequence of this step was that it opened floodgates of pent up foreign investment waiting to enter China. As a result China took a giant step towards economic growth in 1994. Figure 6 shows the changes in the Chinese balance of trade in the following year. This we hypothesize might be partly due to the regulated import and export flows. China maintains a large number of non-tariff administrative controls such as quotas and licensing requirements over imports; such that actual imports do not reflect the real demand for imported commodities.

Case of Spain

The Spanish Peseta was devalued in 1982 following a severe economic crisis in the late 70s and early 80s. The budget deficit has doubled from 605 billion pesetas in 1981 to 1131 billion in 1982, foreign debt had increased by $1.5 billion, unemployment was 17% and about $3.8 billion worth foreign reserves were depleted. Felipe Gonzalez, the Spanish premier, devalued the peseta as part of Saneamiento y reform, aimed at reducing inflation, unemployment, and the budget deficit. Figure 7 shows the effect of the devaluation on the balance of trade, which started improving after a slight dip, showing a surplus by 1984.

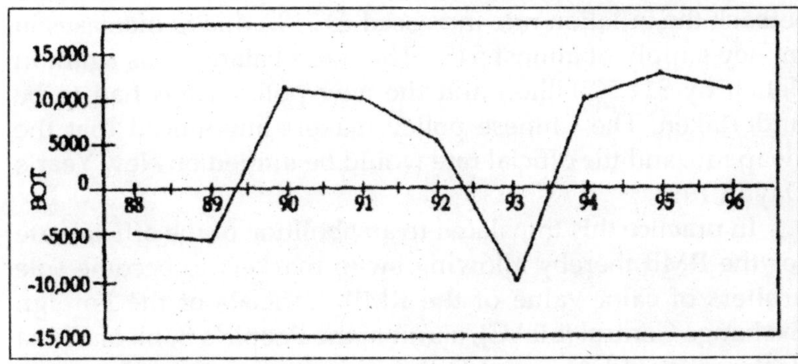

Figure 6: J-Curve and China's Balance of Trade 1988-1991 ($ Millions)

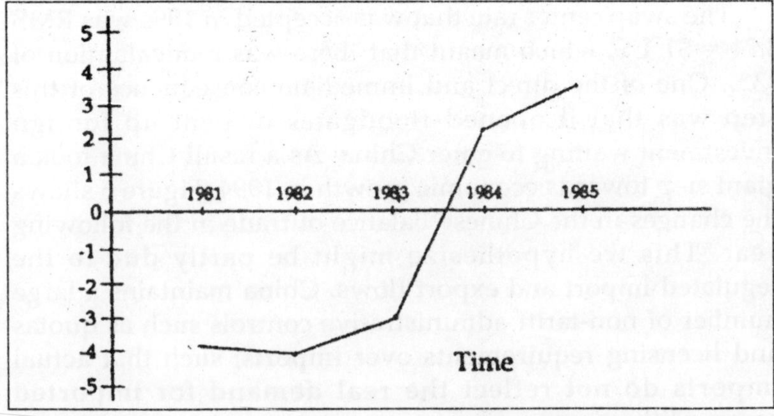

Figure 7: Effect of 1982 Devaluation of the Peseta in Spain from 1981-1985

CONCLUSIONS AND SUMMARY

This chapter intended to empirically examine the existence of the J-curve. For this purpose we chose 7 countries: The Philippines, Kenya, Japan, Indonesia, Mexico, China and Spain. With the exception of China. It is observed that in the latter six countries, dramatic change in the exchange rate leads to a J-curve on the balance of payments, inclusive of Japan, where a revaluation of the yen led to an inverted J-curve phenomenon in the balance of trades. We conclude that the elasticity approach and the Marshall-Lerner Condition are relevant concepts applicable empirically, as the deficit in the balance of trade evaporates only after a time lag. In the long run analysis it makes clear-cut sense that if a country's currency is not valued according to market forces, the government is forced to readjust the currency value, sooner or later. The trade balance after the devaluation behaves according to the J-curve phenomenon which means that deficits in the balance of trade evaporate only after some time. This is a valid and important lesson for future policy actions of countries that resist the freely floating exchange regime.

NOTES

1. Balance of Trade = Price of Exports* Quantity of Exports-Price of imports* Quantity of Imports.
2. The Exchange rate is expressed as pesos per SDR.
3. The Balance of Trade is measured in millions of Dollars.
4. The Exchange rate is expressed as pesos per SDR.

REFERENCES

Balasa, B. and Noland, M., *Japan in the World Economy,* Institute for International Economics, Washington DC, 1988.

Cheng, E., "China of the Cheap", *Far Eastern Economic Review,* May 11, 1992, 42-44.

Das, D. K., *The Yen Appreciation and the International Economy,* New York University Press, New York, 1994.

Glassburner, B., *Indonesian New Economic Policy and it's Socio-political implications,* in Jackson and Pye, eds., Political power and communication in Indonesia, University of California, 1978.

Glyfason, T., *The Effect of Exchange Rate Changes on the Balance of Trade in Ten Industrial Countries,* IMF Staff Papers, 1978, 375--390.

International Financial Statistics, Published by the IMF, 1990-1994.

Killick, T., *'Papers on the Kenyan Economy,* Heinemann Educational Books Ltd., Ibadan, 1981.

Komiya, R., and Suda, M., *Japan's Foreign Exchange Policy 1971-1982,* Allen and Unwin., Ltd., 1991.

Kulkarni, K., *Balance of Payment Changes and the Exchange Rate Devaluation: A Case of India,* Indian Journal of Economics, No. 303, 1996b, 415-425.

Kulkarni, K., *The J-Curve Hypothesis and the Currency Devaluation: Cases of Egypt and Ghana,* Journal of Applied Business Research, Vol. 12, 1996a, 1-8.

Lustig, N., *Mexico: The Remaking of the Economy,* The Brooking' Institute, Washington D.C., 1992.

Lieberman, S., *Growth and Crisis in the Spanish Economy,* 1940-1993 Routledge, London, 1995.

Marquez, J., *Bilateral Trade Elasticities,* Review of Economics and Statistics, Vol. 72, l, 1990, 75-76.

Miller, N., and Yeager, R., Kenya and the Quest for Prosperity, West view Press, 1994.

Myint, H., *The Inward and the Outward looking countries in Southeast Asia, Malayan Economic Review,* Vol. 12, l, 1967.

Sicat, G., *Economic Policy and Philippine Development,* University of Manilla Press, Manilla, 1975, 161-181.

Solis, L., *Economic Policy Reform in Mexico,* Pergamon Policy Studies, 1981.

13

COMPARISON OF 1980s LATIN AMERICAN AND 1990s EAST ASIAN FINANCIAL CRISES

INTRODUCTION

It is generally argued that developing economies are powerless before global market forces. Perhaps recommendations prescribed by international financial institutions to liberalize economies have made some developing economies vulnerable to the effects of the open market. Perhaps the combination of financial liberalization in the developing world, irresponsible domestic monetary policies and anti-inflationary policies of the developed world, particularly the West, have allowed financial crises to occur. Crises have spread from Latin America to East Asia to other regions of the developing world, induced by financial instability (Hirst and Thompson 2004). An international financial crisis is a situation where the international elements considerably exacerbate a crisis in ways that would not occur in a closed economy (Summers 2000).

Typically, a financial crisis occurs as an economy enters a recession that follows a period of productive economic activity fueled by credit and capital inflows. The cycle of over lending, which occurred in both the Latin American financial crisis and

This Chapter is based on an article with the same title co-authored with Ms. Annie Dullum

the East Asian financial crisis, is intensified by implicit or explicit contracts between lenders and borrowers, poor supervision of financial flows, and issues among the banking sector (Kaminsky and Reinhert 1999). Financial crises are accompanied by a depreciation of the economy's currency, weakening exports, loss of financial credibility and negative economic growth.

The financial crises in Latin America and East Asia occurred in different decades and were caused by different external and internal influences. "Throughout the most successful of developing regions, living standards are falling as unemployment rises and the effects of huge devaluations work through into higher import prices. Many millions of people are at risk, and many millions of people who were confident of middle-class status feel robbed of their lifetime savings and security" (Wade and Veneroso, 1998).

Therefore the main question to be answered is "Do international financial crises occur and are they worsened by the exposure of nations to an open world economy?" or "Has Globalization proven to be the primary cause of financial crises in recent decades, or are crises substantially influenced by nations' socio-economic condition?" The causes of the financial crises in Latin America and East Asia vary according to the nation's degree of income equality, maintenance of government budget, extent of foreign borrowing, amount of domestic savings and implementation of effective macroeconomic policies. This paper intends to answer these questions with the following organization. Section 1 explains the causes and circumstances of Latin American crisis, while Section 2 deals with the Southeast Asian Crisis. Section 3 makes contrasts and comparisons of these two crises and Section 4 forms the summary and conclusion.

SECTION - 1

CASE OF LATIN AMERICAN FINANCIAL CRISIS

In the early 1980s Latin America, as a rapidly developing region, abruptly experienced a debt and development crisis. Latin American financial crises began in the 1970s though were more prominent during the early 1980s. During the period, the countries of Latin America were experiencing soaring economies. The advancing economies of Latin America were the result of rising governmental deficits caused by excessive foreign borrowing. In the 1960s and 1970s many Latin American countries, notably Brazil, Argentina, and Mexico, borrowed huge sums of money from international creditors with the intention to develop industries and improve infrastructure. Figure 1 shows the annual growth in public external debt. In the 1970s, Mexico, Venezuela, Brazil and Argentina acquired the most public debt. At the time of borrowing, Latin American economies were exhibiting great performance and development. Nations' large budget deficits were accelerating inflation and the incrementing entry of capital was increasing the economies' vulnerability to violent external shocks. Nations increased resources towards repaying debts which resulted in the reduction of domestic output and consumption (Hirst and Thompson 2004). The economies were no longer capable of increasing their economic growth. Foreign debt of Latin American nations surpassed the amount the economies were able to earn. The large amounts that the government borrowed were careless and corrupt (Wade and Veneroso 1998). Between 1975 and 1982, Latin American debt to commercial banks increased at a cumulative annual rate of more than twenty percent. This heightened borrowing led Latin America to quadruple its external debt from $75 billion in 1975 to more than $315 billion in 1983. Interest payments and the repayment of the principal amount increased rapidly,

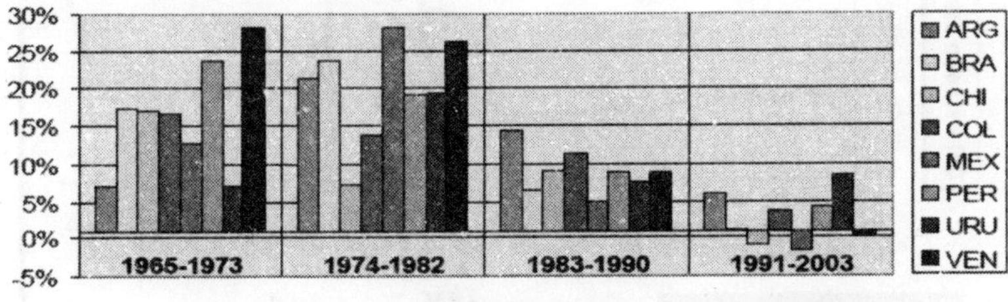

Figure 1: Average Annual Growth in Public External Debt (in current US dollars)

amounting to $66 billion in 1982 compared to only $12 billion in 1975 (Theberge 1999). The Latin American crisis was a result of bad macroeconomic policies and foreign borrowing by governments.

The Latin American financial crisis followed the world economy's recession in the 1970s and 1980s. The world was experiencing a recession in which oil prices were increasing and the interest rate was growing in the United States and among European nations. The United States and Europe became more attractive for foreign direct investment resulting from the growing interest rate. During the global recession, oil prices rose dramatically. Figure 2 shows that during the 1970s, oil prices were increasing with a peak in the early 1980s. Petroleum exporting countries accumulated large amounts of cash due to the increase in the international price of oil. These nations were able to invest more money in international banks. The money invested in international banks provided banks the ability to lend more money. Latin American governments were able to continue borrowing money for domestic purposes. As the interest rates continued to increase in the United States and Europe in 1979, Latin American nations found it

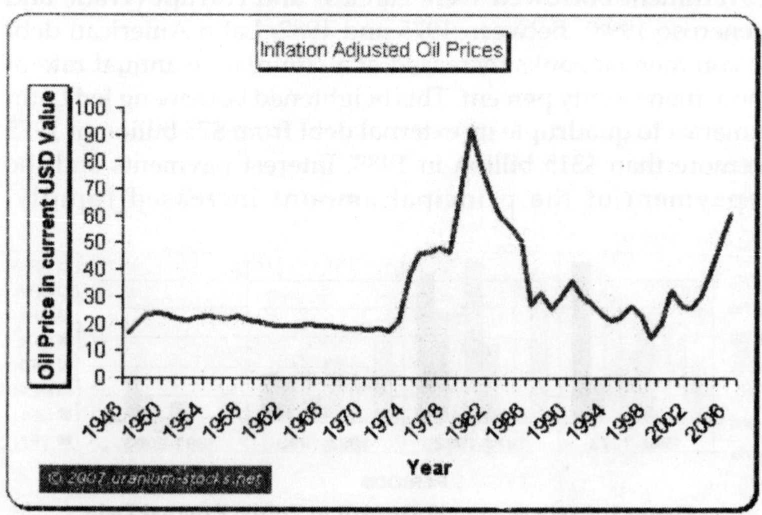

Figure 2

increasingly more difficult to repay loans. While the risky accumulation of foreign debt by Latin American governments occurred over a number of years, the debt crisis began when the international capital markets became aware that Latin America would not be able to repay its loans. Consequently, Latin America's inability to repay the loans was initially revealed by Mexico to the international community.

In August of 1982, Mexico declared that it would no longer be able to service its debt by stating default on its loans. Following this realization, the majority of commercial banks reduced or stopped lending to Latin American nations. Latin America's loans were primarily short-term and the financial crisis ensued when lenders refused to refinance the loans. Billions of dollars of loans that previously would have been refinanced were now due immediately. In response to the crisis most nations abandoned their import substitution and industrialization (ISI) models of economy and adopted an export-oriented industrialization strategy with the exceptions of Chile and Costa Rica which adopted reformist strategies. Consequently, massive amounts of capital outflow occurred, particularly to the United States. Currencies depreciated and the real interest rate continued to increase. During the crisis of the early 1980s, gross domestic product (GDP) growth rate for the region was only slightly more than two percent. In per capita terms, Latin America experienced negative growth of almost nine percent (Palat 2003). The debt crisis is one of the factors which contributed to the collapse of some authoritarian dictatorships in the region, such as Brazil's military regime and the Argentine bureaucratic-authoritarian regime.

SECTION - 2

EAST ASIAN FINANCIAL CRISIS

The East Asian Financial Crisis began in July of 1997. Prior to the crisis, the Asian economies were experiencing a period of progress and prosperity due to immense amounts of capital inflow. The Asian economies performed rapid industrialization, had high values of gross domestic product and export growth in the 1980s and 1990s. They were envisioned as model economies for the rest of the developing world able to offer valuable lessons to other countries seeking to overcome the challenges of late development (Grabel 1999). The process of liberalization in the 1990s failed to implement national financial supervision to control excessive borrowing.

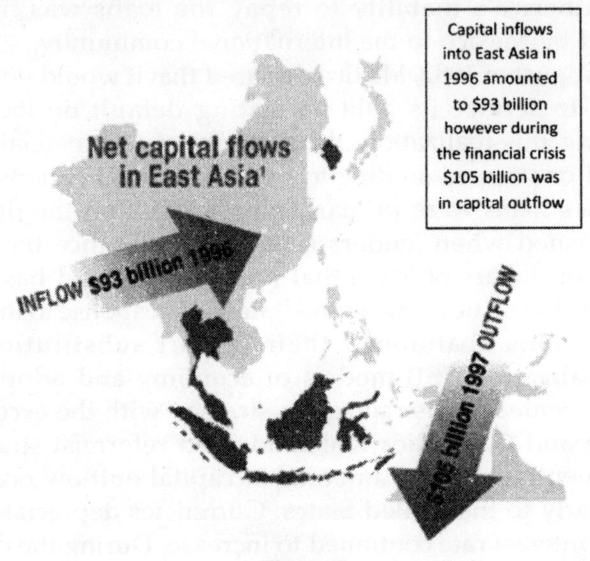

Figure 3

The Asian economies had high interest rates which attracted investors, consequently, large amounts of investment accrued. Hence, individuals and firms acquired large amounts of short-term, private debt (Wade and Veneroso 1998). The Asian economies needed continuous investments in order to sustain productivity and growth (Hirst and Thompson 2004). There has been general agreement on the existence of a crisis and its consequences however the causes of the crisis are less understood. It is debatable what really led to the devaluations of currencies but whether it was a fast outflow of capital from Japanese banks due to their own domestic issues particularly concerning real estate, the United States' interest rate's increase to challenge inflation leading to a more attractive investment region than Asia and/or a final peak of investments into the region led to its decline. Contagion effect resulted by an abrupt withdrawal of short-term funds by Western investors leading to the consequence of many firms' bankruptcies (Hirst and Thompson 2004).

All the causes may not be clearly understood, but the consequences were depreciations of the currencies among the region, inflation, weakening exports, bankruptcies of firms, banks and companies, as well as, declining economic productivity.

The financial crisis was a surprise to leaders, institutions and investors. At the end of 1996, four of the economies which were disrupted by the financial crisis were the world's third, fourth, fifth and sixth top recipients of private foreign capital inflows. In 1996, Indonesia received approximately eighteen billion dollars of private capital inflows. Malaysia received sixteen billion dollars, Brazil acquired approximately fifteen billion dollars and Thailand received more than thirteen billion dollars of foreign capital invested in private ventures prior to the crisis (Grabel 1999). The Asian economies exposure to corruption, flawed assumptions on real estate values, over spending by governments and ineffective government policies were causes of the problem however the financial crisis that spread throughout East Asia came as a surprise to the international community.

The crisis began in Thailand in May of 1997 with the financial collapse of the Thai baht resulting from the Thai government's decision to float its currency and eliminate its peg to the American dollar, a decision based on its domestic real estate crisis. At the time, Thailand had acquired a burden of foreign debt that forced the country into bankruptcy prior to the collapse of its currency. Following the forced devaluation, Thailand's earnings from imports decreased making recovery impossible. The crisis spread to other nations in the region. Most of the currencies in East Asia and Japan depreciated, the value of stocks fell and private debt increased. Indonesia, South Korea and Thailand were the countries most affected by the crisis. Hong Kong, Malaysia, Laos and the Philippines were also considerably affected by the crisis. The

People's Republic of China, India, Taiwan, Singapore and Vietnam were relatively unaffected. Japan was not considerably affected by the crisis however was experiencing its own economic difficulties. In October of 1997, the crisis reached Brazil and Russia. By early December the crisis had reached South Korea. In early 1998, a new cycle of instability disrupted the financial markets of South Korea and Indonesia (Grabel 1999). The crisis, in terms of scope and depth, was very disruptive to the East Asian economies.

All of the East Asian nations saw their currencies depreciate significantly relative to the American dollar. The currency crisis caused Indonesia's gross domestic product (GDP) to decline to fifteen percent in one year. Thailand and Malaysia suffered losses amounting to approximately ten percent of their gross domestic products (Leblang 2005). Although most of the governments of Asia had no national debt and reliable fiscal policies, the International Monetary Fund (IMF) was forced to initiate a forty billion dollar program to stabilize the currencies of South Korea, Thailand, and Indonesia, whose economies were hit particularly hard by the crisis (Jayasuriya & Rosser, 2001). Japan was experiencing its own recession due to a highly inefficient banking system resulting from unmanageable and large quantities of debt. The United States intervened to stop the continual decline of the value of the Yen by purchasing approximately two billion dollars worth of the Japanese currency (King 2000). The regional and global economic crisis resulted in political instability in Indonesia and drastic inflation caused by depreciation of the Indonesian Rupiah. The effects of the crisis lasted through 1998 as the growth in the Philippines dropped to almost zero in 1998 (Leblang 2005). In 1999, however, the economies of Asia were beginning to recover.

The two factors that contributed to the principal outcome of the financial crisis in East Asia was that the private sector had excessive reliance on foreign loans and the economies failed to control portfolio investment flows (Grabel 1999). The Asian economies involved in the crisis of the 1990s were vulnerable to the risks of the withdrawal of currency and investors' actions. Once the risks became apparent, it was too late for the governments to be able to reverse the crisis. During the financial crisis of East Asia the governments were coerced to implement neoliberal policies economically and socially in order to create a financial environment in which private capital would return and entice the IMF to offer financial assistance.

SECTION - 3

CONTRASTING CAUSES OF THE FINANCIAL CRISES IN LATIN AMERICA AND EAST ASIA

Latin American and East Asian financial crises were both a cause of excessive foreign borrowing. The principal lenders to Asia were commercial banks who were also primarily responsible for excessive lending in Latin America during the 1970s (Hirst and Thompson 2004). Prior to the financial crisis, Latin American public debt from commercial banks increased. Latin American economies were driven primarily by high rates of government borrowing.

According to Figure 4, in the period of 1978 to 1982, Latin America had greater capital flows than East Asia. However following 1983, the period in which Latin America was experiencing a currency crisis, East Asia had more capital flows than Latin America (Gavin 1997). When the world economy went into recession in the 1970s and 1980s and interest rates increased in the United States and in Europe, debt payments also increased making it harder for borrowing countries to pay back their debts (Sachs, 1989). The international markets realized the fate of Latin America and the government's inability to repay their loans. The governments in Latin America had borrowed billions of dollars collectively and were forced to repay the loans immediately. The borrowing in Latin America was "wasteful and corrupt" (Wade & Veneroso, 1998) because it was done by governments rather than by private firms operating in competitive markets.

In contrast, most debt in East Asia is private debt, accumulated by private firms and individuals. Corporate debt is much higher in Asian countries, particularly South Korea, than in Western economies (Wade and Veneroso 1998). Until

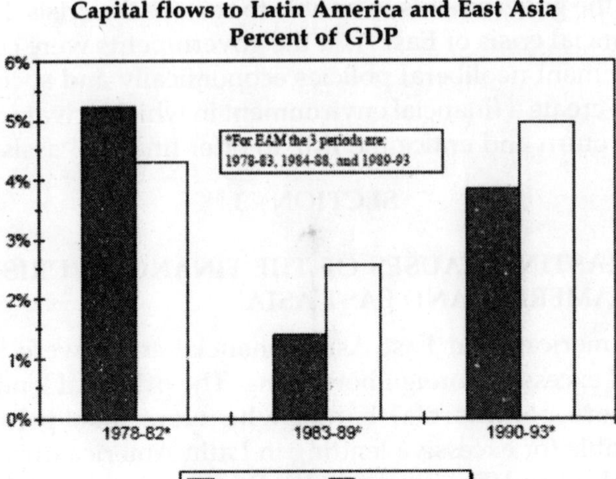

Figure 4

the inception of the crisis, Asia attracted almost half of the total capital inflow to developing countries because the economies of East Asia maintained high interest rates attractive to foreign investors looking for a high rate of return (Radalet & Sachs 1998). The resulting large quantities of credit that became available influenced the economic climate and increased asset prices to an unsustainable level. These asset prices eventually began to collapse, causing individuals and companies to default on debt obligations (Hirst and Thompson 2004). In addition, Japanese banks were the largest lenders in Asia and the key creditor in Thailand. Japanese banks began the contagion effect of withdrawing investments and other foreign commercial banks followed by withdrawing their loans (King 2001). A primary contrast between the financial crises in Latin America and East Asia was the differences in debt accumulated. Latin American foreign debt was accumulated by the government while East Asian debt was a source of revenue for businesses and households.

Governments in Latin America and East Asia managed their balance of payments accounts differently prior to the financial crises. Large budget deficits were common among

Latin American nations whereas the East Asian economies held large amounts of domestic savings. In the debt crisis of the 1980s, Latin American countries displayed strong similarities by all possessing large balance of payments deficits that produced high inflations and internal instability (Sachs 1989). Latin American nations' large deficits are outcomes of populist policies in which governments implemented procedures that rapidly and significantly increased government spending in order to correct inequities in the income distribution and to raise the living standards of the poor in their nations. East Asian nations did not have large budget deficits thus had balance of payments in surplus or in balance.

As both regions were experiencing economic growth, private and public saving was exhibited in one region while the other region struggled to save. The economies of East Asia promoted domestic savings and have proven successful in expanding their savings substantially during the period of economic growth (Hirst and Thompson 2004). In contrast, Latin American nations do not domestically save. "Given the low domestic savings rate in Latin America, much of the budget deficit was financed by borrowing from abroad (Hayami 2003)." East Asian economies have strong governmental reserves and significant domestic savings whereas Latin America has negative governmental reserves and contains small amounts of domestic savings (Sachs, 1989). Figure 5 depicts the relationship between savings rate in East Asia and Latin America. Following the mid 1970s, East Asia possessed a greater savings rate than Latin America (Gavin 1997). These factors exemplify the contrasting differences in the financial system of the two regions possibly explaining how East Asian economies have been able to recover more quickly than Latin American economies.

Financial crises occur as a consequence of governments' mismanagement of macroeconomic policies which are influenced internally by domestic policy makers and externally due to Western influence by the IMF to liberalize economies by deregulating financial institutions. Import substitution industrialization (ISI) is a trade and economic policy on the

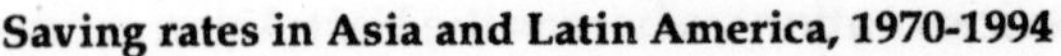

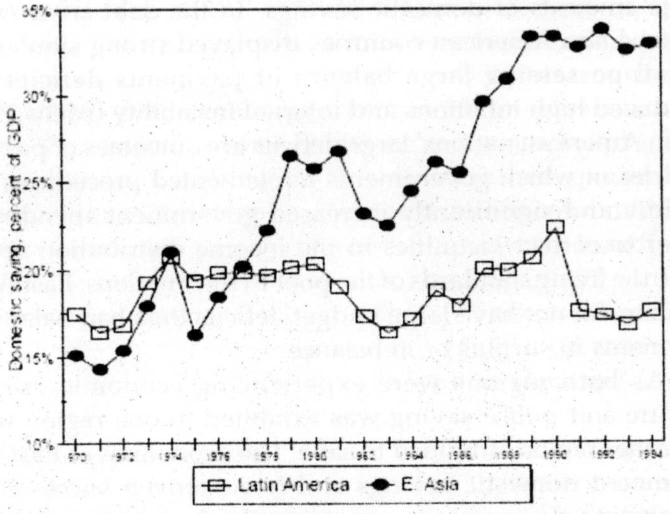

Figure 5

premise that a state should attempt to substitute products imported with domestically produced substitutes. In Asian nations' ISI policies are focused externally by promoting exports whereas in Latin American nations' ISI policies focus on internal conditions among world markets (Krugman & Obstfeld 2005). Prior to the financial crises, the regions promoted diverse economic and trade policies. In the aftermath of the financial crises, Latin America and East Asia experienced drastically different consequences as bankruptcies occurred.

The import substitution industrialization policy in Asian economies focused externally by promoting exports rather than internally. The internal focus of ISI was rejected by many East Asian nations allowing superior economic performance prior to their financial crisis. Many East Asian economies shifted rapidly from ISI policies to an open economic policy. "Asia experienced a crisis because its various countries did not liberalize their financial institutions enough. They failed to turn domestic banks into Western-style institutions (Hirst and Thompson 2004)." They failed to develop appropriate institutions of national financial supervision and to follow cautious policies to control excessive borrowing. "The financial crisis in East Asia was a market failure resulting from liberalizing international capital movements under the fixed exchange rate in the absence of adequate and prudent regulations due to the euphoria created by the extraordinary level of past economic growth (Hayami 2003)." East Asian nations' experience of economic prosperity was a result of their trade and economic policies however these policies also contributed to their decline at the end of the twentieth century.

In Latin America, institutional substitution industrialization (ISI) policy focused on internal economic conditions influencing the promotion of domestic production rather than imports. ISI failed in Latin America because governments did not invest enough in skills and education to increase domestic production. The policies in many of the Latin American nations provided the region with economic development however the policy failures were a cause of the region's financial crisis. The financial crisis in Latin America was caused by the combination of bad macroeconomic policies like populism and corrupt borrowing by governments and was thus a government failure (Hayami 2003). The East Asian financial crisis was caused by market failure because there should have been greater supervision of capital flows and better protection of the national businesses from external risks. In contrast, the Latin American financial crisis was attributable to governments' failure to implement supportive macroeconomic policies and reduce foreign borrowing.

Countries with high income inequality have proven to be especially vulnerable to debt crises. Sachs' research shows that income inequalities in Latin America tend to be much larger then in other regions of the world especially compared to East Asia which has an unusually low degree of income inequality (Sachs 1989). Many of Latin America's economic problems are consequences of income inequality which promotes social unrest and excessive foreign borrowing as a result of social pressures to provide redistributive programs. Figure 6 shows that Latin America has greater income inequality than East Asia. Latin American countries displayed large budget deficits thus creating high inflations and balance of payments crises. Andrew Berg's findings reveal that countries with high income inequality are more likely to reschedule loans (Sachs 1989). Income inequality intensifies political pressure to raise the incomes of the lower classes, which contributes to bad policy choices and poor economic performance. Economic policy in Latin America is challenged by conflicting interests of class, sectors, regions and ethnic groups. Social conflicts lead to weak political institutions and short government tenures (Sachs 1989). The financial crisis in Latin America was partially derived from the internal condition of high income inequalities which led to increased public deficits, rescheduling of loans, poor macroeconomic polices by weak political institutions. Contrastingly, East Asia is characterized by social equality and thusly the social structures of society were not contributing causes to the financial crisis of the 1990s.

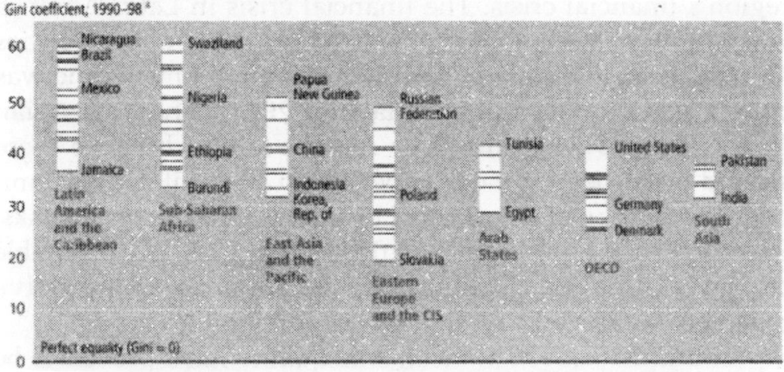

Figure 6

Thus financial crises in Latin America and East Asia have similar yet contrasting external factors. "World real interest rates reached unexpected and unprecedented levels in the 1980s, resulting in an enormous drain of resources from Latin American debtor countries to the creditor world. Commodities prices for Latin America's leading exports collapsed. And in many countries, fragile democratic governments had to try to pick up the pieces in human, political and economic terms—left by earlier military regimes" (Sachs 1989). The effect of world interest rates, including the significant interest of the United States has had major impact on nations competing in the open economy, many times indirectly causing a financial crisis. Figure 7 demonstrates the varying interest rate in the United States where it was at its peak during the financial crises of East Asia and Latin America. In the East Asian economies, the American dollar and interest rate directly affected their ability to compete for foreign direct investment. The appreciation of the American dollar caused an increase in its interest rate which was politically desirable for the United States yet worsened the situation of financial competition for the Asian economies (Wade and Veneroso 1998). The Asian economies were dependent on continued investment in their firms in order to maintain economic growth. The decline of investment in the region as more investors became attracted to the United States and European economies challenged East Asia's development. In East Asia, as country after country fell into crisis, many local

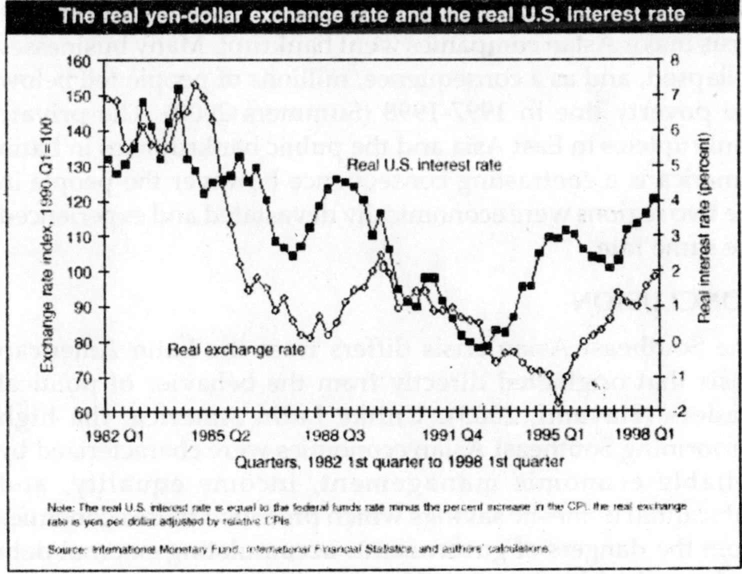

Note: The real U.S. interest rate is equal to the federal funds rate minus the percent increase in the CPI, the real exchange rate is yen per dollar adjusted by relative CPIs.

Source: International Monetary Fund, International Financial Statistics, and authors' calculations.

Figure 7

businesses and governments that had taken out loans in American dollars, which became much more expensive relative to the local currency, became unable to pay their creditors. The dynamics of the situation were similar in the Latin American debt crisis yet it was the governments who had borrowed the loans and were now facing the difficulty of repayment. The primary contrasting external cause of the financial crises involves fluctuating dominant currencies and adjustments of interest rates and how the two regions were affected.

The Latin American financial crisis of the 1980s and the East Asian financial crisis of the following decade have a primary contrasting consequence determined by bankruptcies. Many governments in Latin America went bankrupt following the crisis due to their inability to repay loans to foreign lenders. The contagion effect among lenders stemming from the acknowledgement of the credit crisis led to large withdrawals of credit from the Southeast Asian countries, causing bankruptcies of businesses and financial institutions. A common practice in Asian economies is government protection and intervention of major business enterprises when about to fail to avoid bankruptcy (Hayami 2003). However during the crisis major Asian companies went bankrupt. Many businesses collapsed, and as a consequence, millions of people fell below the poverty line in 1997-1998 (Summers 2000). The private bankruptcies in East Asia and the public bankruptcies in Latin America is a contrasting consequence however the people in the two regions were economically devastated and experienced the same fate.

CONCLUSION

The Southeast Asian crisis differs from the Latin American crisis that originated directly from the behavior of political leaders (Hayami, 2003). Unlike Latin America, the high performing Southeast Asian economies were characterized by reliable economic management, income equality, and substantial domestic savings which protected these economies from the dangers of governments accumulating external debt and eventual bankruptcy (Hayami, 2003). However, the lack of protection and control of external private borrowing resulted in the market failing to protect workers and firms from external forces resulting in the financial crises and bankruptcies of firms. In the case of Latin America, high income inequality, large deficits, considerable public borrowing, lack of domestic savings and dire macroeconomic policies led to the failure of governments to withstand the financial crisis. Many governments went bankrupt in Latin America as a result of the financial crisis of the 1980's. Latin American economies were not able to sustain economic growth after their recovery from the debt crisis. Southeast Asian economies have proven capable of returning to their comfortable path of economic development. Currently, Latin America and Southeast Asia are showing signs of advancement and have returned to the path of economic development. The financial crises of the 1980's and 1990's concerning Latin America and Southeast Asian economies have contrasting and comparable internal and external consequences and causes.

REFERENCES

Gavin, Michael, Ricardo hausmann and Ernesto Talvi. Saving Behavior in Latin America: Overview and Policy Issues. Inter-American Development Bank. Washington D.C.: Office of the Chief Economist. Working Paper 346, 1997.

Grabel, Illene. Rejecting Exceptionalism: Reinterpreting the Asian Financial Crises. 1999.

Kaminsky, Graciela L. and Carmen M. Reinhert. Financial Crises in Asia and Latin America: Then and Now. Washington, D.C.: American Economic Review 88, 1998. 444-448.

Hayami, Yujiro. From the Washington Consensus to the Post-Washington Consensus: Retrospect and Prospect. Asian Development Review. Vol. 20. No. 2. Bangladesh: Blackwell Publishing, 2003. 40-65.

Hirst, Paul Q. and Grahame Thompson. Globalization in Question: The International Economy and the Possibilities of Governance. New York: Polity Press, 2001.

Jayasuriya, Kanishka and Andrew Rosser. Economic Orthodoxy and the East Asian Crisis. Third World Quarterly. Vol 22. No 3. New York: Taylor and Francis Group, 2001. 381-396.

King, Michael R. Who Triggered the Asian Financial Crisis? Review of International Political Economy. London: Routledge, 2000, 438-466.

Krugman, Paul and Maurice Obstfeld. International Economics. New York: Addison Wesley, 2005.

Leblang, David and Shanker Satyanath. Politically Generated Uncertainty and Currency Crises: Theory, Tests and Forecasts. 2005.

Palat, Ravi Arvind. 'Eyes Wide Shut': Reconceptualizing the Asian Crisis. Review of International Political Economy 10:2. New York: Routledge, 2003. 169-195.

Radelet, Steven and Jeffrey Sachs. The Onset of the East Asian Financial Crisis. Working Paper No. 6680. Cambridge, MA: National Bureau of Economic Research, 1998.

Sachs, Jeffrey. Social Conflict and Populist Policies in Latin America. Harvard University: NBER Working Paper #2897. 1989.

Summers, Lawrence H. International Financial Crises: Causes, Prevention and Cures. Richard T. Ely Lecture. 2000.

Wade, Robert and Frank Veneroso. The Asian Crisis: The High Debt Model versus the Wall Street-Treasury-IMF Complex. New Left Review. March/April 1998. 3-23.

14

UNCONVENTIONAL STRUCTURAL TRANSFORMATION IN RECENT INDIAN ECONOMIC GROWTH:

New Lessons and Evidence

INTRODUCTION

Economic development theories are typically structural, Marxist, or neoclassical in nature; each of which presents a slightly different perspective and recommendations for the most effective methods a society can apply to achieve economic development. The study of theory is important; however, it is critical that we understand how to apply the theory and test its validity. This paper examines Arthur Lewis' Structural Change model and its applicability to the country of India.

The Structural Change model by Arthur Lewis provides an explanation of how developing economies move through various stages of development by implementing a balanced growth strategy to help offset the consequences of dualism. The crux of the theory focuses on the efficient allocation of resources, specifically taking surplus labor and transferring it to an industry, which can more efficiently use the labor input and, as a result, boost the total product produced by the

---

This Chapter is based on an article with the same title co-authored with Ms. Meg Hendricks

economy thereby increasing GDP, employment and the standard of living.

In this chapter, the Structural Change Theory is applied to recent Indian economic growth in hopes that some understanding can be gained regarding the country's interesting and impressive development experience. Over the past 10 years, India has become the second fastest growing economy in Asia, just behind China, with both remarkable and consistent increases in its Gross Domestic Product. It is evident that India is becoming an increasingly important part of the global economy such that when a citizen of a developed economy calls for technical support on many top brands of computers, he or she is likely to speak to someone in India. This growth is primarily due to software development and the services industry, which suggests that there has been a transfer of labor from the country's agricultural sector to the service and software sectors.

While Lewis' model directly focuses on labor transfer from agriculture to industry, at first glance it appears that India has not dedicated factors of production to support the growth and development of its industrial sector thereby indicating that the Structural Growth model does not fit the dynamics of change in India. It is true that India does not have a large industrial sector; however if Lewis' model is used as a general application of resource allocation and efficiency, it could be argued that the 14% drop in agricultural labor has reinvested itself into the services sector via more attractive wages and higher productivity. Therefore, it is fair to consider the Structural Change theory as one that accurately describes the growth phenomenon currently occurring in India. The new lesson however is that structural change can occur by reallocating labor from agriculture to services rather than to the industrial sector as Lewis suggested.

The structure of the chapter is separated into two sections. Section One provides an examination of Arthur Lewis' Structural Growth model including strengths and weaknesses of the theory while Section Two applies the economic development model to the Indian economy.

SECTION - 1

An Examination of Arthur Lewis' Structural Adjustment Model

The living conditions endured by the majority of people residing in less developed countries are a global concern. Issues such as low levels of income, capital stock, poor educational systems, limited technology, inadequate infrastructure and inequality between service and industrial base income as well as unstable political and economic institutions characterize less developed countries (LDCs).[1] The drive to improve the economic and political conditions in developing economies has emerged as a complex and highly interesting branch of economics, which has been closely studied since the end of World War II. Determining the best economic policies with the goal of providing higher standards of living in less developed countries was of great interest to economists both in the developing and developed world. Numerous theories and extensions have emerged in the past 40 years, some of which are more influential than others.

Although there has been extensive discussion regarding how to measure the development level of a country, the most common tool of analysis remains a country's Gross Domestic Product (GDP). GDP measures the total market value of all the goods and services produced by an economy. It is assumed that a higher GDP indicates a higher standard of living for the country - a supposition that unfortunately can be untrue. For the sake of comparing levels of development, it is generally considered more effective and appropriate to use Per Capita Income (PCI), which considers the size of a country's population when calculating GDP. While the use of this measure more accurately reflects the productivity of a society, PCI does not provide any indication of income equality in a country and therefore still remains ineffective at determining the actual level of development enjoyed by a nation's general population. It has been proven repeatedly that the benefits of economic development are not distributed evenly which is reflected by the huge disparities between rich and poor in developing economies. The extreme stratification between the rich and poor is just one of the many dualistic features of an LDC. In fact, it became evident to economists that all developing economies had numerous conditions, which could be considered dualistic in nature. This realization engaged the curiosity of economists throughout the world in the 1940's and 1950's.

The concept of dualism is very real in developing countries and indicates an economy in which development occurs unevenly between and within sectors.[2] The disparity between the rich and the poor or the dichotomy between the small industrial sector and the large agrarian, rural sector are just two examples of how dualism exists in LDCs. The traditional or agricultural sector in LDCs is typically responsible for producing the greatest portion of these countries' GDPs, with the industrial sector playing a secondary role. In contrast, the industrial sector in developed economies is dominant and agriculture is but a small contributor to GDP thereby indicating that growth of the industrial sector is positive for development. This distinction and disparity in LDCs between the two sectors precipitated an economic theory referred to as the Structural Growth Theory, proffered by Arthur Lewis in 1954. While dualism is considered to involve opposing forces or extremely different dynamics, structural growth involves creating a development strategy based on balanced growth, which Arthur Lewis' Structural Growth model aims to do by addressing disequilibrium within an economy.[3] The Structuralist approach further attempts to identify specific rigidities and lags in a developing economy that predispose it to ineffective and inefficient resource allocation[4].

Arthur Lewis recognized that the non-commercial agricultural sector is primarily composed of family-owned farms, which are customarily tended to, by the entire family or group of families who rent the land. Consequently, both the labor required to grow the foodgrains and the wages received from the farm's outputs are shared by all members of the family. Economically, this labor sharing technique results in a very low marginal productivity because each additional unit of labor fails to increase the productivity of the farm, which results in the driving down of wages to a subsistence level. For example, Lewis suggested that if there were eight people working on a farm producing 400 units of food, but only five of them were actually needed to produce the same total product, the additional three laborers were not increasing the production and therefore have a zero marginal product. Because of low labor productivity, wages are at a subsistence level. As a result, Lewis' theory proposes that if those three laborers were redirected or reallocated to work in the industrial sector, the marginal productivity of those individuals would be positive and the laborer's wages would be higher than the subsistence level. This improvement in marginal productivity would also contribute to the development of the economy by increasing the country's GDP.

The industrial sector, which is typically underdeveloped in LDCs, would experience an inflow of labor from the agricultural sector, and causes an immediate increase in total product since the industrial sector is characterized by positive labor productivity. As a new, undeveloped sector with positive labor productivity, wages would be higher in the industrial sector, which would encourage labor migration and would increase total product, resulting in higher profits. Lewis assumes that industry owners or "capitalists" reinvest profits into the business by purchasing capital assets or new production technologies. An increase in capital assets and/or an improvement in production technologies enable the capitalists to absorb and utilize additional labor while also increasing the productivity of the current laborers. The total product in industry continues to grow resulting in a balance between the agriculture and industrial sectors while also strengthening the economy's diversification and GDP.

The Structural Growth model is a sensible concept that reallocates resources (labor) to a sector that can more productively use the resource. The objectives of Lewis' Model are threefold: (1) to commercialize a developing country by adjusting the labor surplus through the reallocation of unproductive labor, (2) to implement technology in both the agriculture and industrial sectors to support higher productivity, and (3) to increase privatization to complement government planners.[5] Additionally, Lewis' model has three main assumptions, which mirror its objectives: "technology can be divided between capital using (capitalist) and non capital using (subsistence), the labor supply is elastic at a conventional wage, and saving is done largely by the recipients of nonwage income (capitalists)."[6] In general, these assumptions help to simplify real life conditions and have stood the test of time. Lewis' theory both recognizes that countries develop slowly and in stages but also provides a guide for how to develop - both of which have proven to be significant contributions to the school of development economics.[7]

Lewis assumes that the labor supply is elastic meaning that the labor supply is sensitive to changes in demand and wage rates. In order for labor to migrate from the rural, agrarian parts of the country to urban and industrial jobs, some degree of wage increase must exist in order to attract the surplus labor. "A substantial unskilled labor wage gap is indeed likely to be required, partly to induce the typical agricultural worker to overcome her attachment to soil and family, partly to meet transport costs, and partly as a consequence of such institutional factors as commercialized sector minimum wage legislation, unionization, public sector wage setting, etc., each of which usually do not extend into non-commercialized activities. Once these two wage levels are given within a general equilibrium context, the release of labor by the non-commercialized sector and its absorption by the commercialized sector represents an essential ingredient of balanced growth in the labor surplus economy."[8]

Arthur Lewis' contribution to development economics has received extensive attention, which has uncovered both lines of attack as well as arenas, which have provided further support and credibility for his theory; however, labor surplus has by far been the most debated topic of Lewis' model. Gustav Ranis contributed a strong assessment of Lewis' contributions to development economics in two papers titled "Arthur Lewis' Contributions to Development Thinking and Policy"[9] and "Labor Surplus Economies".[10] Arthur Lewis or Gustav Ranis specifically discusses the concept of labor surplus, which has been attacked and repudiated by many economists, specifically the assumption that labor surplus can be removed and there will be no change in output by the agricultural sector. Ranis reports that Theodore Schultz cites that when a large percentage of the agricultural work force contracted influenza, there was a substantial decrease in agricultural output thereby discrediting the assumption of zero marginal productivity. Amartya Sen (1967) negated Schultz claim by suggesting that in some instances there may be a change in agricultural output, but the laborers who remain in the agricultural sector may need to put in more hours and work harder than they did when the labor surplus existed to achieve equal total product output. It is clear that Lewis thought of labor surplus in terms of the number of human beings that could be reallocated to another more productive sector rather than the total work hours required to produce a set amount. Ranis suggests that a more accurate assessment of the labor surplus debate is that if there is a large withdrawal of labor from a sector, there must be a "reorganization of production by those left behind, i.e., technology change."[11]

Other weaknesses of Lewis' theory include his failure to address the development problems associated with mass migration to urban areas, which typically play host to most of the industrial sector.[12] Cities or large urban areas are associated with challenges and problems such as providing sufficient education for the population, poor infrastructure and sanitation, which can lead to increased disease, as well as heightened levels of crime, and a lack of housing. The notion that labor can continue to infiltrate the urban areas with no negative consequences has proven to be unrealistic. A third weakness found in Lewis' assumption is that wages in the industrial sector will remain higher than those in the agricultural sector; in fact if the inter-sectoral terms of trade shift in favor of agriculture, wages will increase in the agrarian sector and attract labor away from the industrial sector.

Technology provides the means to increase productivity with the same or even less labor resulting in greater efficiency and higher total product. The application of technology in the agriculture and industrial sectors is typically skewed in most developing countries. If the country has access to purchase and can afford new technologies of production, the industrial or manufacturing sectors are typically more prepared to reinvest profits to increase efficiency. The use of technology or improved technologies of production in the industrial sector is considered a given in Lewis' Structural Adjustment model.

Broadly speaking, Lewis' model provides a strategy for developing economies to pursue slow economic growth by reallocating surplus labor in the inefficient sector with low marginal productivity to the sector that promises both higher wages and an ability to grow through the application and implementation of new technologies of production. "While Lewis' theory clearly has its weaknesses, his notion of dualism, especially that focused on the labor market dimension, rural and urban, continues to offer a theoretically valid, empirically relevant and practically useful framework for dealing with some fundamental real world issues of development."[13]

In this paper, however, we argue that the dualism in economic development can be realized when labor is reallocated from agriculture to services in which marginal productivity can be even higher than in the industrial sector. Hence, economic development can result from the attractive force of the services sector as witnessed in the case of India. Thus, when the services sector improves faster than the industrial sector, it offers higher pay-off to the labor, and economic growth occurs but by slightly different means than is suggested by Lewis' model. One of the other major problems of Lewis's model is the assumption (and therefore argument) that growth necessarily occurs in manufacturing or industrial sector alone, which ignores potential growth in the agricultural sector.

SECTION - 2

Applicabilility of the Structural Growth Model in India

India is currently considered one of the fastest growing economies in the world, which is impressive in its own right, but given that X India is still considered a developing economy, its growth is even more remarkable. The country is 1,269,338 square miles and is made up of 28 states. The capital city is New Delhi, located in the northern part of the country and is home to the national government. The official languages are English and Hindi, but there are 22 other scheduled languages plus an additional 415 living languages. The currency is the Indian Rupee (INR) and is currently valued at 45 INR per US dollar. The country's GDP is approximately $1000 billion in 2006 and its Per Capita Income (PCI) for 2006 was approximately $950. In 2006 India was the second most rapidly developing country in the world; however, the country is still ranked in the bottom half of the United Nations Development Report (126 out of 177 countries). This highlights the continued dualistic nature of the country's economy. India's population is 1.1 billion, 20% of which have secondary and post secondary education, 40% are semi-literate and 40% are illiterate.[14]

India, like every society, began with agriculture as the predominant contributor to its GDP, but opportunities for industrialization came in 1854 when India joined the industrial revolution with the use of the cotton and jute mill in Calcutta.[15] During that time agriculture remained the top producer, but industry and mines counted for 7% of the national income. With the slowing of the world economy during World War I, the Great Depression and World War II, India's economy stagnated along with the development of its industrial sector. In 1947, India gained its independence from the United Kingdom and worked to implement economic growth policies. India's growth however began very slowly in the mid-1950's due to high levels of protectionism and an increase in public investment.[16] Few years of the 1960s were encouraging. The interest and commitment to develop India's industrial sector was marked by the Industrial Policy Resolution in 1948 resulting in an industrial production annual growth rate of 7% which lasted until 1965; a remarkable growth rate even by developed economies' standards. However, after 1965 and until the mid 1980's, the Indian economy began to slow with little to no growth, and there was essentially no shift in labor allocation during this time. Even though India had a high savings rate, costly capital assets hindered investment into or in the industrial sector. During this time, India was not considered an exceptional model of growth, but that reputation would soon change.

Increased foreign aid and investment as well as a large surplus of domestic savings provided the impetus for India's second growth surge that began in the mid 1980's.[17] By 1991, India was ready for more profound economic adjustments, which now proves to have been a critical year for India. The minority government implemented a series of market liberalization policies beginning in 1991, which continued throughout the decade. The main economic reforms implemented included:

- A increase in the number of sectors open to private investment, including power, steel, oil refining and exploration, road construction, air transport, telecommunications, ports, mining, pharmaceuticals and the financial sector. Sectors such as garments and textiles were deregulated as well.
- Policymakers encouraged foreign direct investment (FDI) and reduced bureaucratic processes.
- Deregulation of production quotas to increase competition.
- Liberalization of trade policies. Simplification of the tariff system, conversion of quotas to tariffs and a reduction of overall rates were imposed.
- Deregulation of state controls on business decision-making and clousunes of loss-making state enterprises.[18]

The response to the reforms was overwhelmingly positive and has resulted in a significant increase in India's GDP as well as a swell in both the wealthy and middle class sections of society. "In July 1991...with the announcement of sweeping liberalization by the minority government of P.V. Narasimha Rao the country opened the economy, dismantled import controls, lowered customs duties, and devalued the currency and virtually abolished licensing controls on private investment, dropped tax rates, and broke public sector monopolies... [W]e felt as though our second independence had arrived: we were going to be free from a rapacious and domineering state."[19]

While economic growth occured in each sector, the industrial sector was not exploding in the manner that Lewis' model would predict. Industrialization began in India in 1854, but it soon became clear that the country did not hold a comparative advantage in this sector.[20] The price of capital goods was so high that increases in capital stock were very slow, resulting in an industry sector that had limited capital assets for growth. [21] Consequently, capital accumulation in India is not impressive which hampers the country's ability to be competitive.[22] Additionally, stagnation in the industrial sector is due to an exhaustion of the industrial sector's ability to provide import substitutions as well as low investment.[23] As of 2005, the industrial sector provided approximately 27.1% of the country's GDP and predominately consisted of sales in telecom, cement, automobiles, tobacco, beverages, metals and alloys, manufacturing and equipment, textiles, wood and wood products.[24] A very promising and fast-growing industry is that of telecom which grew by 34% in 2005.[25]

Both a barrier to growth as well as a potential industry for significant growth is that of infrastructure.[26] As a developing economy, India's infrastructure is very limited and is in desperate need of rebuilding and reorganization. The cement industry stands to gain significantly if the administrative bottlenecks can be resolved to provide public investments in new roads and transportation options, such as trains or light rails.[27] In addition to these structural limitations, there are still some other bottlenecks to economic growth such as high levels of bureaucracy, corruption, a lethargic legal system, and crude and outdated labor laws. The private sector incentives are still not to the point where manufacturing can grow at a rapid speed. Increase in software and other services were relatively new developments, consequently, the regulatory net was not prepared to slow growth in the services sector. For these reasons the modern Indian economic growth is dominated by service more than manufacturing sector.

The rural areas of India are home to approximately 2/3 of the population, the vast majority of which are also employed in the agricultural industry.[28] As of 2004, 57.8% of the population was working in the agricultural sector[29], which indicates that since 1951 there has been a 14% decrease in the amount of labor involved in the sector. Currently no technology is used in the informal or non-commercialized agricultural sector, which has hindered any significant growth possible in foodgrains.[30] With such a large percent of the population still living in rural areas, it is critical for India to increase its agricultural productivity for the sake of long-term stability and growth.[31] However, it is unlikely that the agricultural sector will be able to absorb additional labor[32] because of "inadequate irrigation facilities, fragmented land holdings, low technology application, increasing input costs, and high levels of debts incurred by farmers and money owed to rural money lenders."[33] The federal and state governments give agricultural subsidies to support the sector; however, the majority of aid is "given to wealthy farmers and results in an increase in the price of food which further stratifies wealth within the country"[34] and contributes to economic dualism. The limited opportunities to earn a living wage in the agricultural sector suggest that the Indian government must strategize job opportunities for those displaced agricultural workers with limited education.

During the 1960's-1970's when industry became a focus of the government specifically with the publication of the Industrial Policy Resolution in 1948, foodgrains actually became more valuable leading terms of trade to shift in favor of agriculture.[35] This resulted in a wage increase in the agricultural sector in comparison to industry, which ultimately contributed to the stagnation of the industrial sector as a whole.[36]

An examination of India's economic situation, specifically the trend of its GDP, the percent of the labor force employed in the agricultural sector, the percent of GDP contributed by agriculture, manufacturing, industry and services provide both a yearly and a trend analysis for sector strength and growth.

These categories allow us to examine the actual data and determine if India's economic growth can be attributed to the Structural Growth Theory.

India's GDP in Current US $

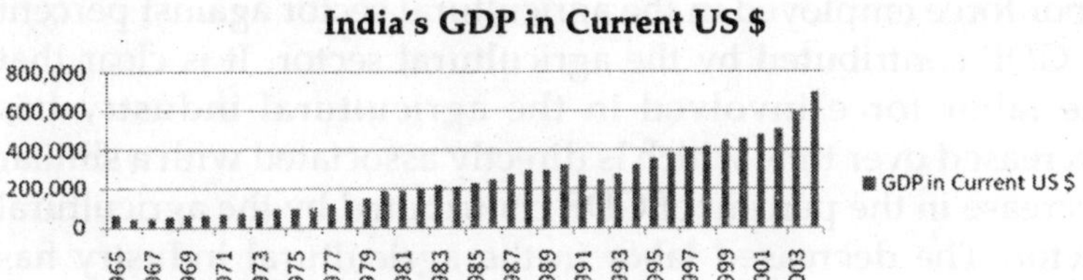

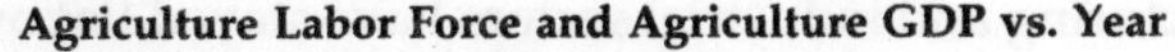
Agriculture Labor Force and Agriculture GDP vs. Year

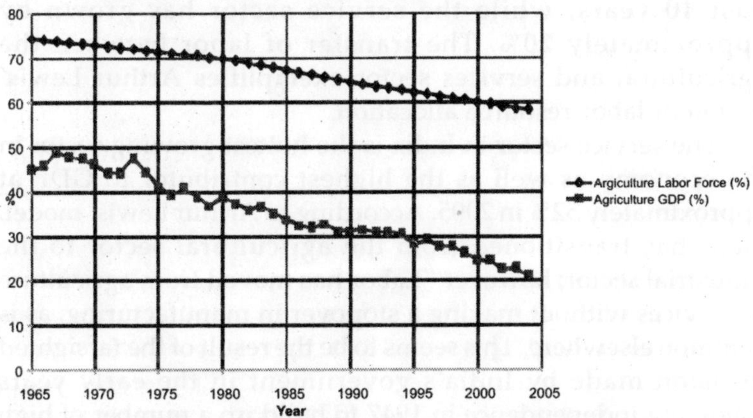

Industry, Manufacturing, and Services GDP vs. Year

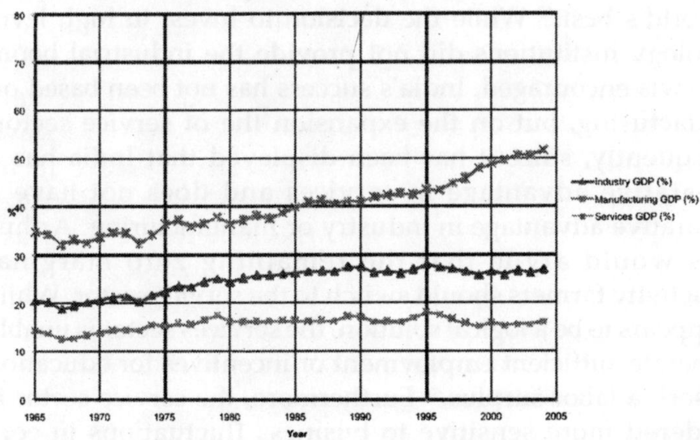

The data indicates that since 1965, India's GDP has grown steadily but has made significant jumps in the past 10 years. A bit more telling is the second graph, which plots percent of labor force employed in the agricultural sector against percent of GDP contributed by the agricultural sector. It is clear that the labor force involved in the agricultural industry has decreased over time which is directly associated with a similar decrease in the percent of GDP contributed by the agricultural sector. The decreased labor in the agricultural industry has been transferred, but graph three indicates that both the manufacturing and industrial sectors have stayed flat over the past 40 years, while the service sector has grown by approximately 20%. The transfer of labor between the agricultural and services sector exemplifies Arthur Lewis' notion of labor resource allocation.

The service sector in India is the hottest growing sector in the economy as well as the highest contributor to GDP at approximately 52% in 2005. According to Arthur Lewis' model, labor has transitioned from the agricultural sector to the industrial sector; however "Labor has moved from agriculture to services without making a stopover in manufacturing, as is common elsewhere. This seems to be the result of the farsighted decision made by India's government in the early years following independence in 1947 to build up a number of high quality institutes of technology to this day that remain among the world's best.[40] While the decision to invest in high level technology institutions did not provide the industrial boom that Lewis encouraged, India's success has not been based on manufacturing, but on the expansion the of service sector. Consequently, since it has been displayed that India has a comparative advantage in services and does not have a comparative advantage in industry or manufacturing, Arthur Lewis would argue that the remaining zero marginal productivity farmers should switch to the service sector. While this appears to be a logical solution, the services sector is unable to generate sufficient employment or incentives for education to absorb a labor surplus.[41] Furthermore, the service sector is considered more sensitive to business fluctuations in core economies, such that if the United State or Europe experiences a depression, the service sector in India is likely to be severely and adversely affected.[42] These two characteristics of the service sector have concentrated the jobs and the wealth in about 20% of the population; also the hands of the individuals with secondary and post secondary education.[43]

Labor in India and Lewis' assumptions regarding the reallocation of surplus labor is diverted by certain cultural, geographical and regulatory dynamics. The fact that 57% of the population remains in rural and agrarian areas of the country suggests that the movement of labor is not occurring to the extent that it could. "The anemic response of cross-state migration to income differentials in India is most likely due to a combination of barriers to the mobility of labor: strong local workers' unions, which act to keep out competing potential employees; rigidities in nominal wages; lack of housing in fast-growing urban areas; and, most important, social, cultural and linguistic barriers to the cross-regional substitutability of labor."[44] Additionally, if the transaction costs of moving away from agriculture are so high, there is little incentive to invest in education.[45]

Certain elements of Indian society have contributed to the existence of surplus labor and low marginal productivity. The labor unions in India are very influential and the surplus labor in manufacturing is due to companies' fear of union unrest and potential backlash. Consequently, firms employ more people than is profitable in order to maintain positive relationships with unions. In some states, the culture is to "shirk" on the job such that productivity is low and more employees are needed.[46] Additionally, low unemployment is an economic priority in India and consequently both the private and public sectors are under pressure from the government to avoid retrenchment of workers.[47] However, that being the case, India's growth rate of output per worker is close to world average.[48]

Due to India's very rigid stubborn labor laws, which are unlikely to change under the current government coalition,"[49] coupled with a population of over 1 billion, full employment is an economic dream for many.[50] "Employment creation is perhaps the most troubling economic and political challenge facing the country. The government has put the issue at the top of its priority list: its employment guarantee scheme has been its main contribution to alleviate the problem so far. The policy prescription for unemployment is to increase the manufacturing sector and to create new jobs in unregistered businesses.[51] In terms of the Structural Growth model, the growth of the labor supply in India makes Lewis' notion of "labor surplus" even more potent[52].

Even though India has skipped over the development of its industrial sector and moved straight to creating a well-respected services sector, India is on its way to becoming a more developed economy. It is clear that this growth can be attributed to reallocation of labor. In order to avoid further stratification of wealth it would be ideal to have a manufacturing industry in India, like there is in China, to provide employment to the 80% of semi-literate or illiterate population.[53]

It is standard practice to compare the two fastest growing economies in Asia, and because of India's lack of industry, the country continues to come in behind China in its potential for future growth. "The main difference in the growth performance of China and India is not the strength of India's service sector, but the weakness of its manufacturing. Until India boosts its industrial productivity, which will require bolder reforms, it is premature to boast that its economic performance is as good as China's."[54] However, it seems unlikely that India will shift or even share its current focus on growing and strengthening the services sector in order to grow its industry sector, in which it ostensibly does not have a comparative advantage in the region of Asia.

CONCLUSION

Arthur Lewis' Structural Growth approach is respected because developing economies continue to struggle to absorb their growing labor force and further because of a worsening of distribution of income.[55] While it does seem that most developing countries are slowly transitioning labor from the agricultural sector to the industrial sector, India is taking a different approach by providing excellent employment opportunities to the highly educated population in the service sector. It is also important to note that this development strategy will not distribute the benefits equally, but will concentrate the wealth into the hands of the 20% of the population that is literate and educated, thereby increasing economic dualism within the country. India deserves respect for being able to develop a highly advanced industry such as software and services, but the problem of stagnant industrial, manufacturing and agricultural industries leaves much of the population without quality employment opportunities. Although India is managing its development differently than other countries, it is clear that Lewis' model is highly applicable as is demonstrated by the shift in labor away from agriculture to a more productive, lucrative and technologically advanced sector.

NOTES

1. Varis, Olli. An Exploration Into an Urbanizing World: Interconnections of Water, Poverty and Urbanizations - Development Theories. 2003.
2. Chenery, Hollis B. "The Structuralist Approach to Development Policy." The American Economic Review, Vol. 65, No. 2, Papers and Proceedings of the Eighty-seventh Annual Meeting of the American Economic Association. (May 1975), pp. 310-316.
3. Chenery, Hollis B. "The Structuralist Approach to Development Policy." The American Economic Review, Vol. 65, No. 2, Papers and Proceedings of the Eighty-seventh Annual Meeting of the American Economic Association. (May 1975), pp. 310-316.
4. *ibid.*
5. Ranis, Gustav. "Arthur Lewis' Contributions to Development Thinking and Policy." Center Discussion Paper No. 891. Economic Growth Center, Yale University. August 2004.
6. Chenery, Hollis B. "The Structuralist Approach to Development Policy." The American Economic Review, Vol. 65, No. 2, Papers and Proceedings of the Eighty-seventh Annual Meeting of the American Economic Association. (May 1975), pp. 310-316.
7. Ranis, Gustav. "Arthur Lewis' Contributions to Development Thinking and Policy." Center Discussion Paper No. 891. Economic Growth Center, Yale University. August 2004.

8. Ranis, Gustav. "Labor Surplus Economies." Center Discussion Paper No. 900. Economic Growth Center, Yale University. December 2004. p. 6.
9. Ranis, Gustav. "Arthur Lewis' Contributions to Development Thinking and Policy." Center Discussion Paper No. 891. Economic Growth Center, Yale University. August 2004.
10. Ranis, Gustav. "Labor Surplus Economies." Center Discussion Paper No. 900. Economic Growth Center, Yale University. December 2004.
11. *ibid* p. 9.
12. Ranis, Gustav. "Labor Surplus Economies." Center Discussion Paper No. 900. Economic Growth Center, Yale University. December 2004.
13. Ranis, Gustav. "Arthur Lewis' Contributions to Development Thinking and Policy." Center Discussion Paper No. 891. Economic Growth Center, Yale University. August 2004. p. 16.
14. Mehra, Rajnish. "Discussion of Sources of Growth in the Indian Economy." University of California Santa Barbara & National Bureau of Economic Research. January 2007.
15. Patnaik, Prabhat. "Industrial Development in India since Independence." Social Scientist, Vol. 7, No. 11 (June, 1979) p. 3-19.
16. *ibid.*
17. DeLong, Bradford J. "India Since Independence: An Analytic Growth Narrative." *http://econ161.berkeley.edu/Econ_Articles/India/India_Rodrik_draft April 2001.*
18. "India - the Country Report" The Economist Intelligence Unit, June 2006.
19. DeLong, Bradford J. "India Since Independence: An Analytic Growth Narrative." http://econ161.berkeley.edu/Econ_Articles/India/India_Rodrik_draft April 2001. p. 3.
20. Kulkarni, Kishore G. Readings in International Economics - Selected Writings of Professor Kishore G. Kulkarni. New Delhi: Serials Publications, 2006.
21. DeLong, Bradford J. "India Since Independence: An Analytic Growth Narrative." *http://econ161.berkeley.edu/Econ_Articles/India/India_Rodrik_draft April 2001*
22. Mehra, Rajnish. "Discussion of Sources of Growth in the Indian Economy." University of California Santa Barbara & National Bureau of Economic Research. January 2007.
23. Patnaik, Prabhat. "Industrial Development in India since Independence." Social Scientist, Vol. 7, No. 11 (June, 1979) p. 3-19.
24. "India - the Country Report" The Economist Intelligence Unit, June 2006.

25. Guerrero, Antonio. "Indian Industry Scales New Heights." Global Finance, February 2006.

26. "India – the Country Report" The Economist Intelligence Unit, June 2006.

27. Guerrero, Antonio. "Indian Industry Scales New Heights." Global Finance, February 2006.

28. "The Other Side of the Indian Growth Story: Confronting Agriculture and Rural Development." June 26th, 2007 Featured Speakers: Arvind Panagariya, Columbia University; Suresh Chandra Babu, International Food Policy Research Institute; Derek Byerlee, World Bank.

29. Food and Agriculture Organization of the United Nations (FAO). 2006. FAOSTAT Online Statistical Service. Rome: FAO. Available online at: *http://faostat.fao.org*.

30. "The Other Side of the Indian Growth Story: Confronting Agriculture and Rural Development." June 26th, 2007 Featured Speakers: Arvind Panagariya, Columbia University; Suresh Chandra Babu, International Food Policy Research Institute; Derek Byerlee, World Bank.

31. "The Other Side of the Indian Growth Story: Confronting Agriculture and Rural Development." June 26th, 2007 Featured Speakers: Arvind Panagariya, Columbia University; Suresh Chandra Babu, International Food Policy Research Institute; Derek Byerlee, World Bank.

32. "India – the Country Report" The Economist Intelligence Unit, June 2006.

33. "The Other Side of the Indian Growth Story: Confronting Agriculture and Rural Development." June 26th, 2007 Featured Speakers: Arvind Panagariya, Columbia University; Suresh Chandra Babu, International Food Policy Research Institute; Derek Byerlee, World Bank.

34. "The Other Side of the Indian Growth Story: Confronting Agriculture and Rural Development." June 26th, 2007 Featured Speakers: Arvind Panagariya, Columbia University; Suresh Chandra Babu, International Food Policy Research Institute; Derek Byerlee, World Bank.

35. Patnaik, Prabhat. "Industrial Development in India since Independence." *Social Scientist*, Vol. 7, No. 11 (June, 1979) p. 3-19. p. 13,15.

36. Ranis, Gustav. "Labor Surplus Economies." Center Discussion Paper No. 900. Economic Growth Center, Yale University. December 2004.

37. Food and Agriculture Organization of the United Nations (FAO). 2006. FAOSTAT Online Statistical Service. Rome: FAO. Available online at: *http://faostat.fao.org*
38. Food and Agriculture Organization of the United Nations (FAO). 2006. FAOSTAT Online Statistical Service. Rome: FAO. Available online at: *http://faostat.fao.org*
39. Food and Agriculture Organization of the United Nations (FAO). 2006. FAOSTAT Online Statistical Service. Rome: FAO. Available online at: *http://faostat.fao.org*
40. Gylfason, Thorvaldur. "Growth – How to India and China Grow." Challenge, Vol. 49, No. 1, Januauary / February 2006, pp. 74-89.
41. Mehra, Rajnish. "Discussion of Sources of Growth in the Indian Economy." University of California Santa Barbara & National Bureau of Economic Research. January 2007.
42. Mehra, Rajnish. "Discussion of Sources of Growth in the Indian Economy." University of California Santa Barbara & National Bureau of Economic Research. January 2007.
43. Mehra, Rajnish. "Discussion of Sources of Growth in the Indian Economy." University of California Santa Barbara & National Bureau of Economic Research. January 2007.
44. Cashin, Paul & Ratna Sahay. "Regional Economic Growth and Convergence in India." Finance & Development, March 1996. p. 59.
45. Mehra, Rajnish. "Discussion of Sources of Growth in the Indian Economy." University of California Santa Barbara & National Bureau of Economic Research. January 2007.
46. Ray, Subhash & Anasua Bhattacharya. "Surplus Labor in Indian Manufacturing: Evidence from the Annual Survey of Industries." Department of Economics Working Paper Series. Working Paper 2003-14, May 2003.
47. Ray, Subhash & Anasua Bhattacharya. "Surplus Labor in Indian Manufacturing: Evidence from the Annual Survey of Industries." Department of Economics Working Paper Series. Working Paper 2003-14, May 2003.
48. DeLong, Bradford J. "India Since Independence: An Analytic Growth Narrative." *http://econ161.berkeley.edu/Econ_Articles/India/India_Rodrik_draft* April 2001.
49. "India – the Country Report" The Economist Intelligence Unit, June 2006. p. 30.
50. "India – the Country Report" The Economist Intelligence Unit, June 2006.
51. "India – the Country Report" The Economist Intelligence Unit, June 2006.

52. Chenery, Hollis B. "The Structuralist Approach to Development Policy." The American Economic Review, Vol. 65, No. 2, Papers and Proceedings of the Eighty-seventh Annual Meeting of the American Economic Association. (May 1975), pp. 310-316.
53. The Other Side of the Indian Growth Story: Confronting Agriculture and Rural Development." June 26th, 2007 Featured Speakers: Arvind Panagariya, Columbia University; Suresh Chandra Babu, International Food Policy Research Institute; Derek Byerlee, World Bank.
54. "Reading the Tea Leaves." *The Economist*, January 25, 2007.
55. Chenery, Hollis B. "The Structuralist Approach to Development Policy." The American Economic Review, Vol. 65, No. 2, Papers and Proceedings of the Eighty-seventh Annual Meeting of the American Economic Association. (May 1975), pp. 310-316.

REFERENCES

Cashin, Paul & Ratna Sahay. "Regional Economic Growth and Convergence in India." *Finance & Development*, March 1996.

Chakraborty, Suparna. "Technology as a Channel of Economic Growth in India." December 18, 2005.

Chenery, Hollis B. "The Structuralist Approach to Development Policy." The American Economic Review, Vol. 65, No. 2, Papers and Proceedings of the Eighty-seventh Annual Meeting of the American Economic Association. (May 1975), pp. 310-316.

DeLong, Bradford J. "India Since Independence: An Analytic Growth Narrative." *http://econ161.berkeley.edu/Econ_Articles/India/India_Rodrik_draft* April 2001.

"Economy-GDP Beats Expectations." Economist Intelligence Unit, Economist Magazine, 2007.

Food and Agriculture Organization of the United Nations (FAO). 2006. FAOSTAT Online Statistical Service. Rome: FAO.

Gylfason, Thorvaldur. "Growth - How to India and China Grow." Challenge, Vol. 49, No. 1, January / February 2006, pp. 74-89.

Guerrero, Anotonio. "Indian Industry Scales New Heights." Global Finance, February 2006.

"India Industrial Production Growth Rates." *http://indiaonestop.com/economy-macro-industry.htmoverview.* Accessed on 7/15/07.

"India: Robust Expansion Augurs Tightening." December 4, 2006. *www.emerging-markets-online.com.* Accessed July 12, 2007.

"India – the Country Report" The Economist Intelligence Unit, June 2006.

Kumari, Anita. "Liberalisation and Sources of Industrial Growth in India: An Analysis Based on Input-Output Approach." Institute of Economic Growth, University of Delhi.

Mehra, Rajnish. "Discussion of Sources of Growth in the Indian Economy." University of California Santa Barbara & National Bureau of Economic Research. January 2007.

Patnaik, Prabhat. "Industrial Development in India since Independence." *Social Scientist*, Vol. 7, No. 11 (June, 1979) p. 3-19.

"The Other Side of the Indian Growth Story: Confronting Agriculture and Rural Development." June 26th, 2007. Featured Speakers: Arvind Panagariya, Columbia University; Suresh Chandra Babu, International Food Policy Research Institute; Derek Byerlee, World Bank.

Ranis, Gustav. "Arthur Lewis' Contributions to Development Thinking and Policy." Center 56Discussion Paper No. 891. Economic Growth Center, Yale University. August 2004.

Ranis, Gustav. "Labor Surplus Economies." Center Discussion Paper No. 900. Economic Growth Center, Yale University. December 2004.

Ray, Subhash & Anasua Bhattacharya. "Surplus Labor in Indian Manufacturing: Evidence from the Annual Survey of Industries." Department of Economics Working Paper Series. Working Paper 2003-14, May 2003.

"Reading the Tea Leaves." The Economist, January 25, 2007.

Sampson, Ben. "India Calling." Professional Engineering, July 12, 2006.

Tyson-Chan, Darlin. "India, not China, the place to be." Money Management. February, 22, 2007.

Varis, Olli. An Exploration Into an Urbanizing World: Interconnections of Water, Poverty and Urbanizations – Development Theories. 2003.

15

INDIA'S BOP: A REVIEW OF CAPITAL ACCOUNT BEHAVIOUR AFTER INDEPENDENCE

A record of international transactions, popularly called balance of payments (BOP hereafter), is of greater significance to the Indian economy in recent times than before because of its newly found affection to openness. As international trade has increased, the need for paying for higher imports has also jumped by a multifold amount. The present paper reviews changes in the capital account of the Indian BOP. A detailed analysis of Indian BOP's current account changes is seen in Kulkarni (1996), hence in the present chapter we concentrate only on the capital account changes Overall one can observe that the current account of Indian BOP has been consistently in deficit, hence on capital account ways to finance the current account deficit had to be found out.

In Section 1 that follows, we initially discuss the process of recording transactions in Indian BOP, and then analyze the overall development of capital account after independence. In Section 2 we summarize our observations and provide conclusions.

This Chapter is based on an article published in Indian Journal of Applied Economics, 1999.

SECTION -1

In the case of India the BOP is divided into two major accounts: current account and capital account. The current account is divided into merchandise, non-monetary gold movement account and invisibles account. Invisibles account is further classified into services (comprising of travel, transportation, insurance, investment income, government transactions, not included elsewhere, and miscellaneous) and transfer payments (unrequited transfers, e.g. grants, gifts etc.)

The capital account includes those transactions that result in changes in foreign financial assets and liabilities. Capital transactions are classified into three main segments: Private, Banking and Official. While private sector's statistics include capital account transactions of resident individuals and private corporate entities, that of banking sector's comprise transactions in foreign financial assets and liabilities of both private and public sector banks, including that of the Reserve Bank of India. Official sector includes capital account transactions of the Central and State governments and public sector undertakings. Movements in foreign exchange assets held by the Reserve Bank are shown under "Reserves."

As one can imagine the capital account changes were a direct reflection of changes in balance of trade. A cursory look at the Indian balance of trade shows that, with very few exceptions, in all years after independence, the trade balance was in deficit. As trade balance goes into deficit, a country needs to find ways to attract the capital to pay for the higher payments of imports than export earnings. Two main ways to do that is to reduce the foreign reserve stocks at home or to borrow from an international lender: either commercial or institutional. India was not a very active player in commercial borrowing until the 1980s and most of the trade balance deficit was financed by international institutional borrowing like from the World Bank and/or IMF. After the 1980s even if commercial borrowing was made, the role played by the World Bank, IMF, Aid India Consortium etc. is still very significant.

At the time of independence Indian foreign reserve holdings were impressive, thanks to the sizable trade surplus with the UK during the WWII period when UK had made large purchases from India to support the war expenditure. Hence the sterling balance in 1947-48 was to the tune of Rs. 1,733 crores. However immediately after independence the demand for imported commodities increased faster than the supply of exportables. Therefore a large portion of jute and cotton producing areas had gone to East and West Pakistan and India became a net importer of jute by 1949. The deficit in balance of trade was initially met by reducing the foreign reserve stock substantially. Moreover the trade imbalance was partly nullified by Rupee devaluation of 1949. Three years after independence there was a net outflow of Rs. 583 crores worth of foreign exchange mainly the pound sterling.

As it is common knowledge, the First Five Year Plan was not a very ambitious plan and hence the imports as well as exports were left without much trade restriction. This created a moderate deficit in the balance of trade (Rs. 541 crores) which was compensated by the surplus of invisible (Rs. 500.6 crores). Thus inflow of capital to the tune of Rs. 13.6 crores was sufficient to take care of the deficit in balance of trade. (See Misra and Puri for greater detail) the story of the Second Five Year Plan (1956-61) was quite contrary. However the first two years of the plan saw a substantial deficit in balance of trade (Rs. 1031 crores) and the surplus of invisible trade was only Rs. 287.3 crores.

Governmental policies resorted to heavy restrictions on imports as only the imports of raw material and capital equipment was seen to be a necessary evil. Thus throughout the Second Plan period the deficit in trade account was substantial (with cumulative figure of Rs. 2261 crores). This deficit had to be financed by foreign assistance and drawing down of foreign reserves. In retrospect, the Second Five Year Plan marked the beginning of a new era of borrowing from the rest of the world. In fact in this time period the Aid India Consortium of a few developed countries was formed to help India finance its deficit in balance of trade. Total foreign loans received in this period were Rs. 910.2 crores and the foreign exchange reserves were drawn down by Rs. 598.8 crores.

The practice of finding ways to finance the trade deficit had to be continued in the Third Five Year Plan as well as in three annual plans that followed the third plan. This was mainly due to the continuously high trade deficit experienced in these years. In the third five year plan the average annual trade deficit was Rs. 462.4 crores. The overall drought conditions in several states made the matter worse as foodgrains had to be imported.

A substantial part of the trade deficit was financed by foreign assistance. International loans in this period amounted to an average of Rs. 535 crores per annum while grants average $ Rs. 29.3 crores per annum. With a minor exception, all the trade deficit of the three annual plan days was financed by foreign assistance. A serious trend of moving into a financial assistance trap for the country began. The total deficit in three years following the third five year plan period was Rs. 3090.9 crores which put even a greater burden on borrowing from external sources.

The fourth five year plan period was characterized by increased imports and stagnated exports. As prices of petroleum products were raised by OPEC the value of imports increased tremendously. In 1969-70, the country imported Rs. 1582 crores of goods and services and in 1973-74 the import bill was Rs. 2729 crores. During this time or specific year span (1973-74) exports only increased from Rs. 1403 crores to Rs. 2350 crores.

Thus the total deficit (comprising current account, capital account, and errors and omissions) in the fourth plan period amounted to Rs. 3964 crores. This was met by foreign assistance that was further divided into the following categories: loans excluding Public Law 480 loans Rs. 3370 crores, P.L. 480 loans Rs. 153.4 crores and grants (excluding P.L. 480) Title I grants amounted to Rs. 432.5 crores. Greater dependence on borrowing further increased in the fourth five year plan period.

A continuation of oil price shock made the matter worse in the fifth five year plan period (1974-75 to 1979-80). Because of a unprecedented rise in the oil price the country experienced a record deficit of Rs. 977 crores in 1974-75 years. Nonetheless a new trend began to materialize in this period. As more lucrative job offers were received in the Middle East countries by the Indian nationals, private remittances started becoming an important entry in the balance of payments of the economy. As a result transfer payments to India on private account aggregated to Rs. 3128 crores over the five years of the fifth plan period.

Second, the large increase in world prices gave a strong boost to Indian exports which also increased greatly in this period. In 1975-76 exports increased by 31 percent over the earlier year and in the next year they increased by 23 percent. The third notable event that occurred in this period was the relatively constant volume of oil imports. The quantity of oil imports was about the same for four years after 1974. Only after 1978-79 when the country attained a comfortable position in its balance of payments and foreign reserves did the import of crude oil pick up. Fourth the international price of gold increased in this time and the difference between the Indian domestic gold price and the international price almost evaporated. This reduced the gold smuggling activities resulting in a better showing in receipts and payments statistics of the Reserve Bank of India. These developments made it suitable for the Indian economy to adjust to the first oil shock rather quickly. The foreign exchange reserve which were Rs. 992.crotes in 1973-74, increased to Rs. 5820 crores in 1978-79. Thus the foreign exchange position was strong enough to finance 9.5 months of imports in 1978-79 as against only 4.4 months in 1973-74.

The second oil shock of 1979 showed its bad effects in the 1980s. Table 1 shows the reflection of continuously high trade deficit of the 1980s. Financing the deficits on current account capital can come from unilateral and bilateral aid programs. However in the 1980s the concessional aid rather than going up, declined progressively. The stringent protectionist policies of government did not offer any incentives for the foreign investors to enter into the Indian market hence the private capital via foreign direct investment did not flow with a very high volume. Indian authorities were left with only one viable option of commercial borrowing in order to finance the current account deficit. After a great deal of initial hesitation India embarked on significant commercial borrowing in 1980. As a result India's borrowing from private sources increased substantially after 1980. This also meant that since the 1980s the total external debt has been made up of a good mix of private, public and international institutions' debt. Nonetheless private borrowing was carried out with a high interest rate and was basically of a short duration. Fortunately for India the debt crisis in other developing countries such as in Latin American countries was more serious and, as seen in Kulkarni-Chakraborty (1989), the relative situation of Indian economy was satisfactory.

Table 1
Movements In Indian Foreign Exchange Reserves: 1980-1992

Column 1 *Year*	*Column 2* *Foreign Currency*	*Column 3* *Foreign Exchange*	*Column 4* *IMF Net*
1980-81	5850	6823	1029
1981-82	3582	4390	639
1982-83	4281	4896	1958
1983-84	5099	5649	1298
1984-85	5482	5952	53
1985-86	5972	6520	-267
1986-87	5924	6574	-690
1987-88	5618	6223	-1123
1988-89	4226	4802	-1175
1989-90	3368	5834	-1183
1990-91	2236	5834	-1183
1991-92	3774	7501	794

Thus the sixth plan period (1980-1985) showed a consistent increase in current account deficit. The sources of financing this increasing deficit are summarized in Table 1. In the first two years of the sixth plan period the total foreign exchange reserves with the Reserve Bank of India were insufficient to finance all of the trade deficit. The difference was covered by borrowing from the IMP, and a newly discovered source of deposits from Non-Resident Indians (NRI). In the last three years of the Sixth Plan however, the capital inflow exceeded the financial needs and therefore the stock of the foreign reserves with the Reserve Bank moderately increased. In general, as it is observed in Holla (1992) for the plan period as a whole 51 percent of the current account deficit was met by way of foreign loans, 40 percent through use of fund resources (including loans from IMP Trust Fund) and 16 percent was met by deposits from NRIs.

Column 3 includes assets at the Reserve Bank of India, gold holdings of RBI and SDR holdings of the Government of India. All figures are in U.S. millions of dollars. Column 2 includes foreign currency assets of RBI at the end of the year. Column 4 denotes net withdrawals from the IMF Trust Fund.

When the Seventh Five Year Plan (1985-1990) was originally designed, the trade deficit was projected to be Rs. 20,000 crores for all five years. Within two years of its operation the alarming figures of trade deficit made tile government revise these projections to Rs. 23,000 crores for the five year.

The actual figures were worse than even adjusted projections. In the first two years the average trade deficit figures were Rs. 12,000 crores per year. The deficit in trade was partly because of liberalized import policy that was started at the behest of Late Rajiv Gandhi administration and partly due to over emphasized export growth that did not quite materialize. The import licenses for machinery, manufactured goods, computer products were distributed liberally, the oil prices worldwide had an upward pressure and the overall trend in increased petroleum products imports did not diminish. The trade deficit that was getting out of hand created an extra-ordinary pressure on foreign debt as witnessed in Table 2.

As seen in Table 2 the total debt from outside sources amounted to Rs. 118,906 crores in 1991. Indian export failed to make a significant dent in the world markets and imports were increasing.

Table 2 also points out that in the period under consideration, the share of external assistance declined and the

Table 2
India's Foreign Debt In Seventh Plan

Year	*External*	*Commercial*	*IMF*	*NRI*	*Total*
1986	26638	7647	5285	5650	45220
1987	32312	10321	5547	7847	56027
1988	36578	12876	4732	10054	64240
1989	46838	18034	3696	14154	83722
1990	54100	22065	2572	17831	96568
1991	66314	26706	5132	20754	118,906

Source: See Misra and Puri in bibliography, page 443. Column 2 records all external assistance, column 3 reports external commercial borrowing, column 4 reports total liability to the International Monetary Fund, column 5 reports deposits by NRIs and column 6 is the total of all debt. All figures are in crores of Rupees.

share of commercial borrowing and NRI deposits increased. This change in the external debt composition raised the average cost of external debt in the late 1980s.

Thus the Seventh Plan period significantly changed the composition of balance of payments of the Indian economy. It not only was clear that the increasing imports were putting added pressure on deficit in current account but also the external assistance to the country was more in the form of repayment obligations rather than external financial assistance as was the case in earlier years. By 1990 therefore the country had a severe capital account crisis to deal with. As seen in Table 2 in 1990 the external assistance reached to Rs. 54,100 crores and the total debt increased to Rs. 96568 crores. In 1991 there was a sign of reversal to this trend as external borrowing further increased to Rs. 66,134 crores and total foreign debt increased to Rs. 118,906 crores.

As a result, could only the country afford imports for three weeks, the Rupee value was arbitrarily kept high, NRI deposits were attracted with unusually high interest rate and there were very few alternatives than to request IMF to give special aid to revert the financial crisis.

1991-92 was the year of several drastic changes. As the new government was elected and a new budget was announced, new path to international trade was charted. With IMF's insistence the Rupee value was devaluated to bring it closer to natural (or market) rate of Rs. 31 = 1$, and a new liberalization program was announced that invited foreign direct investment in the economy with an open heart. A tremendous growth in foreign interest in the Indian economy was witnessed by increased capital inflow, increase in exports (led by exports of computer software), increased business activity and enhanced confidence and clearance of numerous foreign collaborations. Indian economy grew at the fastest rate ever witnessed in the modem era.

Clearly the opening of international trade was the main mantra of the 1990s that solved several of the economic problems. Devaluation of the Indian Rupee improved export performance and reduced imports after 1992. In 1994 and 1995 the Gross Domestic Product increased with a 6% annual rate. Another main benefit of these economic reforms was the tremendous increase in foreign direct investment (FDI hereafter). In 1991-92 the share of FDI was 3.3%, but it increased to 14% in 1992-93 and then to 45% in 1993-1994. Roughly 19,000 foreign collaborative production ventures were sanctioned between 1991 to December 1994 bringing in Rs. 130 billion north of investment.

Other economic indicators also showed positive gains, inflation has been under 10% for two years in a row, employment has been growing and per capita income for the first time increased at a 2% rate. The balance of payments performance thus improved in a significant way after embracing the market oriented policies. As witnessed in Kulkarni (1996) there is a new demand for full convertibility of Indian rupee that can help the balance of payments performance in the future.

SECTION-II

SUMMARY AND CONCLUSION

The main aim of this chapter was to review the capital account changes in the Indian BOP. It was abundantly clear that the deficit in trade balance had to be financed by either borrowing commercially or publicly. The Indian government received a crisis situation when the supply of foreign reserves almost evaporated in 1989 and 1990. The devaluation of the Indian Rupee, together with the newly instituted economic reform helped salvage the situation in 1991. The gains from economic liberalization are witnessed in modern times in terms of the betterment of economic output as well as the increased consumer surplus.

REFERENCES

Agarwal, M., "Liberal Capital Flows and Management of India's Balance of Payments", in Ashok Guha edited, Economic Liberalization. Industrial Structure and Growth in India. New Delhi, India. 1992.

Government of India, Economic Surveys. New Delhi, 1977-78, 1990-91, 1992-93.

Holla, K.R., "Recent Trends in India's Balance of Payments", Chapter 28, in M. Thomas Paul edited, International Monetary, Banking and Trade Systems and Economic Development, National Institute of Bank Management, Pune, India, 1992.

Kochar M.G., "India's Balance of Payments: Problems and Prospects", Chapter 27, in M. Thomas Paul edited, International Monetary, Banking and Trade Systems and Economic Development. National Institute of Bank Management, Pune India, 1992.

Kulkarni, Kishore and Chakraborty Debasish, "India's External Debt: An Exception to the International Debt Crisis", International Journal of Development Banking Vol. '1, No.1, January 1989, pp. 31-39.

Kulkarni, Kishore, "India's Balance of Payments: A Review of Her Current Account Since Independence", paper presented in Association of Indian Economic Studies International Conference in Mumbai, May 1996.

Kulkarni, Kishore, "Full flexibility of Indian Rupee: Sooner the Better", Social Engineer, Vol. 5, No.1, January 1996, pp. 70-78.

MacDougall, Donald, "India's Balance of Payments Problems", Chapter 9 in P.N. Rosenstein Roden Edited, Pricing and Fiscal Policies: A Study in Method, London, George Allen and Unwin, pp. 175-211, 1964.

Misra, S.K., and Puri, V.K., " A Textbook of Indian Economy", Himalaya PUblishing Company Mumbai, 1992, Chapter 29.

Nayyar, Deepak, "India's Exports and Export Policies in 1960s", Cambridge University Press, London, 1977.

Roy Choudhury, S.P., "India's Balance of Payment Position: an Overview of the Trend, Perspective and Consequences", Paper included in M. Thomas Paul edited, International Monetary, Banking and Trade Systems and Economic Development, National Institute of Bank Management, Pune India, 1992.

Sarma, Y.U.K., "India's Balance of Payments 1948-49 to 1984-85: Survey", Journal of the Indian School of Political Economy, Vol. No.2, July-December 1989, pp. 270-301.

Srinivasan, T.N., "India's Economic Reforms: Task Ahead", Address at the Seminar on Structural Adjustment and Policy Reforms: Perspectives from International Experiences, April 4, 1994, New Delhi, pp. 1-22.

16

FULL CONVERTIBILITY OF THE INDIAN RUPEE: SOONER THE BETTER

There has been much discussion about the anticipated full convertibility of the Indian Rupee recently in Indian political and economic circles, but little action has been taken to make the "main" decision. At present time, Indian Rupee is convertible only on the current account, meaning that one can get foreign exchange from a bank only if one has some export to back up for this transaction. The Free Trade Zones (FTZ) established in major cities are the only areas that can have privilege of this restricted trading ability in foreign exchange. Moreover foreign investment in terms of financial assets purchase is strictly prohibited for personal investment.

It is argued in this chapter that for the full benefits from free international trade and exchange, the economically most efficient thing to do is to have full convertibility on the capital account for the financial flows to move freely in and out of the economy. What are the theoretical arguments for a full convertibility? In other words, what are the costs and consequences of limited convertibility in a free trade atmosphere?

Answers to these questions will give some idea of urgency of full convertibility as a policy action on the part of Indian

---

*First draft of this chapter was presented in Association of Indian Economic Studies (AIES) meeting in January 1996 in San Francisco, California. It is based on article published in Social Engineer, 1999.

policy makers. In this paper we also discuss theoretical implications of insistence by the authorities to keep the exchange rate under control. Moreover, Section 1 also discusses theoretical benefits from fully flexible exchange rate. Section 2 makes a case for going to full convertibility of the Indian Rupee as early as possible to avoid further depreciation of the Indian Rupee value in terms of the major currencies. This is accomplished by a review of recent changes in export, import and financial flows of Indian economy.

In the political circles it is many times pointed out that the authorities are successful in holding the value of Indian Rupee equal to 31 Rs. = 1 US$ for the last two-three years. In fact some bold and adventurous analysts have argued that there is a chance that the Rupee may even appreciate after the full convertibility. In this chapter we argue that fixed exchange rate for the last two years has little meaning because trade as well as financial transactions were so severely controlled and the expectation of appreciating Indian Rupee in the near future is over-optimism.

SECTION-I

THEORY OF CONTROLLED EXCHANGE RATE

In simple theoretical terms it can be safely stated that the very fact they authorities find it necessary to control exchange rate, there is a reason to seriously doubt that the real (or natural) exchange rate is higher than the controlled one. Further, we shall also argue that there is a great likelihood of Indian Rupee depreciating by big margins despite the apparent constant value of the last three years in terms of the U5 $. On a preliminary theoretical level, it is very easy to point out a need for full convertibility by using simple analysis of foreign exchange market which determines equilibrium exchange rate. If foreign exchange is defined by the "bunch of foreign currencies," then the market of foreign exchange has two important forces: quantity of foreign exchange demanded and the quantity of foreign exchange supplied. Both these demand and supply forces are derived from forces of export and import. As domestic residents import more they create demand for foreign exchange, and as foreign residents buy more of domestic goods and services (read as "domestic export go up") there is higher quantity of foreign exchange supplied.

Quantities of foreign exchange demanded and supplied determine the "price" of foreign exchange namely the exchange rate. The American way the exchange rate is defined as the number of domestic currency units per unit of the foreign currency (Note that this definition is the inverse of the European way of defining exchange rate which defines exchange rate as the number of foreign currency units per unit of the domestic currency).

When the exchange rate goes up the quantity of foreign exchange demanded is expected to go down because an increase in exchange rate depreciates the domestic currency, and domestic imports are expected to decline (assuming a high enough elasticity of demand for import with respect to the exchange rate).

Thus the demand for foreign exchange curve is sloping downwards from left to right. On the other hand as exchange rate goes up the quantity of foreign exchange supplied is expected to go up because with the increased exchange rate the domestic exports become cheaper, and foreign residents are expected to demand more domestic exports assuming a large enough elasticity of the demand for export with respect to the exchange rate change. This creates an upward sloping supply of foreign exchange curve from left to right as shown in Figure 1.

With the given demand and supply curves of foreign exchange, the equilibrium exchange rate is determined by the point of intersection of these curves such as at point J where the exchange rate is ER_1. Without governmental control over the foreign exchange transactions, the exchange rate is expected to be at ER_1 because of the "Paradox of Flexibility."

The Paradox of Flexibility is simply stated as, "if any price is fully flexible, then it remains at the (same) level of equilibrium." It is proven by the fact that at any exchange rate above equilibrium, there happens to be excess supply of foreign exchange which pushes exchange rate back to the equilibrium

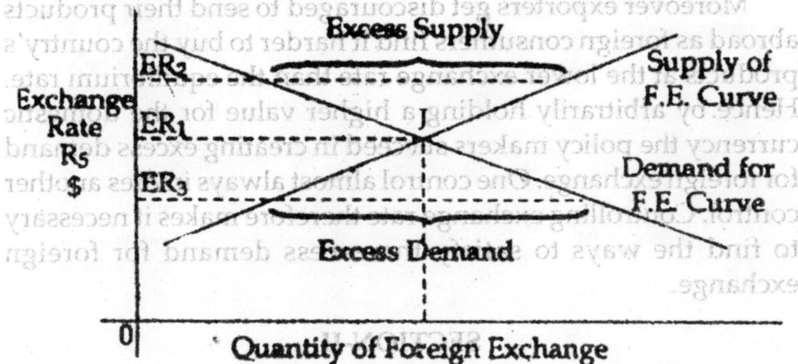

Figure 1 : Foreign Exchange Market Equilibrium

level. At any exchange rate below equilibrium, there is excess demand for foreign exchange that pushes the exchange rate up to the equilibrium. For whatever reasons, if governmental authorities do not allow exchange rate to be decided by the market forces then they have to decide at what level they would keep it controlled. Clearly no control is needed to keep the exchange rate at the equilibrium, as market forces are strong enough to drive it to equilibrium. Hence governmental authorities need to decide whether the controlled exchange rate should be above or below the equilibrium exchange rate.

Notice that at any exchange rate above equilibrium, there is excess supply of foreign exchange, which no controlling authority wants to create on purpose. Also at any rate above equilibrium, the exporters gain and importers lose, hence the domestic production will be artificially driven out of the country. Clearly no controlling authority wants to do that either.

Hence the government would select the controlled exchange rate that is necessarily below the equilibrium exchange rate. Now at any exchange rate below equilibrium, the market of foreign exchange experiences excess demand for foreign exchange. This arises because the importers benefit by the lower exchange rate as they can buy foreign products more conveniently than if the exchange rate was at equilibrium level.

Moreover exporters get discouraged to send their products abroad as foreign consumers find it harder to buy the country's products at the lower exchange rate than the equilibrium rate. Hence by arbitrarily holding a higher value for the domestic currency the policy makers succeed in creating excess demand for foreign exchange. One control almost always invites another control. Controlling exchange rate therefore makes it necessary to find the ways to satisfy the excess demand for foreign exchange.

SECTION-II

INDIAN EXPERIENCE OF CONTROLLED EXCHANGE RATE

There are several policy alternatives that government can adopt to satisfy the excess demand for foreign exchange. They are as follows: (a) There is an option of borrowing foreign exchange from the countries that have excess supply of foreign exchange, or from international lending institutions like the International Monetary Fund. Indian authorities have used both sources extensively in the past.

In fact the Aid India Consortium, a special group of countries that is interested in giving special aid to India, is very active and is helping Indian planners. (b) The second option is to stop the domestic consumer from importing freely from the foreign countries. This calls for strict import licensing and controls. India has used this arrangement from after independence and in a smaller extent even before independence from the British rule. Controls on import transactions and licensing policies give a bigger window of operation to bureaucracy and favoritism.

It becomes a prestige issue to have import licenses and one has witnessed great evidence of this bureaucracy in India over the period of time. (c) The third option is to control the foreign exchange transactions themselves so that even if the demanders are demanding higher amounts of foreign exchange the policy makers will not allow them to have free convertibility of the domestic currency to any other currency. This gives the domestic currency a "soft currency" status and the free transactions of this currency are strictly controlled. Again we get yet another excuse for bureaucracy and additional controls lead to further restrictions on the free transactions of the public. Indian authorities have used these controls very efficiently as well as the other policy alternatives monitored above.

The continuous existence of exchange rate below equilibrium level also makes it mandatory that the country not only save the foreign reserves but also search for resources to acquire the new ones. These efforts usually are in vain because the suppliers of the foreign reserves do not have great intentions of supplying them. All in all the controlled exchange rate makes a country swamped with regulations, controls, rules and bureaucracy. Visitors to India have witnessed all of these consequences first hand. The solution for all this status quo is the acceptance of full convertibility.

Changes in capital account of Indian balance of payments are reported in Table 1 of next page. It is important to notice that while a continuous balance of trade deficit necessitated the Indian economy to either borrow from the Non-Resident Indians (NRI) in terms of loans, the capital outflows have also to be curtailed by limiting the imports of the country.

Since the independence (from the British rule) Indian government has been using the double-edged sword of borrowing from abroad and controlling the foreign exchange outflows. As seen in Table 1. A trade deficit was non-existent only in three years, 1972, 1976 and 1977. In fact the trade deficit to substantial number after 1979 as the Indian economy was beset by the second oil crisis and heavy machinery and other technologically essential goods had to be imported. The exchange rate vis-a-vis U.S. dollar depreciated significantly after 1990 and the deposits of NRI were substantial after 1986. They continued to grow in 1994 before marginally declining in 1995.

In a recent paper Srinivasan (1995) has commented on the issue of convertibility with a different angle. He mentions, "A policy event of major significance is the adoption of the IMF section 8 convertibility of the Rupee in September 1994. The Finance Minister (Dr. Manmohan Singh) is reported to have said than even full convertibility is likely within a year or two since in his view fundamentals for such decision are in place. I am not entirely persuaded. Full convertibility involves freeing capital markets. Unless the Rupee freely floated, this would complicate the task of exchange rate management." (see Srinivasan (1994) listed in bibliography).

Table 1
India's Balance of Payment: Exchange Rate, Trade Balance and Foreign Reserves From NRI Investment

Year	*Exchange rate Rs./U.S. dollar*	*Trade deficit millions of dollar*	*Foreign Reserves*
1970	7.57	131	612
1971	7.27	372	778
1972	8.08	-68	280
1973	8.20	191	512
1974	8.15	625	-824
1975	8.93	286	1007
1976	8.88	-787	884
1977	8.20	-932	21
1978	8.18	884	607
1979	7.90	2222	533
1980	7.93	5644	647
1981	9.09	5711	609
1982	9.63	4820	322
1983	10.49	4098	1371
1984	12.45	4025	2064
1985	12.16	5616	1692
1986	13.12	5438	2244
1987	12.87	5777	4208
1988	14.94	6581	5284
1989	17.03	6110	4899
1990	18.07	5151	4141
1991	25.83	1610	5242
1992	26.20	3310	4491
1993	30.50	3924	5140

Source: International Financial Statistics, (IFS) Yearbook, publication of International Monetary Fund, 1994.

Nonetheless he goes further to emphasize that the situation is not ripe enough to embrace full convertibility right away.

While we agree with the overall zest of Prof. Srinivasan's argument, we have in this chapter pointed out that the time has been most suitable for the full convertibility ever since the foreign reserve stock had reached a comfortable level. In fact the sooner Indian authorities allon freely floating Rupee with full convertibility on capital as well as current account. The better it is for the foreign investment attraction. Moreover politically it makes sense to show the rest of the world community the full extent of the policy commitment that started in 1991.

As one can easily point out the Indian economy has a long road ahead in terms of liberalization. While much ado has been made in terms of sanctioning the foreign investment projects there are still areas that need much work in terms of further liberalization. More specifically, the banking and financial sector is still heavily controlled, import licensing is still not easily available to a common person, and the insurance industry needs to take several strides before it can be called fully open for free competition.

Nonetheless in many respects 1995 was an year of encouraging news. Even though agricultural growth rate was moderate of 2.2% the industrial sector improved production with an impressive rate of 8.0%. This is reflected in real GDP growth rate of 5.3%. Foreign Exchange reserves reached to $19.5 billion and foreign direct investment amounted to $4.00 billion. With a trade balance deficit of $2.03 billion, there was a clear need for increasing exports from $26.22 billion. The imports were $28.25 billion which obviously were the highest ever in the history of India.

Imports increased basically because of a sharp decline in the average tariff rate that was on the average 50% in 1995, much lower than the 300% that Indian importers paid in as late as 1991. Thus there is enough statistical evidence to believe that the Indian economy is doing much better in 1995 than in 1991. However what lies in future is as hard to predict as the election results of January 1996. In economic terms it is seen that flexible exchange rate can attract much needed capital at least in short run and in the long run export performance of

Indian economy is expected to be much improved because of competition from outside.

SUMMARY AND CONCLUSIONS

In this chapter we intended to show by using basic economic theory, effects of a controlled exchange rate and compared them with the consequences of a freely floating exchange rate. The main conclusion is that while controlled exchange rate, by its very nature, invites more restrictions on trade and foreign exchange transactions, the freely floating exchange rate can enable governmental authorities to reduce the plethora of regulations on trade and foreign exchange transactions. Also it is recognized that controlled exchange rate is always less than the equilibrium (or market determined) exchange rate and any attempt to make a full convertibility of a currency will raise the exchange rate further, irrespective of the foreign reserve holding by the government. Nonetheless an increase in exchange rate lowers the quantity of imports and raises the amount of exports of the economy. This further reduces a burden on deficit in balance of trade and imposes natural limits on goods and services bought and sold in international markets. The time is ripe for Indian authorities who quite possibly have a real inclination of market freedom and economic liberalization to take a quick action in terms of making Indian Rupee fully flexible. The longer we wait worse it gets in terms of expectational changes and market adjustments.

BIBLIOGRAPHY AND REFERENCES

IMF Survey, "Full Convertibility is Important Goal in An Independent Global Economy", April 8, 1995, pp. 113-117.

International Monetary Fund Publications, *International Financial Statistics Yearbook*, Washington D.C 1994.

Kulkarni, Kishore "India's Foreign Trade and Balance of Payment", A chapter in J.S. Uppal edited, India's Economic Problems, Fourth Edition, Tata-McGraw Hill Publications, New Delhi, 1996.

Kulkarni, Kishore, "Balance of Payment Changes and the Exchange Rate Devaluation: A Case of India", a paper presented in Association of India Economic Studies Meeting, Washington D.C, January 1995.

Marathe S. S., "Economic Reform: Some Lessons from the Past", Sixth CD. Deshmukh Endowment Memorial Lecture, National Insurance Academy, June 7, 1995.

N. Chandra Mohan, "Rupee Devaluation: A Wise Idea?", *Business Inditl,* March, 13-26,1995, pp. 41-42.

Srinivasan, T.N., "India's Economic Reforms: Developments Since the Budget for 1994-1995", Paper Presented in Association of Indian Economic Studies meeting, Washington D.C, January 1995.

17

LESSONS FOR INDIA FROM THE RECENT FINANCIAL AND ECONOMIC CRISIS IN SOUTHEAST ASIA

INTRODUCTION

That the much-celebrated "Economic Miracle" in Southeast Asia came to a chaotic end in 1997 is now widely accepted in the academic community. Few would argue that after three decades of unbridled economic expansion, five Southeast Asian economies-Thailand, Indonesia, Malaysia, Philippines, and South Korea saw their currencies and stock markets crash and their financial systems collapse, all within a matter of months. Explanations of Asia's financial ruin have ranged from allegations of financial mismanagement and crony capitalism to IMF complacency and negligence in dealing with the crisis. Subsequent financial turmoil in Russia and Brazil has only served to intensify the criticisms against the IMF.

This chapter attempts to weave through the alternate theories of the crisis by utilizing economic data in order to conduct a critical and comparative analysis of the same. The chapter specifically considers the case of the Indian economy in order to answer two main questions. First, can other economies (especially India) learn any lessons from the

This Chapter is based on an article published in Journal of Business and Economic Perspectives (Co-author: Dr. Meenakshi Rishi).

financial crisis in Southeast Asia? And second, are there any steps that policy makers can take in order to avoid similar financial woes?

The chapter is organized as follows. The next section examines several competing perspectives on the onset and spread of the financial and economic crisis in the above-mentioned Southeast Asian economies. This section also establishes the importance of analyzing external debt statistics of the affected countries in order to gain a better understanding of the crisis. This is followed by a cross-country comparison of key external debt indicators for the involved countries and the Indian economy. The motivation is to ascertain whether external debt statistics such as total debt service paid in recent years, the commitments of repayment, interest paid on loans, the duration on loans from abroad, and recent balance of payment changes provide (any) indications of impending financial crisis. The implications of this cross-country analysis for the Indian economy are discussed in the concluding section of the chapter that also offers a policy perspective on the efficacy of capital controls in financially vulnerable economies.

THE FINANCIAL AND ECONOMIC CRISIS IN SOUTHEAST ASIA

The contrast in academic attitude toward Southeast Asia is obvious even to the casual observer. Economic publications of the early 1990s that had touted the achievements of the "tiger" economies were pondering the causes for and the extent of the "Asian flu" in the late 1990s. While it is hard to ascertain the authenticity of the erstwhile Asian miracle, even skeptics agree that the economies of South Korea, Malaysia, Indonesia and Thailand had all generated impressive growth rates and recorded fiscal surpluses with moderate current account deficits and low rates of inflation over the years 1994 to 1996. In fact, Indonesia, Korea, and Thailand had also registered capital account surpluses and increases in reserves prior to the emergence of the currency crisis and the ensuing financial panic in the second quarter of 1997. Thus, judging solely on the basis of macroeconomic indicators, it would appear that the Asian economic crisis was quite different from the financial crisis of Central and Latin America, where the latter were fuelled by domestic demand and current account deficits.

All of the above-mentioned Southeast Asian economies had embarked on a process of capital account liberalization during the 1980s and 1990s in an effort to attract short and medium term capital. Since interest rate yields were relatively high in these countries and because their currencies were tied to the U.S. dollar, private capital flows to these countries soared, surging to $93 billion for the five affected economies in 1996. At the same time, domestic banks and financial intermediaries also began borrowing internationally in order to lend locally.

While there was nothing outwardly wrong with this scenario, signs of trouble began to emerge in the late 1990s as the pace of economic activity faltered. These countries started amassing current account deficits which resulted in an erosion of their international competitiveness. In the second quarter of 1997, Thailand recorded a deficit in its capital account, which in combination with a deficit in the current account led to harried currency stabilization attempts by the central bank. However, despite a concerted effort to maintain the value of the Baht, the fourth quarter of 1997 saw reserve losses and increased capital outflows from the economy. At this juncture, the central bank had no choice but to let the domestic currency float to an all-time low. This "flu" soon spread to Indonesia, South Korea, and Malaysia that suffered similar capital outflows and currency collapses. The World Bank has estimated that between June 1997 and January 1998, private capital outflows from Southeast Asian economies totaled $12 billion and that the median currency devaluation for the affected economies was close to 80 percent.

Economists have now attempted to identify the exact causes for the capital account reversals experienced by Southeast Asian economies. The Bank of International Sentiments (1998) theorizes that short-term debt fuelled over investment and created speculative bubbles that caused these economies to become vulnerable to "swings of sentiment in international capital markets." Interestingly enough, almost seven decades before the Asian crisis, Taussing (1928, p. 130) had highlighted the potentially destabilizing role of capital outflows in precipitating financial crises. The following quote from the author is illustrative.

Loans from the creditor country begin with a modest amount, then increase and proceed to a crescendo. They are likely to be made in exceptionally large amounts towards the culminating stage of a period of activity and speculative upswing continues. With the advent of crisis, they are at once cut down sharply or even cease entirely. The interest payments on the old loans are no longer offset by any new loans; they become instantly a new charge to be met by the borrowing country. A sudden reversal takes place in the debtor country's international balance sheet; it feels the consequences abruptly, in an immediate need of increased remittances from creditor country, in a strain on its banks, high rates of discounts (interest) and falling prices. When this period of irregular movements has run its course, the debtor country has more to remit on its interest account than to receive on principal account and that remittance is effected by an excess of merchandise exports over imports.

Insofar as other explanations of the crisis are concerned, Ryan (1999) doubts whether the Asian "miracle" was genuine and attributes the 1997 crisis to non-historical economic events, such as, fiscal prudence in anticipation of overheating due to capital inflows. In this regard, Ryan's analysis is in marked contrast to Krugman's (1998) hypothesis that faults money financed budget deficits for reserve depletion and the eventual collapse of exchange peg in the Southeast Asian economies. However, both Ryan (1999) and Krugman (1998) agree that the Southeast Asian prosperity of the 1980s was more due to a tremendous spurt in resource mobilization and less due to any shifts in productivity. This line of reasoning suggests that the financial crisis of the 1990s is largely attributable to the diminishing returns to scale that accrued the amassed resources in this region.

Theories aside, it is a matter of fact that in the second quarter of 1997, Southeast Asian economies began to show signs of strain in their trade deficit situation and an increase in their foreign debt burden, all of which contributed to the chain reaction that culminated in the loss of investor confidence in these countries. The loss of confidence in turn contributed to capital outflows, depreciating currencies, and decline in asset values. Once the "bubble" burst, the crisis escalated into a full-blown financial meltdown that was fueled by perceptions of weakness in the Southeast Asian economies. There is evidence that supports the fact that domestic investors were the major participants in the outflow of capital that precipitated the financial crisis-an experience not unlike that of Mexico facing its Peso crisis of 1994-95. The similarities between the Southeast Asian crisis and the Mexican crisis have been aptly prophesied by Jackson (1996, page 39).

A massive current account deficit, a crippling foreign debt burden and excessive monetary growth encouraged speculators to attack its currency. This is a description of Mexico before its financial meltdown in December 1994 but could now sum up several fast growing Asian economies. Thanks to economic woes and political turmoil, the currencies of Thailand, Malaysia and Indonesia have all been attacked this year.

As the crisis situation deteriorated, the IMF stepped in and imposed its fiscal austerity plan on the afflicted economics that called for cutbacks in government spending, increases in interest rates, the immediate shutdown of failed financial institutions, and the repayment of foreign creditors. In return, the Fund provided $4 billion to Thailand, $10 billion to Indonesia and $21 billion to Korea and additional assistance came from the World Bank and the Asian Development Bank. However, the IMF's handling of the Asian crisis came under sharp attack as restrictive macroeconomic policies plunged these economies into a deep recession and poverty. In the winter of 1998, the IMF was forced to renegotiate its economic plan with the crisis-affected economies. While specific details varied from country to country, the IMF relaxed its demand for restrictive fiscal policies and immediate bank closures, although it defended its stance on interest rates.

THE ASIAN CRISIS AND INDIA: A CROSS-COUNTRY COMPARISON

To date the Indian economy has successfully escaped the phenomenal financial crisis faced by Thailand, Malaysia, Philippines, South Korea, and Indonesia. Some argue that this is due in part to strict financial control, a responsible monetary policy, and a stable, albeit increasing trade imbalance. Nonetheless, a balance-of-payments crisis in 1991 and a subsequent structural adjustment program, a continued increase in capital inflows, as well as a worsening trade deficit have all been areas of concern for many scholars. As Parchure (1998) warns, "Any country which is internationally indebted and whose current account is in deficit is already in crisis. If, in addition, the government of that country has tacitly or explicitly promised her citizens and/or international investors to maintain the external value of her currency, the crisis can be precipitous." Of special concern to Indian economists is the fact that the balance of foreign reserves with the Indian Reserve Bank is largely illusionary since it reflects external borrowing and does not constitute any real earnings for the country. In light of the above, several economists have averred that the Indian economy is on the verge of a financial crisis that can be averted only by a devaluation of Indian Rupee. For instance, Kulkarni (1997) has recommended an explicit devaluation of the currency to ensure that the value of the Rupee is set by market forces as opposed to being determined by the whims of policy authorities.

The question before us then, is to determine how the Indian situation compares with that of the crisis-ridden Asian economies. The cross-country comparison is intended to shed light on some of the issues raised above. In particular, the remainder of this section utilizes statistics on external borrowing, balance-of-payments data, and the burden of external debt in order to investigate whether these debt indicators suggest any warning signs for the Indian economy. The following cross-country analysis will also focus on the nature of India's external debt, particularly with respect to its composition and its term to maturity.

Table 1 lists debt service payments (and for some years debt service due) for each of the Southeast Asian economies under review and for India over the 1980 to 1997 time period. The table indicates that total debt serviced for Indonesia has registered a consistent increase since 1987, almost tripling over the 11-year period from 1987 to 1997. While the Malaysian, Philippine, and South Korean figures are not as alarming; the case of Thailand suggests that total debt service has almost doubled over the 1990s, reaching a record $11.7 billion in 1997. In this context, the Indian situation is also somewhat worrisome. In 1986, India's debt service paid increased substantially (to $5.6 billion dollars) and remained at high levels throughout the late 1980s. Following a steady increase from 1988 to 1995, the total debt service totaled $12.66 billion in 1996, although the amount has since declined to $10.8 billion in 1997. A rising debt service burden is open to interpretation. On one hand, when a higher amount of debt is retired every year, it perpetuates the image of solvency and translates into greater investor confidence and a higher future supply of external credit. On the other hand, an increasing debt service burden also signifies an increasing level of indebtedness, which can constrict the supply of external credit. In the Indian case, the increased debt service payments can be taken as a sign of greater strength rather than weakness. This is largely due to the liberalization of the economy since 1991 and the mostly optimistic view regarding the economy in lending circles.

Table 2 provides information on total debt service expressed as a percentage of export earnings and as a percentage of GNP. Similar to Table 1, this table also highlights the tremendous burden of debt on the Indonesian economy, which has the highest debt service to GNP ratio among all five Southeast Asian economies. The latest (1997) data suggests that while South Korea and Thailand recorded marginal increase in their debt service to GNP ratio, Malaysia and the Philippines were successful in reducing the same. Insofar as the Indian economy is concerned, debt service as a percentage of GNP has declined from a peak of 10 percent in 1989 to approximately 3 percent in 1997. An examination of India's total debt service

Table 1
The Servicing of Total External Debt

Total Debt Service Paid (U.S.$ million)-X
Total Debt Service Due (U.S.$ million)-Y

Country	*1980*	*1981*	*1982*	*1983*	*1984*	*1985*	*1986*	*1987*	*1988*	*1989*	*1990*	*1991*	*1992*	*1993*	*1994*	*1995*	*1996*	*1997*
Indonesia																		
X	3083	3501	3870	4024	4746	5822	5985	7003	8641	9709	9922	11461	12578	14267	14972	16416	21459	19736
Y										9269	9416	10645	1141	13428	13650			
Malaysia																		
X	934	1145	1524	1924	2731	5399	3526	4453	6057	4338	3571	3042	3099	4205	5042	6021	7657	7109
Y										4139	3402	2854	2924	3921	4648			
Philippine																		
X	2171	2958	3498	3019	2687	2539	2958	3365	3397	3245	3592	3398	4302	4908	4534	5337	5778	4541
Y										4811	4767	4508	5192	4881	4132			
S. Korea																		
X	4449	5920	6348	6429	7161	9048	11222	181%	10461	8765	8279	6051	6973	9173	7923	13081	14750	14548
Y										7895	7366	5076	6222	8385	7815			
Thailand																		
X	1608	1865	1930	2204	2669	3263	3655	3463	4386	4394	5294	4918	5907	9121	9237	8608	8652	11716
Y										3903	4644	4044	5073	8132	7770			
India																		
X	1379	1519	1975	2563	2938	3534	5274	5694	5952	7033	7888	7502	7323	8453	10516	13349	12669	10832
Y										6464	6989	6676	6925	8086	10047			

Note: Total debt service paid is debt service payments on long-term debt (public and publicly guaranteed and non--guaranteed and private non-guaranteed), use of IMF credit, and interest on short-term debt. Total debt service due is contractual debt service payment on long-term debt (public and publicly guaranteed and private non-guaranteed) and the use of IMF credit beginning with 1989.

Source: World Bank, World Debt Tables, Tables, Global Development Finance, various issues.

as a percentage of its export earnings suggests that on average during the 1990s, around 27 percent of the economy's export earnings were diverted toward debt servicing. The corresponding debt service ratio is higher only for Indonesia, averaging 33 percent over the 1990s. While the Malaysian and South Korean debt service ratio was below 10 percent through the 1990s, the Philippines and Thailand averaged debt service ratio was below 10 percent thrcugh the 1990s, the Philippines and Thailand averaged debt service ratio was below 10 percent through the 1990s, the Philippines and Thailand averaged debt service ratios of 20 percent and 14 percent respectively, over the same time period.

Table 2
Total Debt Service as a Percentage of GNP-X Total Debt Service as a Percentage of Export Earnings-Y (U.S. $ millions)

Country	*1989*	*1990*	*1991*	*1992*	*1993*	*1994*	*1995*	*1996*	*1997*
Indonesia									
X	38.4	33.4	343	32.6	33.6	30.7	30.9	36.8	30.0
Y	2.5	2.8	3.2	3.2	3.3	3.6	4.1	3.6	9.5
Malaysia									
X	15.1	12.6	7.4	9.1	8.4	9.0	7.0	8.2	7.5
Y	12.1	10.5	6.5	7.7	7.7	9.2	7.4	8.1	7.6
Philippines									
X	25.4	27.0	23.0	24.4	25.6	18.9	16.0	13.7	9.2
Y	7.7	8.0	7.4	7.9	8.8	7.0	7.0	6.6	5.3
S. Korea									
X	10.8	7.2	7.8	9.4	7.9	8.6	9.4	8.6	
Y	3.3	2.0	2.3	2.7	2.4	2.9	3.0	3.3	
Thailand									
X	16.4	16.9	13.0	13.8	13.7	13.5	11.6	11.5	15.4
Y	6.2	6.2	5.1	5.4	5.6	5.7	5.2	4.8	7.8
India									
X	28.6	31.4	28.6	28.7	26.6	27.6	28.1	24.1	20.4
Y	10.1	9.1	9.4	9.4	9.3	8.4	8.5	9.9	2.9

Source: World Bank, World Debt Tables, Global Development Finance and various issues:

Total debt stocks as a percentage of GNP are reported in Table 3. The table suggests that India has been fairly successful in reducing its debt to GNP ratio over the period under study. In 1993 Indian total debt outstanding was 36.3 percent of GNP, however, this percentage has since registered a significant decline and stood at 25 percent of GNP. However, this percentage has since registered a significant decline and stood at 25 percent of GNP in 1997. By contrast, the other Southeast Asian economies reveal a consistently rising trend of debt stock to GNP and 1997 data places the statistic at greater than 30 percent in every case. Specifically for Indonesia, debt stock as a percentage of GNP has increased from a low of 25.4 percent in 1981 to a high of 65.3 percent in 1997. In Malaysia the percentage registered an all time high in 1986 (84 percent) and has since declined to 50.5 percent in 1997. For the Philippine economy too, the crucial year was 1986-the debt stock to GNP ratio increased to a record 96 percent in 1986 and continued to be high until 1993, registering only a moderate decline over the following four years. In the case of Thailand a steady rise in the debt stock to GNP ratio is suggested by the sharp rise in the statistic from 25 percent in 1980 to 62.6 percent in 1996.

Table 4 presents the ratio of short-term debt to the total debt of a country. It also provides statistics on the ratio of short-term debt to export earnings. A high ratio of short-term to total debt is warning signal for an economy. This is because from the debtor's perspective, long-term debt is preferred to short-term loans because with longer-term debt, the borrower is allowed more time to adjust repayment capability. As a consequence long-term loans typically have a smaller risk of default, which is also beneficial from the creditor's standpoint. Similarly, the smaller the ratio of short-term debt to export earnings, the greater is the ability of a country to repay her debt. In this context, Table 4 reveals that Indonesia has fared the worst as compared to India and other Southeast Asian economies. In 1997, for instance, the ratio of Indonesian short-term debt to export earnings rose to 55 percent, which is higher than the corresponding debt to export earning statistic recorded for every other economy under review. Insofar as the short-term debt to total debt ratio is concerned, both Thailand and South Korea reveal a moderately declining trend since 1995.

Table 3
Total Debt Stocks as a Percentage of GNP

Country	*1980*	*1981*	*1982*	*1983*	*1984*	*1985*	*1986*	*1987*	*1988*	*1989*	*1990*	*1991*	*1992*	*1993*	*1994*	*1995*	*1996*	*1997*
Indonesia	28.0	25.4	29.4	38.9	39.5	40.9	52.2	73.0	63.9	61.3	64.1	65.1	66.4	58.7	63.3	64.6	59.7	65.3
Malaysia	28.0	38.2	52.4	63.6	59.4	69.9	84.5	77.1	56.7	45.6	39.3	39.9	36.4	38.7	36.9	42.5	42.1	50.5
Philippines	53.8	54.3	62.3	71.3	76.8	89.2	96.5	91.3	77.3	68.3	68.8	70.4	60.8	64.1	59.3	51.8	47.3	53.0
S. Korea	48.7	49.3	52.3	50.8	48.4	52.5	45.5	29.8	19.9	14.9	13.9	13.6	14.4	14.4	15.3	25.4	27.4	32.8
Thailand	25.9	31.5	34.8	35.3	36.8	47.8	45.5	40.9	35.7	32.9	33.3	36.9	36.2	37.1	43.1	50.4	50.3	62.6
India	11.9	12.6	14.9	16.0	17.5	19.3	21.3	21.9	20.8	26.4	27.1	31.5	33.6	36.3	34.2	29.2	25.6	24.9

Source: World Bank, World Debt Tables, Global Development Finance, various issues.

Table 4

Ratio of Short Term Debt to Total Debt (%)-X Ratio of Short Term Debt to Export Earnings (%)-Y

Country	*1980*	*1981*	*1982*	*1983*	*1984*	*1985*	*1986*	*1987*	*1988*	*1989*	*1990*	*1991*	*1992*	*1993*	*1994*	*1995*	*1996*	*1997*
Indonesia																		
X	13.2	14.4	18.1	15.4	17.0	10.6	9.0	12.1	12.4	13.4	15.9	17.9	20.5	20.1	17.7	20.9	25.0	26.4
Y	12.5	13.1	22.5	23.3	24.3	17.9	22.5	33.6	31.3	31.1	35.3	42.5	45.3	42.5	34.7	48.9	55.3	54.7
Malaysia																		
X	20.5	17.6	12.9	16.8	13.5	13.2	12.4	10.3	8.6	14.0	11.9	11.6	18.2	29.8	25.0	21.2	27.8	31.6
Y	9.1	11.7	12.0	18.6	13.2	15.1	16.7	11.1	6.52	7.8	5.5	5.2	7.7	12.9	9.4	8.4	11.7	15.6
Philippine																		
X	43.4	45.6	46.9	39.5	38.8	34.4	19.1	12.7	13.3	13.8	14.5	15.2	15.9	14.0	14.5	13.4	19.3	26.0
Y	92.1	107	139	115	116	114	61.2	40.5	35.0	31.0	33.3	33.4	29.8	26.2	23.4	15.9	18.8	24.0
S. Korea																		
X	35.8	31.0	33.3	30.0	27.1	22.8	19.8	23.3	27.4	29.9	30.9	28.2	27.0	25.8	25.5	5.13	39.9	37.5
Y	46.7	37.5	43.8	39.8	33.9	32.4	22.0	16.5	13.7	132	13.9	13.1	13.0	12.2	11.9	38.9	41.7	31.8
Thailand																		
X	43.4	45.6	46.9	39.5	38.8	34.4	19.1	12.7	13.3	13.8	14.5	15.2	15.9	14.0	14.5	49.4	41.4	37.3
Y	92.1	107	139	115	116	114	61.2	40.5	35.0	31.0	33.3	33.4	29.8	26.2	23.4	55.5	49.9	15.7
India																		
X	4.5	5.3	6.9	8.3	8.4	7.6	6.8	6.3	10.9	10.2	10.4	8.4	7.1	3.9	5.1	5.3	7.5	5.3
Y	6.2	8.2	13.3	17.2	17.8	20.1	20.0	29.3	30.5	31.5	32.6	26.1	23.6	11.5	10.9	10.6	12.7	9.5

Source: World Bank, World Debt Tables, Global Development Finance, various issues.

However, these countries currently have the highest percentage of total debt tied up in short term borrowings when compared to all the other Southeast Asian economies and India. In the Indian case, the ratio of short-term debt to total debt is very low and has not exceeded 10 percent since 1991. The ratio of short-term debt to export earnings is also low, although there has been an upward movement in the same over 1995-1996. This increase may have been the result of new governmental initiatives that allowed international financial institutions to sell short-term bonds to non-resident Indians (NRIs).

Table 5 presents the ratio of confessional debt as a percentage of total external debt. Naturally, it is beneficial for debtor governments to borrow more on "confessional" as opposed to "non-concession" terms. Additionally, a greater share of confessional debt to total debt also enables better external debt management for the debtor country. Table 5 indicates a slow reduction in the concessional debt to total debt ratio for all the countries under review. The table also reveals that until 1994, India had done a good job of acquiring concessional debt. Since 1994, the percentage of concessional debt has declined somewhat, although it still compares favourably with the corresponding percentage for the other Southeast Asian economies. The author of this book is of the opinion that the modest decline in the concessional debt portion of India's total debt is mostly due the higher increase in total external debt (denominator) rather than to an actual decline in concessional debt (numerator). Given the political situation in the country in the last two years and India's recent actions in terms of nuclear tests, the concessional debt element of total external debt may be an intriguing area of observation in the near future. Obviously, sustained declines in these ratios can signal a loss of international confidence in the economy.

Table 6 reports data on multilateral debt as a percentage of total external debt. Again, a high percentage of multilateral debt to total debt is preferred as it is beneficial for a borrower to borrow from as many sources as possible in order to minimize risk. A high multilateral debt component also attests

Table 5

Concessional Debt as a Percentage of Total External Debt.

Country	*1980*	*1981*	*1982*	*1983*	*1984*	*1985*	*1986*	*1987*	*1988*	*1989*	*1990*	*1991*	*1992*	*1993*	*1994*	*1995*	*1996*	*1997*
Indonesia	36.4	34.2	30.0	26.7	24.6	27.1	27.3	27.6	27.8	26.7	26.7	26.7	25.4	27.9	29.9	22.5	20.3	17.7
Malaysia	10.1	7.4	4.9	4.1	5.1	6.0	6.9	8.7	10.5	10.9	13.9	14.3	13.0	12.1	13.5	10.6	6.4	4.3
Philippines	6.7	5.8	5.3	6.0	6.4	9.5	11.3	15.2	18.6	19.3	22.7	24.6	27.0	29.0	28.7	26.3	22.8	21.9
S. Korea	9.7	9.4	8.0	7.5	6.7	6.5	7.2	9.5	10.4	10.5	12.8	11.8	10.3	10.0	9.0	3.8	2.8	2.2
Thailand	10.0	9.8	9.6	9.9	10.0	11.5	14.1	17.1	16.9	15.3	15.1	12.6	11.9	11.0	10.2	8.5	7.9	7.1
India	75.3	68.5	59.9	53.5	51.0	48.5	46.2	44.8	42.4	48.6	47.6	46.2	47.0	47.3	48.2	45.8	43.4	41.0

Source: World Bank, World Debt Tables, Global Development Finance, various issues.

Table 6

Multilateral Debt as a Percentage of Total External Debt

Country	*1980*	*1981*	*1982*	*1983*	*1984*	*1985*	*1986*	*1987*	*1988*	*1989*	*199C*	*1991*	*1992*	*1993*	*1994*	*1995*	*1996*	*1997*
Indonesia	8.8	9.9	10.8	11.6	12.2	15.5	17.4	18.4	19.8	20.0	20.4	20.0	18.6	19.9	19.8	16.1	13.4	11.6
Malaysia	11.3	9.2	7.3	6.1	5.5	5.9	6.1	6.9	7.9	9.0	11.3	10.9	9.3	7.0	6.0	4.8	3.5	2.6
Philippines	7.5	8.8	8.7	11.7	11.7	13.1	14.9	16.8	16.5	17.3	20.5	20.5	20.9	21.3	21.2	21.5	19.3	16.1
S. Korea	80	8.3	9.0	9.5	9.1	9.7	11.4	14.8	12.8	11.7	10.8	9.0	7.5	6.8	5.7	2.5	1.8	4.8
Thailand	12.0	12.4	14.7	16.5	16.0	17.7	20.4	21.8	16.8	14.2	13.2	9.9	7.4	6.6	5.1	3.9	3.3	3.8
India	29.5	32.0	31.3	30.7	30.9	30.3	29.5	29.8	80.9	26.8	26.6	28.5	29.1	30.2	31.8	45.8	44.7	31.1

Source: World Bank, *World Debt Tables, Global Development Finance,* various issues.

to the credit-worthiness of the debtor and as such signals a greater willingness to lend on part of the creditor. In this respect, India has done an impressive job in attracting debt from multilateral sources as compared to other Southeast Asian economies. Table 6 indicates that the multilateral portion of India's external debt has steadily increased from 27 percent in 1990 to 46 percent in 1995. The ratio has since declined to 31 percent in 1997. By contrast, all the other Southeast Asian economies under review record a comparatively smaller proportion of multilateral debt to total external debt for the period under observation.

As mentioned above, the ability of an economy to garner long-term loans rather than accumulate short-term debt signifies a well-managed external debt situation. This is because short-term loans need short-term solutions that may be hard to find while long-term loans can be repaid over a longer time period. Further, a higher component of short-term to total debt can easily precipitate a balance-of-payments crisis as explained above in the context of the Asian crisis. Data on the maturity periods of the external borrowing for several Asian economies are presented in Table 7. The table indicates that India is in a comfortable position with regards to the maturity of its external borrowing. In particular, the term period of new commitments for India is on average much higher (some times two to three times higher) than that of the other five Southeast Asian countries from 1980 to 1997. As an illustration, the average terms of new commitments for Indonesia, Malaysia, the Philippines, and Thailand are in the 15-21 year range over the 1980 to 1997 time period. In South Korea the maturity periods are even shorter, averaging approximately 13 years over the 1990s. Insofar as the Indian economy is concerned, table 7 reveals a shortening of the average term of new debt commitments in India over the 1990s (24 years) as compared to the 1980s (26 years). Indeed, Indian policy makers should treat this finding with some degree of concern.

In addition to the average term of new commitments, the interest rate paid on the new commitments is also important

Table 7

Average Terms of New Commitments-Maturity Periods of External Borrowing (In Years)

Country	*1980*	*1981*	*1982*	*1983*	*1984*	*1985*	*1986*	*1987*	*1988*	*1989*	*1990*	*1991*	*1992*	*1993*	*1994*	*1995*	*1996*	*1997*
Indonesia	19.4	16.0	15.0	15.0	16.0	17.2	15.7	19.6	20.6	20.2	20.7	19.1	18.1	18.5	20.3	17.6	19.2	16.2
Malaysia	13.8	14.0	11.0	11 .0	15.0	21 .5	14.4	14.8	17.5	12.1	18.5	18.5	20.9	11 .4	17.81	18.3	18.2	12.8
Philippine	16.6	16.0	16.0	16.0	15.0	10.7	23.4	21.4	22.4	20.1	21.9	22.9	18.6	15.8	16.0	21.8	17.3	25.5
S. Korea	15.3	15.0	14.0	14.0	13.0	11.8	13.0	14.1	19.7	19.7	17.6	11.3	13.0	10.1	11.8	11.6	14.3	16.5
Thailand	16.8	17.0	19.0	20.0	16.0	18.0	16.2	19.1	16.9	12.9	21.3	19.0	17.9	20.0	16.7	14.5	18.4	12.4
India	33.5	33.7	34.4	25.4	2.3.4	25.6	20.2	24.8	22.4	21.3	25.7	20.9	25.0	25.4	27.3	25.9	20.9	22.9

Source: World Bank, *World Debt Tables, Global Development Finance,* various issues.

Table 8
Average Terms of New Commitments-Interest Rate Paid on External Loans

Country	*1980*	*1981*	*1982*	*1983*	*1984*	*1985*	*1986*	*1987*	*1988*	*1989*	*1990*	*1991*	*1992*	*1993*	*1994*	*1995*	*1996*	*1997*
Indonesia																		
Official Creditors	5.4	7.9	8.8	8.5	8.5	6.7	7.0	5.5	4.9	5.6	5.7	6.1	5.2	4.9	4.9	5.1	4.8	6.3
Private Creditors	12.4	9.4	9.1	8.8	9.7	7.7	6.5	6.9	7.0	7.6	7.5	6.3	7.1	6.2	5.0	6.8	6.6	4.9
A11 Creditors	8.1	8.6	9.0	8.7	9.0	7.2	6.7	5.8	5.3	6.1	6.1	6.2	5.9	5.5	4.9	5.7	5.4	5.6
Malaysia																		
Official Creditors	6.7	7.6	8.0	7.1	7.4	8.4	7.5	7.8	4.9	7.0	4.0	6.8	4.7	5.3	7.5	3.4	0.0	7.4
Private Creditors	14.1	13.6	12.4	9.6	9.9	8.8	6.6	5.9	5.7	7.9	9.5	7.6	7.0	5.2	6.4	6.3	6.6	5.9
All Creditors	11.2	12.0	11.6	9.3	9.4	21.5	14.4	6.5	5.2	7.6	5.9	7.4	5.8	5.2	6.8	5.8	6.6	5.9
Philippines																		
Official Creditors	7.1	7.8	9.1	8.5	8.0	7.4	5.2	5.2	4.6	5.5	5.3	4.6	5.8	4.9	5.4	4.3	4.9	3.7
Private Creditors	14.4	14.5	13.4	9.9	9.3	9.0	7.4	8.4	8.0	5.7	9.2	7.3	5.4	5.6	5.3	6.3	7.4	5.9
All creditors	10.2	10.9	11.2	9.1	8.3	8.5	5.3	5.4	5.1	5.5	6.3	5.1	5.7	5.2	5.4	5.1	6.2	4.5
S. Korea																		
Official Creditors	7.4	8.3	10.8	9.0	8.4	7.9	8.4	6.0	6.8	7.0	6.2	7.8	6.9	7.4	6.6	7.1	0.0	6.4
Private Creditors	14.1	13.7	11.4	9.7	9.7	8.6	7.3	7.6	9.0	8.5	8.9	7.7	7.1	5.6	6.0	6.8	6.6	6.8
All Creditors	11.3	12.1	11.3	9.5	9.5	8.5	7.6	7.1	7.6	8.2	7.9	7.7	7.1	5.7	6.0	6.8	6.6	6.6
Thailand																		
Official Creditors	7.1	7.5	8.6	8.0	7.8	5.6	4.5	4.5	4.4	6.4	4.4	3.6	6.0	4.1	4.2	3.8	4.0	5.9
Private Creditors	13.8	13.7	11.1	8.9	9.5	5.6	6.0	6.0	6.6	7.9	6.4	7.7	7.3	5.3	5.6	6.2	6.1	6.6
All Creditors	9.5	10.0	9.3	8.2	8.8	8.3	5.6	5.2	5.5	7.4	5.1	5.0	6.5	4.3	4.8	5.2	4.6	6.0
India																		
Official Creditors	2.1	3.8	6.1	4.6	6.1	5.1	5.2	4.8	5.4	4.6	4.0	4.2	3.9	3.6	3.5	3.2	4.5	3.9
Private Creditors	15.5	11.8	10.2	10.3	9.6	8.3	6.5	7.3	8.0	8.1	8.3	9.5	7.2	7.3	7.6	5.0	5.5	7.0
A1l Creditors	8.8	7.8	8.2	7.5	7.9	5.8	5.7	5.7	6.5	5.8	5.8	5.8	5.3	4.7	4.6	3.4	4.8	5.1

Source: World Bank, *World Debt Tables, Global Development Finance,* various issues.

for a cross-country analysis of external debt. Table 8 reports the interest rates paid by Southeast Asian economies on the new commitments from official as well as private creditors. In terms of a cross-country comparison, the Indian economy appears to in a much better shape than the other economies under consideration. India recorded its highest interest rate payment of 15.5 percent to private creditors in 1980, and its lowest interest rate of 2.1 percent was paid to official creditors in the same year. In 1997 India paid an average interest rate of 3.9 percent to official creditors, 7 percent to private creditors, and 5.1 percent to all creditors combined together. This latter percentage is the lowest when compared to all other Southeast Asian economies in 1997. Insofar as individual countries are concerned, Indonesia paid an interest rate as high as 12.4 percent to private creditors in 1980 and was able to bring the same down to 4.9 percent by 1997. Malaysia had no interest rate commitments to official creditors in 1996. The picture changed in 1997 with Malaysia recording the highest official interest rate (7.4 percent) among all the countries under review. For the Philippines, the lowest interest rate paid was 4.6 percent to official creditors in 1988. However, it also had to borrow at an interest rate of 14.5 percent from private creditors in 1981. South Korea paid its lowest interest rate of 5.6 percent to private creditors in 1993, and its highest interest rate of 14.1 percent was paid out to private creditors in 1980. Thailand's highest interest rate was 13.8 percent and was paid to private creditors in 1980, while its lowest interest rate of 3.6 percent was paid to official creditors in 1991.

Table 9 provides information on interest payments as a percentage of export earnings and reveals that India has recorded a relatively high interest to export earnings ratio in recent years. For instance, the ratio of interest payments to export earnings averages at approximately 12.3 percent for India as contrasted with 2.5 percent for Malaysia and 3.5 percent for South Korea. For Indian economic observers, a high ratio of interest payments to export earnings can be very disturbing. The higher ratios obviously mean that India has consistently paid more interest than any other debt-affected

Table 9

Ratio of Interest Payments to Export Earnings (%)

Country	*1980*	*1981*	*1982*	*1983*	*1984*	*1985*	*1986*	*1987*	*1988*	*1989*	*1990*	*1991*	*1992*	*1993*	*1994*	*1995*	*1996*	*1997*
Indonesia	6.5	6.9	9.1	10.1	11.0	11.9	16.8	15.6	15.6	15.0	12.7	13.6	11.5	11.8	11.1	11.7	11.4	10.2
Malaysia	4.0	5.1	6.5	7.1	8.1	9.0	9.3	7.9	6.7	4.6	3.6	3.1	2.5	2.4	2.1	1.8	1.9	3.0
Philippines	18.2	24.7	29.8	24.5	23.9	21.9	18.5	19.1	18.1	16.9	13.3	11	8.6	11.1	8.6	7.0	5.4	4.5
S. Korea	12.7	14.1	14.7	12.2	12.0	12.8	9.2	5.7	4.2	3.8	3.4	3.2	3.0	2.9	2.7	4.5	4.6	4.1
Thailand	9.4	12.6	11.7	12.5	11.7	13.3	11.0	8.4	7.1	6.0	6.5	7.0	6.3	5.7	5.6	5.7	5.8	7.3
India	4.2	5.0	7.3	9.2	10.6	12.6	14.2	14.0	13.4	17.1	18.2	16.5	15.1	12.8	11.3	9.7	8.5	6.9

Source: World Bank, *World Debt Tables, Global Development Finance*, various issues.

economy in this study. However, current data also suggest a reversal of trend – since 1990 the ratio of interest payments to export earnings has steadily declined and in 1997 it settled down to a fifteen year low of 7 percent.

Table 10 summarizes many of the arguments made above. The table reports the present value of external debt expressed as a percentage of export earnings (PV/XGS) and as a percentage of GNP (PV/GNP). In terms of this analysis, the performance of the Indian economy is mixed at best. For instance, over the 1992-94 time period, the PV/XGS ratio for India was highest among all other Southeast Asian economies. However, over the 1994 to 1996 time period, India's economic performance shows marked improvement, especially in comparison to Indonesia and the Philippines (data for South Korea are not available for these years). The PV/XGS ratios for Thailand and Malaysia indicate better external debt management over the 1994 to 1996 time period. Data for 1997 indicate that although India has succeeded in bringing down its PV/GNP ratio, the PV/XGS remains relatively high when compared to other Southeast Asian economies. In this regard,

Table 10
Key Indebtedness Ratios 1992-1997 (US $ millions)

	1992-1994		*1994-1996*		*1997*	
	PV/XGS	*PV/GNP*	*PV/XGS*	*PV/GNP*	*PV/XGS*	*PV/GNP*
Indonesia	186	54	236	64	215	62
Malaysia	38	34	38	34	48	49
Philippines	163	56	163	56	106	52
S. Korea	45	14			85	30
Thailand	96	39	96	39	121	56
India	214	26	152	22	151	21

Note: PV/XGS is the present value of external debt as a percentage of export earnings.

PV /GNP is the present value of external debt as a percentage of GNP.

Source: World Bank, World Debt Tables, Global Development Finance, various issues. Data for South Korea are not available for the years 1994-1996.

Indian policy should pay attention to boosting export earnings in order to better manage external borrowing and debt servicing.

CONCLUSIONS AND LESSONS FOR INDIA

The purpose of this study was to compare the performance of the Indian economy with that of other debt affected Southeast Asian economies. The comparison was intended to provide us with some answers to the question of the proximity of a financial crisis for the Indian economy. The foregoing analysis suggests that the current Southeast Asian economic crisis may have been abetted by a sustained deficit in the balance of trade that got out of hand well before the onset of financial panic in these countries. Moreover, the reliance on short term borrowing in order to finance the trade deficit probably exacerbated the financial vulnerability of these economies. The increased financial flows were further mismanaged as the Southeast Asian economies allowed domestic money supplies to grow, leading to severe devaluation of their currencies. Finally, as is now clear, the crisis was precipitated by a collapse of confidence, which then led to a downward spiral of capital flight, restricted credit and consequent fragility of the real sector in these economies.

A cross-country comparison of external debt statics indicates that on several accounts the Indian economy is in a much more comfortable position than the Southeast Asian economies considered in this chapter. India's total debt stock in relation to GNP is not alarming, Indian external borrowing is more long-term in nature and Indian external debt has a high multilateral and concessional element, which attests to the credit-worthiness of the economy. Nonetheless, current trends suggest otherwise. This is particularly true with respect to India's declining export earnings and consequent significant rise in the present value of external debt as well as in interest payments as a proportion of export earnings. In this context, it may be accurate to say that the Indian external debt situation exudes an aura of cautious optimism and that external debt management should be an area of policy priority.

Finally, the role played by domestic investors in precipitating the Asian crisis should make Indian policy makers more aware of the issues surrounding the flight of private capital abroad. According to Bidwai, (1997, p. 99) economists at Florida International University have estimated Indian capital flight at $4.4 billion in 1993, $5.8 billion in 1994 and $5.5 billion in 1995 (totaling $15.7 billion). Several scholars and indeed the IMF have now realized the tremendous domestic opportunity cost of such financial outflows and have begun to advocate capital controls in order to stem the outflow of capital.

Capital controls can be of various kinds ranging from restrictions on specific transactions, requirements for foreign investors to keep funds in domestic financial institutions for a specified period of time, or limits on the ability of residents to enter international capital markets. Such capital controls, once widely used, were lifted in many countries on the urging of the IMF. However, the Asian crisis has inspired renewed interest in the experience of countries like Chile, which have maintained some form of controls. In particular, Malaysia imposed capital controls on September 1, 1998. The latter banned transfers between domestic and foreign accounts, and between foreign accounts, shut down the offshore Ringgit market by forcing repatriation of all domestic currency, and enforced tougher regulations on foreign exchange transactions. Ironically, such stringent regulations on the outflow of capital have earned grudging but sure praise for Malaysian Prime Minister Mahatir Mohamad, by none other than the IMF.

However, most academicians agree that the imposition of capital controls is not without substantial costs to the economy. Capital controls limit many of the benefits that arise from the free flow of capital, such as, risk sharing, diversification, growth and technology transfers. Further, controls result in an administrative burden on banks and poorly designed regulations often adversely affect investor confidence and foreign direct investment. Lastly, the corruption creation by evasion of controls itself becomes an unintended cost of the same. In light of the above, economists agree that it is better to attack macroeconomic problems at their source rather than to treat resultant symptoms through capital controls.

Although the crisis in Southeast Asia is now "officially" over, it has provided invaluable lessons to other emerging economies. India in particular needs to realize that short-term capital flows are fair-weather friends and that a consistent slowdown in its export earnings may be enough to cause investor unease, which in turn can propel the economy closer to a flight-fueled financial and economic disaster.

This chapter is based on an article published in Journal of Business and Economic Perspectives co-authored with Dr. Meenakshi Rishi.

REFERENCES

Bank for International Settlements, "68th Annual Report," BIS: Basle, 1998.

Bidwai, Prafulla, "Preventing Capital Flight: Why FERA Must Not Go", Frontline, June 27, 1997, pp. 98-99.

Coresetti, Giancario, Pesenti, Paolo, and Roubini, Nouriel. "What Caused the Asian Currency and Financial Crisis?" NYU working paper (*http://www.stern.nyu.edu*) January 1998.

Hoeing, Thomas, M., "The International Community's Response to the Asian Financial Crisis", Federal Reserve Bank of Kansas City. Economic Review. Second Quarter, 1998 Volume 83, No. 2, pp. 5-8.

Jackson, Sally, (edited), "Asia's Alamo? Terrific Tigers or Ailing Aztecs?" The Australian September 4, 1996.

Krugman, Paul, "What Happened to Asia?" Paul Krugman Homepage, *http:///222.mit.edu/-krugman/*, 1998.

Kulkarni, Kishore, "Full Flexibility of Indian Rupee: Sooner the Better", Social Engineer, January 1996, Vol. 5, No. 1, pp. 70-78.

Marshall, David, "Understanding the Asian Crisis: Systematic Risk as Co-ordination failure". Federal Reserve Bank of Chicago. *Economic Perspectives.* Third Quarter, 1998, pp. 13-28.

Parchure, Rajas, "South East Asian Crisis: Anatomy and Implications", Dyanajoti, National Insurance Academy Publication, Pune publication, January 1998, pp. 1-15.

Ryan, Liam, "The 'Asian Economic Miracle' Unmasked: The Political Economy of the Reality", an Unpublished Paper Presented in the Association of Indian Economic Studies meeting, New York, January 1999, pp. 1-23.

Talele, Chaitram, "The Asian Economic Debacle and India", an Unpublished Paper Presented in the Association of Indian Economic Meetings in New York, January 1999, pp. 1-13.

Tausing, Joseph, "International Economics", New York, Dryden Press Inc., 1928, p. 130.

World Bank, "World Debt Tables", Washington D.C., various issues.

World Bank, "Global Development Finance", Washington D.C., various issues.

18

TWIN DEFICITS REVISITED
Evidence from India, Pakistan and Mexico

INTRODUCTION

In recent years the twin deficits has been subject of investigation for Darrat (1988), Day (1998) and Evans (1986) among others. The decade of 1980s when deficits in budget and trade in case of the U.S. economy behaved more like twins rather than distant cousins, the interest in this topic increased further. However the evidence of twin deficits has not been observed as commonly as the identity of total expenditure and total income would suggest. Moreover the causality of relationship between these deficits is not always observed in any specific direction. However, when the volumes of these deficits are large, the probability of the relationship between them increases significantly.

In this chapter we select countries that traditionally have observed large trade and budget deficits to explore causality between them. India, Pakistan and Mexico have experienced large trade and budget deficits in recent years. The chapter is divided into four sections. Section 1 describes the basic identity in international macroeconomics, which argues that the deficits should have a twin like relationship. It carries out related

This Chapter is based on the paper presented in Western Economic Association meeting in San Diego, CA on July 8-10, 1999.

literature survey to bring out the importance of the problem. Section 2 describes the data from three countries and explains the evidence of twin deficits in India, Pakistan and Mexico. Annual data series for 30 years will be used because it is believed that effect of one deficit on the other is more significant in yearly data than in quarterly data. A summary of economic conditions in these countries is also undertaken in Section 2. Section 3 uses the Granger causality test and VAR technique to find out which deficit affects the other more significantly. Data are tested for stationarity and the regression results are presented. Section 4 serves as a summary and conclusion of the results.

SECTION - I

REASONS FOR EXISTENCE OF TWIN DEFICITS

In simple Keynesian terms the total expenditures of the economy are defined as C + I + G + X – M where C is the consumption on the final goods and services by the consumer sector, I is the investment of the producer sector which includes the expenditure on purchase of machinery tools and equipment, construction activities and an increase in stock of inventories, G stands for the government expenditure on such activities as the welfare payments, defence, transportation etc., X is the value of nation's exports of goods and services and M is the value of nation's imports of goods and services expressed in the domestic currency. The GDP (Y) of an economy can also be defined from sources side as equal to C + S + T*x* where S is the saving and T*x* is the tax revenue of the government.

As it is elaborated in any macroeconomic textbook, [one is Kulkarni (1997, chapter 7)] the level of GDP at which the total expenditure is equal to total income, the equilibrium level of GDP is defined. In terms of Figure 1, it means that Y*e* is the equilibrium level of GDP where the 45-degree line and total expenditure line intersect. [For more information about the specific reasons for the shape of total expenditure line, please refer to Kulkarni (1997, Chapter 7)].

It can be effectively prove that an economy will always produce equilibrium level of GDP. If an economy produces any level of GDP that is higher than equilibrium, say Y_1, then

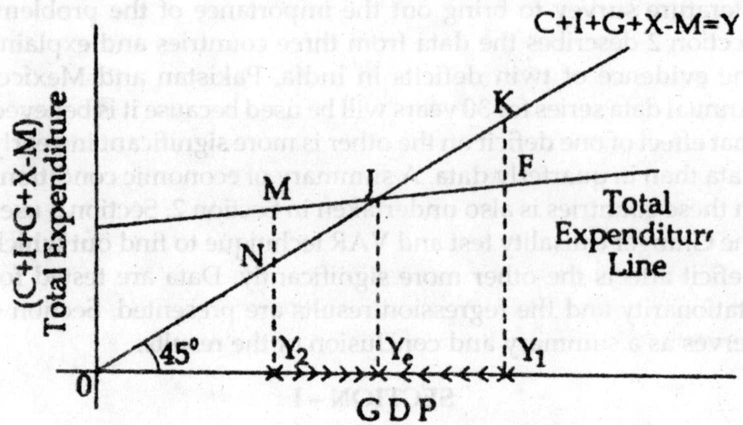

Figure 1: Keynesian Cross and Equilibrium Level of GDP

at Y_1 GDP level, there is higher total income than total expenditure leading to excess supply of goods and services. Due to the excess supply, the prices in the economy will start declining, the expected profit rate or the marginal efficiency of capital will become low, the investment will start declining, future output will decline, unemployment will go up and there will be overall recessionary force in this economy. This recessionary gap will be responsible for making the economy produce the future GDP at lower level than Y_1.

Similarly if the economy by mistake produces GDP less than the equilibrium GDP, say Y_2 then at Y_2 level of GDP the total expenditure is higher than total income leading to excess demand for goods and services. This excess demand is responsible for higher prices leading to higher expected profit rate, higher investment, and higher future output. This condition of the economy because of higher prices is called "inflationary gap". Thus inflationary and recessionary gaps are responsible for making the economy produce no more and no less than the equilibrium level of GDP.

Hence the economy sooner or later has total expenditure equal to total income leading us to write the following fundamental identity

Total Expenditure = Total Income

$$C + I + G + X - M = C + S + Tx \quad (1)$$

Cancelling consumption on both sides of equation (1) and rearranging the terms we get

$$(I - S) + (G - Tx) = (M - X) \quad (2)$$

Assuming stability of the first term in equation (2), and recognizing that second term is the deficit on government's budget, and third term means the trade deficit, we can deduce that the two deficits would be always equal to each other. In fact if one goes up, then the other one would go up too and vice versa. This leads to the conclusion that these deficits act like twins, hence they are called, "Twin deficits".

Equation (2) also forms the basis for Alexander's famous Absorption Approach to the balance of payments. The original formation of this approach is found in Alexander (1952). According to absorption approach, the trade deficit is closely related to budget deficit. Hence any change in other economic variables, (say, for example, change in exchange rate) can bring about a decline in trade deficit, only if it is associated with "austerity program" (meaning reduction in Government Expenditure) on the part of government. Thus success of exchange rate policy is dependent upon how strongly it is supported by the restrictive fiscal policy. More importantly, if trade balance defines the balance of payments (BOP), like it does in cases of underdeveloped countries where capital flows either are severely restricted or are of negligible volume then BOP is in deficit as long as fiscal policy is of expansionary kind. This was also one of the important criticisms of traditional total Keyensian economics which rarely paid attention to the trade balance effects of the expansionary fiscal policy. (For more information on this please see Kulkarni (1983).

The relevance of twin deficits can also be explained in terms of IS-LM-BP curve analysis. Consider Figure 2, which shows the general equilibrium of the economy at point J, where all three markets of the economy: money, goods or commodity, and foreign trade market are in equilibrium. The IS curve shows the locus of combinations of interest rate and GDP at which commodity market is in equilibrium. The commodity market equilibrium is defined by the equality of total expenditure (C + I + G + X - M) and total income.

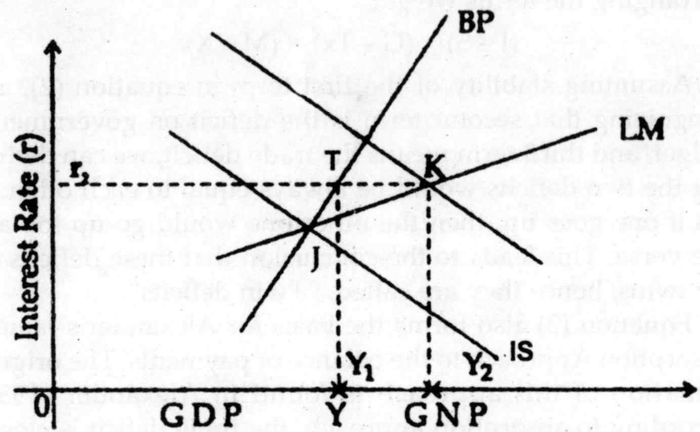

Figure 2: IS–LM–BP Curve Analysis

Similarly LM curve shows the combinations of interest rate and GDP at which money market is in equilibrium. As it is well known in macroeconomic literature, the money market equilibrium is defined by a point at which there is equality of quantity of money demanded and quantity of money supplied.

The combinations of interest rate and GDP that are needed to have BOP = 0, are traced by BP curve. BP curve slopes upwards because if current account and capital accounts are considered to be the main balances on BOP, then a higher GDP is responsible for higher imports which make current account deficit. To compensate this current account deficit by a capital account surplus (and to have BOP = 0) we need to have higher interest rate which would be responsible for capital inflow. Hence higher GDP has to be associated with higher interest rate to have BOP = 0. The point at which all three (IS, LM, and BP) curves intersect is a point where all three markets are in equilibrium simultaneously.

Now consider a change in fiscal policy. If government sector decides to adopt an expansionary fiscal policy (by raising the level of government expenditure, or by lowering the taxes) then first there is a budget deficit created and second this change in terms of Figure 2 is shown by a shift in the IS curve to the right. With the shift of IS curve to the right, the new equilibria of commodity and money market are achieved at point K. At point K however, one can see that there is deficit in BOP. At point K, deficit in balance of payment exists because at point K, GDP is Y_2 and interest rate is r_2. With r_2 interest rate, to have BOP = 0, the GDP required is Y_1. This is evidenced by point T which is on BP curve with r_2 interest rate. At point K we have higher GDP than that is required for BOP = 0. There is a deficit in BOP at point K. Thus an expansionary fiscal policy that necessarily leads to deficit in the budget is also responsible for leading to deficit in the trade. Hence there is another reason to believe that there will be an existence of twin deficits.

On empirical basis, twin deficit has been a favorite topic for researchers in recent times as several authors have attempted to estimate the relationship between these two deficits. Rossensswerg and Tallman (1993) examine the causal relationship between budget and trade deficits for U.S. by using five variable Vector Auto Regressive (VAR) system. They use the variables of government purchases, government balance, trade balance, interest rate and exchange rate. Using the "Levels" of variables (as against the differences) they conclude that there is in fact evidence of twin deficit phenomenon.

Mohammad and Skaggs (1996) find the link between two deficits in U.S. using five variables of real budget deficit, growth of M_2 money supply, real current account balance, real income and real exchange rate. They test for multivariate co-integration and estimate vector error-correction (VER) model. They also examine effects of using different data transformations and of estimating the VAR model. When they use only two variables of trade and budget deficits, they find no evidence of co-integration in them. However when other variables are included in the model there is sufficient evidence of co-integration between two deficits. They also predict that a reduction of budget deficit by $86 billion in the first quarter of 1990 would have reduced the current account deficit in the fourth quarter of 1992 by approximately $37 billion.

Vamvoukas (1997) uses bi-variate and tri-variate models to investigate the relationship between budget and trade deficits based on co-integration analysis and error correction model (ECM) strategy. He uses Greek annual data for period between 1948 and 1993. When he estimated bi-variate model he found no existence of co-integration between two deficits but when he used GDP as the third variable he found strong and stable co-integration between two deficits. However his empirical evidence showed one-way causality from budget to trade deficit. In order to estimate the evidence of twin deficits using some developing countries' data, we move to the next section.

SECTION – II

EVIDENCE OF TWIN DEFICITS IN INDIA, PAKISTAN AND MEXICO

All three countries we selected in this study have a few common characteristics : These are all developing countries, all have adopted a continuously expansionary fiscal policy in the period under study, and all have experienced trade deficits of different magnitude in this time period. Table 1 presents the annual data of these three countries for the time period between 1969 and 1996. By using simple regression model in first two equations and the Granger's test (for more information on this technique, see Granger (1969) in the bibliography) in equations 3 and 4, we estimated the causality in the trade and budget deficits. Our results were as follows:

(a) Table 2 lists the results for Mexico for the available data from 1979 to 1996 (sample size of 19). Four types of tests were performed in all three cases.

In their general forms, the estimated equations can be written as follows:

1. $TDi = kBDi$ where $i = 1, 2, 3$. TD and BD represent trade and budget deficits respectively, and k is expected coefficient.
2. $BDi = jTDDi$ where $i = 1, 2, 3$ j is the expected coefficient.

3. TDi(t) = lBDi(t–1) + mTDi(t–1) where i = 1, 2, 3. L and m are the expected coefficients, and (t) and (t – 1) represent current and past time periods respectively.
4. BDi(t) = nBDi(t - 1) + pTDi(t - 1) where I = 1, 2, 3. (t) and (t - 1) present the time periods.

It appears from the first set of results for the case of Mexico, that not only R square was extremely low (.087) but also there is no sign of causality from either direction between trade and budget deficits of the Mexican economy.

Therefore we do not see unidirectional causality between trade and budget deficits in Mexico in the given time period. Nor do we see any feedback as reported in the second set of results in Table 2. Thus in case of Mexico there is no evidence of causality in twin deficits. Detail results of all regressions are reported in Table 2.

Table 2
Regression Results for Mexico: 1979-1996

1. TD3 = -.185BD3
   R square =.087. Standard Error of the Estimate = 9137.4
   T statistic = - 1.27
2. BD3 = -.471 TD3
   R square =.087. Standard Error of the Estimate = 14591.9
   T statistic = - 1.27.
3. TD3(t) =.654 BD3 (t - 1) -.0148 TD3 (t - 1)
   (3.176) (-.115)
   R square =.426, Standard Error of the Estimate = 7701.64
   Figures in the parenthesis represent the t statistic of the estimated coefficient.
4. BD3(t) = -.008237 TD3(t - 1) +.794 BD3 (t - 1)
   (-.313) (4.805)
   R square =.634 Standard error of the estimate = 9840.86
   Figures in the parenthesis represent t statistic of the estimated coefficient.

In case of India the results are vastly different than in Mexico. All tests have shown better results, and the R square is considerably higher than in case of Mexico. All four equations' estimated results for India's case are listed in

Table 3. While the simple regression analysis shows the relationship between trade and budget deficits, the Granger test indicates that causality runs from budget deficit to trade deficit in case of India. As seen in equation 3 results in Table 3, trade deficit is dependent upon budget deficit, the relationship that is expected by our macroeconomic analysis. Hence in case of India, we can witness with a great confidence internal an evidence of deficits acting more like twins rather than distant cousins.

Table 3
Regression Results for India: 1979-1996

1. TDl = 12.02 BDl
   R square =.722. Standard Errror of the Estimate = 2195.75 Durtiin Watson statistic =.363, t statistic = 8.684.
2. BDl = -.006 TDl
   R square =.722. Standard Error of the Estimate = 155.1
   T statistic = 8.684.
3. TDl(t) = 3.11 BDl (t - 1) +.87 TDl (t - 1)
   (2.14) (8.418)

   R square =.922, Standard Error of the Estimate = 1207.5
   Figures in the parenthesis represent the"t statistic of the estimated coefficient.
4. BDl(t) = 1.045 BDl(t - 1) +.00034 TDl (t - 1)
   (19.96) (.916)
   R square =.98 Standard error of the Estimate = 43.5
   Figures in the parenthesis represent t statistic of the estimated coefficient.

(b) In case of Pakistan as evidenced in four pages of Table 4, there is in fact an evidence of causality between budget and trade deficits, but the direction of causality runs exactly opposite of the Indian case. In Pakistan therefore, the relationship between the deficits run from trade deficit to the budget deficit. The R square values are decent for all equations, and the relationships are justified, but the causality implies that the values of trade deficit affect the values of budget deficit. This is contrary to the traditional belief of the twin deficit idea, and exactly opposite of the results obtained for India.

Table 4
Regression Results for Pakistan: 1979-1996

1. TD2 =.00369 BD2
   R square =.63, t statistic = 6.908
   Standard Errror of the Estimate = 1363.98
2. BD2 = 17.03 TD2
   R square =.63, t statistic 6.908, Standard Error of the Estimate = 1363.98
3. TD2 =.989 TD2 (t - 1) +.000134 BD2(t - 1)
   (16.05) (.45)
   R square =.964, Standard Error of the Estimate = 443.93
   Figures in the parenthesis reprnsent the t statistic of the estimated coefficient.
4. BD2 = 2.862 TD2(t - 1) +.935 BD2(t - 1)
   (2.64) (13.96)
   R square =.960 Standard error of the Estimate = 9989.46
   Figures in the parenthesis represent t statistic of the estimated coefficient.

SECTION - III

SUMMARY AND CONCLUSIONS

In this chapter our main objectives were to summarize the theoretical argument of twin deficit, review the existing literature, and apply the twin deficit idea to the three country data to test for empirical evidence. It was interesting to see that in case of Mexico there is no evidence of twin deficit. occurring because of one another. In fact there was no evidence of causality running in either direction. One reason for this could be that the budget deficit and trade deficit values for Mexico have fluctuated wildly and there were some problems in getting a long run data for Mexican economy.

In case of India there was a strong evidence of twin deficits. Moreover as expected by textbook explanation there was a reason to believe that budget deficits create trade deficits. Hence the traditional theory works efficiently in case of India. But the positive results of India were discredited by the experience of Pakistan where we find that twin deficits existed, but the causality ran in an exactly opposite direction than in Indian case. In Pakistan therefore there is an evidence of trade deficits creating the budget deficits. With three country cases showing different evidences, the twin deficit idea has a little or no evidence in this time period.

BIBLIOGRAPHY AND REFERENCES

Abel, John D., "Twin Deficits During the 1980s: An Empirical Investigation", *Journal of Macroeconomics*, Winter 1990, pp. 81-96.

Alexander, Sydney, "Effects of Devaluation on a Trade Balance", IMF Staff Papers, 1952, pp. 263-278.

Darrat, Ali F., "Have Large Budget Deficits Caused Rising Trade Deficits?", *Southern Economic Journal*, April 1988, pp. 879-87.

Day, Edward A., "Twin Deficits Revisited", Paper presented in Southern Economic Association meeting, November 1998, pp. 1-15.

Dewald, William G. and Ulan, Michael, "The Twin Deficit Illusion", Cato journal, Winter 1990, pp. 689-707.

Enders, Walter and Bong-Soo Lee, "Current Account and Budget Deficits: Twins or Distant Cousins?", *Review of Economics and Statistics*, August 1990, pp. 373-81.

Granger, C. W. J., "Investigating Casual Relations by Econometric Models and Cross Spectral Methods", *Econometrica*, July 1969, pp. 424-438.

Kawai, Masahiroa dn Maccini, Louis J., "Twin Deficits verses Unpleasant Fiscal Arithmatic In a Small Open Economy", *Journal of Money Credit and Banking*, August 1995, pp. 639-658.

Kulkarni, Kishore, "First Principles of Macro-Monetary Theory", Third Edition, Kendall/Hunt Publishing Company, Dubuque, Iowa, 1997.

Miller, Stephen and R. Frank S., "Are the Deficits Really Related?", Contemporary Poticy Issues, October 1989, pp. 91-115.

Mohammadi Hasan and Skaggs Neil T., "US Fiscal Policy and Trade Deficits: A Broad Perspective", *Southern Economic Journal*, Vol. 62, No. 3, January 1996.

Rosensweig, Jeffrey and Tallman, Ellis W. "Fiscal Policy and Trade Adjustment: Are the Deficits Really Twins?", *Economic Inquiry*, October 1993, pp. 580-594.

Vamvoukas G. A., "Have Large Budget Deficits Caused Increasing Trade Deficits?: Evidence From A Developing Country", *Atlantic Economic Journal*, Vol. 25, No. 1, March 1997.

19

HAS INTERNATIONAL TRADE BENEFITED LDCs? — INDIA'S CASE

INTRODUCTION

There are three major aims of writing this chapter. First, it intends to summarize the main arguments of less developed countries (LDCs) against the policy of accepting totally free trade with other nations; second, it examines the development of trade transactions of India's economy in the light of these arguments; and, third, it provides some policy implications of the findings on India's experience.

In brief, the main arguments for restricted instead of completely free trade are: (1) Free trade forces LDCs to specialize in labour intensive agricultural goods and raw materials, such as metal ores, cotton, sugar and jute—increased production of which does not bring in rapid economic growth. For the developed nations, on the other hand, the argument goes further, *viz.*, they specialize in high cost, better priced finished products—increased production of which leads to rapid economic growth. Thus, totally free trade leads to unequal, biased economic growth; (2) free trade does not guarantee a stability of demand for exports of LDCs, which leads to a severe problem of export instability for them, (3) free trade, over a period, leads to a higher increase in the price of imports of LDCs than their exports, so that their terms of trade (TOT) deteriorate compared to the TOT of the developed countries, and (4) free trade policies are undesirable because of imperfections in the international financial market that does not provide enough aid to even the most deserving of LDCs, especially after the international debt crisis that started in the 1980s.

There are three sections that follow. Section 1 surveys the literature on the main arguments of less developed countries that follow restricted trade with other nations. Section 2 evaluates the performance of India's economy in the light of the main theoretical arguments of section 1. Section 3 summarizes the results and makes some policy conclusions. The essential conclusion is that the policy of severe restrictions on free trade had led to decline in India's export share in world trade. If China's economic reform experiment of a few years ago can serve as any guide, then free trade can increase the share of exports in the total world trade.

SECTION I

ARGUMENTS FOR CONTROLLED TRADE

The Ricardian argument of comparative advantage that forms the basis of all other arguments for free trade, implies that a country should export and at least incompletely specialize in production of those goods that can be produced at a comparatively lower cost domestically than abroad. Even the Heckscher-Ohlin thesis claims that the country should export and specialize in the products that use the more abundant factor of production in the country with higher intensity. When we apply these basic principles of free trade to LDCs that have an abundant labor supply and a comparative advantage in the production of raw materials, we realize that they should specialize and export only such products as jute, sugar, cotton, iron ore and tea.

The Ricardian principle and Heckscher-Ohlin theorem also imply that developed countries with all their abundant capital and a comparative advantage in the production of capital intensive advantage in the production of capital intensive finished products, such as automobiles, manufactures, computers, aeronautics, etc., should export (and specialize in) these goods to LDCs. The free trade of this nature as the international trade theory shows, leads to higher world welfare and gains from trade to both partners of the exchange. To put it in Haberler's terms, free trade of this sort can have several advantages, such as fuller utilization of resources, increase in the market size, transmission of new ideas, new technology and new managerial skills. (See Haberler, 1964, for further details.) However, the supporters of controlled trade are anxious to point out that production of same raw materials and the primary agricultural products do not benefit the people of LDCs. Therefore, it would be worthwhile to test India's performance in the light of these arguments.

As a second point of disagreement between them, the supporters of free trade and controlled trade observe the extent of export fluctuations of LDCs. The main concern is that exports of an LDC seem to be very unstable because they are so much dependent upon the economic conditions of the developed countries. As there are changes in demand patterns, the export instability is a normal occurrence for LDCs. There are several reasons for the unstable exports of LDCs. First, the exports of the developed world are not very price sensitive because many of these finished goods have a low price elasticity of demand. The exports of the developing world are believed to be price sensitive because the minerals and the agricultural products have close substitutes. Moreover, the demand conditions of developed countries change according to their business fluctuations, and the supply of exports from. LDCs have several natural or artificial constraints. It would be beneficial to observe the export stability (or the lack of it) in the case of India to evaluate the validity of this argument.

As a side argument, several economists believe that even though the increase in prices of export make the economy grow its export sector, this export growth is not necessarily beneficial for the economy. A classic theoretical analysis is found in Bhagwati's hypothesis of Immiserizing Growth. The argument is that when the export growth of an economy is associated with the decline in prices of exports, then the deterioration in Terms of Trade (TOT) can lead to reduced welfare for the economy. Thus, growth in the export sector is not necessarily beneficial to an economy. Hence a close observation of the terms of trade behavior is warranted.

The third argument for supporting controlled rather than free trade is the unfavorable change of Terms of Trade (TOT) of LDCs after trade transactions have taken place. It is generally believed that free trade causes deterioration of LDC's terms of trade, because the prices of their imports increase faster than the prices of their exports. Hence, if the terms of trade are defined as the ratio of prices of exports to the prices of imports, then the TOT of LDCs deteriorate over a period of time when completely free trade is allowed. The reasons for this argument are as follows: It is safely believed that the cost of production, which reflects the living standards of labor in the economy, is positively tied up to the prices of exports in developed countries, but not in LDCs. Hence the cost of labor (and therefore the cost of production) in developed countries goes up. It is reflected in the higher prices of their exports (that are LDCs' imports). On the other hand, the elastic demand for exports of LDCs does not allow any increase in prices of LDCs' exports. This keeps LDCs' standard of living as low as before. Thus, the deterioration of TOT is a direct result of low standard of living in LDCs. It is, therefore, crucial to know the direction in which the TOT of Indian economy are headed in the last few years.

The last criterion, that we use to observe the international performance of Indian economy, is her ability to borrow in international financial markets. Even if the Indian government has not gone in for private (or commercial) borrowing from the international banks to the extent that several debt ridden Latin American countries have, the international financing to India, in several instances, does not come without some undesirable policy consequences. The devaluation of Indian rupee in 1966, the pressure from the World Bank to open up the economy and several policy recommendations from the IMF when it was given aid to other economics are, the examples of outside pressure associated with international lending. Several LDCs resent being told by outsiders the optimum policy solutions for them. It is thought to be a worth-while exercise to examine the international aid to Indian economy in relation to its need for it.

SECTION II

THE CASE OF INDIA

In this section we evaluate the arguments of Section 1 with the help of Indian economy's performance in the last few years. It is possible to argue that India has adhered to controlled rather than free trade to a large extent. And to evaluate the Indian case as a case of free trade may seem contradictory. However, this is a case of a glass being half full or half empty. Indian trade is clearly not completely controlled; there are trade directions given, amounts restricted and foreign exchange is controlled. The real trade flow is still determined by the demand structure. Morever, the trade restrictions are not successful for a long time as a policy instrument. Hence, it is counter-argued that the Indian case is studied here for what progress it has made, rather than searching for answers to how and why it has developed the way it has developed in the last three decades.

Once the above point is cleared, as expected by our first argument, Indian economy should specialize in goods that are classified as raw materials and agricultural products and exports more of these goods, because in a capital-intensive manufacturing sector Indian economy does not possess a comparative advantage. There are several related studies about the export performance of the Indian economy, notable among them being Agarwal (1985) and Ahuja and Pahariya (1986).

Agarwal's conclusion is that Indian economy's share in the whole world has considerably declined during the period 1965 to 1980. (The recent data show that the trend has continued in the 1980s). However, the main reason for this decline is on the supply side. This is because the shares in all regions of the world either increase or decrease together. If exports are divided into agricultural products, raw materials and manufactures, Indian economy experienced an increase in the share of manufactures and decline in the share of raw materials in its exports to the world. Agarwal contends, however, that

Indian economy's share in the world exports of the same products has declined in the last 40 years because of the increasingly protectionist policies, reduction in the openness of the economy, and the greater direct or indirect trade barriers applied by the government. Thus, international trade has not forced the Indian economy to specialize only in the labor intensive raw materials production. On the contrary, the policy of controlled trade has led to shrinkage of India's export share in the world trade.

Ahuja-Pahariya apply the Heckscher-Ohlin-Samuelson model to the Indian economy to explain the commodity pattern of her trade. Their conclusion is that physical capital intensity does not seem to be a good predictor of India's trade patterns, as a single explanatory variable of India's pattern of trade, the human capital does a better job than any other variable. The share of manufactures in aggregate exports has increased from 47.5% in 1960 to 59.2% in 1974 and 63.4% in 1988. The role of non-traditional items, such as engineering goods, chemicals, etc., in India's trade has increased in modern times. Recently, India has emerged as an important exporter of turn-key projects which include, besides the material and equipment, the supply of Indian expertise and technical know-how. In the last few years there has been a new trend of increase in computer related software exports to other developing countries.

It is interesting to note that the commodities that have seen decline in the export share in the 1980s are tea, species, rice, sugar, and jute, while the commodities that experienced an increase in the total export share are coffee, marine products, fruits and vegetables, gems and jewellery, machinery, transport equipments etc., even though in absolute figures the traditional commodities like tea, sugar, cloth and raw materials have ranked considerably higher than other goods.

In terms of the import composition, there has been a considerable shift in the post-independence era. Significant reduction has been achieved in the imports of industrial machinery, paper, chemicals, etc., which shows that self-reliance is formed in important areas. All in all, it is quite clear that whatever trade was allowed in the last 40 years, the Indian economy has neither specialized in its exports of only raw materials nor has it imported consistently only the finished products as expected by the opponents of free trade.

The second criterion used for the evaluation of India's international trade is the performance of its Terms of Trade (TOT) over a period of time. Table 1 indicates the TOT of Indian economy from 1960 to 1987. As can be witnessed in the last column of Table 1, the TOT have not deteriorated by any significant amount. The terms of trade, as the ratio of unit value of exports and the unit value of imports, amounted to 1.41 in 1960, deteriorated to 1.33 in 1965, improved to 1.62 in 1972, and then rapidly deteriorated to 1.04 in 1974. Needless to say, this acute deterioration was a direct result of OPEC's oil-price shock. The terms of trade fluctuated between 1975 and 1980, reaching the lowest point in 1980. However, after 1980 the terms of trade improved steadily up to 1986 to reach almost the same figure as in 1960. This observation by no means supports the arguments that the TOT of a developing country steadily deteriorates under free trade. Despite the trade regulations of different degrees imposed by the Indian government, the terms of trade have not deteriorated. Hence there is no apparent welfare loss of Indian economy from the wide trade with the rest of the world.

Obviously, if the terms of trade have not deteriorated by a significant degree, then the theoretically convincing argument of Immiserizing Growth does not apply to the Indian situation. One has to keep in mind, however, that there are other ways to define the terms of trade, such as commodity terms of trade, weighted terms of trade, income terms of trade, etc. (For more information on these definitions, please refer to Salvatore, 1989, page 317, or any other international trade textbook.) Nonetheless, all terms of trade measurements move in same direction, hence an observation of the movements of one of them is a good proxy for the movements in any other.

The somewhat non-existent deterioration of Indian terms of trade is also observed in several other studies of TOT for developing countries by other researchers. Kindleberger (1956)

Table 1
Terms of Trade of India's Economy during 1960 to 1987

Year	*Exports*	*Increase in %*	*Imports*	*U.V. Exports*	*U.V. Imports*	*Trade Balance*	*Terms of Trade*
1960	6341		10968	24	17	–719	1.41
1961	6601	4.0	10884	24	17	–537	1.41
1962	6682	1.2	11248	23	16	–647	1.44
1963	7741	13.6	11796	23	17	–621	1.35
1964	8118	4.6	13693	23	17	–937	1.35
1965	8032	–1.0	13516	24	18	–1037	1.33
1966	11714	45.8	20373	32	22	–957	1.45
1967	12097	3.2	20796	37	26	–861	1.42
1968	13209	9.1	19273	35	25	–387	1.40
1969	13763	4.1	16589	37	26	–8	1.42
1970	15198	10.4	15933	37	26	–131	1.42
1971	15256	.38	18155	38	25	–372	1.52
1972	18568	21 7	16844	42	26	68	1.62
1973	22591	21.6	24893	51	34	–191	1.50
1974	31786	40.7	41596	64	54	–625	1.19
1975	36412	14.5	53388	71	68	–286	1.04
1976	49702	36.4	50738	75	71	787	1.06
1977	55734	12.13	57937	85	65	932	1.31
1978	54564	–2.0	64387	85	66	–884	1.29
1979	63445	16.2	79820	92	85	–2222	1.08
1980	67517	6.0	116771	100	100	–5644	1.00
1981	71780	6.3	133379	96	86	–5711	1.12
1982	88416	23.17	139691	110	88	–4820	1.25
1983	92430	4.5	142012	117	90	–4098	1.30
1984	112744	21.9	163035	134	83	–4025	1.61
1985	114098	1.2	198587	149	107	–5616	1.39
1986	119777	4.9	194280	151	105	–5438	1.44
1987	147413	23.0	216758	NA	NA	NA	NA

Note: Export and import figures are in millions of rupees, and 1980 is treated as the base year for index numbers. U.V. stands for 'unit value' and the source of the data is International Financial Statistics Year book published by the International Monetary Fund, Washington, D.C., 1988. Percentage calculation of Column 3 is authors.

concluded that TOT of developing countries vis-a-vis Western Europe declined only slightly between 1870 and 1952. Lispey (1963) concluded that TOT of developing nations in relation to the U.S. did not suffer any continuous deterioration from 1880 to 1960. In a more recent study by Grilli and Yang (1988) the terms of trade observed for developing countries for the primary products and manufactures declined only by 6 percent per year between 1900 and 1986 period. Thus, all these studies confirm the observation about India that TOT deterioration is not a major problem in the growing trade of a less developed economy.

In order to test the behavior of Indian terms of trade statistically, we hypothesize that it is determined by the export growth rate, import growth rate and growth in the trade balance. If the argument of deteriorating TOT is true, then the export and import growth rates would have a significant impact on the behavior of TOT. More specifically, an increase in import growth rate would reduce the price of imports and improve TOT, an increase in export growth would reduce the price of export and make TOT deteriorate, and the increase in trade imbalance would deteriorate TOT. To test the validity of these arguments, we tested the equation of the following form:

$$TOT = a1 + a2 \log EX + a3 \log IM + a4\ TRBGR \qquad (1)$$

where TOT = terms of trade (last column in Table 1)

log EX = logarithm of exports

log IM = logarithm of imports

TRBGR = growth rate of trade balance.

By using the data in Table 1 we ran the regression, and the ordinary least square estimates of equation (1) were received as follows:

$$\begin{aligned} TOT &= \underset{(5.62)}{1.979} + \underset{(.4771)}{.0783} \log EX - \underset{(-.842)}{.1367} \log IM \\ &\quad \underset{(-.04624)}{-.00000626}\ TRBGR \end{aligned}$$

R square = .1429,

Durbin Watson Statistic = .6981,

Standard Error of the Regression = .1659

It is apparent from the above results that the hypothesis of TOT dependency on the imports and export growth rates (same as the logarithms of the variables), and the trade balance growth rates, is not empirically supported. The R square value is very low (that shows little correlation), the Durbin Watson statistic is unacceptably low, and none of the statistic values of the estimated coefficients pass the *t* test. (Which in econometric terms means the hypothesis that the estimated coefficients are different from zero, cannot be rejected even in 75 per cent confidence interval.) It is therefore confirmed that TOT of the Indian economy did not deteriorate significantly, and they were not significantly determined by the imports, exports and trade balance of the economy in the period between 1960-1987.

The third criterion we use to observe the Indian economy's trade is the export instability inhibited in it. The argument (as mentioned in Section 1) is that the demand for exports of an LDC is unstable primarily due to the business fluctuations in the Western world. The export performance of Indian economy is seen in column 2 of Table l. In terms of percentages of the nominal export volume, the highest increase in export was registered in the year 1966 and the highest decline in export was registered in the year 1966 and the highest decline in export volume was observed in 1978. A careful observation shows that these were years when very impressive export growth was followed by the drastic decline in growth rate (observe for example, the years 1977, 1978 and 1984, 1985, 1986). However, a reverse case of a drastic increase in the growth rate of export succeeding the moderate increase is also visible (see, for example, the years 1971, 1972 or 1978, 1979 or 1981, 1982). In general, the export instability is very much evident in the case of Indian exports. Other studies have shown that the export instability in the case of India is determined more by supply factors than influenced by demand factors. Postulating that the Indian export instability is a function of commodity concentration index, geographic (or regional) concentration index, the export market share coefficient, the share of manufactures in total export and exchange rate variability,

Kulkarni *et al.*, conclude that Indian export instability is satisfactorily explained by these explanatory variables for the period between 1970 and 1985. Even though this observation does not automatically exclude the demand factors as another explanatory variable of the export instability, this does partly confirm the fact that India's export instability is determined by policy variables (like exchange rate) and supply variables (like commodity concentration in exports). Second, when commodity composition in exports is changing (as is the Indian case), export instability is a natural result. This is partly because the new commodities entering into the export stream have a completely different market structure than the old ones. The segmented market structures add to the export instability.

Even if the above-mentioned argument is inconclusive, the studies of export instability of other LDCs have mixed results. For example, a study by MacBean (1966) found that the index of export earnings instability was 23 for the group of 45 developing nations while the same index was 18 for the 18 developed countries he considered. Thus, on an absolute scale, the instability of export earning in developing countries should not be of any concern. Further, MacBean argued that the effects of unstable exports of an LDC on its GNP or any other economic variable are not so drastic as to interfere with its development efforts.

Thus, in the case of India, also, the main question is whether the experience of unstable exports, as in column 3 of Table 1, is responsible for any adverse effects on the development of the economy. The whole issue of economic development in India is so complex that it is hard to conclude that export instability is the main reason for slow economic growth. Again the economic development in India is determined by supply constraints, hence the monsoon (or the lack of it), the fiscal and monetary impetus, the rate of capital accumulation, etc., are better determinants of the Indian economy's growth than export instability. Hence, concentrating on the betterment of factors that are predominant in economic development determination is a more urgent strategy than complaining about export instability.

The fourth point of LDC's argument for controlled trade, as mentioned in Section I, is the unavailability of international aid in the international financial market. On this front the Indian economy has done much better than many other developing countries. Both the International Monetary Fund (IMF) and the International Bank for Reconstruction and Development (more popularly called the World Bank) have generously offered low-interest aid in billions of dollars to India over the four decades of Independence. Moreover, the democratic Western countries have always regarded India as a deserving recipient of their aid forming such special groups as Aid-India Consortium.

Also, the Indian economy's debt service ratios have consistently been better than several seriously indebted countries like Ecuador, Brazil, Chile and Argentia. In fact, as a result of her better payment performance, the Indian economy did not have to go for commercial borrowing in the international financial market in a big way. The October 1990 World Economic Outlook by IMF classifies India into "Diversified Borrowers" list, meaning that India is neither an official nor a serious market borrower. This fact is confirmed by noticing that out of the total annual world debt of $800 billion, the Indian borrowing amounts only to $2 billion. This also implies that India was excluded from such lists as "72 countries with recent debt-servicing difficulties", or "15 heavily indebted countries". Thus, if the IMF statistic is a reliable guide, the Indian economy continues to be an attractive place of international lending.

However, assuming that the IMF survey was based on the figures of 1989, it has to be pointed out that the political and religious troubles in the country have induced Moody's Investment Service to reduce India's credit rating to BAAI from the earlier classification of A2 level for the long-term loans and the Prime-2 level from the earlier Prime-1 level for the short-term loan in October, 1990. Thus, India came down from just below the US and Japan to be placed with China and Thailand. The second source of credit rating, Standard and Poor, gave India the rating of BBB, to have it placed with Turkey and

Hungry. A rating of BBB means that the country has only "adequate" capacity to repay the interest and the principal of the loans to be borrowed.

As a result of these lower credit ratings, the loans would be harder to come by, but loans will still be available. The interest rate to be charged for India's loans would be higher by .15 to .20 percent than before the ratings were announced. Therefore, while India could borrow sufficient amounts with an interest rate .25 to .30 percent above LIBOR (London Inter-Bank Offer Rate) before the ratings, the new interest rate would be .4 to .45 percent above LIBOR. How does it transfer into absolute values? Assuming the annual additional borrowing to be Rs. 15 billion, it only means an extra annual burden of Rs. 30 million. Thus, the situation is not terribly bad, but an effort towards improving the rating would help.

In the future India may want to consider commercial borrowings of greater percentage or ask more aid from institutions like IMF. India has already borrowed $ 1 billion from IMF and additional $ 700 million is borrowed from another source in IMF. But both these aid programmes are without any conditions attached to them. Any additional aid from IMF would not be achieved without some strings attached to policy co-ordination. This can be a grey area on the political basis. In any case, unless the foreign remittances by Indians abroad dry down considerably, (in the last five years the non-resident liabilities have increased from Rs. 38.19 billion to Rs. 190.00 billion), unless the BOP deficit grows further (In 1990, it is said that the country has enough foreign reserves to finance only two months of imports), and unless the economy is engulfed with other politically severe problems, there are signs that the India's international creditworthiness would not deplete by any significant amount.

SECTION III

SUMMARY AND CONCLUSIONS

All in all, it is concluded that the complains about free trade and the arguments for controlled trade are not strong enough not to adopt further trade liberalization. The country is classified as the "Exporter of Manufactures", since the export of manufactures accounted for more than 50 percent of the total exports in 1990, the export instability is not a prime determinant of economic development, the rate of international financial aid is not depleting, and the terms of trade have not deteriorated by any significant amount to cause serious worry. If further gains in international trade are to be sought, the wider liberalization of trade policies can benefit the economy. We observe no evidence for increased protectionism.

BIBLIOGRAPHY AND REFERENCES

Agarwal, Manmohan, "A Comparative Analysis of India's Export Performance: 1965-1980", *Indian Economic Review*, Vol. XXIII, No. 2, June, 1985, pp. 231-262.

Ahuja, Kanta and Pahariya, N.C., "Changes in Determinants and Structure of India's Foreign Trade", *The Indian Economic Journal*, Vol. 34, No. 3, 1986, pp. 13-33.

Balassa, Bela, "Exports, Policy Choices and Economic Growth in Developing Countries After the 1973 Oil Shock", *Journal of Development Economics*, January 1985.

Bhagwati, J. N., "Immiserizing Growth", *Review of Economic Studies*, June 1958. Reprinted in R. E. Caves and H. G. Johnson edited, "Readings in International Economics", Homewood, Illinois: Irwin Publishers, 1968.

Greenaway, D., edited, *Economic Development in International Trade*, Macmillan Publishers, London, 1987.

Grilli, E., and Yang, M. C., "Primary Commodity Prices, Manufactured Goods Prices, and Terms of Trade of Developing Countries; What the Long Run Shows", *World Bank Economic Review*, January 1988.

Haberler, G., "Comparative Advantage, Agricultural Production and International Trade", *The International Journal of Agrarian Affairs*, May 1964.

International Monetary Fund, World Economic Outlook; A Survey by the Staff of the IMF, October, 1990, pp. 107-108.

Jones, R. W., and Kenen, Peter, edited, *Handbook of International Economics*, Vol. 1, North-Holland Publishing Company, New York, 1984.

Kindleberger, Charles P., *The Terms of Trade: A European Case Study*, Willey Publications, New York, 1956.

Kulkarni, Kishore G., Nandakumar, P., and Pradhan, Hemanta K., "Export Instability Revisited: The Link From Exchange Rate Variability", *Journal of Foreign Exchange and International Finance*, Vol. III, No. 4, pp. 341-353.

Lipsey, R. E., *Price and Quantity Trends in the Foreign Trade of the Limited States*, Princeton University Press, Princeton, NJ, 1963.

Love, J., "Export Instability in Less Developed Countries: Consequences and Causes", *Journal of Economic Studies*, January 1987.

MacBean, A. I., *Export Instability and Economic Development*, Harvard University Press, Cambridge, Massachusetts, 1966.

Myint, H., "The Classical Theory of International Trade and the Underdeveloped Countries", *Economic Journal*, June 1958.

Prebisch, R., *Towards a New Trade Policy for Development*, United Nations Publications, New York 1964.

Ram, Rati, "Exports and Economic Growth in Developing Countries: Evidence From Time Series and Cross Sectional Data", *Economic Development and Cultural Change*, October 1987.

Reidel, J., "Trade as an Engine of Growth in Developing Countries", *Economic Journal*, March 1984.

Salvatore, Dominick, *International Economics*, Third Edition, Chapter 11, Macmillan Publishing Company, New York, 1989.

Spraos, J., *Inegualizing Trade?* Claredon Press, Oxford, England, 1983.

Taneja, Shiv and Thakurta, P.G., "Moody Blues: India's Image Crashes", *India Today*, October 31, 1990, pp. 56-57.

20

THE RECENT INDONESIAN CURRENCY CRISIS UNDERLYING FACTORS AND IMPLICATIONS

BACKGROUND AND INTRODUCTION

Indonesia was among the South-East Asian countries that were hit by the currency crisis spread-out in July 1997. The Thailand Baht was the first currency devaluated after several months to defend the speculative attack by currency traders. On July 2, the Thailand government decided to float the exchange rate of baht and the exchange rate was immediately increased by around 16 percent. The next currency devalued after the Thailand baht was the Phillipine peso whose exchange rate was increased by around 11 percent, on July 11, 1997. Three days after the Phillipine peso devaluation, the Malaysian ringgit exchange rate was depreciated by 2 percent.

Since the Indonesian economy shares the fundamental macroeconomic problems that have led to the devaluation of the other country currencies, the pressure to devaluate the Indonesian Rupiah was increasing. From the fixed exchange rate of 1644 Rupiah per U.S. Dollar in September 12, 1986, the Rupiah exchange rate has been depreciated to 2478 Rupiah per U.S. Dollar, or around 51 percent in 10 months. On July 11,

---

This Chapter is based on an article published in Journal of Foreign Exchange and International, Finance (co-author: Iravati, Irdina).

1997, the Indonesian government widened the intervention band from 8 to 12 percent, which resulted in a new intervention band of 2678 to 2374 Rupiah per U.S. Dollar from the previous intervention band of 2612 to 2430 Rupiah per U.S. Dollar. By July 20, 1997, the Rupiah has depreciated to around 2612 Rupiah per US Dollar, or around 5.4 percent in 10 days. At last, in August 14, 1997, the government announced the policy decision to float the Rupiah exchange rate to follow the market forces. Since then, the Rupiah has been depreciated to the lowest exchange rate of around 3500 Rupiah per U.S. Dollar in the middle of October, and temporarily stabilized at around 5000 Rupiah per U.S. Dollar. In 1998, the depreciation of Rupiah continued reaching to 12,000 Rupiah per U.S. Dollar.

Following the decision to float the Rupiah exchange rate, to suppress further depreciation of the currency the government took two measures to tighten money supply. The first measure was increasing the interest rate of Bank of Indonesia certificate (sertifikat Bank Indonesia) from 10.5 percent to 20, 22, 28 and 30 percent respectively for one week, two weeks, three weeks, and one-month maturity. And second, the government drew the government-owned companies' deposits from the bank. Due to these government decisions, the interest rate of deposit and inter bank call money market were increased.

Although the recent devaluation of the Indonesian Rupiah is not the first major devaluation of the currency, the underlying causes and implications of the devaluation is broader than the previous devaluation cases. The underlying cause of the devaluation was not limited to the macroeconomic situation of Indonesia, but also involved the regional situation. The implications of the devaluation will also be much broader because the Government of Indonesia has decided to float the exchange rate of Rupiah since the time of the devaluation. Before discussing the possible causes and implications of the Rupiah devaluation to the Indonesian economy, a review of the country's previous currency devaluation causes and implications will be presented.

Analysis of Indonesian Rupiah devaluations prior to 1997 since the establishment of single exchange rate in April 1970 that integrate the previous different exchange rates, until August 14, 1997, Indonesia has had four major devaluations. The first two devaluations were in the 1970s, in August 1971 and in November 1978, and the other two devaluations were in the 1980s, in March 1983 and September 1986.

The objective of the first devaluation of Indonesian Rupiah was to close the gap between the exchange rate fixed by the government and the free market rate and thus creating a fully convertible Rupiah (Ranuwihardjo, 1972). When the devaluation took place on August 23, 1971, the exchange rate was increased from 378 Rupiah per U.S. Dollar to 415 Rupiah per U.S. Dollar, or an increase of around 10 percent. At that time, the government of Indonesia adopted the fixed exchange rate system by pegging the Rupiah to the U.S. Dollar hence the exchange rate was kept at the same level until 1978 when the next devaluation of the Rupiah took place.

Hill argued in his book "The Indonesian Economy Since 1966" that under that situation the Rupiah value should have appreciated, otherwise the fixed exchange rate policy will result in high inflation. As illustrated in Figure 1, the large increase in money supply has indeed increased the inflation rate to more than 50 percent in 1975 and on an average the inflation rate during 1972-1977 period was around 20 percent.

The second devaluation in 1978 when the exchange rate was increased from 415 Rupiah per U.S. Dollar to 625 Rupiah per U.S. Dollar was unexpected. In the period of 1975-1977, prior to the devaluation, inflation was relatively low because of the government tight fiscal and monetary policy. Although the balance of payment showed a deficit, it was relatively strong because the deficit was small. The devaluation was motivated by the concern to increase non-oil and gas export, which was justified by the increase in non-oil and gas export in the years following the devaluation. On the other hand, the devaluation has led to a rapid monetary expansion due to the high oil price caused by the Iran-Iraq dispute, which further created a high inflation. The domestic inflation soared to another peak of around 45 percent in 1980. This situation eroded the beneficial effects of the devaluation (Hill, 1996).

Source: IMF, International Financial Statistics, various issues.

Figure 1: Indonesian Growth of Money Supply and Inflation Rate

The third devaluation occurred in March 1983 with the objective of curing the deficit in current account. The exchange rate was increased by around 38 percent, from 702 Rupiah per U.S. Dollar to 970 Rupiah per U.S. Dollar. The government objective to cure the current account deficit was achieved by the devaluation as the current account position in 1985 and 1986 was improved.

In 1986, the government was forced to devaluate the Rupiah also with the expectation of lowering the current account deficit, since it was estimated that the 1986 export would be lower than what has been projected. Although imports of goods and services were expected to be lower than the projection that has been made, oil export was estimated to fall by half of the projected value, yielding a current account deficit. The fall in oil export was mainly due to the fall in price because the volume of export continued to increase. It was estimated that the deficit could not be fully covered by aid and private inflows net of debt repayments. Hence to cover the remaining deficit the government had to either get another government borrowing or draw down reserve. These options would have brought negative implications to the country, instead the government took the decision to devaluate the Rupiah.

Realizing the destabilizing effect of devaluation to the economy, in 1986 the government decided to change the exchange rate system from the fixed exchange rate to managed floating exchange rate. The government expected that by maintaining the constant real effective exchange rate toward the U.S. Dollar, an uncertainty in the business sector could be reduced (Hill, 1996). Since then the Rupiah depreciation was gradual, creating a small inflationary impact. To maintain a low inflation rate, the government conducted a concretionary monetary and fiscal policy. Money supply growth was kept between 10-20 percent annual growth, which was also supported by a sharp decrease in oil export due to the sharp decline in oil price.

Rupiah value has a long-term decreasing trend, which means that the exchange rate will be increasing in the long-term. To keep the monetary stability the government tried to manage the Rupiah exchange rate at a realistic level. Since 1990, the Rupiah exchange rate has been related to a basket of currency. Prior to that, the movement of Rupiah was compared against the movement of the U.S. Dollar. From the last devaluation in 1986 to around the middle of this year, the Rupiah exchange rate has been depreciated from 1644 Rupiah per U.S. Dollar to 2487 Rupiah per U.S. Dollar or around 5 percent per annum.

The underlying considerations of the previous devaluation cases have been the improvement of the balance of trade and balance of payment. Although the past devaluation cases have brought negative impact upon the economy such as high inflation, basically the objective of the decision to devaluate can be achieved. Based on the past experiences, it seemed that the government had become more cautious making the decision to devaluate the currency by combining the exchange rate policy with monetary and fiscal policies.

UNDERLYING FACTORS OF 1997 INDONESIAN RUPIAH DEVALUATION

The underlying factors that have caused the recent devaluation of the Indonesian Rupiah can be classified into two categories:

the pressures from the outside of the economy and the internal factors. The pressures from outside of the economy were mainly arising from the attack of speculators from the world foreign exchange market, while the internal factors that supported the decision to devaluate the currency was the macroeconomic condition of the Indonesian economy.

Pressures from the Outside of the Economy: The foreign exchange market in the South-East Asian region has been characterized by currencies that were considered as overvalued. Since the inflation rate in most of the countries in the region was higher than the inflation rate of the countries which currencies included in the basket of currencies for comparison, it is expected that the change in the exchange rate would be higher than the current exchange rate depreciation. The change in the nominal exchange rate of the Indonesian Rupiah for example, was only around 5 percent per annum, while the market exchange rate was decreasing twice as fast.

Under the situation in which most countries have large trade deficits, as shown in Figure 2, devaluation would be a logical measure to eliminate or decrease the trade deficit in each economy. This situation increased the speculation within the foreign exchange market since the situation opened opportunities to make profits. Pilbeam (1991) pointed out that speculators could make profits in an inefficient market. He took Eugene Fama's definition of an efficient market as a market in which prices "fully reflect" available information. In the case of foreign exchange market, the market participants can use all available information to predict the value of the exchange rate that reflects its underlying determinants (Pilbeam, 1991). This implies that the foreign exchange market in South-East Asia can be perceived as inefficient since the nominal exchange rate do not reflect the underlying determinants. Under this situation, according to Friedman as pointed out by Pilbeam (1991), speculators can take an action toward the stabilization of the exchange rate by moving the exchange rate toward a more appropriate value. Speculators have forced economies in South-East Asian region, including Indonesia, to devalue

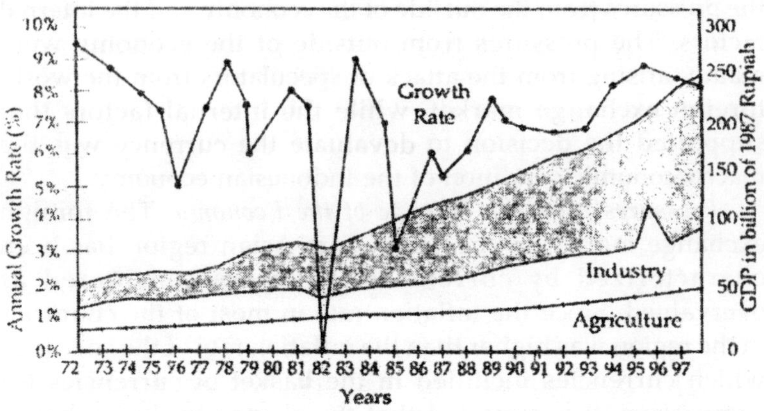

Source: World Bank, World Tables, 1994. Central Bureau of Statistics, Indonesia.

Figure 2: Indonesian GDP by Sector and Growth Rate

their currencies toward a more appropriate value and gained profits from the action.

Internal Factors: Although Indonesia has recorded a high GDP growth in 1996 and estimated to have a high GDP growth in 1997 alongwith a decreasing trend of inflation, there are concerns regarding increasing deficits in both current account and balance of payments that could lead to the devaluation of the Rupiah.

Indonesia has achieved approximately 7.8 percent GDP growth in 1996 and is estimated to achieve GDP growth of around 7.7 percent this year. The 1997 economic growth is supported by high investment as a result of the small decrease in the interest rate, high demand of export, and high capital inflow.

The inflation that has always daunted the economy also showed a decreasing trend partly due to the decline in the inflation from food price that used to have a large effect on inflation. However, high inflation was still possible due to the high inflow of foreign capital that was attracted to the high interest rate and the increase in money supply despite the effort of the government to conduct a restrictive monetary policy.

The government conducted a tight monetary policy by restricting bank lending. The central bank has raised the reserve requirement from 3 to 5 percent, after having already raised it from 2 to 3 percent in 1996. However, the government has not been entirely successful in reducing credit expansion. Although below the levels of previous years, credit expansion in 1996 was surpassing the Bank Indonesia target of 17 percent.

The growth of money supply was another indication of the limited success of tight monetary policy. Narrow money (M1) increased by 21.7 percent by the end of 1996, while growth in broad money (M2) was 29.6 percent. This not only exceeds the Bank Indonesia target of 16 percent, but also the growth rate recorded in 1995.

Although the economic growth was quite high alongwith a relatively low inflation rate, there is a growing concern on the rising current account deficit. The current account deficit reached US $8.8 billion at the end of 1996, increased from US $7.6 billion in 1995. This trend will probably continue on to 1997-1998, when the current account deficit will total US $9.8 billion or roughly 4 percent of GDP. Figure 3 records the growth of Indonesian export and import since 1972. As can be observed, the rising current account deficit was resulting from

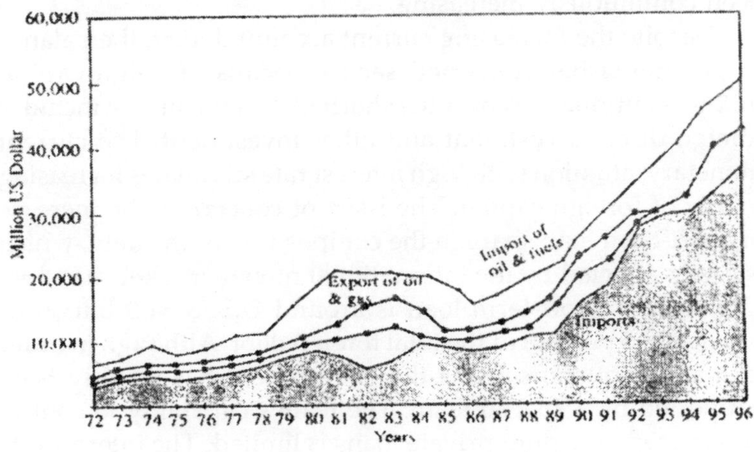

Sources: IMF, International Financial Statistics, various issues.

Figure 3: Indonesian Export and Import

the slow export growth, which in turn increased imports, and thus creating a deficit in the services sector. Over 1994 to 1997 period the trade surplus has plunged. In 1996, total exports were growing by around 8.3 percent, while the imports surged to 12.2 percent. The non-oil and gas export growth was 11.7 percent, while non-oil and gas imports increased by approximately 14.6 percent. This high import content of inputs has become a concern for its possibility to dampen the economic growth.

The remaining sources of foreign exchange earnings that can be tapped are tourism and worker's remittances because most of the other Indonesian non-oil and gas export products rely on competitiveness born out of pricing rather than quality, putting them at a distinct disadvantage. The export commodity becoming vulnerable with new competitors offering better prices, tariff or non-tariff barriers, and problems arising from reliance on imported raw materials.

The current account deficit was pushed by the increase in the services sector deficit. In 1995, services sector deficit was around U.S. $ 13.3 billion, and it was increased to U.S. $ 14 in 1996. The projected services sector deficit for 1998 is U.S. $ 15.2 billion. Efforts to reduce this deficit by reducing debt interest payments are impossible since total foreign debt has been continuously increasing.

Despite the increasing current account deficit, the balance of payments has remained secure because foreign capital inflows continued to cover the shortfall. Capital inflow includes foreign direct investment and other investment. The current monetary situation with high interest rate stimulates increasing inflow of foreign capital. The issue of concern is the increase of short-term loan share in the composition of the debt, which is easily affected by the international money market situation. The current short-term loan is around U.S. $ 34.3 billion or around 28.5 percent of the total foreign debt. Although in order to manage offshore loans the government has already been supported by a special team. The team's capability to control and manage the pure private loans is limited. The interest rate on private loan is higher and the repayment period is shorter compared to the government loan.

The increasing current account deficit over the past two years has made the government's task of managing the balance of payments increasingly difficult. Realizing that large balance of payments deficit has wide-ranging implications on the economy, policy makers and economists focus their attention on the problem of current account deficit. Over the entire 1987 to 1997 period, the government has proved not to resort to devaluation, putting repeated rumors to the contrary. However, these Indonesian macroeconomic conditions have turned to be among the rationale of the recent devaluation.

OBSERVATION OF INDONESIAN RUPIAH DEVALUATION IMPLICATIONS

Blanchard (1997) listed three effects of the real depreciation of a currency to the trade balance, those are the increase of export, increase in demand of domestic goods, and decrease in import. Export of domestically produced goods of a country whose currency is depreciated, or the exchange rate is increasing, is increased because the country's goods becoming relatively cheaper in the foreign market. On the other hand, prices of foreign goods are becoming more expensive for the country's domestic market, and hence the demand of domestically produced goods in the domestic market is increasing and the import of foreign goods is decreasing. Overall, depreciation of a currency could lead to the improvement of the country's trade of balance provided that the increase in exports and decrease in imports are sufficiently offset the increase of the value of imports (Blanchard). This condition is called the Marshall-Lerner condition.

Besides improving the trade balance, depreciation of a country's currency also results in the increase of the domestic output (Blanchard). As the prices of domestically produced goods are relatively decreasing in the foreign market because of the depreciation, export of domestic goods is increasing. On the domestic market, as the prices of foreign goods are relatively increasing due to the currency depreciation, the demand of domestic goods as the substitute is increasing. Hence, demand for domestically produced goods is increasing both in the foreign and domestic markets and this will result in the increase of the domestic output.

Observations on the effect of currency depreciation to the trade balance have shown that a time lag occurred between the time of the depreciation and the time at which the trade balance showed the effect. During this time lag, the quantity of goods being exported and imported is adjusted to the new price. Hence, in the initial period after the depreciation, trade balance will still show a decline, however in the following periods, if the Marshall-Lerner condition holds, trade balance will show an increasing trend. This process will produce a curve that appears like a letter 'J' and is called the 'J-curve' (Blanchard).

Figure 4 shows that the J-curve hypothesis occurred in Indonesia, after the devaluations in 1971, 1978, 1981, and 1986. Kulkarni (1997) pointed out that there is an empirical evidence of the occurrence of J-curve hypothesis in the case of Indonesia. After the 1971 devaluation, the Indonesian balance of trade was increasing during the 1972-1974 period. In 1975, a sharp decrease of the balance of trade occurred because of the decrease in both oil and gas export and manufactured goods export due to the world recession. After 1975, with the increasing condition of the world economy, the balance of trade was increasing slowly as a result of the increase in Indonesian exports.

The balance of trade was again increasing sharply, after the major devaluation in 1978. In 1979, the trade balance had more than doubled, and the growth from 1979 to 1980 was around 30 percent. This high growth of the balance of trade was supported by the high oil price in the 1980. After this peak, the Indonesian balance of trade during 1981 to 1983 period slumped to the level of the early 1970s. The Indonesian export of oil and gas was still high, but there was a sharp decrease in the export of manufactured goods which was accompanied by a sharp increase in the imports of manufactured goods. The sharp decrease in the export of manufactured goods resulted from the tight money policy conducted by the government. This restrictive monetary policy was considered necessary to prevent a high inflation rate due to the excessive money supply. High export of oil and gas has brought a sharp increase in the domestic money supply.

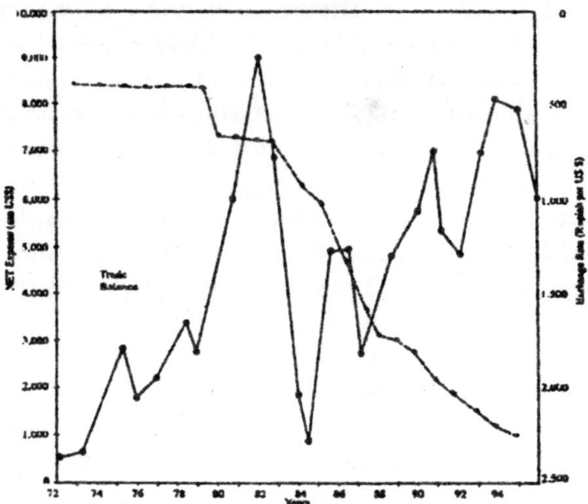

Source: World Bank, World Tables, 1994.

Figure 4: Indonesian Balance of Trade

After the devaluation in 1981, an increase in the balance of trade during 1984 and 1985 can be observed. The devaluation has increased the Indonesian competitiveness and hence increased the export in manufactured goods which was also coupled by the decrease in imports of manufactured goods. In 1986, a large decrease in the balance of trade occurred as a result of the sharp decrease in oil export.

After 1986, the year in which the government devalued the Rupiah and changed the exchange rate policy from the fixed exchange rate policy to the managed floating exchange rate, large increases of trade balance can be observed during 1987 to 1989. From 1989 to 1995, the export of oil and gas was almost constant while export of manufactured goods was growing steadily. The decline of trade balance in 1993-1995 period was resulting from the growing import of manufactured goods.

The possibility of the occurrence of the relationship between the devaluation of the Rupiah and the improvement of the Indonesian balance of trade that can be detected in Figure 2 can be statistically examined. Bahmani-Oskooee (1989) noted in his article "Devaluation and the J-Curve: Some Evidence from LDC's" that statistical relationship between devaluation of a currency with the improvement of trade balance of a country has been investigated by numerous authors. He identified that the variables being accounted as the explanatory variables between investigations. Cooper (1971), Connolly and. Taylor (1972), Laffer (1974) and Salany (1974) only consider the exchange rate as the explanatory variable. Miles (1979) added income and money supply as the explanatory variables. However, the conclusion of Miles' observation on the relationships between devaluation and exchange rate, income, and money supply was quite contrary to the original hypothesis. Miles concluded that the improvement of balance of trade and balance of payment could not be explained by using exchange rate as the only explanatory variable. Further, although all of the three explanatory variables considered in the observation, the result cannot explain the improvement in the balance of trade. They can only explain the improvement in the balance of payment (Bahamani-Oskooee, 1989).

The statistical relationship between devaluation and improvement of balance of trade that has been studied by Bahamani-Oskooee for Greece, India, Korea, and Thailand, will be developed for Indonesia in this paper. Bahmani-Oskooee used the following relationship that has been developed by Krueger:

$$TB = f(Y, E/P)$$

Where TB is the trade balance, Y is the level of real output, E is the exchange rate, and P is the domestic price level. Bahmani-Oskooee extended the relationship to include world income (YW) and high powered money of the country being analyzed (M) and rest of the world (MW), and considered exchange rate variable as a lag variable.

The equation developed by Bahmani-Oskooee that will be used in this paper is:

$$TB_t = \alpha_0 + \alpha_1 Y_t + \alpha_2 YW_t + \alpha_3 M_t + \alpha_4 MW_t + \sum_{i=0}^{n} \beta_i (E/P)_{t-1} + u_i$$

Trade balance is defined as the net-export or exports minus imports. Following Bahmani-Oskooee, α_1 is expected to be negative, as increase of income will increase imports that leads to the decrease in trade balance. However, Bahmani-Oskooee also took into account the Magee (1973) argument that the sign of α_1 be positive if the domestic production of importables rises faster than consumption so as to reduce the volume of imports. α_2 is considered to be either negative or positive. Bahmani-Oskooee followed Miles defining that money supply is not defined as M1 or M2, but as the level of the domestic portion of high-power money that is under the control of the monetary authorities. α_3 is expected to have a negative sign since with the increase of money supply, an individual will perceive an increase in wealth that resulted in an increase in imports which in turn decreases the trade balance. α_4 to the contrary, is expected to have a positive sign, as the trade balance is expected to increase with devaluation. Coefficient b, which is the summation of the lag coefficients, is expected to have a positive sign since an increase in the exchange rate, which is defined as the number of domestic currency unit per unit of foreign exchange, is expected to have a positive impact on the balance of trade.

Table 1 shows the result of the regression to estimate the coefficient of the trade balance equation. The following Indonesian data from 1972 to 1992 were used in the analysis:

- TB = Index of domestic currency value of exports minus imports, 1980 = 100.
- Y = index of yearly real GDP, 1980 = 100.
- YW = index of U.S. and Japan real income, 1980 = 100. U.S. and Japan were chosen because they are Indonesia's main trading partner. Equal weights are assigned to both countries.
- M = index of domestic high power money, 1980 = 100.
- MW = index of U.S. and Japan money supply, 1980 = 100. Equal weights are assigned to both countries.

Table 1
Coefficient Estimates of the Trade Balance Equation

Independent Variables	*Expected Sign*	*Greece*		*India*		*Thailand*		*Indonesia*	
		Coefficient Estimates	*t-statistic*	*Coefficient Estimates*	*t-statistic*	*Coefficient Estimates*	*t-statistic*	*Coefficient Estimates*	*t-statistic*
Constant		–127.200	0.77	566.700	0.54	-1985.000	2.67	-551.600	-2.07
Y	–/+	1.074	0.85	–0.115	0.45	-1.497	0.66	0.727	1.56
YW	+/	1.897	2.36	2.360	0.94	2.118	0.52	1.401	1.34
M	-	–0.489	0.88	0.181	0.16	6.165	2.69	–0.112	-1.22
MW	+	–1.046	1.12	–5.630	2.05	–4.783	1.52	4.015	1.92
E/P	+	–0.769	1.28	–1.709	0.20	16.740	2.68	22.110	
E/P Lag 0		2.933	2.19	5.262	2.57	2.083	0.79	-67.36	-1.44
E/P Lag 1		1.271	2.35	1.855	1.73	1.114	0.89	77.900	1.17
E/P Lag 2		0.145	0.57	-0.271	0.22	0.863	1.12	109.780	1.63
E/P Lag 3		-0.535	1.46	-1.160	0.81	1.113	1.48	-143.760	-2.84
E/P Lag 4		-0.861	2.13	-1.220	0.86	1.648	1.97	45.55	1.56
E/P Lag 5		-0.925	2.54	-0.859	0.63	2.252	2.13		
E/P Lag 6		-0.818	2.56	-0.485	0.38	2.711	2.01		
E/P Lag 7		-0.632	2.00	-0.505	0.48	2.807	1.89		
E/P Lag 8		-0.456	1.54	-1.328	2.03	2327	1.82		
E/P Lag 9		-0.384	1.66	-3.362	2.16	1.052	1.47		

contd. table

Independent Variables	Expected Sign	Greece		India		Thailand		Indonesia	
		Coefficient Estimates	t-statistic	Coefficient Estimates	t-statistic	Coefficient Estimates	t-statistic	Coefficient Estimates	t-statistic
E/P Lag 10		-0.506	1.22			-1231	0.81		
E/P Lag 11									
Summary and diagnostic statistics									
Number of Observations		n.a.		n.a.		n.a.		17	
R squared		0.28		0.52		0.77		0.80	
F		1.96		3.16		9.16		3.15	
Durbin-Watson statistic		2.1364		3.1349		2.2786		2.35	

Source: Bahmani-Oskooee, Mohsen.

Notes: Devaluation and the J-Curve: Some Evidence from LDCs Errata", *The Review of Economics and Statistics,* Volume 71, Issue 3 (Aug. 1989), pp. 553-554.

E = index of Rupiah exchange rate, 1980 = 100.
P = Indonesia Consumer Price Index, 1980 = 100.

The value of the trade balance equation R-squared is 80 percent that means the change in the explanatory variables included in the equation can explain the change in the trade balance variable by 80 percent. The *t*-statistics show that the explanatory variables which can explain the change in the trade balance are domestic income, income of U.S. and Japan, domestic money supply, money supply in U.S. and Japan, and all of the exchange rate variables. Coefficient of the domestic income variable is positive, meaning that higher domestic income leads to higher trade balance, or the increase of import due to the higher income is still less than the increase in export. As expected, the sign of the coefficient of U.S. and Japan income variable is positive which means that higher income of U.S. and Japan will lead to higher exports from Indonesia. The domestic money supply variable has a negative sign which implies that the increase in the domestic money supply leads to the decrease in balance trade. The money supply variable also has a coefficient with a positive sign, which shows that higher money supply in the U.S. and Japan leads to higher imports from Indonesia. The sign is positive, showing that overall exchange rate variable has a positive relationship with the balance of trade. The exchange rate lag variable implies the occurrence of the J-curve hypothesis by first having a negative sign, and both 1-year and 2-year lag variables have positive signs, and then another negative and positive sign. This observation is consistent with the observation from the graph that the effect of devaluation is quickly eroded by some other factors within a short period after the devaluation. For comparison, result of Bahmani-Oskooee investigation on Greece, India and Thailand is included in Table 1. The regression result for Indonesia is similar to the Greece result, since the signs of estimated coefficients are comparable.

However, it should be noted that the data used for this observation are annual data while Bahmani-Oskooee observation is using quarterly data. Nonetheless, as seen above, conclusions of both studies are same.

The effect of the devaluation of Rupiah in 1997 to the trade balance may not be as high as what has been experienced in the previous devaluation cases considering the current composition of Indonesia's export and import commodities. Indonesia's export and import commodities can be categorized in two major commodities for the purpose of analysis. The first category is oil and gas commodity and the second category is non-oil and gas commodities or manufactured goods.

In 1978, oil and gas export accounted for 65 percent of the total Indonesian export manufactured goods accounted for 35 percent of the total. The devaluation of the Rupiah alongwith high oil price boost the government export revenue, hence, the increase of trade balance reached 130 percent and 50 percent in two subsequent years following the devaluation. When the Rupiah was again devaluated in 1981, the proportion of oil and gas export was higher because of the decrease in manufactured goods export. As a result, after the devaluation in 1981, the trade balance increased five fold.

By comparison, in 1986 the composition of oil and gas and manufactured goods export were almost equal when the government devalued the Rupiah. The increase of balance of trade in three subsequent years following the devaluation were 90 percent, 22 percent and 17 percent, respectively, which were lower than before.

It should also be noted that import of manufactured goods is consistently higher than export of manufactured goods, resulting in a consistent deficit of balance of trade in the absence of oil export. With the current composition of oil and gas and manufactured goods exports of approximately 25 percent and 75 percent respectively, plus the fact that import of manufactured goods is higher than its export, the improvement of trade balance will not be as substantial. High import content of manufactured goods for export leads to the increase in cost for producing the goods, which in turn drive the increase of export price. Besides, the usual increase in competitiveness due to the devaluation is eroded by the fact that the neighboring countries in the region which are competitors of Indonesia in the export market are also devaluing their currencies.

The other effect of devaluation is that the increase in inflation can be observed shortly after the devaluation for two reasons. The first reason is the increase of imported goods prices, which leads to cost-push inflation. The second reason for the increase in inflation resulted from devaluation is the increase in money supply as a result for the increase in export revenue. The past devaluation cases show that this was particularly true when the share of oil and gas export in the total export was high. Both after 1971 and 1978 devaluations, the inflation rose to 41 percent in 1974 and 20 percent in 1979. However, following the 1981 devaluation, the increase in inflation was moderate, because having past experiences of the increase in inflation following the devaluation, the government fixed prices of basic commodities to control the inflation after the devaluation. An effort to curb the increase in inflation is one of the reasons for the government to take the concretionary monetary policy following the recent devaluation.

As an effort to manage inflation, the government decision to tighten the money supply following the devaluation is to keep the further decrease in the Rupiah value. The demand for the U.S. dollar was excessive due to the high portion of uncovered offshore borrowing made by the private sector. The private sector has been under an illusion of a stable Rupiah value with the managed depreciation of 5 to 6 percent per year when they borrowed. This uncontrolled high domestic money supply has driven the increase of demand for the U.S. dollar and under a limited supply of the U.S. dollar this high demand has led to the shortage of U.S. dollar which in turn increases the U.S. dollar price or will devalue the Rupiah.

However, the contrationary monetary policy may decrease the country's future economic growth because of its effect on consumer spending, interest rate, and bank loans. The consumer spending is reduced because under a decreased money supply situation, people perceive that their income is less, hence decreasing their consumption. Through the multiplier process, the decrease in consumption will eventually decrease investment, which in turn decreases the economic growth of the economy.

As a result of the decrease in the money supply, the interest rate is increased. Interest rates in September and October, two months following the devaluation, was doubled from the rate in August, prior to the devaluation. High interest rate has two prong effects. The first effect is decreasing the investment because of the high price of bank credits coupled with depressed market situation, and the second effect is the increase in bad bank debt. Both effects of increasing interest rate result in a diminishing effect toward investment that further decrease the economic growth.

It is also observed that the decrease in investment was caused by the decrease in bank credits. Due to the limited money supply, banks have limited capability to give credits for investment. And the decrease in investment is expected to affect the economic growth.

Overall, Indonesia is facing a condition of decreasing growth in the near future, unless the government could formulate an appropriate policy mix and implement the policy consistently. Given the inefficiency, bureaucracy, and administrative drawbacks, it seems that a short-term solution is hard to find.

CONCLUSION

Although Indonesia has had four major devaluations in the past 25 years, the possible implications resulting from the recent major devaluation should be evaluated cautiously since the situation encountered would be entirely different from what has happened in the past. Past devaluation of the Rupiah which used to show its effectiveness in improving the balance of trade and balance of payment, might not be effective any more for the currency devaluation was also conducted by the other economies. Hence, Indonesia should seek other fundamental measures to cure the deficits in the balance of trade and balance of payment. Formulation of an appropriate policy mix is becoming challenge for the government in the near future. As the events of 1998 have proven, the efforts by governmental policy actions at best are inadequate. Moreover, the overall crisis in 1998 has pointed out that responsible policy-making and efficient work-culture are a precondition for economic growth. Without drastic solutions, this drastic problem can not be solved.

REFERENCES

Bahmani-Oskooee, Mohsen, "Devaluation and the J-Curve: Some Evidence from LDCs", *The Review of Economics and Statistics,* Volume 67, Issue 3, The MTT Press, August 1985, pp. 500-504.

——"Notes: Devaluation and the J-Curve: Some Evidence from LDCs Errata", *The Review of Economics and Statistics,* Volume 71, Issue 3, The MIT Press, August 1989, pp. 553-554.

Blanchard, Olivier, *Macroeconomics,* Prentice-Hall, Inc., New Jersey, 1997.

De Grauwe, Paul, "Paradigms of Macroeconomic Policy for the Open Economy", *Macroeconomic Policy in Open Economies,* Edited by Michele U. Fratianni, Dominick Salvatore, and Juregen von Hagen, Greenwood Press, Westport-Connecticut, London, 1997.

Gie, Kwik Kian, "Bagaimana Nilai Rupiah", *Kompas Online,* 4 August 1997.

——,"Tertular atau Letupan dari Dalam", *Kompas Online,* 11 August 1997.

——, "Rupiah Mengambang Total"? *Kompas Online,* 18 August 1997.

——, "Kenali dan Dadapilah Kenyataan", *Kompas Online,* 8 September 1997.

Hill, Hal, *The Indonesian Economy Since 1996: Southeast Asia's Emerging Giant,* Cambridge University Press, Australia, 1996.

Husted, Steven L. and Mishael Melvin, *International Economics,* Harper Collins, New York, 1995.

Kulkarni, Kishore, *First Principles of Macro-Monetary Theory,* Kendall/ Hunt Publishing Company, Dubuque, Iowa, 1997.

Kulkarni, Kishore, "Empirical Evidence of J-Curve Hypothesis in Eight Countries", Working Paper, 1998.

Miles, Marc A., "The Effects of Devaluation on the Trade Balance and the Balance of Payments: Some New Results", *The Journal of Political Economy,* Volume 87, Issue 3, University of Chicago, June 1979, 600-620.

Pilbeam, Keith, *Exchange Rate Management,* St. Martin's Press, New York, 1991.

Ranuwihardjo, Sukadji, "Exchange Rate Experience and Policy in Indonesia since World War II", *Exchange Rate Policy in Southeast Asia,* Edited by Herbert G. Grubel and Theodore Morgan, Lexington Books, Toronto, London, 1972.

World Bank, World Tables, The Johns Hopkins University Press, Baltimore and London, various issues.

DATA SOURCE

Balance of Payments Statistics Yearbook, International Monetary Fund, Washington D.C., various issues.

Indonesia: EIU Country Report 3rd quarter 1997, The Economist Intelligence Unit: London, 1997.

Indonesia: EIU Country Profile 1996-97, The Economist Intelligence Unit: London, 1996.

International Financial Statistics, International Monetary Fund, Washington D.C., various issues.

Kebijakan Ekonomi Tak Bisa Diisolasi, Bisnis Indonesia, Dari Diskusi Ahli Bisnis Indonesia, 24 September 1997.

National and Regional Income - Statistical Tables, Central Bureau of Statistics (BPS Online), September 1997.

STATISTICAL SECTION*

List of Tables

Special Tables

---

* Prepared by Ms. Manisha Bhosale, Research Assistant for JFEIF, National Institute of Bank Management, Pune.

21

ECONOMIC GROWTH AND INCOME DISTRIBUTION IN MALAYSIA:

A Test of the Kuznets Inverted U Hypothesis

INTRODUCTION

Defining economic growth solely in terms of per capita income is inadequate because there is no indication of its effect on the welfare of the population. One way to evaluate the effect of development on the economic well being is through the study of income distribution. By way of a metaphor, one can pose some highly relevant questions. As the economic pie becomes larger, in how many ways can the pie be divided among the people? Do all the people get equal portions? Do some get bigger slices than others? How well is country's wealth divided among the population? This is the essence of the problem.

A common fallacy is to assume that an increase in the per capita income necessarily means that everyone is better off economically. Even if some sector of the economy were not benefiting, so the argument goes, it is only a matter of time before the benefits of economic development begin to trickle down. In reality, income distribution for the less developed countries is persistently less equal compared to the developed countries. This problem of unequal income distribution needs to be addressed.

This chapter is based on article published in 'Prajnan', 1997-1998, Co-authors: G. Subrahmanyam, R.I. Hadi Ali, Zarina Othman.

What are the ramifications for a persistently unequal income distribution? Besides the more obvious social injustice of the phenomenon where the rich become richer and the poor become poorer, this unhealthy state of affairs promises social as well as political tensions. The very fabric of society is threatened.

For many years there is a continuing debate regarding the relationship of economic growth and income distribution. In 1955, the noted Harvard economist Simon Kuznets, proposed that this relationship between the level of per capita income and inequality in the distribution of income may take the form of an inverted 'U'. According to his hypothesis, as the per capita income rises, inequality may rise initially, reach a maximum at an intermediate level of income, and declines as the income levels, typical of an industrial country are reached.

The purpose of this chapter is to observe the relevance of Kuznets' inverted U. hypothesis in the economic development experience of Malaysia. Is Kuznets' hypothesis applicable for this developing country?

THEORETICAL ASPECTS OF THE KUZNETS INVERTED U HYPOTHESIS

Before embarking on a discussion of Kuznets' hypothesis, a general discourse on the measurement of income inequality will precede. Economists measure income inequality with the Lorenz Curve, named after the American statistician C. Lorenz.

A survey collects income data from representative households and is projected over all households in the country. Once these statistics have been collected, the next step is the analysis of the data, commonly arranged using the Lorenz method. To draw a Lorenz Curve, income recipients are ranked from the lowest income to the highest income along the horizontal axis. The vertical axis represents the cumulative percentage of income, also ranked from the lowest to the highest. The Lorenz Curve itself indicates the percentage of total income accounted for by any cumulative percentage of recipients. The shape of this curve shows the degree of inequality in the income distribution with reference to a 45 degree line drawn diagonally from the origin. This hypothetical line represents equal income distribution. The inequality of the distribution of income is greater the further away the curved line bends away from the 45 degree line. (Please see Figure 1.)

In an effort to obtain a single numerical indicator of inequality of income distribution, the Gini Coefficient was developed. It is derived from the areas on the Lorenz Curve diagram. If *I* A' represents the area bounded by the curve and the 45 degree line, and *'B'* the areas not covered by 'A' (see Figure 1 above), the Gini Coefficient can be calculated using the formula *AI* A + B. Thus the bigger the area covered by *'A'*, the higher will be the Gini Coefficient. Theoretically, the value of the coefficient can range from 0 (representing perfect income equality) to 1 (depicting perfect inequality).

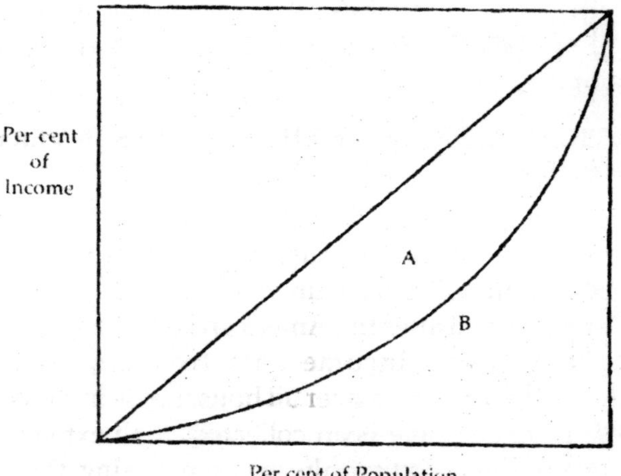

Figure 1: The Lorenz Curve

The use of Gini Coefficients as comparative measures must take into account its problems. For instance, Lorenz Curves can intersect, so that different curves can generate the same Gini Coefficient but reflect entirely different income distribution patterns. In such cases, there is no clear measure of relative inequality. The World Bank, for instance, publishes income distribution figures in the form of quintiles; the population being divided into ordinal 20 percentage divisions according to the percentage of income received. Instead of looking at the composite whole, analysts who are interested in the lower income groups can concentrate on the lower 40 percent bracket of the population. Likewise comparisons can be made of the top 10 percent of the population, which is the sector that receives much of the wealth of the nation in the developing countries. Comparison along these lines would be fair but at the risk of ignoring what goes on in the rest of the distribution.

Simon Kuznets was the first to express the view that income inequality tends to increase during the first stages of the economic growth, then levels off and finally diminishes during the later stages.[1] (Please see Figure 2). He demonstrated that the inequality of the distribution of personal income is more pronounced in the developing countries than the developed ones. Another characteristic difference noted was that the share of the higher income groups in the developing countries was larger compared to the developed countries. Five percent of the population of the developing countries record of 20-25 percent of the income for the same population base.[2]

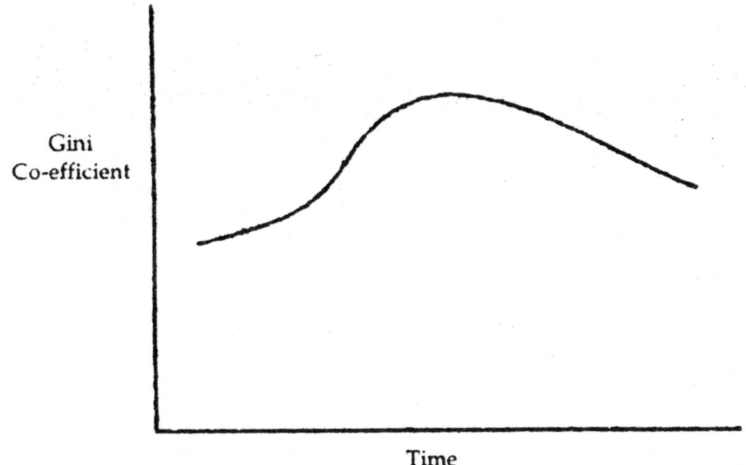

Figure 2: The Kuznets Inverted U Hypothesis

What are the sources of these income inequalities? Kuznets concentrates his attention first to the factors that contribute to the higher share of the top income groups in the undeveloped than the developed countries and secondly to the factors that may account for the lower share of the lower income groups in the developed than in the developing countries.

For the first category, he proposed two reasons, *viz.*, "the existence of occupational groups that, because of their high level of training and responsibility, need a substantial minimum income to enable the participant to pursue his activity effectively and to attract an adequate supply of new entrants."[3] One similarity of developed and developing countries pertain to the prevalence of high income groups in the urban centres. The difference being in the nature of the contrast between the urban and rural centres in the developed and the developing countries. This is the second reason. Kuznets notes that the "differentials in productivity and per worker income between the countryside and the city are significantly wider in the underdeveloped than in the developed countries, reflecting their far greater economic backwardness in the agricultural than in the non-agricultural sectors .... Thus the larger share of income of the top groups in the underdeveloped countries reflects in part the greater contrast between the rural and the urban incomes."[4]

How do you account for the shares of the low income groups? The developed world has a lower share compared to the developing countries. Kuznets points to the high average per capita income of the former. This being the result of generally divergent income differentials between the two regions. He points to the " different skills of the occupations and differences in the distribution of income yielding assets..."[5]

According to Kuznets structural differentials also contributes to this fact. Developing countries have an extended family non-income generating dependants exhausting this is not the case in the developed countries, more characterized by independent separate family units, a nuclear family with a higher per capita income, provided for by social security and a greater opportunity' to accumulate savings for retirement.[6]

Kuznets findings were supported by research undertaken by Irving B. Kravis. Using the United States as the reference he found inequality in Italy, Puerto Rico, El Salvador and Sri Lanka. The United States had comparable inequality in Britain, Japanan and Canada. Denmark, Netherlands and Israel had less inequality. Kravis concluded that the developing countries have relatively greater inequality than the developed countries.[7]

Adelman and Morris gathered data from forty-three developing countries. Using analysis of variance, they found six explanatory factors of income inequality. Among the factors was the level of economic development.[8] Adelman and Morris's work was refined further by Paukert by the incorporation of more reliable data. He tabulated income distribution and per capita GDP data from fifty-six countries. Empirical evidence showed that inequality begins at a comparatively low level, reaches a peak in countries with per capita income of $301-$500, then diminishes at higher incomes.[9]

Oshima opined that the major determinants of income inequality, at least in Asian countries, appears to be the weight of the rural or farm sector in the total economy. He maintains that other factors are trival.[10] This dualism is characterized by the coexistence of a low-productivity subsistence agricultural sector and a high-productivity agri business and the industrial sector in the developing society. This distinct dualism generates great income inequalities that many people in the developing countries are worse off during development compared to the pre-industrial stage.

In case of Malaysia our approach is to use time series data for a particular country to prove the above relationship. Unfortunately good estimates of measure of income distribution for each country are difficult to come by.

A preliminary survey of the social and economic statistics of Malaysia unearthed Gini Coefficients dating from Independence Day in 1957 to 1989, albeit calculated every few years. This affords an opportunity to observe the relevance of Kuznets Inverted U Hypothesis as it applies to the Malaysian development experience.

Table 1
Estimates of Inequality in Relation to GNP Per Capita

Country groups	*Number of countries*	*Gini coefficient*	*GNP per capita ($)*
1. Low-income	11	0.427	256
2. Lower-middle-income	16	0.505	867
3. Upper-middle-income	12	0.428	2,623
4. Industrial market economies18	0.331	8,664	

Source: Adapted from Montek S. Ahluwalia, "Inequality, Poverty and Development", Journal of Development Economics, 3, 1976, pp. 340-341 and World Bank, Development Report 1985, pp. 228-29. GNP figures for 1975 at 1983 base year.

ECONOMIC DEVELOPMENT AND INCOME DISTRIBUTION IN MALAYSIA: 1957-1990

On the eve of independence in 1957, Malaysia (then known as Malaya) was a country heavily dependent upon tin and rubber, which together accounted for 85 percent of total exports and 45 percent of the GDP.[11] The narrow and non-diversified base of the economy was not the only problem. The country was also plagued by poverty, an unequal distribution of income among the major ethnic groups as well as between regions.[12] The non-homogenous ethnic character of the country presented special political problems, an additional complication not faced by other homogenous countries as they confront the spectre of unequal income distribution. The incidence of poverty was most prevalent among the Malays, the majority of which lived in the rural areas and were engaged in such activities as fishing, cultivation of rice, coconuts and farming in general. Not surprisingly, the average annual income per capita among the Malays was M$367, about 43 percent of the annual per capita income of the Chinese.

Even after ten years of independence, the average Malay earned about M$l,770 while the non-Malay received M$3,200 annually,[13] This was because the non-Malay dominated the more lucrative economic sectors such as mining, commerce and construction. These are all concentrated in the urban areas. During the Communist Insurgency (1948-60), many

Chinese were resettled from the jungle fringes into 'new villages' a strategy to deny the predominantly Chinese communists logistic and manpower support. In the new villages, all modern infrastructure as well as basic amenities were provided by the government. The inhabitants of these new villages also had better access to educational facilities.

The colonial administration in Malaya, brought in Chinese and Indian labourers to develop the lucrative tin and rubber industries. While these two category of workers were concentrated in the more progressive geographic areas, the Malays were left in the rural areas with little opportunity to develop economically or socially, although they maintain political power. Ishak and Ragayah[14] viewed the problem of income inequality as a consequence of earning differentials among the three ethnic groups, brought about by differences in skill and education. Their work provides a brief overview of the prevailing socio-economic scenario in the period after independence and leading to the bloody ethnic riots of May 13, 1969.

One bitter lesson drawn from the experience is the importance of achieving a balance between socio-political progress and a fair distribution of the country's wealth. Although economic progress was impressive, income distribution was sadly lopsided. Occupied and Economic activity was identifiable according to ethnicity. This state of affairs remains a stumbling block in efforts at racial harmonization and integration. Against this background of imbalances, the 1969 national elections were thrown into turmoil by elements within the political parties to instigate upheavals challenging the political rights and special position of the Malays, a condition agreed upon by all immigrant groups prior to obtaining automatic citizenship in a newly independent Malaysia.

The ethnic riots of 1969 awakened the government to the need to take an active role in resolving the country's imbalances. The programme of action was formulated within the New Economic Policy (NEP).

THE NEW ECONOMIC POLICY (1971-1990)

The NEP is essentially a programme of socio-economic engineering, which address certain structural and destabilizing imbalances inherent within the economy. Over the twenty years of its implementation, it was undoubtedly a stunning success. Before the NEP, the incidence of poverty stood at 49.3 percent. Of this, the largest number of poor households was in the rural areas, 58.7 percent compared to 21.3 percent in the urban areas. The Malays still constitute the majority of the poor, 65 percent compared to 26 percent for the Chinese and 39 percent for the Indians.

With respect to ownership of the corporate share capital, the Malays control only 2.4 percent of the total, compared to 34.3 percent of the other Malaysians. (Please see Table 2).

The NEP has a two-prong objective, *viz.:*

(a) to reduce poverty irrespective of race, and

(b) to restructure Malaysian society by eliminating the identification of race with economic function.[15]

Table 2
Selected Socio-economic Targets Under Nep

Incidence of Poverty	*1970*	*1976*	*1990 (Achieved)*	*1990 (Targeted)*
Peninsular Malaysia				
Overall	49.3	-	15.0	16.7
Rural	58.7	-	19.3	23.0
Urban	21.3	-	7.3	9.1
Malay	65.0	-	20.8	-
Chinese	26.0	-	5.7	-
Indians	39.0	-	8.0	-
Others	44.8	-	18.0	-
Sabah	-	58.3	-	34.4
Sarawak	-	56.5	21.0	-
Ownership of Equity Malays	2.4	-	20.3	30.0
Other Malaysians	34.3	-	54.6	40.0
Foreigners	63.3	-	25.1	30.0

Source: Adapted from Government of Malaysia, The Second Outline Perspective Plan, 1991- 2000, Kuala Lumpur, National Printing Department, 1991, pp. 34-46.

The redistribution was to take place through the growth of the economy, so that one ethnic group would not benefit at the expense of the others. This essentially means that efforts were geared towards upgrading the economic status of the Malays 'while at the same time not neglecting the rest of the population. Efforts were made to:

(a) reduce poverty by providing opportunities for the poor to move into more productive employment and by setting up industries especially in the rural areas;

(b) provide better and more efficient services in the areas of housing, transportation, public utilities, education, health, nutrition and family planning; and

(c) accelerate the creation of productive employment opportunity in the secondary and tertiary sectors.[16]

The first target of the NEP was to reduce the incidence of poverty to 16.7 percent by the year 1990. An important element of this is the creation of the Bumiputera Commercial and Industrial Community (BCIC). This is to ensure the participation of Bumiputera (literally sons of the soil) individuals in the modern sectors of the economy. By the end of the NEP, the Bumiputeras should own and manage at least 30 percent of the total commercial and industrial activities of the economy.

It was hoped that the above programmes would bring about a greater integration and a more equitable distribution of wealth among the various ethnic groups as well as correct, the imbalances in regional development. It was the firm belief of the government that the goals of the NEP should be implemented within the context of rapid economic growth. Real GDP growth was targeted to grow at an annual rate of 8 percent, a level thought necessary for generating a sufficiently high rate of employment. With an 8 percent growth, it was projected that the unemployment rate would be gradually reduced from 7.4 percent to 3.6 percent by 1990, thus reaching full employment.

At the end of the implementation period in 1990, indicators show that the NEP fell short of its targets due in part to the global recession in the mid-1980s. Although the overall incidence of poverty in Peninsular Malaysia decreased from 49.3 percent in 1970 to 15 percent (improving on the objective by 1.7 percent), poverty is still concentrated within the traditional primary sectors and the rural areas.[17]

In terms of occupation, the small rubber holders, paddy farmers, small coconut holders and fishermen still constitute a large proportion of the poor. Since the Btimiputera dwell mostly in the rural areas and work in these sectors, the incidence of poverty within this ethnic group has improved but remains high. The restructuring of the society to remove the identification of economic activity with ethnicity still needs further policy stress.

THE KUZNETS INVERTED U HYPOTHESIS: THE MALAYSIAN CASE

Malaysia is a rapidly developing country on the threshold of moving into the ranks of the Newly Industrialized Economies. Except for 1985, when the GDP decreased by M$2 billion (due to the global recession), Malaysia has shown a consistent pattern of economic growth averaging 8 percent annual growth in the late 80s and the 90s. It presents an opportunity to observe the relevance of Kuznets hypothesis as it relates to the Malaysian development experience. Table 3 details the growth in GDP and the trend of the associated Gini Coefficients over time.

Figure 3 is a graphical representation of Table 3 and provides a classic Kuznets inverted *V*. With Independence, the income inequality was not pronounced, reflected in a low Gini Coefficient. As the government embarked on successive five-year development plans, the income inequality worsened as a portion of the population began to reap a bigger share of the nation's wealth. Following the debilitating 1969 ethnic riots; the government formulated and implemented the NEP, basically a socio-economic restructuring programme. Consistent with Kuznets hypothesis/. income inequality continues to worsen even as the economy grew. The Gini Coefficient peaked in 1976 at 0.532. With continuing economic growth and the NEP, development programmes aimed at

Table 3
Economic Growth and the Gini Coefficient 1957-1989

Year	*GDP Million of $M*	*Gini Coefficient*
1957/1958	NA	0.412
1967/1968	NA	0.438
1970	12,155	0.502
1973	18,723	0.530
1976	28,085	0.532
1979	46,426	0.508
1984	79,550	0.480
1987	79,625	0.456
1989	102,587	0.445

Note: Adapted from International Monetary Fund, International Financial Statistics Yearbook, 1995/ Washington, IMP/ 1996. Base year for GDP is 1990. Gini Coefficient figures for 1970-1989 obtained from Economics Planning Unit, Prime Minister's Department, Malaysia. Figures for 1957/58 and 1967/68 taken from David Um, Readings on Malaysian Economic Development, London, Oxford University Press, 1975/ pp. 4243 and p. 272 .

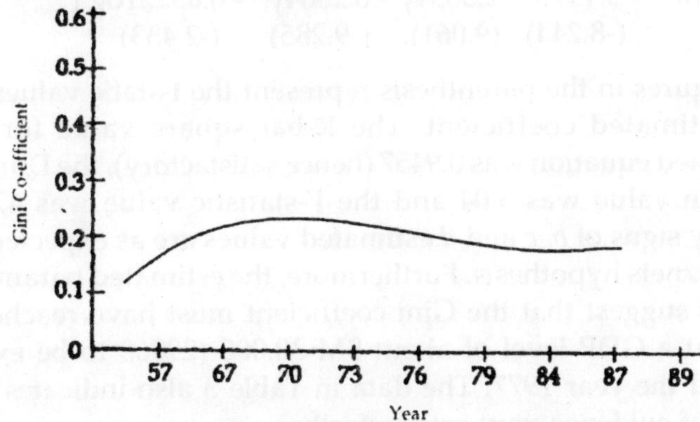

Figure 3: Malaysia: Gini Coefficient Over Time

eradicating poverty begins to take effect. The Gini Coefficient continually declines well into the early 1990s as the inequality improves.

In order 'to justify the observation of Figure 3 we decided to run a regression of the following form:

$$\text{Gini} = a + by + cy'' + dt'$$

where *a, b,* c and *d* are coefficients, y is the logarithm of per capita real GNP, y" is the square of y and t' is time period of one year and t′ is the logarithm of time period. Hence the time of the sample period becomes 1, 10, 13, 16, 19, 22, 27, 30 and 32. Clearly by running the regression parameters to be estimated are *a, b, c* and d. If the Kuznets hypothesis is true, then, in econometrics terms, the value of *b* will be positive and c will be negative.

This means, as developing economies grow, 'the higher value of per capita income leads to higher Gini values which means income inequality grows. This will be the net impact of growth; notwithstanding the inequality reducing influence of any social and institutional factors inherent to the economy. But income inequality necessarily declines as per capita income increases beyond a threshold level. When the above equation was estimated by using the data in this paper with the ordinary least squares technique, the following results were obtained:

$$\text{Gini} = -\ 5.1375 + 2.5634y - 0.2864y'' - 0.0522\log t$$
$$(-8.244)\quad (9.061),\quad (-9.285)\quad (-2.433)$$

Figures in the parenthesis represent the t-static values for the estimated coefficient. The R-bar square value for the estimated equation was 0.9457 (hence satisfactory), the Durbin-Watson value was 3.04 and the F-statistic value was 47.42. Clearly signs of *b, c* and *d* estimated values are as expected by the Kuznets hypothesis. Furthermore, the estimated parameter values suggest that the Gini coefficient must have reached a peak at a GDP level of about $M 30,000 (29868 to be exact) around the year 1977. The data in Table 3 also indicates this piece of evidence very satisfactorily.

Hence, the econometric analysis supports the overall claim in this paper that Kuznets' hypothesis is eminently suitable for the economy of Malaysia.

CONCLUSION

The Malaysian development experience provides empirical evidence in support of Kuznets Inverted U Hypothesis, in addition to the studies conducted by Kravis, Adelman and Morris, Paukert and Oshima. Indeed, with economic growth, the income distribution worsened initially and bottomed in 1976 and thereafter steadily improved.

Malaysia's basic problem is one of dualism. The economy is divided into two sectors, an impoverished traditional, rural agricultural sector and the more affluent urban sector. Although the New Economic Policy has shown positive gains, the results are- far from satisfactory. The majority of the poor Malay have not benefited as much from development policies as those in the higher income bracket. While the NEP does provide additional venues of employment for the poor Malay, some distracters have pointed out that the fundamental reasons for rural poverty have yet to be tackled. While this category of the population is still relatively poor compared to the rest of the society, the development agencies have contributed to their economic betterment. Agricultural research agencies for instance have produced disease resistant and high yielding strain of crops. Better irrigation and fast maturing hybrids have enabled rice to be harvested twice in one year, essentially doubling the income of the paddy farmers. These are significant achievements.

Nevertheless, ethnicity continues to be associated with occupation. The creation of a Malay business community and the restructuring of economic occupation can indeed eliminate the identification of economic activity with ethnicity but a word of caution is forthcoming. The overzealous promotion of Malay interests should not ignore the needs of the non-Malays for it can breed discontent and aggravate ethnic tensions. So far, economic growth has benefited cost of the target groups. Everyone got a bigger slice of the economic pie. As the adage goes, everyone rises with the tide. So long as economic development continues, more time will be available for better integration of the populace, contributing eventually to political stability. Political stability, it must be stressed is a prerequisite for economic development. We confirmed our results by completing an econometric analysis to test the behaviour of Gini Coefficient.

NOTES

1. Sumon Kuznets, "Economic Growth and Income Inequality", *The American Economic Review,* XIV, No.1, March 1955, pp. 1-28.
2. Simon Kuznets, *"Economic Growth and Structure - Selected Essays",* New York, W.W. Norton & Company, 1965, pp. 257-287.
3. *Ibid.,* p. 295.
4. *Ibid.,* p. 297.
5. *Ibid.*
6. *Ibid.,* p. 299.
7. Irving B. Kravis, "International Differences in the Distribution of Income", *Review of Economics and Statistics,* November 1960, pp. 408-16.
8. Irma Adelman and Cynthia Taft Morris, *"Economic Growth and Social Equity in Developing Countries"*, Stanford, Stanford University Press, 1973.
9. F. Paukert; "Income Distribution at Different Levels of Development: A Survey of Evidence", *International Labor Review,* August-September 1973, pp. 97-125.
10. H.T. Oshima, "The International Comparison of Size Distribution of Family Incomes with Special Reference to Asia", *Review of Economics and Statistics,* Vol. 44, No.4, November 1962, pp. 439-445.
11. David Urn, *Readings on Malaysian Economic Development,* London, Oxford University Press, 1975, p. 11.
12. The population is categorized according to Bumiputera and non-Bumiputera. The former group consists of 55.25 percent Malays and 3.75 percent other indigenous people. The latter consist of the Chinese who make up 32.1 percent, the Indians 8.2 percent and others 0.7 percent. The statistics are from the 1980 and 1991 Census Report cited in *Malaysia* 1994 *Yearbook,* Kuala Lumpur, Berita Publishing, 1995, p. 53.
13. Sudhir Anand, *"Inequatity and Poverty in Malaysia: Measurement and Decomposition,* New York, Oxford University Press, 1983, pp. 4-6.
14. Ishak Shari and Ragayah Hj. Mat Zain, "Patterns and Trends of Income Distribution in Malaysia: 1970-1987", *Journal of Singapore Economic Review, 35,* 1990, pp. 103-104.
15. Government of Malaysia, *The Second Outline Perspective Plan, 1991-2000;* Kuala Lumpur, National Printing Department, 1991, p. 31.
16. Felix Gagliano, *Communal Violence in Malaysia* 1969: *The Political Aftermath,* Ohio, Center for International Studies, 1971, pp. 31-35.
17. Government of Malaysia, *The Second Outline Perspective,* p. 46.

BIBLIOGRAPHY

Ahluwalia, Montek S., "Inequality, Poverty and Development", *Journal of Development Economics, 3,* 1973.

Alderman, Irma and Cynthia Taft Morris, *Economic Growth and Social Equity in Developing Countries,* Stanford, Stanford University Press, 1973.

Anand, Sudhir, *Inequality and Poverty in Malaysia: Measurement and Decomposition,* New York, Oxford University Press, 1983.

Berita Publishing, *Malaysia* 1994 *Yearbook,* Kuala Lumpur, Berita Publishing, 1995.

Frank, Charles L. and Richard C. Webb, eds, *Income Distribution and Growth* ill *the Less Developed Countries,* Washington, The Brookings Institute, 1977.

Gagliano, Felix, *Communal Violence in Malaysia* 1969: *The Political Aftemlath,* Ohio, Centre for International Studies, 1971.

Government of Malaysia, The *Second Outline Perspective Plan, 1991-2000,* Kuala Lumpur, National Printing Department, 1991.

International Monetary Fund, *International Financial Statistics Yearbook 1995,* Washington, IMF, 1996.

Kravis, Irving B., "International Differences in the Distribution of Income", *Review of Economics and Statistics,* November 1960.

Kuznets, Simon, "Economic Growth and Income Inequality", The *American Economic Review,* Vol. XIV, No.1, March 1955.

Kuznets, Simon, *Economic Growth and Structure - Selected Essays,* New York, W.W. Norton and Company, 1965.

Lim, David, *Readings on Malaysian Economic Development,* London, Oxford University Press, 1975.

Oshima, H.T., "The International Comparison of Size Distribution of Family Income with Special Reference to Asia", *Review of Economics and Statistics,* Vol. 44, No. 4 November 1-2.

Paukert, F., "Income Distribution at Different Levels of Development: A Survey of Evidence", *International Labor Review,* August-September 1977.

Shari, Ishak and Ragayah Hj. Mat Zain, "Patterns and Trends of Income Distribution in Malaysia 1970-1987", *Journal of Singapore Economic Review, 35,* 1990.

World Bank, *Development Report* 1985, Washington D.C., World Bank, 1986.

22

A CASE OF PROTECTIONIST POLICIES AND ECONOMIC WELFARE:
Some Evidence from Syria's Economy

INTRODUCTION

This chapter attempts to summarize the effects of import tariffs on a small economy and it revisits the arguments for protectionist policies. It then examines the case of Syria, which has had a long history of trade restrictions. As a small country, Syria's protectionist tariffs have impeded its economic growth and have had an overall negative impact on its economy. This impact can be fully realized when Syria's economic policies and performance are compared to other countries in its region. Although it would make economic sense to reform trade policies, there are numerous political reasons why the government chooses to maintain its protectionist stance.

Less developed countries (LDCs) have in the past justified protectionist tariffs by a variety of arguments, including market failure arguments; particularly those affecting the labor sector and unemployment, protection of domestic industries (especially "infant industries"), social benefits not realized in the free market model, and the need for government revenue to provide public services. The theory goes that smaller, less

---

First draft of this paper was presented in the Federation of Business Disciplines (FBD) meeting in march 2003 in Houston TX. (Co-author: Roger Dowd, University of Denver).

developed countries need protection from the larger developed countries, or their industries, workers and *societies* will suffer. Protectionist *policies,* then, are designed to help producers and government increase revenue while workers get to keep their jobs.

Free trade theorists argue that this tinkering with markets can often lead to undesirable effects. Recent studies and empirical experience suggest that protectionist strategies have been counterproductive. Syria's experience is a particularly striking example of the negative effects of these policies. While most other LDCs around the world, and even in the Arab region, have been liberalizing their economies and experiencing resulting growth, Syria has remained highly restrictive, and its growth has been stunted as a result.

The following section outlines the effects of tariffs on an economy and goes into further detail on protectionist arguments and free trade counter arguments. Section III evaluates Syria's protectionist strategies and its resulting economic performance. Section IV examines economic data of other countries in the region as a point of comparison, and discusses some of the political reasons that Syria's government has failed to implement reforms. Section V summarizes the results and offers a conclusion.

THE EFFECTS OF TARIFFS AND JUSTIFICATIONS FOR PROTECTIONISM

The standard trade model advanced by neo-classical economists relies on a cost-benefit analysis of the value to each group impacted by protectionist trade policies like tariffs. When a tariff is imposed, consumers lose overall surplus due to increased prices. That lost consumer surplus is partially regained by increased producer surplus, and partially by increased government revenues (the amount of the tariff times the quantity imported.) However, there is a portion of the lost consumer surplus that is not regained by any sector of the economy (the *efficiency* or *deadweight loss).* In a large country, this may be offset by the resulting gains in terms of trade. Therefore, a common justification for protectionist trade policies is that free markets are likely to damage their terms of trade, and instruments like tariffs can help improve a country's terms of trade. But, as Krugman and Obstfeld state, "most small countries have very little ability to affect the world prices of either their imports or other exports, so that the terms of trade arguments is of little practical importance" (Krugman, 224).

Therefore, justification for protectionism in small countries like Syria must lie with market failure arguments. Market failures in the labor sector, for instance, could account for high levels of unemployment; as labor might not easily be transferred from one sector to another, particularly extensive retraining or relocation were involved. Protectionist policies like tariffs could also increase a country's marginal social benefits something not accounted for in the neoclassical measures surplus. For instance, certain projects (like dams and railroads) may create external economies that would not be factored into producer gains in the classical market model and external diseconomies (like pollution) that would not re-factored as costs (Perkins, *et al., 152-154)*.

Further justification for tariffs in LDCs comes from the infant industries argument, which states that developing industries need protection from global competition with already-developed industries in the same sector, or they will not survive (like a "law of the manufacturing jungle".) The off-forgotten premise to this argument is that once the industry reaches maturity, its need for protection disappears.

Tariffs are also a crucial source of government revenue for many LDCs (Balassa, 94); they may be either unwilling or unable to effectively collect revenue from more typical resources in developed countries, like income or corporate taxes. Thus, the provision of public services may be dependent on tariff revenue. But the important factor here is what the government actually does with the revenues collected from the tariffs. Bhagwati (1969) noted that a country's terms of trade are likely to deteriorate if the government itself spends the tariff revenue as opposed to redistributing it to the private sector.

In effect, protectionist theory argues, government must intervene in some sectors of the economy to offset market failures elsewhere. This theory of the second best (the best being where markets operate as they should) is designed to increase the overall welfare of the country's economy, and has long provided justification for protectionist governments (Krugman, Obstfeld, 2001). But, one must ask, how good is second best? The increasingly poor comparative performance of small protectionist governments like Syria's has caused a major paradigm shift among economic development theorists, who are now more likely to adopt the standard model of protectionist effects outlined at the beginning of this section.

Ingco (1997) found that removing trade policy distortions in the agricultural sector in LDCs could convert the relatively small loss in terms of trade to potential gains, but that those countries that failed to liberalize their trade policy lost the opportunity for such gains. Rutherford and Tarr (1998) found that larger tariff cuts in developing -countries have produced "larger estimated welfare gains at least proportionate to the size of the cut". And the costs of trade liberalization, particularly in the form of unemployment, seem to be relatively short-term and are minimal compared to the relative benefits, as Matusz and Tarr (1999) discovered. In fact, normal labor turnover is often greater than unemployment resulting from trade liberalization. In addition, the unemployment doesn't tend to last long, and there is usually an increase in manufacturing employment in LDCs a year after liberalization.

The benefits of revenue to the government are dubious at best. As Perkins, *et al.*, note, "a major source of inefficiency in taxation is excessive costs of tax administration. In some countries and for some taxes these costs have been so high that they call into question the desirability of using certain taxes for any purposes" (472). With each tariff that is introduced comes a layer of bureaucracy that carries real costs.

Studies focusing on the Arab world in particular indicate the need for badly needed reform in the region. Blavy's study of Arab nations in the Levant (2001) finds them to be far more restrictive than most other LDCs, with resulting lower rates of growth and economic welfare. Both Abdalla and Tahir (1997) found that trade intervention policies in the Arab world have had negative impacts on economic growth, and advocate for free market reforms to liberalize imports and promote exports (though they note that these should be preceded by deflationary fiscal policy and devaluation of exchange rates). Yet even in the economically restrictive Arab world, Syria has some of the highest rates of protectionism and the poorest economic indicators.

CASE STUDY: SYRIA

The desired effects of the protectionist arguments outlined above are as follows: 1. Producers will gain by increasing market price, particularly in infant industries; 2. Governments will gain in the form of revenues, which would then be, theoretically, redistributed back to society via the public sector; 3. Workers will gain by retaining their jobs, and 4. The populace will gain from increased social benefits that would not be realized in the free markets competition. One would expect, then, to see countries with protectionist policies exhibit vibrant developing industries that bolster continual national economic growth, a government that promotes public welfare, redistributing income through effective social programs, low unemployment and decent standards of living for its people.

The above is far from the case in Syria. As Gambill notes, Syria is "one of, the poorest countries in the Middle East (per capita GNP being a mere $1010 in 1999), saddled by one of the highest rates on annual population growth in the region (2.7%), negative economic growth (-1.7% in 1999), skyrocketing unemployment (estimated at 20%), a negative balance of trade, and dwindling oil reserves (2.5 billion barrels)" (Gambill, 1).

Syria is indeed a small country in economic terms in just about every sector. With a GDP of under $20 billion, it can hardly consider itself a major player on the world economic stage. Even in sectors like petroleum, it makes up only a fraction of the world market, unlike many of its Arab neighbors. Probably its biggest sectors relative to world markets, are in some agricultural crops and industries like textiles; although these can hardly be said to have a significant impact on world prices.

It is also a labor abundant country, with high unemployment rates indicating a surplus of labor. Syria's exports reflect this labor abundance: only three commodities (oil, cotton and wheat) comprise 81% of total exports, all of which are labor-intensive raw materials (ArabicNews.com, 4/24/99).

Syria also has one of the highest rate of trade restrictions in the world. These restrictions take the form of tariffs, quotas, licenses and red tape barriers. Informally, Syria's high rates of corruption, intellectual piracy and black market activity also constitute barriers to free trade.

The average tariff rate in Syria is 45.44 per cent (Heritage Freedom Index). The U.S. State Department reports that customs duties are progressively taxed from 1 to 100 percent, and for finished products rates can be extremely high – exceeding 200 per cent for passenger cars!

Licensing and red tape barriers offer further restrictions. While the State Department notes merely that customs procedures are "cumbersome and tedious", some of the anecdotal evidence of hindrances to free trade approaches the ridiculous:

"The SARG requires that export and import licenses be obtained for every single item imported and then re-exported, regardless of value. Several company representatives recalled that documentation for even minor items, such as paint cans and used spark plugs, had to be kept to prove to customs officials that they had not been illegally re-exported or sold locally. Likewise, foreign companies must acquire temporary permits for each item of equipment intended for temporary use and subsequent re-export to avoid paying import duties. These permits can be difficult to extend if the company's service contract has expired, and if it wants to keep the equipment in country for stand-by usage. Delays in the re-export of equipment after a temporary permit expires have drawn heavy fines" (Country Watch.com, 44).

Just how well are these policies faring? In the production sector, economic growth has trouble keeping pace with high rates of population growth. "Some economists estimate that Syria needs to achieve a seven per cent growth rate-a huge increase on the current rate-to accommodate the army of young people entering the employment market each year" (BBC, 1). The largely centrally controlled export sector set plan for 1998 called for exports of U.S. $238 million, but fell far short at U.S. $131 million, achieving only 56% of the goal (Arabic News.com, 4/24/99). The infant industries argument does not seem to hold up well here.

The government has certainly gained from the protectionist policies. The problem is that little of the revenue collected gets redistributed to the private sector (which can cause deterioration in the terms of trade noted by Bhagwati above). In addition, much does not even make it into the public sector due to the high levels of corruption:

"Syria's outmoded custom regulations are another area where elite interests have blocked reform. Syria has one of the highest custom rates in the world, yet the government's customs revenue is very small. The amount of money skimmed off by corrupt officials before it reaches the treasury has been estimated at $1 billion per year. In some cases, customs regulations are specifically tailored to enrich well-connected elites. Tobacco imports are banned, for example, precisely because figures close to the regime profit from smuggling cigarettes into the country. Imports of a variety of other consumer goods are prohibited outside the so-called 'free zone,' an enclave in Damascus managed by two of Bashar (al Assad)' maternal cousins, Rami and Ihab Makhlouf. Not surprisingly, the government has not made any significant efforts to reform the customs systems" (Gambill, 3).

As noted earlier, the workers certainly seem not to have benefited from Syria's trade restrictions, based on unemployment figures of around 20%. The societal benefits of such policies seem unclear: 54 per cent of the rural population lives in poverty, while 25 per cent of the urban populations are below the poverty line (al-Qudsi, in Tahir, 224).

So who does benefit from restrictions on trade in Syria? Clearly, it is the elites who control such policy. The government benefits, especially through corruption, cronyism, nepotism and clientelism in the state sector. And the producers of protected industries also benefit. But can one say that Syria's economy is better off than it might be due to protectionist policies? One could argue that its economic status is due to problems in the region, which leads us to an analysis of other countries in the Middle East and North Africa (MENA) region for comparison.

COMPARISON WITH OTHER ECONOMIES IN THE REGION

Syria ranked 15th among 18 countries in the MENA region based on economic performance indicators. Worldwide, Syria came immediately *behind* Bangladesh, Ukraine and Honduras. (Syria Report, 7/5/02). Being ranked so low in the MENA region is significant, for that region is marked by some of the most restrictive trade policies and poorest economic development in the world. An IMF Working paper by Blavy (2001) examining trade in the Mashreq (the Levantine region of the Middle East encompassing Syria, Lebanon, Israel, Jordan and Egypt) found that "intra-regional trade is at very low levels, especially when compared with other regions" ... which was largely due to the fact that "trade restrictions in the Mashreq are higher than in other developing regions" (Blavy, 3). He goes on to note:

> "Over the last two decades the Mashreq (excluding Israel) has lost one-half of its share in world exports ... while developing countries as a whole broadly held their share constant. At the same time, Israel increased its share of exports by 50 per cent, while East Asia doubled its share. As a result, the share of the Mashreq region in world exports in 1999 was ... only 0.2 per cent when Israel is not included. As measured by the share of trade in GDP, the Mashreq region has in fact become less open between 1980 and 1999. Only Jordan and the West Bank and Gaza experience levels of openness that are comparable to the average developing country (70 per cent of GDP). When only exports are considered, the gap is even wider, with exports amounting to 13.4 per cent of GDP in Mashreq countries (excluding Israel, where exports as a per cent of GDP reach 26.1 per cent) compared to 37.1 per cent in the average developing country" (Blavy, 4).

Blavy cited the IMF trade restrictiveness (Trest) index (ranked 1 to 10), which measured the levels of a nation's protectionist trade policies: Syria ranked 10. The scores of others in the region: Israel 4, Egypt 8, Jordarumd Lebanon, 7. Blavy's study estimates that a reduction of Syria's trade restrictiveness to sample average levels of 4.7 (along with exchange rate and political reforms) would have an impact of a 106% improvement in Syria's economy. "If the index of trade restrictiveness were to decline by 1 unit (toward a less restricted regime), the model suggests that exports would be increased by 20 per cent... the potential impact for comprehensive trade liberalization would be substantial" (Blavy, 14). The following chart compares relative levels of trade restriction and economic indicators in Syria's geographical region.

The chart shows levels of protectionism in Mashreq countries against GDP growth (factored against population growth). There does seem to be an inverse correlation between the two figures: the higher the levels of protectionism, the lower the rates of real GDP growth.

Country	*Trest* Score*	*Trade policy-*	*Govt. Interv**	*GDP growth***	*GDP per cap*
Egypt	8.0	5.0	3.0	1.6%	$1,420
Israel	4.0	2.0	3.5	2.2%	$16,400
Jordan	7.0	4.0	3.0	3.1 %	$1,650
Lebanon	7.0	4.0	3.0	0.8%	$2,900
Syria	10.0	5.0	5.0	-1.9%	$1,100

* Trade restrictiveness, scale 1 (least restrictive) to 10 (most restrictive). (Source: IMF Trade Restrictiveness Index).

** Scale of 1 (low level of protectionism) to 5 (high level of protectionism) (Source: Heritage Foundation Economic Freedom Index).

* Level of Government Intervention: Scale of 1 (low) to 5 (high) (Source: Heritage Foundation Economic Freedom Index).

** Factored against population growth.

However, other countries in this region have been gradually loosening their trade restraints in the last few years, and have been experiencing resulting growth, while Syria has continued its protectionist patterns. " ... the government has made It clear that full liberalization is not on the cards. The government is unwilling to privatize the loss-making state sector, which employs around a quarter of the workforce. In addition, there is a formidable group in government, often referred to as the 'old guard', who have profited from the current system and have no wish to see reforms flourish" (BBC, 2).

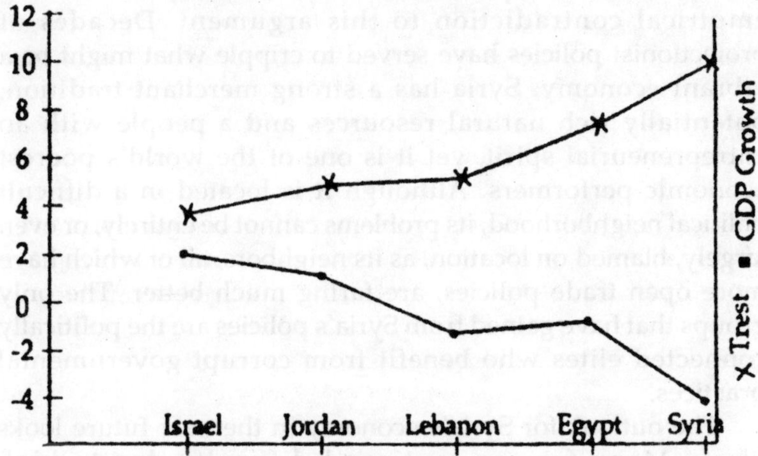

Chart 1: Mashraq Trade Restrictiveness v GDP Growth

This last group is one of the key reasons why Syria has continued its protectionist policies despite the large amount of evidence that they are not successful. While there would be many winners as a result of reform, including the consumers at large, people in rural areas, and small business owners in the private sector, the potential losers, as a result of reform, including businesses who receive subsidies and protection, those in the government bureaucracy and state-run sectors and the elites who benefit from corruption, as well as the "military-mercantile complex" discussed by Gambill (2001), are the ones in charge. They are not likely to want to change the system, and given the lack of political freedom in the country, they are able to squelch economic reform movements. The presence of the Israeli-Palestinian conflict and the worldwide climate of the war on terror give the government political justification for crushing reform movements of any kind.

SUMMARY AND CONCLUSION

Protectionists would have us believe that trade restrictions are necessary to protect consumers, infant industry, workers and society in less developed countries. The case of Syria is a strong empirical contradiction to this argument. Decades of protectionist policies have served to cripple what might be a vibrant economy. Syria has a strong merchant tradition, potentially rich natural resources and a people with an entrepreneurial spirit, yet it is one of the world's poorest economic performers. Although it is located in a difficult political neighborhood, its problems cannot be entirely, or even largely, blamed on location, as its neighbors, all of which have more open trade policies, are faring much better. The only groups that have gained from Syria's policies are the politically connected elites who benefit from corrupt governmental practices.

The outlook for Syria's economy in the near future looks bleak. Many foresee continued difficulty due to high population growth and levels of defense spending, in addition to the low production and export incentives due to the protective nature of the economy (Arabic News. com, 5/22/99). In fact, Syria is one of the few nations on the globe that is continuing to expand its public sector, while most LDCs are moving toward privatization and open markets (tradeport.org). As reported recently in an online news journal specializing in the Middle East:

> "Syria's economic system and inward-oriented development strategy has not helped its economic integration objectives. They, in fact, hindered integration in the following ways. First, the central planning model that Syria and several other Arab states followed were feared by Arab states that followed a free enterprise economic model. Second, the import substitution strategy pursued by Syria was chosen over an export-oriented strategy that could have mobilized Syria's resources to meet the demands of the Arab region for food and manufacturing. Third, Syria's manufacturing products

produced under a protective trade regime were unable to compete in quality and price in the

Gulf markets which became in the last twenty years the largest and most buoyant in the Arab world. The Gulf States adopted open trade regimes, importing goods from all over the world almost duty free. Fourth, the private sector was constrained and was not able to grow enough to explore opportunities for trade with other Arab states" (ArabicNews.com,5/22/99).

The current political situation compounds Syria's economic problems even further. The Middle East crisis allows the Syrian government to justify repressive measures and protectionist policies. Since the government itself is benefiting from the status quo, there seems little reason to change. Once again, it seems that economic reform and political reform must go hand in hand. In the end, it is the people who suffer from restrictions on political and economic freedom.

BIBLIOGRAPHY AND REFERENCES

"1997 Country Reports on Economic Policy and Trade Practices: Syria", US State Department *website,www.state gov.*

Abdalla, Adil, "Recent Developments in Trade Issues", in Tahir, Jamil, ed., *Economic Theory Underlying Adjustment Policies in Arab Countries,* Elsevier, Amsterdam, 1997.

Al-Qudsi, Sulayman, "Labor Markets and Structural Adjustment Policies: Implications to Developing and Arab Countries", in Tahir, Jamil, ed., *Economic Theory Underlying Adjustment Policies in Arab Countries,* Elsevier, Amsterdam, 1997.

"Analysis: Syria's Economic Challenge', *BBC News Online,* http:/ / news.bbc.co.uk, July 17, 2001.

Balassa, B. *et al.* eds., *The Structure of Protection in Developing Countries,* Baltimore: Johns Hopkins University Press, Baltimore, 1971.

Bhagwati, Jagdish, *The Economics of Underdeveloped Countries,* McGraw-Hill, New York, 1966.

Bhagwati, Jagdish, *Protectionism,* MIT Press, Cambridge, MA, 1988.

Bhagwati, *Trade, Tariffs and Growth,* MIT Press, Cambridge, MA, 1969.

Blanford, Nicholas, "Hopesfor Political Reform Eclipsed in Syria", *Christian Science Monitor,* May 20, 2002.

Blavy, Rodolphe, "Trade in the Mashreq: An Empirical Examination", IMF Working Paper WP /01/163, International Monetary Fund, October, 2001.

"Country Reports on Economic Policies and Trade Practices: Syria", US Department of Commerce-National Trade Data Bank, *www.tradeport.org,* September 3, 1999.

"Index of Economic Freedom", The Heritage Foundation, *http:// cf.heritage.org, 2002.*

Ingco, Merlinda, "Has Agricultural Trade liberalization Improved Welfare in the Least-Developed Countries? Yes", World Bank Working Paper WPS1748,1997.

Gambill, Gary, "The Political Obstacles to Economic Reform in Syria", *Middle East Intelligence Bulletin,* v. 3, n. 7, July, 2001.

Krugman, Paul, and Obstfeld, Maurice, *International Economics,* Fifth Edition, Addison-Wesley Longman, 2000.

Matusz; Stevn, and Tim, David, "Adjusting to Trade Policy Reform", World Bank Working Paper WPS2142, 1999.

Perkins, Dwight, *et al., Economics of Development,* Fifth Edition, Norton, New York, 2001.

Political Risk Yearbook, "Syria, The PRS Group, Oct. 2001.

Rutherford, Thomas, and Tarr, David, "Trade liberalization and Endogenous Growth in a Small Open Economy: A Quantitative Assessment", World Bank Working Paper WPS 1970; 1998.

"Syria Country' Review", Country Watch.com March 13, 2001.

"Syrian Public Sector's Exports Decline By 30%", *ArabicNews.com,* April 24, 1999.

"Syria Ranks 15 in Economic Performance in the MENA region, The Syria Report, *www.syria-report.com.* July 5, 2002.

"Syria's Economic System", *ArabicNews.com,* May 22,1999.

Tahir, ·Jamil, ed., *Economic Theory Underlying Adjustment Policies in Arab Countries,* Elsevier, Amsterdam, 1997.

23

IMPACT OF DUTCH DISEASE ON AN ECONOMY
A Case of Nigeria

INTRODUCTION

There is a widespread feeling amongst the lay public that economic growth is directly related to the available stock of natural resources. Without natural resources there can be no economic growth. Natural resources, defined in broader terms, may include all the stocks of physical assets, minerals, stocks of basic metals such as zinc, cooper, gold and silver and bed of such important ingredients as oil and natural gas. Many supporters of this hypothesis point out that the vulnerability of developing countries to consistent stagnation is because of the unavailability of natural resources.

In reality, however, there are several cases which disprove this belief. In the real world, some countries that have reserves of oil, and plentiful natural resources and which, should be supra-rich if the above analysis is true, survive very poorly. On the other hand, some other countries that lack natural resources have prospered to an extent that is envied by the whole world. Nigeria, Mexico and Argentina can be taken as the countries with plentiful resources, but lacking in growth.

This chapter is based on an article published in the 'Journal of Foreign Exchange and International Finance' Co-author: Erick Erickson.

And South Korea, Japan and Taiwan can be taken as the countries that lack resources, but are very prosperous in recent years.

Nonetheless, one can easily observe that natural resources historically have played an important role in the economic growth of some other countries. In modern times however it seems that human and capital resources are more important than natural resources. It is also important to see what type of economic policies the country has adopted to improve (or retard) economic growth. No wonder then that even Saudi Arabia, despite all the oil resources possesses has, has experienced economic difficulties. The best-known illness that afflicts the resource rich countries is called "Dutch disease" ... a term originated to describe the Netherlands' experience after her discovery of abundant natural gas reserves in the late 1970s.

The main purpose of this chapter is to examine the epidemic of the Dutch disease afflicted developing countries in general and Nigeria in particular. Compared to several other countries that experienced hardships, only Indonesia has apparently used her windfall cleverly to boost her economic growth. Nonetheless, the recent Asian crisis has hit the Indonesian economy very hard leading to the suspicions about her earlier gains from the oil windfall. The present chapter is organized in the following manner: Section I considers the theoretical explanation of the Dutch disease. Section II explains the appearance of the Dutch Disease in Nigeria from an increase in gasoline prices and increased foreign reserves that created economic hardships. Section III makes the summary and concludes our findings.

SECTION-I

THEORETICAL EXPLANATION OF THE DUTCH DISEASE

From the theoretical point of view the Dutch disease-occurs in the following sequence; as its main national export enjoys increased demand from the rest of the world, a nation's foreign reserves increase, its currency appreciates and its other exportable commodities see much decline in their demand. "Briefly, it refers to the situation whereby massive increases of revenues from primary product exports by a country produce paradoxes. It suffocates the' growth of other export sectors; and causes various economic problems such as unemployment, inflation and international payment imbalance". (See Harrison, 1993, page 194). In the case of the Netherlands, when major reserves of natural gas were discovered in the 1960s, an initial export boom and balance of payments surplus appeared to promise prosperity. Instead, during the 1970s the Dutch economy suffered from rising inflation and unemployment declining export of manufactures and lower rates of income growth. This experience taught the economists that the Dutch disease can be a very general phenomenon especially if the country depends upon only a few exports whose price and demand are increasing worldwide.

The oil boom of the 1970s and the early 1980s produced similar paradoxes in a number of other countries. Because it is the influx of foreign reserves that causes the Dutch disease, the syndrome can also result from large inflow of capital in any form (See Gillis and Perkins in the reference list, page 434).

If we define the nominal exchange rate (ER) as the actual exchange rate and real exchange rate (RER) as the one adjusted for inflations in both countries, then we can write the real exchange rate as

$$RER = ER\ (P^* / P)$$

where P is the foreign country's price level and P is the domestic price level.

To explain the effect of real exchange rate change on the balance of payments of the economy consider the impact of a real exchange rate decline on export industries. Suppose further that with a fixed exchange rate, domestic inflation is in excess of foreign inflation which causes exporters' profits to decline especially if domestic wages and the prices of domestic inputs rise faster than the price of exported goods. Hence, as domestic price level increase faster than the foreign price level, the real exchange rate decreases even if the nominal exchange rate stays the same.

As a result of the decrease in exporters' profits, exporters may reduce the quantity produced of exportables which can reduce the income and employment in the export sector. Thus, a reduction in the exchange rate can reduce the profits of the export sector. The appreciation of the real exchange rate can occur due to several reasons. First, the surplus of foreign currency caused by domestic economy's increased export earnings can reduce the domestic real exchange rate leading to appreciation of the domestic currency. Second, the booming exports can feed into the domestic money supply leading to higher domestic prices.

Thus, as exports go up, international reserves go up and the broadly defined domestic money supply increases.

Let MS= D + R,

where MS is money supply, D is the domestically originated money supply and R is the foreign reserves. With an increase in either D or R there is an increase in the money supply. An increase in money supply becomes the main cause of inflation in the economy that has experienced the increased export price. These are disturbing vital signs of the Dutch Disease. A · boom in primary exports after spurring faster domestic inflation and after causing an appreciation of real exchange rates can also make other exportable less competitive in the world markets. Added to this decline in competitiveness is the rising cost of production with increased prices of such products as utilities, wage rate, raw materials and transportation. This may lead to reduction in future production and therefore employment. Thus, another result of a rapid increase in an export price is a depression in the production of tradeable goods.

SECTION - II

DUTCH DISEASE: A CASE OF NIGERIA

As a major oil exporter and a member of the OPEC, Nigeria is expected to meet her basic requirements without much trouble. Moreover, one expects that Nigeria should have enough resources for capital development and investment in future of the country. Nonetheless, before becoming a major oil exporting country, Nigeria was mainly an agrarian country with mining as the second most important sector. Until 1972, oil was not the primary export of Nigeria. Table 1 lists the sectoral contributions to the total product of the Nigerian economy. In 1970, the agriculture sector pitched in 48.8 per cent of the total output which was a fall from 62.9 per cent in 1960. However the 1966-70 Civil War affected agricultural production. In 1980, agriculture share had fallen dramatically to 20 per cent and the government had to resort to a Green Revolution programme to revitalize the agriculture sector.

Table 1
Sectoral Contribution to Gross Domestic Product in Nigeria: 1960-1986

Year	*Agriculture*	*Petrol/ oil*	*Other Mining*	*Manufacturing*	*Construction*	*Transportation*
1960	62.9	0.2	1	4.8	4.8	4.9
1965	54.5	3.4	1.2	6.9	5.7	4.5
1970	48.8	9.3	1	7.2	5.8	2.8
1974	26.5	31.3	1.4	3.6	7.2	2.8
1980	20.6	29.1	1.8	8.4	7.6	3.5
1983	28.6	17.2	1.3	11.2	6.1	4.5
1986	36.3	11.4	0.7	11.4	2.4	4.9

Note: All figures are in percentages, and they do not add upto 100 per cent because of the smaller contributions of other unmentioned sectors.

The minor increase in agriculture's contribution from 1983 (with 28.6 per cent share) to 1986 (with 36 per cent share) was impressive but much less than expected by the governmental authority. As expected, the oil sector posted a sharp increase in its share in the total output of the economy. While oil contributed only 0.2 per cent of gross domestic output in 1960, it contributed 34 per cent in 1974. The share of oil declined mildly in 1980 to 29 per cent and to 11 per cent in 1986 when oil prices got stabilized. This reflects the impact of newly found oil resources in the Nigerian economy, and also oil price rise in 1973-74 when the oil prices quadrupled. This increase in gasoline price was further fuelled by another doubling of oil prices in the 1979-80 period. In Nigeria, the oil resources made for a windfall of 23 per cent of the non-mining Gross Domestic Product in 1974 and 12 per cent in 1979. Of course the main challenge was in use of these available resources. As it is well known, the Nigerian political system was marred by ethnic violence and competition among different ethnic groups to hold more resources. Added to these political burdens were the economically ill-fated decisions of a tremendous increase in government expenditure and the tax distribution. Thus, the Nigerian government used this windfall to expand its role in the provision of infrastructural facilities, free social services and capital expenditure for industrial development. As evidenced in Table 2, public expenditure increased from 4 per cent of GDP to 30 per cent of GDP. This obviously put pressure on the budget deficit that averaged annually to 12 per cent of the nominal GDP from the 1981 to 1984 period.

Table 2
Nigerian Total Expenditures as a Percentage of GDP

Year	*Consumption*	*Investment*	*Government Expenditure*	*Exports*	*Imports*
1960	71.55	14.07	5.12	14.82	13.92
1962	68	14.89	5.05	18.85	12.74
1964	67	18.77	5.32	19.27	13.51
1966	72.82	16.46	5.73	20.75	14.18
1970	66.14	18.99	8.27	21.61	14.82
1974	68.83	21.23	7.96	20.18	17.87
1978	69.77	32.74	15.66	19.23	44.24
1981	87.77	35.12	11.84	13.1	52.59
1982	92.91	27.27	11.65	9.27	41.03
1983	91.47	21.56	12.3	9.47	33.38
1984	87.56	16.52	13.04	11.62	27.38
1985	81.89	.23 ,23.55	11.14	13.55	29.69
1986	82.01	15.37	11.93	13.84	21.31

Note: AU figures are percentages. They do not add upto 100 because of small error and omission.

With the help of governmental biased policies towards the capital-intensive industrial sector, the oil boom era did not help much in agricultural growth. As the rural sector was politically weak, it received a smaller share of the windfall gain and agriculture suffered a setback. A case is easily made by an observation that before the oil price increase the Nigerian economy was a net exporter of such agricultural products as palm produce, cocoa, timber, cotton and rubber. However, this high production in a agriculture changed by mid-1980s as the resources were transferred to industrial development and oil production. In 1985, Nigeria had lost her lead in palm oil and cocoa exports. Ironically, the country had to resort to food imports of upto 58 per cent of total food consumption by 1986. Nigeria also imported 72 per cent of her industrial raw materials. This new development raised the overall price level of the economy and led to limited exports in future years. The decade of the 1980s saw a 90 per cent decline in exports of non-oil products ... a classic symptom of the Dutch disease!

On the other hand, the booming oil exports and the influx of foreign exchange also pushed down the exchange rate for a short duration. This resulted in an increase in imports and a decline in exports. From 1974 to 1984 the imports increased from 17.8 per cent of GDP to 33 per cent of GDP. Hence, imports almost doubled in 10 years. While imports were increasing, exports were declining. By 1983 Nigerian exports had fallen from 20 per cent of GDP to 9.47 per cent of GDP in only 10 years. Moreover the diversification of exports, which was a major characteristic before the oil boom, disappeared. The increase in imports over exports had to be financed by some outside source, in the Nigerian case the financing arrived from external borrowing. The country's total external debt amounted to only $570 million in 1970 but it dramatically increased to $24.5 billion in 1986.

As the figures in Table 3 show the modern times data of the Nigerian economy become even more interesting in the macroeconomic terms. While there has been a boost to the economy in terms of an increase in nominal GNP from 1992 onwards, the social conflicts and an unstable political situation

Table 3
Recent Data of the Nigerian Economy: 1986-1995

Year	*Nominal GNP*	*Foreign Exchange*	*CPI*	*Interest rate*	*Govt. Exp.*	*ER (nominal)*
1987	97,225	1165	40.1	12.75	22,018	4.14
1988	132,503	651	61.9	12.75	27,749	5.35
1989	207,173	1765	93.1	18.5	41,028	7.65
1990	238,624	3863	100	18.5	61,149	9.00
1991	299,511	4435	113	15.5	67,530	9.86
1992	485,408	967	163.4	17.5	107,703	19.64
1993	627,911	1372	256.8	26	174,524	21.88
1994	848,626	1386	403.3	13.5	141,615	21.99
1995	1,133,435	1443	696.9	13.5	189,231	21.88

Note: International Financial Statistics; Yearbook, International Monetary Fund (IMF) publications, 1994 edition, Washington D.C.

Source: Nominal GNP, Government Expenditure and Foreign Reserves Figures are measured in million of Naira. Exchange Rate is expressed as the number of domestic currency units (Naira) per unit of foreign currency (US dollar). The interest rate is the nominal interest rate.

retarded growth in the 1987 to 1992 period. In fact, the highest increase in nominal GNP was experienced only in 1989. It is important to notice, that the price increase has contributed substantially to the growth in nominal GNP. With the CPI figure of 100 in 1990 the price increase in the last six years was 696 per cent. This dearly has inflated the nominal GNP figures.

The Nigerian economic troubles seemed to have continued during the 1990s decade. The interest rate level reached to 26 per cent in 1993, and the exchange rate depreciated by 400 per cent in 8 years. The world economy therefore has lowered the expectations of a firm and stable economic situation in Nigeria. We tested the presence of the Dutch Disease in Nigeria by conducting a Two Stage Least Square regression of real GNP against the Nigerian exchange rate and crude oil production. Our data covered the years from 1996 through 1994. Over this period of time, the Nigerian exchange rate was closely correlated to its CPI (Observed R square = 0.999). To avoid multicollinearity, only the · Exchange Rate was used as a predetermined variable.

Let

RGDP = Real Nigerian Gross Domestic Product

ER = Nigerian Exchange Rate in terms of Naira per US dollar

CPP = Index of Crude Oil Production (1990 = 100)

FE = Foreign Exchange Holdings in Nigeria.

The model simultaneously estimated coefficients of the following simple RGDP estimator:

RGDP = aD + al.ER + a2.CPP + e (1)

where exchange rate is explained as a function of oil production and foreign currency holdings

ER = bO + bIFE + b2CPP + e_1 (2)

The annual data were collected from the International Financial Statistics of the International Monetary Fund's yearbooks. When the computer programmes were run, the non-biased second stage regression results of equation (1) and (2) were observed as listed in Table 4.

Regression results of equation (3) in Table 4 clearly explain 41 per cent of the variation in real GDP in Nigeria over about 30 years using only two explanatory variables. In our opinion this is a significant Percentage explained by these two explanatory variables.

Table 4

RGDP = 59996.16 -13448.85ER + 2172CPP (3)
Standard error of the regression = 85320.23

"T" statistics are 1.303, - 1.666 and 4.086 respectively
R square = 0.41, Adjusted R square = 0.368

"F" value = 9.17 ER = -2.058 - 0.001 (4)
FE - 0.0991 CPP

Standard error of the regression = 6.175
"T" statistics are -598, -1.712 and 2.183 respectively

R square = 0.162
Adjusted R square = 0.98

Further the "F" statistic is significant at a 99 per cent confidence level, indicating that the model is useful, if not precise. As expected by our theory, oil production is a significant and positive contributor to real GDP of the Nigerian economy. Since the exchange rates have a negative effect on real GDP, and from "T" statistic it is significant in 99 per cent confidence level, the presence of "Dutch Disease" in Nigerian case is vindicated. (The significance level of "T" statistic of 4.09 is 0.107).

It should be further noted that exchange rates and oil production are not strongly correlated (their R2 is-Q.065), so the model is unlikely to suffer from multicollinearity. Heteroscadisticity between error terms and CPP is indicated by simple Durbin-Watson tests and the heteroscadisticity apparent between error term and ER is corrected by the Two-Stage Least Squares estimation.

Thus our regression results confirm what our theory predicts in terms of the presence of Dutch Disease in Nigerian economy in the given time period.

SECTION-III

SUMMARY AND CONCLUSION

In this chapter, we intended to review the theory of the Dutch Disease that has its roots in the 1960s' hypothesis of Immiserizing Growth Hypothesis made popular by Jagdish Bhagwati. After reviewing theory, we wanted to test whether the tremendous increase in oil price has created any symptoms of Dutch Disease in the Nigerian economy. By investigating the Nigerian data, we confirmed that increase in major export price has created foreign reserve inflow that has become inflationary and has retarded the growth in real GDP. Our regression results confirm the expectations from our theoretical arguments.

REFERENCES

Gillis, Malcolm and Perkins D.H., *Economics of Development,* W.W. Norton and Company, New York, 1992.

Harrison, Ezeela Fidel, "Structural Re-adjustment in Nigeria", *American Journal of Economics and Sociology,* Vol. 52, No.2, April 1993.

International Monetary Fund, *International Financial Statistics Yearbook,* Nigeria Section, Washington D.C., 1996.

Nyatepe-Coo, A.A., "Dutch Disease, Government Policy and Import Demand in Nigeria", *Applied Economics,* Vol. 26, 1994, pp. 327-336.

O'Sullivan, Edmund, "Learning to live with Cheap Oil", *Middle East Business Weekly,* January 1994.

"Ungenerous Endowments: The Natural Resources Myth", *The Economist,* December 23,1995 issue.

24

TEST OF DUTCH DISEASE PHENOMENON IN BRAZIL, NIGERIA, MALAYSIA AND RUSSIA AND LESSONS FOR INDIA'S TRADE POLICY

INTRODUCTION

Many countries around the world have experienced economic growth that was either wiped out by a sudden short term financial or other non-economic crisis (e.g. Venezuela, Chile, the Philippines, Argentina Indonesia, Malaysia, Mexico) or have developed a new phenomenon of "growth with increased unemployment of labour" (e.g. Brazil, India, Nigeria). The main question to be answered is, "How does an economy suffer from hardship amongst plenty?" This paper has main aim of pointing out the economic linkages that lead to higher economic hardships if the economy is unable to buffer the external pressures. Hence, in the initial part of this paper, we explain the origins of Dutch Disease. Several economists have already tested (and have attempted to explain) theoretical points that lead to Dutch Disease phenomenon. We devote first section to reviewing relevant applications of this topic done by other researchers. We include in it the review of these studies' findings and summarize their conclusions.

This Chapter is based on an article co-authored with Mr. P. Brijesh, and Mr. Arvind K. Jha

Next section of our work involves explaining and testing the Dutch Disease phenomenon for Brazilian economy. Other sections that follow, carry out similar tests for Malaysia, Nigeria and Russia. While studying the experience of these economies is beneficial, learning from these experiences seems to be even more important. Therefore in the section that follows these experiences, we discuss the relevance to the Indian economy. Our conclusion is that unless policy makers keep a careful eye on external disturbances, the international trade dominated economic growth, as in case of India, has a future potential of putting greater challenges in front of policy makers. Our specific recommendations are listed at the end of this paper.

Findings of each section on Brazil, Malaysia, Nigeria, Russia and India are complemented by Vector Auto Regression (VAR) analysis to test the validity of effects of Foreign Reserves on Price Level (CPI), and on real GDP (Y), and effect of Exchange Rate on real GDP. In a standard VAR model, dependent variable is regressed with two time period lagged value of dependent variable, and two time period lagged value of explanatory variable whose impact on the dependent variable is to be observed.

Hypothesis testing is done with 99 percent, 95 percent, and 90 percent confidence intervals by observing Z values. Standard error of regression, the duration of the data set and R squared values are reported at the end of respective sections along with our observations about these results.

The variables used in the text sections for different countries and respective econometrics sections sometimes are not same. This is because of non-availability of longer time series data on required variables. We tried numerous ways to come up with a reliably estimable model and have reported the best possible results. Hence, we used foreign exchange reserves (FR) as proxy to test for overall effect on economy (both price level (P) and GDP). A negative effect of the stock of foreign exchange reserves on the level of GDP is a sign of the presence of Dutch disease effect. Our concluding section is followed by the bibliography and references. Lags are used to see if the effect of independent variables is any more significant if some time is allowed to elapse.

SECTION - 1

Explanation of Problem of Dutch Disease and Survey of Literature

The term, "Dutch Disease" appears to have been coined originally in the weekly magazine, "The Economist" in November 26, 1977 issue. It is the phenomenon of early 1970s when prices of oil increased; the Dutch economy experienced growth in her major export of Natural Gas. This led to increase in foreign exchange reserves which increased the domestic money supply leading to inflation. Simultaneously there was an increase in Dutch economy's major imports which led to the increased cost of production and the overall decline in aggregate supply. As the aggregate supply decreased, there was an increase in domestic unemployment. Thus in late 1970s, despite the growth in export sector, the Dutch economy experienced the stagflation phenomenon which is popularly called the "Dutch Disease".

Interestingly, the "Dutch Disease" is a misnomer because the Netherlands economy did not take very long to recover from this disease in 1980s. It is also not a norm to name a disease after a patient. In fact, if a disease has to be judged by a patient, and is to be named after the most serious patient, then many other countries had more resemblance to this disease and the disease lasted longer in countries such as Nigeria.

In terms of studies that concentrate on developing countries, Spatafora and Warner (2001) in their data set made up of 18 oil countries between years 1965 and 1989 found that favorable terms-of-trade shocks boost non-tradable output but that Dutch Disease effects are remarkably lacking. While some countries have found a way to keep the Dutch Disease out of their economies, some others such as Nigeria could not do so. A study by Stokke (2005) indicated how the gold price boom can help explain the de-industrialization and disappointing growth experience in South Africa.

According to IMF (World Economic Outlook, 2005), remittances from foreign countries, like any other foreign exchange inflow, carry a potential for the Dutch Disease-type issues. In general, this does not appear to have had major adverse effects on economic performance. This argument is relevant in case of India where remittances from Non-Resident Indians (NRIs) have increased tremendously and foreign reserves have reached to record levels in recent years.

Latsis (2005), in the case of Russia, indicates that the symptoms of Dutch Disease are more acute as export trade expands due to the soaring prices of export commodities. Russia's fuel and energy sectors alone account for nearly two-thirds of total exports.

Oomes and Kalcheva (2007) in their study examined whether recent economic developments in Russia have been symptomatic of Dutch Disease. The four main symptoms the study tested include (1) an appreciation of the real exchange rate; (2) a slowdown in manufacturing growth (deindustrialization); (3) an increase in service sector growth; and (4) an increase in wage growth. In this context, the study pointed out that there is evidence that oil prices have strengthened the real ruble exchange rate. However, it is not clear that this real exchange rate appreciation has been responsible for the observed slowdown in manufacturing growth. The study finds clear evidence of high real wage growth in all sectors since 2000, which is consistent with both the resource movement and the spending effect.

Acosta, Lartey and Mandelman (2007) using data for El Salvador (a country for which remittances amounted to 16 percent of the GDP in 2005) found that the inability of the economy to absorb remittances leads to the Dutch Disease phenomenon.

Lopez, Molina and Bussolo (2007) recognize that while remittances have a positive impact on a good number of development indicators of recipient countries, however, they may bring a number of undesired problems (appreciation of exchange rate); especially if flows are large relative to the size of the recipient economies (Latin American countries).

According to Stiglitz (2004), an easy way to avoid currency appreciation is as follows: keep the foreign exchange earned from oil exports out of the country. And further, invest the money in other developed countries or bring it in only gradually. But in most developing countries, such a policy is viewed as using oil money to help someone else's economy.

Thus, from the above discussion, it is clear that the symptoms of Dutch Disease are observed all over the world.

SECTION - 2

The Case of Brazil

The main theme is to recognize that the possibility of the Dutch Disease is higher when trade is dependent upon only few commodities. Hence, higher is the commodity concentration in trade, greater is the possibility of economic problems created by international trade. Second, we shall see that the higher concentration of trade to a specific country or a region creates a greater chance for economic disturbance.

Description of Brazilian Economy

The Brazilian economy is expected to have symptoms of the Dutch Disease because of the importance of coffee in her traditional exports during 1960s and growing concentration in manufactured exports in recent years. In the early 1960s, coffee accounted for around 60 percent of the total exports, with manufactured exports negligible.

Brazil had some major economic concerns in 1980s, especially the hyperinflation that was primarily caused by tremendous increase in domestic money supply. Brazilian policy makers followed Import Substitution Industrialization (ISI) strategy until the 1980s, but eventually started to open up the economy in the 1990s. The problems that ISI created were numerous: the neglect of agriculture and other exports which brought along Balance of Payments (BOP) issues; the low productivity and quality, etc. One of the main policies adopted to restore equilibrium was to introduce significant exchange rate devaluations that ultimately contributed to the acceleration of inflation.

Brazil's International Trade in Recent Years: Rise of Manufacturing Sector

When Brazil liberalized its trade regime in the early 1990s, its overvalued exchange rate discouraged exports. It was only after 2000, a tighter fiscal policy and greater exchange rate flexibility improved Brazil's external competitiveness, laying the basis for rapid export growth. Brazil has one of the highest proportions of manufacturing exports to GDP in Latin America, and has been able to penetrate a wide range of markets. Brazilian merchandise exports reached to $137.8 billion in 2006. Manufactured products were the key driver of this result and it is highly diversified. Currently, Brazil is home to large manufacturing plants making it an important player in the world aerospace industry. The Embraer (aircraft manufacturing company) is one of the largest exporters in the country. Further, the share of agriculture in total exports of Brazil has also gone up to 11.7 percent in 2003 from 9.3 percent in 1992. Thus the available data in Table 1 show that currently there is no significant domination of any particular sector in Brazilian exports.

Table 1
Brazilian Exports in 2006 (Main Products)

	US $ Billion	*Share in percent*
Total Exports	137.8	100
Iron ore and concentrates	8.9	6.5
Petroleum oils, crude	6.9	5.0
Soybeans, including grinded	5.7	4.1
Passenger motor vehicles	4.6	3.3
Other	4.2	3.1
Cane sugar, raw	3.9	2.9
Airplanes	3.2	2.4
Meat of bovine animals, fresh, chilled or frozen	3.1	2.3
Transmission and reception apparatus, and components	3.1	2.2
Parts and accessories for motor cars and tractors	3.0	2.2
Coffee, not roasted	2.9	2.1
Meat and edible offal of chicken, fresh, chilled or frozen	2.9	2.1
Iron or nonalloy steel flat-rolled products	2.7	2.0

Source : Banco Central Do Brasil, website

The disaggregated data on manufacturing sector exports for the year 2003 indicate that metal manufactures constituted maximum share of 25.9 percent of the total exports of manufacturing sector, followed by food, beverages and tobacco with 17.6 percent. Among the manufacturing sector exports there is no substantial domination by any particular industry leading to Dutch Disease (Table 2). Thus we see that there is no significant evidence of Dutch Disease like phenomenon in Brazil in recent years.

Table 2
Disaggregated Exports of Manufacturing (Percent of Total Exports under Manufacturing)

	Food, beverages, tobacco	*Textiles*	*Wood & products*	*Paper & products*	*Chemicals*	*Basic metals*	*Metal manufactures*
1995	19.9	7.3	2.1	6.1	9.9	13.4	22.0
2000	13.7	6.3	2.5	4.8	10.6	10.1	31.1
2001	17.1	6.2	2.5	3.9	10.4	8.0	29.7
2002	17.4	5.8	2.8	3.6	10.4	9.2	27.3
2003	17.6	5.5	2.7	4.1	10.8	9.5	25.9

Source: United Nations, International Trade Statistics Year book, Various Issues

Currency Fluctuations in Recent Years in Brazil

The system of exchange mini-devaluations functioned up until February 1990. In March 1990, the dirty flotation exchange rate system was adopted and used until June 1994. Beginning in July 1994, Brazil implemented a limited flexible exchange rate system.

Dutch Disease in Brazil, Are There Any Symptoms?

Strictly speaking, the Dutch Disease is not really a disease if the higher inflows are expected to be permanent. In these cases, the Dutch Disease may simply represent the economy's adaptation to its new found wealth, making the term 'disease' a misnomer. A shift in the production from the tradable to the non-tradable sector is simply a self-correcting mechanism, a way for the economy to adapt to an increase in domestic demand. Thus the increased foreign reserves and fluctuating exports are not serious reasons to worry about, and self correction is a natural process.

Further, the rise of manufacturing sector in recent years (2008) has not led to any substantial erosion in Brazil's traditional coffee export sector causing major unemployment in that industry.

To test the evidence of the Dutch disease, in this section as well as in other sections, we decided to run Vector Auto-Regression (VAR) which essentially measures an effect of one variable on the other variable by calculating direct "Impact Multipliers". There is also an adjustment made by taking a lagged independent variable to measure the last time period's effect of change in independent variable on this time period's dependent variable value.

Hence in equation form the following models were tested:

$$P(t) = a1P(t-1) + a2P(t-2) + a3FR(t-1) + a4FR(t-2) \quad (1)$$

$$Y(t) = b1FR(t-1) + b2FR(t-2) + b3Y(t-1) + b4Y(t-2) \quad (2)$$

$$Y(t) = c1Y(t-1) + c2Y(t-2) + c3ER(t-1) + c4ER(t-2) \quad (3)$$

Where

P = general price level (measured by Consumer Price Index (CPI))

Y = real GDP

FR = stock of foreign reserves

ER = Exchange rate measured as domestic currency units per unit of the foreign currency, increase in this rate would make a depreciation of the domestic currency. (t-1) and (t-2) represent lagged values of the variable by one and two time periods respectively.

To be economically consistent, and to observe the presence of the Dutch Disease, the expected signs of the estimated coefficients (a1, a2, a3, a4, b1, b2, b3, b4, c1 c2, c3, c4) are as follows:

a1, a2, a3 and a4 > 0, b1 and b2 < 0, c3 and c4 < 0.

We shall use the same expected values for all country cases. The annual data for tests of all countries were collected from International Financial Statistics (IFS) published by International Monetary Fund (IMF).

VAR was run for Brazil for the period of 1970-2007 on the annual data series and the econometrics tests for this country show that, General Price Level (P) is positively affected by foreign reserves indicating presence of effect of foreign reserves on the prices (Table 3). The estimated coefficient however is not significant. What is significant is the positive effect of foreign reserves on the real GDP, making it clear that increased foreign reserves have aided the economic growth. Hence, increased foreign reserves have helped Brazilian economy in the period studied to prosper indicating no evidence of Dutch Disease in that sense of the term. Increased exchange rate,

Table 3
Statistical Results for Brazil

Brazil	*Price Level*	*GDP*	*GDP*
Price Level(lagged)	1.431***	.	.
	(0.16)	.	.
Price Level (twice lagged)	-0.447***	.	.
	(0.16)	.	.
Foreign Reserves (lagged)	1.24E-04	0.011***	.
	(1.90E-04)	(0.00)	.
Foreign Reserves (twice lagged)	5.21E-05	0.002	.
	(2.07E-04)	(0.00)	.
GDP (lagged)	.	0.154	0.385
		(0.27)	(0.55)
GDP (twice lagged)	.	0.375*	1.095**
	.	(0.21)	(0.53)
Exchange Rate (lagged)	.	.	-62.026
		.	(198.00)
Exchange Rate (twice lagged)	.	.	362.759**
	.		(170.54)
Observations	36	10	10
R-squared	0.988	0.9041	0.8532

Note: * denotes significance at the 10 percent level, ** at 5 percent, and * at 1 percent

however, has a positive and significant effect on real GDP; meaning that higher Exchange Rate (depreciation of domestic currency) has increased real GDP via increased exports. The high value of estimated coefficient for Exchange rate can be explained by the continuous depreciation of Brazilian currency in late 1980s and in early 1990s. Table 3 also shows that with number of observations of 36, the R-squared is pretty high, indicating a pretty decent model fit and the relationship.

SECTION - 3

The Case of Malaysia

Review of Malaysian Economy

In the case of Malaysia, the propensity to the Dutch Disease experience was mainly due to increasing exports based on electronic components in recent years and the emphasis of policy makers on international trade as the engine of economic growth. In this section, we review the experience of Malaysian economy and investigate if it is consistent with our story of the Dutch Disease.

Malaysia's investment ratio between 1970 to the mid-1990s, was one of the highest in the Asian region, resulting in a dramatic shift in the structure of the economy from agriculture and mining to manufacturing. Much of the investment went into electronics and other export-oriented industries, while large portion also went into non-tradable sectors including capital-intensive infrastructure and the real estate sector. Malaysia's strong economic performance continued during the early 1990s, but then the unexpected crisis of 1997 hit hard. Before 1997, the Real output (GDP) growth averaged 8.5 percent a year, unemployment was below 3 percent, prices and the exchange rate remained stable, and international reserves were robust. However, there were also signs of economic stress as exports decelerated and a large current account deficit developed in the context of a gradual depreciation of the effective exchange rate. While the investment-led growth strategy was successful in raising output and income, the quality of investment projects had deteriorated. This eventually led to major balance sheet weakness in the banking and corporate sectors, exposing the economy to the contagion of the Asian crisis. Similar to its neighbors, Malaysia went through a currency crisis and a banking crisis, but its low level of external debt spared it from a major external debt crisis.

Malaysia's recovery in 1999-2000 was one of the strongest amongst the Asian crisis ridden economies; led by buoyant world demand for electronics and supported by accommodating macroeconomic policies.

In 2003, the marked appreciation of the dollar led to an appreciation of the East Asian currencies, thereby eroding the competitiveness of Malaysian exports and the GDP growth picked up to 5.2 percent. In 2004, however, as a result of Ringgit' peg to the weakening dollar, the value of domestic currency declined by 6.0 percent against a trade-weighted basket of currencies. This was good news for exporter. The improvement in the global economic environment in the second half of the year, coupled with the ringgit's depreciation, led to a doubling

Table 4
Major Indicators for External Sector of Malaysia

	Current account balance (percent of GDP)	*Foreign direct investment, net inflows (percent of GDP)*	*Manufacturing, value added (percent of GDP)*	*Total reserves in months of imports*	*Short-term debt (per cent of total reserves)*
1980	-1.1	3.7	21.6	4.6	23.5
1985	-1.9	2.2	19.3	3.7	47.3
1990	-2.0	5.3	24.2	3.6	17.9
1995	-9.7	4.7	26.4	3.2	29.5
2000	9.4	4.2	32.6	3.3	16.0
2002	7.6	3.4	30.5	4.0	24.8
2003	12.9	2.4	31.1	5.0	19.5
2004	12.1	3.7	30.4	6.2	17.2
2005	14.6	2.9	29.8	5.9	18.7
2006	16.3	3.9	29.8	6.2	14.2
2007	16.0	..	..	6.7	..

Source: World Bank Online Database

of growth in merchandise exports to 12.4 percent. The buildup in Malaysia's reserves in 2004 was reinforced by a rise in portfolio investment resulting from renewed interest by international investors in Asian equities, and the apparent undervaluation of the ringgit.

The rapid export-led growth in post 2002 however, supported by foreign investment, stimulated a steady rise in manufacturing in Malaysia. In the Malaysian context, there are many incidences that prove that the export growth has strongly contributed to GDP growth. The rapid rise of the manufacturing sector is also reflected in both the sectoral distribution of growth and employment patterns.

Is Malaysia Prone to the Dutch Disease?

Even though we cannot point out any direct harmful consequences of large increase in electronics exports of Malaysia, the serious shortcoming of Malaysian export sector was her high degree of concentration in the electronics sub-sector. The electrical machinery sub-sector, including production of semiconductors and other electronic components, computers and peripherals, telecommunications and consumer electronics, accounted for 67.5 percent of manufactured exports of Malaysia in 1995. As we noticed in the case of Brazil in the earlier section, a high concentration on few manufactured products to drive exports is inherently risky, leaving the extremely open Malaysian economy vulnerable to cyclical downturns in prices of these products. The high degree of dependency on foreign capital has left Malaysia with little indigenous capability to continue her export-led growth if the foreign FDI companies change their location or strategy. The U.S. continues to be the major export market for Malaysia and decrease in demand for Malaysian import from the United States can have a significant effect on Malaysian economy.

Table 4 and 5 indicate that the share of agricultural raw materials and food exports in total exports of Malaysia has come down drastically, but the share of manufactured exports is showing a steep increasing trend.

Table 5
Composition of Exports
(As a percentage of merchandise export)

Year	*Agricultural raw materials exports)*	*Food exports*	*High-technology exports*	*Manufactured exports*
1980	31.0	15.0	..	18.8
1985	18.4	17.4	..	27.2
1990	13.8	11.7	38.2	53.8
1995	6.2	9.5	46.1	74.7
2000	2.6	5.5	59.5	80.4
2002	2.2	7.5	58.2	79.7
2003	2.4	8.6	58.9	76.9
2004	2.4	8.0	55.6	75.7
2005	2.5	7.0	54.7	74.6
2006	2.7	7.0	53.8	73.7

Source: World Bank Online Database

According to Doraisami (2004), the downturn in the global electronics demand cycle adversely affected the Malaysian exports. In late 1995 and early 1996, an acute glut in semiconductor production developed and this led to an outright collapse in U.S. dollar prices. Malaysia is one of the top exporters of semiconductors in the world. 1995, had approximately 10 percent of world's market share in semiconductors.

Table 6
Export by Manufacturing Sector
(as a percentage of Total Value)

	(Total) Manufacturing	*Food, beverages, tobacco*	*Textiles*	*Wood and products*	*Chemicals*	*Metal manufactures*
1992	79.9	8.8	6.4	6.1	4.8	47.6
1995	89.6	8.5	4.9	5.1	5.7	59.4
2000	90.1	4.8	3.7	2.7	7	66.9
2002	91.3	6.7	3.3	2.4	7.9	65.5
2003	89.9	7.9	3.1	2.2	8.7	62.4

Source: United Nations, International Trade Statistics Year book, Various Issues

Malaysia was particularly hard hit by worldwide decline in the prices of electronic sector in 1992-1997, given exports of semiconductors (corresponding to Standard Industrial Trade Classification (SITC) 776) is its top export earner and that exports from the electronics sector also strongly feature in its top ten exports (Table 7).

Table 7
Semi Conductor Industry in Malaysia
(in US $ million)

	Thermionic, Microcircuits, transistors, valves, etc.	*Total Export*	*Share in percent*
2000	18,729	81,290	23.0
2001	15,929	73,079	21.8
2002	19,208	78,674	24.4
2003	22,417	82,741	27.1

Source: United Nations, International Trade Statistics Year book, Various Issues

Econometrics Test for Malaysia

As mentioned before, we use the same data source (IFS – IMF) and same VAR equation forms to estimate the coefficients for Malaysia on annual data series for the period of 1970 – 2006 as in case of Brazil (Table 8). In case of Malaysia, there is no evidence of effect of foreign reserves on price level. However, the positive effect of foreign reserves on real GDP is significant. Thus in Malaysia, just like in case of Brazil, the increased stock of foreign reserves has helped boost the economic growth. Exchange rate does not have effect on real GDP, the R squared value is high and the number of observations is 35.

Hence, our conclusion is that just like in case of Brazil, there is no significant evidence of the Dutch Disease in case of Malaysia. In fact, there is a remarkable recovery of the Malaysian economy from the credit crisis of the late 1990s. It is possible that the absence of the disease is mainly due to the commodity diversification of the international trade and a well managed trade policy.

Table 8
Statistical Estimates for Malaysia

Malaysia	*Price Level*	*GDP*	*GDP*
Price Level (lagged)	1.365***	.	.
	(0.14)	.	.
Price Level (twice lagged)	-0.399***	.	.
	(0.14)	.	.
Foreign Reserves (lagged)	-7.12E-06	0.583**	.
	(4.31E-05)	(0.20)	.
Foreign Reserves (twice lagged)	6.74E-05	-0.499*	.
	(5.27E-05)	(0.27)	.
GDP (lagged)	.	1.041***	0.841**
	.	(0.16)	(0.26)
GDP (twice lagged)	.	-0.033093	0.222
	.	(0.16)	(0.28)
Exchange Rate (lagged)	.	.	-9366.669
	.	.	(7647.76)
Exchange Rate (twice lagged)	.	.	8928.832
	.	.	(6102.75)
Observations	35	35	35
R-squared	0.998	0.9955	0.9947

Note: * denotes significance at the 10 percent level, ** at 5 percent, and * at 1 percent

SECTION – 4

The Case of Nigeria

Introduction to Nigerian Economy

Nigeria is the most populous and third largest country of African continent. Oil dominates the economy, traditionally accounting for roughly 30 percent of GDP and 95 percent of foreign exchange earnings. Agriculture is another dominant economic activity in terms of labor employment. The principal agricultural export crops are cocoa and rubber, which together account for nearly 60 percent of non-oil merchandise exports. Nigeria has vast oil reserve estimated at 18 billion barrels and proven natural gas reserves of 3.4 trillion cubic meters (with energy content slightly higher than the country's oil reserves). Export of gas is expected to increase in this decade.

Reasons for Dutch Disease in Nigeria

According to International Monetary Fund's World Economic Outlook (1997), in case of Nigeria in 1969, the oil sector accounted for less than 3 percent of GDP and 42 percent of exports. By 1980, the oil sector had accounted for nearly 30 percent of GDP and oil exports contributed 96 percent of total exports. The steady decline of competitiveness of the non-oil tradable goods sector was reflected in the substantial decline of agricultural exports, which began in the mid 1960s and continued through 1976, when oil production reached its peak.

Notwithstanding, the dramatic rise in oil revenue in the 1970s, the Government failed to strengthen public finances. The excessive public expenditure, from an average of 13 percent of GDP during 1970-73 to 25 percent in 1974-80, moved the fiscal balance from a small surplus to deficit, averaging two and a half percent of GDP a year. The monetary financing of these deficits contributed to a rapid growth in broad money and a sharp acceleration of inflation.

The oil boom created disincentives for agricultural exports through its impact on relative product and factor prices, including the appreciation of the exchange rate and enhanced profitability of investments in non-tradable commodities and services. As a result, the rising wages in the public sector drained labor from rural areas and put an upward pressure on rural wage rate. Nigeria's real effective exchange rate appreciated by 63 percent between 1970 and 1980 and further by 84 percent between 1980 and 1984. Another consequence of the oil boom was the high level of effective demand that it induced, which grossly curtailed exportable output. Increases in nominal incomes that are not matched by increased productivity and output, led to inflationary pressures. Kulkarni-Erickson (1999) tested the presence of Dutch Disease in Nigeria by conducting a Two Stage Least Square regression of real GDP against the Nigerian exchange rate and crude oil production. They confirmed that increase in major export price has created foreign reserve inflow which became inflationary and has retarded the growth in real GDP.

Analysis of sectoral contributions to long-term growth indicates that the services sector has been the most consistent, with an average growth of 5 percent per annum. By contrast, the performance of the agricultural sector has been highly cyclical: decline (1965-1969); sharp rise (1970-1974); decline (1975-1985), and steady rise (1985-2000). Continued neglect of the agriculture sector, while oil exploration was prioritized, amounted to misplacement of emphasis in the country's economic development effort. It signaled to people that only participation in the oil-based urban sector provided viable employment opportunities. This resulted migration from the agriculture sector to oil sector. Thus, the rural agriculture sector, that was the major source of domestic food supply and industrial raw materials, suffered severe manpower loss. This was one factor that made the economy readily vulnerable to the Dutch disease later in the early 1980s. The structure of the Nigerian economy before the redirection of priorities during the 1970s was that of a strong agrarian economy. Damachi and Seibel (1973) show that before the oil era, Nigeria was not only self-sufficient in domestic food production (up to 85 percent), but also was the world's leading exporter of palm oil, the world's second largest exporter of cocoa, and ranked among the top ten in the world in the production and export of timber, cotton, rubber, groundnut, hides and skin. This, however, all changed by the mid-1980s. By 1985, Nigeria had lost its lead in palm oil and cocoa exports. Oshikoya (1990) reported that by 1986, Nigeria had to rely on import for 58 percent of its food, and 72 percent of its industrial raw material. It was clear that the country's economic structure had become seriously maladjusted.

Nigeria's foreign exchange earnings are more than 90 percent dependent on crude oil export receipts (Chart 1). As the oil prices increased in 1970s, there was influx of foreign reserves, but in 1980s that influx was replaced by scarcity as the oil prices stabilized. In fact the export of agriculture and manufacturing sector is almost negligible. Due to this, volatility of the world oil market prices has a direct impact on the supply of foreign exchange.

Diversification of the economic output away from oil and enhancing productivity growth in a stable macroeconomic environment were at the centre of Nigeria's Structural Adjustment Programme (SAP) adopted in 1986.

Econometrics Test for Nigeria

In the case of Nigeria, Consumer Price Index data were not easily available, so we tested only the effect of foreign reserves on real GDP (Equations 2 and 3 in our models) which happened to be positive and significant. Observing the economic conditions of Nigeria however, it was clear that the inflation rate increased, as unemployment rose and the real GDP growth slowed down in last 30-40 years. Hence, the economic hardships were clearly witnessed, which can indicate the advent of Dutch Disease.

Econometrics exercise (VAR) was run on annual data of GDP, Foreign Exchange Reserves and Exchange Rate for the period of 1970 - 2007. It was clear from the test that in Nigeria the foreign reserves inflows have improved the economic growth only after one time period (one year here). However the effect of foreign reserves on real GDP is negative after 2 time periods, (albeit non-significant) as witnessed in our results. Exchange rate changes (possibly because they were controlled by the monetary authorities in Nigeria) have not shown any significant effect on the real GDP. Again, R-squared value is high and the number of observations is 29 (Table 9). This may also prove that the non-economic factors such as administrative bottlenecks, corruption and mismanaged policies in Nigeria have contributed greatly to the economic slowdown.

Thus, the phenomenon of the Dutch Disease is most evident in case of Nigeria. This is partly due to inefficient policies to internalize the economic growth and partly due to excessive reliance on only one good for economic prosperity namely minerals and fuels. The vast mineral (including fuels) wealth of some countries has not always translated into benefits for either the country's economy or for her trading partners. In fact, it has become a 'resource curse', as it curtailed economic development.

Table 9
Statistical Estimates for Nigeria

Nigeria	*GDP*	*GDP*
Foreign Reserves (lagged)	1.199**	.
	(0.21)	.
Foreign Reserves (twice lagged)	-0.247	.
	(0.21)	.
GDP (lagged)	-1.023	1.085***
	(1.15)	(0.17)
GDP (twice lagged)	1.442	0.119
	(1.05)	(0.18)
Exchange Rate (lagged)	.	-9366.669
	.	(7647.76)
Exchange Rate (twice lagged)	.	8928.832
	.	(6102.75)
Observations	29	29
R-squared	0.9476	0.9456

Note: * denotes significance at the 10 percent level, ** at 5 percent, and * at 1 percent

According to United Nations Report (1998), despite the fact that agriculture is the dominant economic activity in developing Africa in terms of its share in GDP (and in terms of the labour force), mineral fuels and related materials account for more than two thirds of the exports. Nigeria is a typical case for this influence of minerals and oil on economy's exports.

SECTION - 5

The Case of Russia

Introduction to Russian Economy

Russia holds the world's largest natural gas reserves, the second largest coal reserves and the eighth largest oil reserves. Russia is also the world's largest exporter of natural gas, the second largest oil exporter and the third largest energy consumer. In this section, we present the experience of Russian economy in recent years in the context of rising oil price. Some of the information in this section is based on an informative paper by Smirnova and Kulkarni (2005) on a similar topic.

One of the main issues on the Russian development agenda is the creation of infrastructure that will ensure the sustainability of growth. Current economic progress provides certain reasons to worry about Russian economy's endurance. Numerous incidences indicate that the success of the Russian economy is generated exclusively by a favorable external situation rather than internally evolved economic mechanisms. High gas and oil prices over the past five years are considered to be the major source of current GDP growth. However, these sources of income are rather unreliable and cannot be regarded as a reasonable base for sustained economic growth. Russia is considered to be experiencing the so-called "Dutch Disease" when a booming export sector increases the relative price of non-tradable goods and services, thus hurting the rest of the tradable goods sector. As we know from the experience of Nigeria, throughout the 1980s and 1990s, some resource abundant countries have suffered from low growth.

It is useful to consider some background information of Russia's foreign trade in recent year. Russian foreign trade balance has been strongly positive since 1998, mainly due to the high world prices of oil. The most important trading partners for the Russian economy are Germany, Belarus, U.S.A and Ukraine (OECD, 2004). Russia's foreign trade reached $370.4 billion in 2005. Minerals and fuels were 51.1 percent of total exports, industrial products, 46.9 percent, and agricultural exports, 2.0 percent. World prices continue to have a major effect on export performance, since commodities, particularly oil, natural gas, metals, and timber, comprise 80 percent of Russian exports. Russian GDP growth and budget surplus/deficit are closely linked to world oil prices.

Using trade margins from statistics of other countries (U.K., Canada, Denmark) along with input-output table of Russian economy World Bank re-estimates the shares of industries and finds that the share of oil and gas industries could be as large as 25 percent of GDP (Table 11). The oil and gas sectors in Russia account for more than 30 percent of total government revenues. Such strong dependence on resource revenues is a common characteristic of resource-rich countries.

Table 10
Russian GDP 2000 by Sector of Origin, Basic Prices

	Share in published Russian GDP, percent	*Adjusted Russian GDP*			
		UK margins		*Dutch margins*	
		Share in GDP, per cent	*Change in share, percent*	*Share in GDP, per cent*	*Change in share, percent*
Industry–total	31.8	51.6	19.8	54.6	22.8
Electro energy	2.8	2.8	0.0	2.8	0.0
Oil and gas total	8.8	25.2	16.4	24.9	16.1
Oil extraction	6.5	12.9	6.4	12.9	6.4
Oil processing	1.2	5.0	3.8	4.7	3.5
Gas	1.1	7.3	6.2	7.3	6.2
Coal	0.5	1.2	0.7	1.0	0.5
Chemicals	1.9	2.9	0.9	3.1	1.1
Machinery	5.1	5.3	0.2	5.2	0.0
Trade	30.8	11.0	-19.8	9.4	-21.4

Source: World Bank Country Reports, Russian Economic Memorandum (2004)

Rautava (2002) supports the view that Russia's output and fiscal policy are sensitive to changes in international oil prices and real exchange rate of Ruble. He uses quarterly data on Russian GDP, budget revenues, real exchange rate and oil price and shows that a 10 percent permanent increase in the level of international oil prices would in long run cause the level of real GDP to increase by 2.2 percent and 3.0 percent increase in change in federal real revenues. Analyzing short-run consequences of oil price change.

The data on sectoral output dynamics do not support significantly the existence of a "Dutch Disease" effect in modern Russian economy. The lagging growth of services and retail turnover relative to machinery does not completely fit the overall story behind the "Dutch Disease". The possible explanation for such counterfactual results can be that the reallocation of resources does not follow relative price movement. The reason for this could be low factor mobility that is well documented in case of Russia. However, even if the Dutch Disease in the modern Russian economy may seem insignificant, one may not conclude that it did not exist at all. The analysis in the time periods of 1995-1998 and 1999-2001 of the Russia's economy proves some presence of the Dutch Disease, the economic crisis of 1998 presenting the strongest proof of it.

Policy Responses to Avoid Dutch Disease in Russia

Many of the potential macroeconomic problems arising from resource dependence can be resolved by the right macroeconomic policies. A stable set of institutions and policies have helped Russia use resources in a better way. Attempts should be made to avoid sharp movements in exchange rates in relatively short time-spans as it can be justified in case of Indian policy intervention. Fiscal policy can be counter cyclical to the oil price, a substantial stabilization fund can be established, and wide range of monetary sterilization mechanisms can be instituted (OECD, 2004). The tax structure of the economy can be used to assist the development of the non-resource sector. There should also be attempts to increase taxation of not only oil industry but also other resource related sectors. Taxing a larger part of resource rent could also lead to relatively lower wages in the resource sector. This will also enable to reduce the general tax levels which will boost other sectors. But this is a prerequisite for a fairly efficient and non-corrupt administration. Further, the non-resource tradable sector must increase productivity and restrain unit labour costs to stay competitive in order to increase export. The recent improvements in efficiency must be sustained if Russia wants to maintain high growth rates and achieve a more diversified industrial structure. However, for the foreseeable future, Russia is almost certain to remain highly dependent on natural resource exports. Long term solution will be provided by diversification of industries.

Econometrics Test for Russia

In case of Russia, mainly due to the restricted inflows of capital, due to non-existence of market structures and due to severe foreign exchange controls, significant results were neither expected nor were received. Only significant effect is the one of Exchange rate movement on real GDP which happened to be negative (for two time periods lagged variable). In case of Russia, we were further constrained for Dutch Disease like experience because the phenomenon was quite recent and we therefore had only 12 annual observations for the period 1993-2006. R-squared value is high, however.

Russian oil price data show close link between the oil price and the level of fixed investments in Russian economy. Therefore, it is not only the level of GDP that is influenced by oil price but the growth rate of economy that is subject to variation due to oil price fluctuation on the world market. Most researchers attribute high growth rates that Russia achieved over last four years to high oil prices (Rautava 2002). At the same time the 4-fold increase in oil price over last 4 years also causes worry with respect to Dutch Disease effect that can influence the further development of the country: real wages grew three times faster than productivity over 2003-2004. Sosunov and Zamulin (2006) have demonstrated that the real appreciation of the Ruble in 1999-2005 is fully consistent with the growth of the oil export revenues that took place during this period. Therefore, we could expect the "Dutch Disease" effect to be quite important for future policies of Russian economy.

SECTION - 6

Case of India

Background

The experience of Brazil, Nigeria, Russia and Malaysia provides an important lesson for an emerging economy like India. In India, we look at movement in its foreign exchange reserves, exchange rates, behavior of exports and diversification in trade and foreign exchange receipts to examine the potential of Dutch disease. India in recent time has shown enormous growth

Table 11
Statistical Results for Russia

Russia	*Price Level*	*GDP*	*GDP*
Price Level(lagged)	0.969***	.	.
	(0.27)	.	.
Price Level (twice lagged)	0.144	.	.
	(0.32)	.	.
Foreign Reserves (lagged)	-2.80E-04	30.179	.
	(3.08E-04)	(161.10)	.
Foreign Reserves (twice lagged)	3.00E-04	-7.137	.
	(4.31E-04)	(186.04)	.
GDP (lagged)	.	0.745***	1.906***
	.	(0.23)	(0.24)
GDP (twice lagged)	.	-0.503**	-0.743***
	.	(0.22)	(0.27)
Exchange Rate (lagged)	.	.	1206.539***
	.	.	(470.23)
Exchange Rate (twice lagged)	.	.	-894.8482*
	.	.	(496.90)
Observations	12	12	12
R-squared	0.9879	0.9707	0.9538

Note: * denotes significance at the 10 percent level, ** at 5 percent, and * at 1 percent

potential which is supported by acceleration in service sector led by software and associated industries. In this context it may be noted that the traditional role of developing countries are changing- from mere recipients of developed countries finished product to important providers of long distance services (Jalan (2002)).

An important reason for this is the 'services revolution' in which geography and levels of industrialization are no longer the primary determinants of the location of facilities for production of services. Most of the developing countries, in recent years, have undergone a significant structural shift in their economy. The share of agriculture in total value added has significantly declined; correspondingly, the share of manufacturing and services sector has increased with the share of manufacturing sector growing at a faster pace than that of services sector. However, India has undergone a slightly different kind of shift. In India, rather than the manufacturing sector, services sector picked up fast and it now accounts for more than 50 percent of the GDP (Chart 3). This trend seen in the developing countries is in agreement with the world trend, i.e. rising share of services in world transactions.

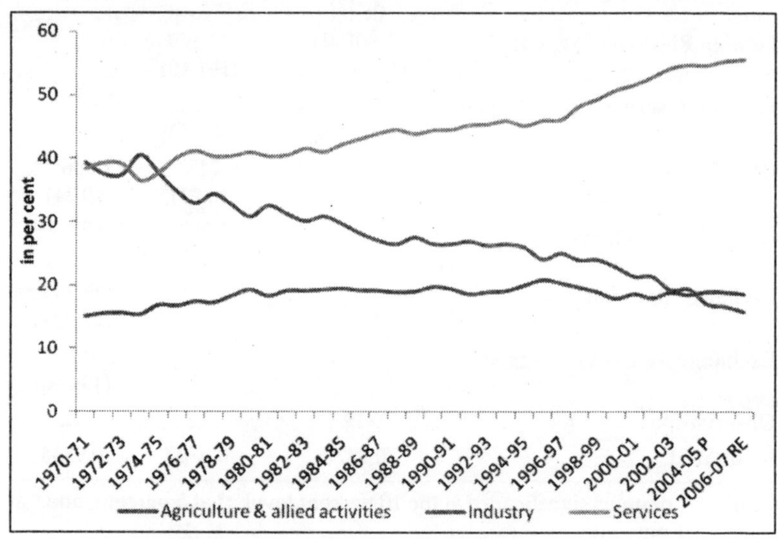

Chart 3: Trends in Sectoral Share of GDP

Potential for Dutch Disease in India

As mentioned earlier, one of the major reason for Dutch disease is inflow of foreign exchange leading to appreciating currency and decline in competitiveness and growth of other tradable sectors. India's foreign exchange reserves started rising steeply since the beginning of this decade (Chart 4).

The traditional economic theory indicates that when reserves accumulate, currency will appreciate and exports will suffer if other things remain the same. However, India's merchandise exports registered a high growth rate of more than 20 percent per annum between 2002-03 and 2007-08. The growth rate stood high, even if the exports of petroleum products, which grew at more than 50 percent annum, are

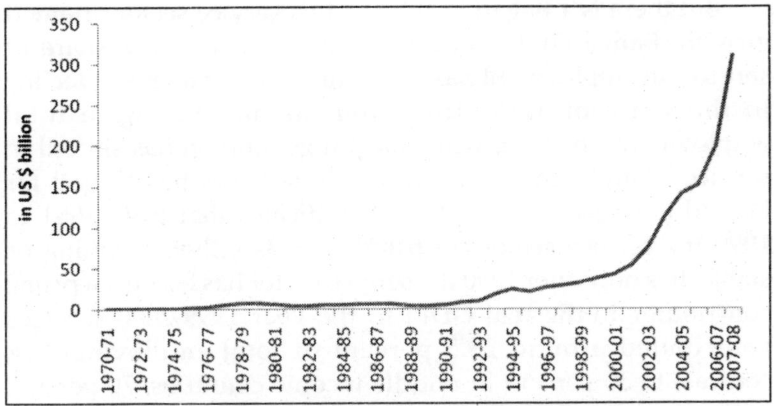

Chart 4: Trend in India's Foreign Exchange Reserves

excluded from the total goods exports. Further exports of services sector also continued to show a good performance. The important point is that this high export growth occurred despite some appreciation of the real effective exchange rate (REER) (Table 12). However, it is said that the actual growth of exports might have been larger had the REER not appreciated (Veeramani, 2008). India continue to be one of the fastest growing economy in the world with average real GDP at factor cost growing by 7.3 percent between 2000-01 and 2007-08.

Table 12
India's Exports and REER

	REER	*Appreciation/ Depreciation*	*Merchandise Exports (US $ million)*	*Growth Rate (in percent)*	*Service Exports (US $ million)*	*Growth Rate (in percent)*
2001-02	98.59	-0.1	43,827	-1.6	17,140	5.4
2002-03	95.99	-2.6	52,719	20.3	20,763	21.1
2003-04	99.07	3.2	63,843	21.1	26,868	29.4
2004-05	98.30	-0.8	83,536	30.8	43,249	61.0
2005-06	100.54	2.3	1,03,091	23.4	61,404	42.0
2006-07	97.42	-3.1	1,26,361	22.6	76,181	24.1
2007-08	104.52	7.3	1,59,007	25.8	87,687	15.1

Note: 36-currency export weighted REER (base 1993-94=100)
Source: Reserve Bank of India, Hand Book of Statistics on Indian Economy.

But there is a negative side for this service sector oriented growth. Banga (2005) indicates that the rise in the share of services in employment has been much slower than the decline in the share of agriculture and manufacturing in total employment. In short, while output generation has shifted to services, employment generation in services has lagged far behind (Table 13). Table 16 also indicates that from 1951 to 1990 the service sector contribution was either declining or stable. It is only after 1990 the service sector has become a prime contributor to the real GDP. In the year 1999-2000 services contributed around 28.5 percent of total employment in contrast to 30 percent in middle income countries, 70 percent in Singapore and 39 percent in Indonesia. A probable reason for fall in employment in faster growing services can be improvements in their labour productivity. Gordon and Gupta (2004) also attribute the slow rise in employment in services to the fact that growth in services has concentrated in those services where labour productivity has risen or are skilled labour intensive. A substantial manufacturing base is essential to absorb the workforce moving out of agriculture.

Table 13
Industrial Distribution of Total Workforce in India

	1951	*1961*	*1972-73*	*1993-94*	*1999-00*
Agriculture	74.6	76.2	73.9	64.7	59.9
Mining &Quarrying	0.4	0.5	0.4	0.7	0.6
Manufacturing	8.2	8.6	8.8	10.5	11.0
Services	16.8	14.7	16.9	24.1	28.5

Source: Banga (2005)

Diversification in India's Trade

In recent times, India's merchandise export growth was broad based across major sectors (Table 18) even though it is dominated by manufactured sectors (Chart 5). Agricultural and allied commodities exports witnessed a sharp acceleration in recent years. The commodity composition of manufactured exports has witnessed a notable shift with engineering goods emerging as the key driver of growth. This is attributable to the growing competitiveness and increasing technological sophistication of India's manufacturing exports. In 2007-08, engineering goods exports remained as the mainstay, accounting for the highest share of 23.1 percent of the total exports.

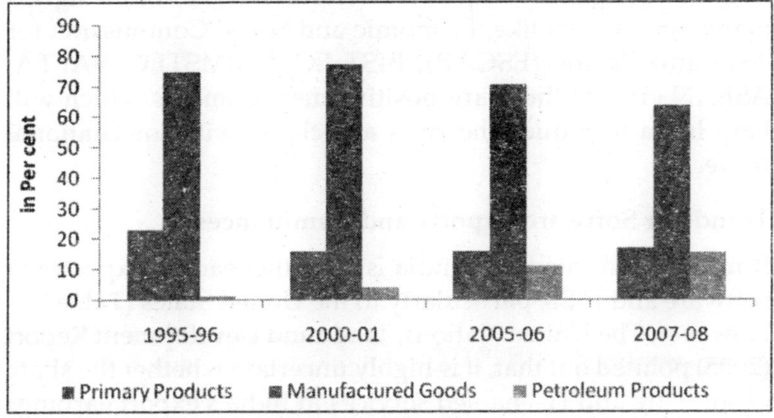

Chart 5: India's Exports by Industry of Origin (Share in Total Exports)

Table 14
Industry Share in India's Total Exports (in percent)

	Agriculture and allied products	*Chemicals and related products*	*Engineering goods*	*Textile*	*Gems and Jewellery*	*Petroleum*
1990-91	18.5	9.5	12.4	23.9	16.1	2.9
1995-96	19.1	11.3	13.8	25.3	16.6	1.4
2000-01	13.4	13.2	15.3	25.3	16.6	4.2
2006-07	10.0	13.7	23.4	13.7	12.6	14.8
2007-08	11.4	12.9	23.1	12.0	12.4	15.6

Source: Directorate General of Commercial Intelligence and Statistics, Government of India.

Destination-wise, India's merchandise trade has moved increasingly towards developing countries. In the recent years, the Asian economies are emerging as major trading partners of India. India's trade has grown faster with these countries than its overall trade growth. These changes (diversification)in India's trade is attributable to deliberate policy measures, involving trade liberalization, reduction of tariffs, promotion of SEZs and regional cooperation efforts. Regarding regional cooperation efforts in Asia, India signed many agreements like, Economic and Social Commission for Asia and Pacific (ESCAP), BIST-EC / BIMSTEC, SAFTA, ASEAN etc. All these are positive developments which will help India to reduce the risks associated with international trade.

Trends in Software Exports and Remittances

It may be indicated that India is now the leading exporter of software and ITES, particularly to the United States (Table 15). However, The United Nations, Trade and Development Report (2005) pointed out that, it is highly uncertain whether the share of software and IT-enabled services in India's export earnings will continue to rise substantially over the medium term. This is because of strong competition in the software market from producers with equally well-educated labour forces (in Central and Eastern Europe, as well as elsewhere in Asia). Also, greater automation of software development may reduce the scope of outsourcing such activities from developed to developing countries. However, as of now, India remains an attractive source for software exports mainly due to lower cost, high quality and favorable time zone. Further, Indian companies have started moving up the value chain.

Another major item in India's invisible items is private transfers from non-resident Indians (Table 16). Remittances from Indians working in the US, UK, South-East Asia and Europe have expanded in comparison with the traditional base of the Middle-East. In this regard, recent surveys conducted by RBI indicate a shift from Middle East to North America as the most import source region of remittances to India (about 44 percent of total remittances) indicating the increasing diversification.

Table 15
India's Software Exports

Year	*US $ million*	*Annual growth (percent)*
1995-96	747	53
2000-01	6,341	57.9
2004-05	17,200	34.4
2005-06	23,600	37.2
2006-07	31,300	32.6
2007-08	40,300	28.8

Source: Reserve Bank of India, Annual Report, Various issues

Table 16
Inward Workers' Remittances to India

Year	*Total Remitt. (US $ billon)*	*Share in (percent) current receipts*	*As a percent of GDP*
1990-91	2.1	8.0	0.7
1995-96	8.5	17.1	2.4
2000-01	13.1	16.8	2.8
2004-05	20.7	13.4	3.0
2005-06	24.6	12.5	3.1
2006-07	28.9	11.9	0.7
2007-08	42.6	14.0	0.9

Source: Reserve Bank of India, Annual Report, Various issues

In capital account, foreign investment flows into India, comprising foreign direct investment (FDI) and foreign portfolio investment, have risen sharply during the 1990s reflecting the policies to attract non-debt creating flows. India has steadily improved its rank of both inward and outward FDI performance index (World Investment Report, 2005) indicating improved investment climate and better growth prospects. Foreign investment flows have increased from negligible levels during 1980s to around U.S. $ 62-billion by 2007-08. In the same year, FDI (U.S. $32-billion) which is relatively non-volatile is more than portfolio investment (U.S. $29 billion) to India. As a proportion to FDI flows to emerging market and developing countries, FDI flows to India have shown a consistent rise from 1.6 percent in 1998 to 3.7 percent in 2005.

Scope for Stabilization Fund

Many countries world over are setting up separate stabilization fund using a part of growing foreign exchange receipts to absorb the excess inflow. The stabilization fund is expected to help stabilize exchange rate. The stabilization fund of Russia was established in 2004 to serve as an important tool for absorbing excessive liquidity, reducing inflationary pressure and insulating the economy from volatility of oil and gas export earnings. The investment and spending pattern of the stabilization fund will lead to capital outflows when oil prices are high and capital inflows when they are low. In Russia these flows will be an important mechanism to counteract current account pressure on the exchange rate; thus, shielding the economy from potentially damaging sharp exchange-rate fluctuations. Surplus revenues resulting from high oil prices (about US $20/bbl (Ulras) are accumulated in the fund automatically). The legislation in Russia stipulate that until the fund accumulate a total of Ruble 500 billion, the revenues accumulated in the stabilization fund may be spent only to finance the federal deficit arising from oil price below the baseline US $ 20 level for Ulras crude. If the fund exceeds Ruble 500, the Government may use such revenues to repay foreign debt. World Bank (2008) indicates that Brazil is planning to set up sovereign wealth fund using its growing reserves. There are indications that government can use a part of these reserves for funding education and health care in Brazil. Nigeria is having Excess Crude Account which acts as a stabilization fund, closing budget deficits that are a product of oil price.

There have been suggestions that India should consider setting up a wealth fund on the lines Stabilization Fund which will smooth the revenue flows arising out of volatility in export proceeds. In this context (Reddy, 2007) pointed out that India has experienced consistent current account deficits, barring a modest surplus for few years. Hence, stabilization fund may not be justified in India's case. India import more than 70 percent of its petroleum requirements and rising oil price is matter of concern. Its food grain production is still dependent on unpredictable monsoon conditions. Further, large part of the capital flows to India are portfolio flows and a significant component of Foreign Direct Investments is utilized for acquisition of existing firms and not in Greenfield projects. It is also pointed out that it is difficult to judge how much is 'adequate reserves' to divert part of 'excess' reserves to special funds. Further, India is having a negative international investment position (liabilities exceeding assets). It is also said that increasing reserves reflect, in part, the lower absorption capacity of the economy, which may pick up with the economy moving on to a higher growth trajectory (Reddy, 2008). All this point towards likely vulnerabilities of India to various shocks and a reasonable stock of foreign exchange reserve is very much required to cushion the impact. Therefore, consideration of separate stabilization fund for India may ideally await 'more comfortable economic situation'.

Econometrics Test for India

The Econometrics exercise (VAR) for India is run for the period of 1970 –2006 on annual data series. The positive and significant effect of foreign reserves on price level is evident for one time period lagged value, but non-significant for two time period lagged value of the foreign reserves. Hence after one time period in India there is an upward pressure on price level, something policy makers can be careful about. It is interesting to point out that foreign reserves in case of India have a negative (significant) effect on the real GDP which means the increased foreign reserves can retard the real GDP after one time period, but the effect is reversed after 2 time periods. Our important conclusion is that the foreign reserves inflow therefore helps economic growth in case of India only in the long run (after two years). As can be seen from Table 21, the effect of exchange rate movement on real GDP is non-existent. The R-squared value is high and satisfactory while the number of observations is 35.

Table 17
Statistical Results for India

India	*Price Level*	*GDP*	*GDP*
Price Level (lagged)	0.602***	.	.
	(0.16)	.	.
Price Level (twice lagged)	0.319**	.	.
	(0.15)	.	.
Foreign Reserves (lagged)	8.02E-07*	-1.251	.
	(-4.7 E-07)	(1.61)	.
Foreign Reserves (twice lagged)	-5.96E-07	3.84**	
	(-4.91 E-07)	(1.64)	
GDP (lagged)		0.555***	0.936***
		(0.14)	(0.15)
GDP (twice lagged)	.	-0.145	0.080
	.	(0.15)	(0.16)
Exchange Rate (lagged)	.	.	16482.760
	.	.	(10228.57)
Exchange Rate (twice lagged)	.	.	-15606.250
	.	.	(10027.50)
Observations	44	44	43
R-squared	0.9924	0.9593	0.9345

Note: * denotes significance at the 10 percent level, ** at 5 percent, and * at 1 percent

CONCLUSION

Lessons for Indian Policy Makers from the Dutch Disease

The main observation from the Dutch disease phenomenon, as it is made clear in our analysis of Brazil, Nigeria, Malaysia and Russia, is that the worldwide events and the unbalanced international trade are capable of inflicting serious hardships to the economy. Economy of Nigeria and Russia depends heavily on oil price and oil exports even in recent years. Malaysia depends heavily on semiconductor exports, while the study of Brazilian case point that diversification of economy may help in a great way to avoid Dutch disease like syndrome. The experience of Nigeria point out that quick revenue from one sector should not lead to neglect of traditional sectors. Further quick revenue may aggravate the problem of corruption. In India's case the rise in software and related exports should not lead to neglect of agricultural sector which employ a majority of its population. A review of Malaysia's economy taught us the lesson that dependence on a single export commodity is risky as international prices are subjected to cyclical downturns. Further, high concentration of FDI in nations primary export sector creates an undesirable dependency. Russian experience taught the lesson that sharp movements in exchange rates in relatively short time-spans can create severe problems for smaller but emerging sectors of the economy. However, India has done well in this regard by not allowing wide fluctuations in its exchange rate.

Russia also shows how stabilization fund and other fiscal measures like taxation can help stabilize an unbalanced growth. Even though we do not recommend a stabilization fund for India at this stage, it will be useful to monitor the experience of other countries with such funds.

Policy steps have to be taken before the damage is done. As a precaution and prevention, policy makers should avoid excessive dependence of international trade on only one commodity or a sector. One can point the finger towards the increased and substantial role of software exports in Indian international trade in recent years. While the leading sector can bring increased foreign reserves, a set-back in its growth can also bring lower economic welfare. The first thing noticeable is the dependence of international trade on one sector and commodity concentration. A solution to this discomfort is not to restrict the exports of increasing, dominant and leading commodity, but to make special efforts in commodity diversification by inventing new channels of other trade patterns. While Indian trade in software sector has increased magnificently, we do not think that it is right to label it as the serious concentration problem. Nonetheless, new avenues for higher trade have to be invented by considering comparative advantage in production of such finished products as fruit products, agricultural food processing, scooter, toys, computer products, refined petroleum products, machinery equipment etc.

A second sign of major concern is the regional concentration of the trade. If country is exporting same good to same region for a long time and has the major part of her trade created by this dominant sector, event of Dutch Disease is more likely to occur. Hence besides the commodity diversification one has to look for regional diversification of trade. Recent attempts by Indian government such as a call for number of Free Trade Agreements are encouraging in this respect. Even if the theoretical concepts of trade creation and trade diversion (made popular by Jacob Viner) have practical meaning in signing new trade agreements, deliberate regional diversification in international trade is a precondition for avoiding symptoms of Dutch Disease. A casual observation of efforts by Indian policy makers in this regard shows that Indian has already taken many actions in this regard.

A third area of concern is the foreign reserves inflow. In our model, this can become a culprit if left unchecked by the monetary policy. While the studies show that Indian monetary policy has done an impressive job of sterilizing the foreign reserve inflow so far, in future more attention has to be paid to its influence on the domestically originated money supply. The movement in REER and exports growth clearly point that, besides exchange rate, other policy measures like implicit subsidies related to exports can play major role in preventing crisis in export sector. In the last two decades inflation has been impressively low in Indian economy and the money supply growth has been moderate, but care needs to be taken that the inflow of foreign reserves does not affect these notable developments. Our study shows that this effect of foreign reserves so far has not been adverse.

The skilled student/research/labour supply to other important sectors should not get eroded because of the lure of quick money from the software -ITES sector. Further, the rise in pay and incentives in software sector may lead to demonstration effect and increase in cost of production in other sectors. Already there are reports indicating IT companies recruiting even from outside the area of specialization to compensate for temporary shortages. However, this is an area for further study to arrive at concrete conclusion.

Last, but not least, the Dutch Disease is one of the consequences of increased cost of production that is created by worldwide increase in import prices. An increase in import prices (such as price of oil imports or price of other energy substitutes) can take place for a variety of reasons. Political environments can also play a part in this shock of increased import prices. Natural disasters, "man-made" conflicts, and supply constraints in foreign countries are responsible for a disruption in imported goods' supply. Hence the old idea of keeping some stocks for rainy days and finding ways to substitute the dominant imports (such as oil exploration) in the most economical ways is another policy option government can consider. In recent years, besides the oil dependence the Indian economy is free from such drastic influence. Nonetheless, we expect a close watch on such import dependence and avoidance of getting into the trap of such commodity dependence in international trade. All in all, one has to be aware of the reasons for avoidance of Dutch Disease in case of India and continue the impressive record for the future.

REFERENCES

Abeysinghe, Tilak (2000), "Electronics and Growth Cycles in Singapore", *Applied Economics*, Volume 32, Number 11, September 15, 2000.

Abreu, Marcelo and D. Verner (1997), "Long-term Brazilian Economic Growth 1930-94", Organisation for Economic Co-operation and Development.

Acosta, P. A., E. K. K. Lartey and F. S. Mandelman (2007), "Remittance and the Dutch Disease", Federal Reseve Bank of Atlanta, Working paper 2007-8, April 2007.

Adam, C. S. and D. L. Bevan (2003), "Aid, Public Expenditure and Dutch Disease." University of Oxford, Working paper 184.

African Development Bank (2000), "African Development Report 2000", Oxford University Press.

Atkins, F. (2002), "Jamaica's Terms of Trade: A Problem of Resource Curse or Dutch Disease ?" Birkbeck College, London, 2002.

Auty, R. M. (1990), "Sowing the Oil in Eight Developing Countries", New York: Oxford University Press, 1990.

Banga, R. (2005), "Critical Issues in India's Service's Led Growth", Indian Council for Research on International Economic Relations, Working Paper No.171, 2005.

Bean, C. (1987), "The Impact of North Sea Oil", in R. Dornbush and R. Layard (edited) 'The Performance of the British Economy', Clarendon Press: Oxford, 1987.

Bruno, M. and J. Sachs (1982), "Energy and Resource Allocation: A Dynamic Model of the Dutch Disease", *Review of Economic Studies* 49, 1982, 845-859.

Buiter, W. and M. Miller (1983), "Changing the Rules: Economic Consequences of the Thatcher Regime", Brookings Papers on Economic Activity 2 (1983), 315-380.

Central Bank of Nigeria (CBN) Annual Report, 2005.

Corden W. (1992), "Booming Sector and Dutch Disease Economics: Survey and Consolidation." Oxford Economic Papers 36 (1984): 359-380. Reprinted in International Trade Theory and Policy, W. Corden. Northampton MA: Edward Elgar Publishing, 1992.

Corden W., and J. Neary (1982), "Booming Sector and De-Industrialisation in a Small Open Economy." *Economic Journal* 92 (December 1982): 825-848.

Damachi, U. G. and H. D. Siebel (1973), "Social Change and Economic Development in Nigeria", New York: Praeger.

Doppelhofer, G., R. Miller and X. Sala-i-Martin (2000), "Determinants of Long-Term Growth: a Bayesian Averaging of Classical Estimates (BACE) Approach." NBER Working Paper, 7750 *http://www.eia.doe.gov/emeu/cabs/russia.html*

Doraisami, Anita (2004), "Trade Causes of the Asian Crisis: The Malaysian Experience", The World Economy, Volume 27, May 2004.

Gelb, A. H. (1988), "Oil Windfalls, Blessing or Curse" Oxford: Oxford, 1988.

Gordon, J. and P. Gupta (2004), "Understanding India's Services Revolution", IMF Working Paper WP/04/171, September.

Goskomstat. "Russia's Exports, Imports in 2005." *http://www.balticdata.info/russia/macro_economics/russia_macro_economics_russia_foreign_trade_basic_information.htm*

Government of India, Directorate General of Commercial Intelligence and Statistics.

Gylfason, T. (2001), "Natural Resources and Economic Growth: What is the Connection?".

Hamilton, J. (1983), "Oil and the Macroeconomy Since World War II," *Journal of Political Economy*, 91, No. 2, (April 1983): 228-48.

Hardt, J. (2003), "Russia's Uncertain Economic Future". New York: M. E. Sharpe, 2003.

Hutchison, M. M. (1994), "Manufacturing Sector Resiliency to Energy Booms: Empirical Evidence from Norway, the Netherlands, and the United Kingdom." Oxford Economic Papers, New Series, 46, No. 2, (1994), 311-329.

International Monetary Fund, World Economic Outlook, Washington D.C. various issues.

International Monetary Fund, International Financial Statistics (IFS), Publication Unit, Washington D.C., Various Issues.

Jalan, B. (2002), "India's Economy in the New Millennium: Selected Essays" New Delhi: UBS Publishers, 2002.

Jadhav, Narendra (2003), "Capital Account Liberalisation: The Indian Experience", Paper Presented at *A Tale of Two Giants: India's and China's Experience with Reform and Growth,* New Delhi, November, 2003.

Kim, Y. (2003), "The Dutch Disease, Russian Style: New Dependency or Global Capitalism?" In The Resource Curse in a Post-Communist Regime: Russia in Comparative Perspective, Kim, Younkyoo: 41-71. England: Ashgate Publishing Limited, 2003.

Kulkarni, K. G. and E. L. Erickson (1999), "Impact of Dutch Disease on an Economy: A Case of Nigeria", Journal of Foreign Exchange and International Finance, Vol. XII, No. 4, pp. 297-204. Also included in "*Readings in International Economics*", Serials Publications, New Delhi, Second Edition, 2006.

Kulkarni, K G. (2006), "*Readings in International Economics,*" Serials Publications, New Delhi, Second Edition 2006, Chapter 3.

Lal, D., S. Bery and D. K. Pant (2003), "The Real Exchange rate, fiscal deficits and capital flows India; 1981-2000, *Economic and Political Weekly*, November 22, 2003.

Lam, R. and L. Wantchekon (2003), "Political Dutch Disease" April 10, 2003.

Latsis, Otto (2005), "Economic Growth has Predictably Slowed Down Due Government Policies", *http://www.cdi.org/russia/johnson/9173-16.cfm*

Lopez, Anthony (2006), "The Case for Dutch Disease in the Republic of Kazakhstan", an Unpublished Working Paper, University of Denver, Graduate School of International Studies, pp. 1-28.

Lopez, H., L. Molina and M. Bussolo (2007), "Remittances and the Real Exchange Rate" World Bank Policy Research Working Paper 4213, April 2007.

Martin, Xavier-sala-I and Arvind Subramanian (2003), "Addressing the Natural Resource Curse: An Illustration from Nigeria", May 2003.

Mallik, Jayanta Kumar (2005), "India's Exports: Policy Defeating Exchange Rate Arithmetic." *Economic and Political Weekly*, December 24, 2005, Volume 40, Number 52.

McMahon, G. (1997), "The Natural Resource Curse: Myth or Reality?" Economic Development Institute, The World Bank, October 21.

Matsen, E. and R. Torvik (2003), "Optimal Dutch Disease." Norges Bank, Working paper ANO 2003/3.

Meesook, K., H. Lee II, L. Liu, Y. Khatri, N. Tamirisa, M. Moore, and M. H. Krysl (2001), " Malaysia: From Crisis to Recovery", International Monetary Fund, Occasional paper No 207.

Mohan, R. (2007), "Capital Account Liberalisation and Conduct of Monetary Policy-the Indian Experience", *International Monetary Seminar*, June 14, 2007.

Moser, G., S. Rogers, R. H. Van Til, R. D. Kibuka and I. Lukonga (1997), "Nigeria Experience with Structural Adjustment" IMF Occasional Paper 148, March 1997.

OECD. "OECD Economic Survey: Russian Federation." September 2004. *http://www.oecd.org/document/39/0,2340,en_2649_201185_324118151111,00.html*

Oomes, N. and K. Kalcheva (2007), "Diagnosing Dutch Disease: Does Russia Have the Symptoms ?" IMF Working Paper, WP/07/102, April 2007.

Prati, A. and T. Tressel (2006), "Aid Volatility and Dutch Disease: Is There a Role for Macroeconomic Policies ?", *IMF Working Paper* 06/145.

Rautava, Jouko (2002), "The Role of Oil Prices and The Real Exchange Rate in Russia's Economy", Bank of Finland, Institute of Economies in Transition, Discussion Papers No. 3.

Reddy, Y. V. (2007), "Forex Reserves, Stabilisation Funds and Sovereign Wealth Funds: Indian Perspective", Reserve Bank of India Bulletin, November 2007.

Reddy, Y. V. (2008), "Government-owned Investment Vehicles and Capital Flows: Indian Perspective", Reserve Bank of India Bulletin, May 2008.

Reserve Bank of India. Hand Book of Statistics on Indian Economy 2006-07.

Reserve Bank of India. "Invisibles in India's Balance of Payments: an Analysis of Trade in Services, Remittances and Income", Reserve Bank of India Bulletin, February 2008.

Reserve Bank of India. Report on Currency and Finance, various issues.

Rosenberg, C. B. and T. O. Saavalainen (1998), " Dealing with Azerbaijan's Oil Boom." Finance and Development, IMF, September 1998, Volume 35, Number 3.

Rosenfielde, S. (1998), "Efficiency and Russia's Economic Recovery Potential to the Year 2000 and Beyond", Brookfield, US: Ashgate Publishing, 1998.

Rotemberg, J. and M. Woodford (1996), "Imperfect Competition and the Effects of Energy Price Increases on Economic Activity." *Journal of Money, Credit and Banking* 28 No. 4 (1996): 550-77.

Sachs, J. and A. Warner (1997) "Fundamental Sources of Long-Run Growth." *The American Economic Review* 87 No. 2 (1997): 184-188.

Sachs, J. and A. Warner (1999), "The Big Push, Natural Resource Booms and Growth." *Journal of Development Economics* 59, (1999): 43–76.

Sachs, J. and A. Warner (1999), "Natural Resource Intensity and Economic Growth", in Mayer, J., B. Chambers and A. Farooq (edited) 'In Development Policies in Natural Resource Economies', Cheltenham, UK: Northhampton, MA: Edward Elgar, 1999.

Sala-i-Martin, X. (1997), "I Just Run Two Million Regressions." The American Economic Review, Papers and Proceedings, May 1997.

Sanusi, J. O. (2003), "Developing the Non-Oil Sector in Nigeria", Central Bank of Nigeria, August, 2003.

Santos, P. F. P. dos (2005), "Brazil's Remarkable Journey" *Finance and Development*, 2005, Volume 42, Number 2.

Sanusi, J. O. (2004), "Exchange Rate Mechanism: The Current Nigerian Experience", Central Bank of Nigeria, February, 2004.

Smirnova, Olga and Kulkarni Kishore (2005), "Dutch Disease in Case of Russia: Analysis and Empirical Evidence", an Unpublished Research Paper, pp. 1-26.

Sosunov, Kirill and Oleg Zamulin (2006), "Can Oil Prices Explain the Real Appreciation of the Russian Ruble in 1998-2005?", Centre for Economic and Financial Research at New Economic School, Working Paper No 83.

Spatafora N. and A. Warner (2001), "Macroeconomic and Sectoral Effects of Terms -of-Trade Shocks - The Experience of the Oil-Exporting Developing Countries", November 2001.

Stiglitz, Joseph (2004), " We Can Now Cure Dutch Disease." Guardian, August 18, 2004.

Stijns, J. P. (2003), "An Empirical Test of the Dutch Disease Hypothesis Using a Gravity Model of Trade." Berkeley: University of California Press, 2003. *http://econwpa.wustl.edu:8089/eps/it/papers/0305/0305001.pdf*

Stokke, H. E. (2005), " Resource Boom and Dutch Disease Effects in South Africa." Norwegian University of Science and Technology, May 30, 2005.

Swerdfeger, N. (2004), "Diagnosing Symptoms of Dutch Disease in the Russian Economy", April 2004.

The Economist (2007), The Economy of Heat: Nature has been Almost too kind to Brazil, "*The Economist*", April 14-20, 2007.

The World Bank Country Report (2004), "Russian Economic Memorandum", Washington D. C.

United Nations (2005), "Trade and Development Report 2005, UN Publications, New York.

Van, P. H. (2005), "Dutch Disease in the Labour Market: Women, Services and Industrialisation", University of Missouri, August 2005.

Veeramani, C. (2008), "Impact of Exchange Rate Appreciation on India's Exports." *Economic and Political Weekly*, May 31, 2008, Volume XLIII, Number 22.

Warner, A. (1992), "Did the Debt Crisis Cause the Investment Crisis?" *Quarterly Journal of Economics* 107 (1992): 1161-1186.

Warner, A. (1994), "Mexico's Investment Collapse: Debt or Oil?" *Journal of International Money and Finance* 13 No. 2 (1994): 239-256.

World Bank Country Report (2004), "Is Dutch Disease Responsible for Russia's Energy Dependent Industrial Structure?" Washington D.C. *http://siteresources.worldbank.org/INTRANETTRADE/Topics/Accession/43873.*

World Bank Press Review (2008), "Brazil Plans Special funds for Revenue from New Oil Fields", Washington D.C. August 21, 2008.

Zadeh, C. E. (2003), "Back to Basics: Dutch Disease: Too Much Wealth Managed Unwisely." *Finance and Development*, 2003, Volume 40, Number 1.

25

ANALYSIS OF DUTCH DISEASE PHENOMENON IN CASE OF VENEZUELA

INTRODUCTION

This paper investigates how the Venezuelan economy has evolved since the international oil price increases of the early 1970s, with particular reference to the Dutch disease. As a major oil exporter and member of the Organization of Petroleum Exporting Countries (OPEC), Venezuela provides an interesting setting to investigate the symptoms and impacts of Dutch disease in an open, developing economy. The Dutch disease is perhaps the most well-known effect of natural resource rents on the real economy, and numerous scholarly contributions reveal that countries relying on a sizable amount of any valuable tradable resource for their exports should concern themselves with the possibility of Dutch disease and the impact that its extraction will have on the economy.

This paper provides a necessarily simplified overview of some broad trends in the Venezuelan economy that have accompanied surges in the international price of oil in the early 1970s and more recently in 2003. It is not intended to be a definitive account of structural changes and their causes, but to inform readers of the broad changes occurring in the economy once resource booms have been realized. The study

---

This Chapter is based on an article co-authored with Mr. Stace Nicholson

employs formal monetary theory to illuminate these changes, but it also recognizes that government policy is an intervening factor in this process. In particular, government action explains to a great degree whether a country will suffer from immiserizing growth or can adjust to a new equilibrium once Dutch Disease is present. It appears that developing countries do not have the capacity to deal properly with the large inflow of foreign exchange following a resource boom. Therefore, where appropriate, the paper sheds light on how government policy in Venezuela has managed any effects brought about by Dutch disease.

SECTION - 1

Theoretical Foundations

The Dutch disease, defined broadly, is an economic phenomenon whereby a natural resource boom gives rise to a host of economic problems, including unemployment, inflation, and imbalances in international payments. While it tends to affect countries upon the discovery, extraction, and exploitation of large amounts of natural resources—most notably oil or natural gas—it can also occur once international demand for a country's export item spikes or the world price of the resource rises. As the name suggests, the term was first used to describe the decline in manufacturing activities and competitiveness in the Netherlands following its discovery and sale of natural gas in the 1970s. According to Kulkarni et.al, the growth in the natural gas export sector was responsible for an influx of foreign reserves into the Dutch economy. This increased domestic money supply resulted in high inflation. Simultaneously, there was an increase in the Dutch economy's major imports given an appreciation of the exchange rate, which led to increased cost of production and the overall decline in aggregate supply. Domestic unemployment increased as the aggregate supply decreased, and a short-term economic crisis ensued.[1]

Although the concept itself was not codified until the 1970s, the theoretical foundation explaining why and how Dutch disease can occur was laid forth by Jagdish Bhagwati in the

1960s via the "Immiserizing Growth" hypothesis. Succinctly, this hypothesis formally demonstrates that an open economy experiencing an expansion in its productive capacity, due to factor accumulation and/or technological progress, can become worse off if its terms of trade deteriorate sufficiently. If certain conditions hold, economic growth leads to a sufficiently acute deterioration in the country's terms of trade, which imposes a loss of real income that outweighs the initial gain in real income attributable to the preliminary economic growth process.[2] In the context of a developing country, immiserizing growth occurs once the nation has started economic growth but encounters unfavorable international demand conditions as it increases its traditional exports.

Beyond the significant insights of Baghwati, Corden and Neary are credited with formulating the core model of Dutch disease economics. They consider a small, open economy comprising three sectors: a tradable, non-traditional manufacturing sector, a tradable natural resource/energy sector, and a non-traded sector.[3] It should be made clear that a traded item is one that is available for export and import, while a good that is not tradable refers to something which is not traded with other countries, such as services. Hence, the first two sectors of the economy in this model are available for import and export, while the third is not. Under the assumptions that all goods are for final consumption, labor is mobile, trade is always balanced, and that commodity and factor prices are competitive, a resource boom affects the economy in the short-term through two main channels: the resource movement effect and the spending effect.

Literature Review for Dutch Disease Phenomenon

The resource movement comes to fruition as an export boom following the use of a natural resource, such as oil, raises the marginal productivity of the mobile factor employed in that sector. In the Corden and Neary model, this mobile factor is labor. This higher factor return in the booming natural resource sector raises the equilibrium wage rate in that sector and attracts labor from the other sectors. The excess demand for labor by the resource sector should cease when real wages are equalized across all sectors at a higher level. The movement of resources would reduce the supply capacity of the other sectors. The non-booming manufacturing and non-tradable sectors, therefore are stagnated or contracted following this factor movement.[4] Obviously, the magnitude of the resource movement effect depends upon the extent to which the resources used by the booming tradable natural resource sector are compatible with the other sectors in the economy. This movement would not be particularly severe if the resource sector forms an 'enclave' within a developing country's economy with few links to other sectors.

It is practical to describe the spending effect by assuming that the resource sector does not demand labor from other sectors, and to concentrate on how the increased income from the natural resource export boom is spent. In short, this effect occurs as the boom in the natural resource sector increases real income in the country. This extra income should increase demand for both traded and non-traded goods, provided that both the tradable non-traditional manufacturing and non-tradable sectors produce normal goods. Given their relative prices in the economy, there will be excess demand for the non-tradable sector, which needs to be met via an appreciation of the real exchange rate. In other words, because the prices of traded goods are fixed internationally, the prices of non-traded goods rise relative to the prices of traded goods. The real exchange rate subsequently appreciates. In mathematical terms, the real exchange rate (RER) may be defined as:

$$q = e - \frac{P_{NT}}{P_{T^*}}$$

In the equation above, *e* is the inverse of the nominal exchange rate, representing the number of foreign currency units required to purchase one unit of domestic currency, and P_T and P_{NT} are the prices of tradable goods expressed in foreign currency and the prices of non-tradable goods expressed in domestic currency, respectively. A rise in the RER as conceptualized here represents a real appreciation of the currency, and it can occur via an increase in P_{NT} or e, or both, relative to P_T*. The rise in e can be produced by the increase in demand for domestic currency following the natural resource boom, while the increase in the relative prices of non-tradable goods/services may come about due to the excess demand for the non-tradable sector.[5]

Kulkarni, *et al.*, affirms that this currency appreciation raises the return to the non-traded sector relative to the tradable manufacturing sector, leading mobile factors of labor and capital to move from the tradable sector to the non-tradable and traditional natural resource sectors. This process thereby facilitates an expansion of the non-tradable sector through the resources it draws from the tradable manufacturing sector. Moreover, the appreciation of the domestic currency lowers the international competitiveness of the manufacturing sector, which reduces its export volume.[6] Likewise, the domestic competitiveness of the manufacturing sector is eroded. Assuming that consumers spend their incomes in two ways—on imports and non-traded services, which suffer no loss from an increase in income—they expend modest sums on traded manufacturing produced locally because the appreciation of the domestic currency causes those goods to be relatively more expensive. This appreciation elevates the production costs and the prices of these products. Consequently, the imports of other countries are priced significantly lower in relative terms, making them much more competitive to the domestic consumer. Furthermore, as Gross Domestic Product (GDP) rises, the transactions demand for money also grows within the country and interest rates rise. Thus, it is more expensive for firms within the traded manufacturing sector to borrow money for investment, which also leads to a decrease in net exports and a reduction in tradable manufacturing consumed domestically.

The interaction between the resource movement and spending effects determines the likely impact of the natural resource boom on sectoral output and real wages. Corden and Neary analyze three static models. The first of these models is illustrative of the short-term, as it assumes that each sector uses one specific factor that is immobile, such as capital, and one mobile factor, such as labor. In this scenario, the resource sector should unambiguously expand because of the resource movement effect, while output from the tradable manufacturing sector should shrink as both the resource movement effect and the spending effect lead to the flight of labor from the manufacturing sector. In sum, Corden and Neary make the distinction between direct de-industrialization and indirect de-industrialization. The former describes the movement of labor from the manufacturing sector to the booming resources sector, whereas the latter refers to the further shift of labor from the manufacturing sector to the non-tradable sector once the spending effect increases the demand for goods from that sector, causing a further appreciation of the real exchange rate.[7]

The combined impact of both the resource movement and spending effects on the non-tradable sector, however, is ambiguous since this would depend on which of the two effects is larger. For example, the spending effect would lead to an expansion of this sector, but the resource movement would cause it to contract. In a country where the resource sector is an enclave in the economy, the resource movement effect would be circumscribed and the non-traded sector would likely expand. The impact of the natural resource boom on real wages is also uncertain in theoretical terms. At one level, the resource movement effect tends to increase the real wage in the resource sector, as output of both the non-tradable and manufacturing sectors shrinks. Yet, the spending effect causes the wage measured in terms of the manufacturing sector to increase, while the wage in terms of the non-tradable sector decreases. The net impact, will rely on the relative magnitude of the two effects, as well as on the relative weight of the non-tradable and manufacturing sectors in the overall consumption profile of the economy. Generally, the real wage is expected to decrease as the share in consumption of the non-tradable sector rises.[8]

As the experiences of many countries having contracted the Dutch disease attest, the economy may experience a significant improvement in performance in the short-run after a natural resource export boom. The current account is likely to record a surplus, or at least improve, if the increase in natural resource exports is larger than the decrease in manufacturing exports. However, it is important to point out that the theory does not make any ex-ante prediction about the evolution of the current account. We can only assert that the real appreciation of the currency has important potential effects on the country's current account through its influence on the pattern of its international trade.

Sachs and Warner (1997) present a cross-country empirical study of economic growth that considers explicitly the effects of natural resource production and/ or natural resource booms on long-term economic growth. They find that countries with a high value of resource-based exports with respect to their GDP have, on average, a tendency for low growth. This seems to confirm the postulate that resource abundance does have adverse effects on economic performance in the long-run.[9] A subsequent study by the same authors, in which they analyze several natural resource booms in Latin America bears outs these findings. They conclude, once more, that most of these booms in Latin America had negative long-lasting effects on growth. Sachs and Warner explain this observed negative relationship between natural resource abundance and growth by emphasizing the crowding out of the manufacturing sector's dynamic effects that result from the biases brought about by the natural resource boom. According to this line of reasoning, manufacturing yields positive production externalities that are crucial for long-term development, such as learning-by-doing.[10] Learning-by-doing refers to the knowledge workers gain as they experience new tasks, gain new skills, and innovate while on the job. Ultimately, this learning-by-doing contributes to the development of human capital, which is the combined skill set of all workers in a country. Hence, the manufacturing sector is an important form of employment because it contributes to the expansion of human capital—more so than the resource or non-traded sectors. By shifting labor away from this high learning-by-doing sector(s), the natural resource boom stymies economic growth in the long-run as the loss of employment due to the decreased sales of tradable manufacturing reduces the value of human capital in the country, which ultimately lowers the rate of growth.

The assertion that natural resource production systematically disembowels the manufacturing sector and negatively affects long-term economic growth is not without its detractors. Benjamin *et al.* (1986) was among the first observers to rebuff this assumption, arguing that the non-tradable sectors might be those negatively affected sectors by a natural resource boom. They argue, that the theoretical framework expounded by Corden and Neary does not take into account the trade determinants for an open economy, nor the behavior of government with respect to its using or wasting the windfall.[11]

These critiques have continued in recent years. Stijns (2003) challenges the assumption held by Sachs and Warner, and others who accept the resource curse thesis, by demonstrating empirically that an abundance of certain types of natural resources—including oil, gas, and minerals—may affect economic growth through both positive and negative channels. Stijns finds that oil and gas reserves tend to be positively associated with better education, more market-oriented economic policy, and more favorable investment-saving characteristics.[12] His analysis also finds that aggregate saving and investment rates, as well as the rate of investment in equipment and other structures, are higher for countries with abundant oil, gas, and mineral reserves.[13] The long-run effects of a natural resource boom would, need to be considered in light of the nature of the country's learning process in exploiting and developing natural resources.

In line with the findings by Stijns, Deaton (1999) insists that temporary commodity price booms can provide a potential source of investment funds which are important for sustained growth. He argues that production revenues from oil, gas, and minerals can help fund public investment projects which may be used to offset the long-run loss associated with decreasing amounts of non-natural resource exports, thereby helping those shrinking economic sectors identified by policymakers as important for long-run growth, and to buffer future terms of trade shocks related to commodity price volatility.[14]

Thus, as Stijns and Deaton suggest, the influence of a natural resource boom on a country's long-run economic growth prospects will be a function of how the windfall revenues accrued from that boom are managed. These resources will have very different effects whether they are used to increase productivity or to boost consumption demand.

Upon review of the relevant literature, one finds evidence to support each of these perspectives. Kulkarni, et.al, provides a comprehensive examination of the broad empirical literature on the Dutch disease published since the 1980s and early 1990s, but a few deserve mention here. A number of these studies confirm the presence of Dutch disease in a variety of oil- or gas-exporting countries in the aftermath of the oil price shock of the 1970s, while also commenting on the failure of resource-driven development. Gelb (1988) tentatively concludes in a case study analysis that the oil price rises of the 1970s may have made several of the oil exporters worse off in the long-run than they would have been with constant real oil prices. According to Gelb, volatility and poor price prediction translates, on average, into a poorer use of resources during the cycle, which may more than offset the increment to resources from the windfall.[15]

Auty (1993) also finds that selected hard-rock mineral exporters did not respond well to terms-of-trade shocks induced by the oil price shocks of the 1970s.[16] In Forsyth's analysis of the effects of North Sea oil exports on the British economy, the author concludes that Dutch Disease effects were apparent in the 1980s, but he adds the proviso that it is difficult to isolate the impact of the natural resource boom on structural changes because of the poor macroeconomic background over which they took place.[17]

Usui (1998) draws a comparison between Indonesia and Mexico in their policy adjustments to the oil boom, with special reference to the Dutch disease. He uncovers a striking contrast between the two countries—especially in their fiscal, foreign borrowing, and exchange rate policies. Whereas Indonesia acted conservatively in its macroeconomic management to avoid the Dutch Disease, Mexico was more carefree in its spending. Equally significant, the investment of oil revenues to strengthen the tradable sector was another factor responsible for Indonesian success throughout the boom and bust cycle. Hence, although Mexico provides a straightforward example of the resource curse thesis, Indonesia is an exception.[18]

Davis (1995) also seeks to identify whether mineral endowments have in fact contributed negatively to the historical long-run growth and development of mineral-producing countries, but he examines the data on a broader scale by comparing twenty-two mineral economies as a group with other non-mineral developing economies. Based on mean and median economic performance between 1970 and 1991, the mineral economies as a group actually outperformed other non-mineral developing economies.[19]

It is quite apparent from the preceding literature review that disparate views of the long-run effects of Dutch disease often arise in the context of the open-economy model. Indeed, this is only a sampling of the rich array of literature on the Dutch Disease. Nonetheless, it is sufficient in relaying the theoretical foundations of the phenomenon, while also laying forth its short-run effects and the uncertainty surrounding its long-run structural effects. One strand of literature emphasizes how specialization in resource-intensive goods can harm growth, while another accentuates the manner in which governments react to the influx of revenue. However, although they are frequently thought to be synonymous, the Dutch Disease and the resource curse thesis are two separate issues. There is nothing inherently growth-inhibiting in mineral booms and any resulting Dutch disease phenomena. The Dutch disease is simply a description of the causes and structural effects of boom-induced growth, and the only problems associated with it is resource reallocation and the burden of adjustment.[20] For the purposes of this paper, we will focus only on the topic of Dutch Disease as it applies to Venezuela.

SECTION – 2

Venezuela: Background of an Oil Economy

Venezuela was characterized as principally an agrarian economy with coffee as its main export item before becoming a major oil exporter. The first commercial drilling for oil occurred in 1917, and the wide-scale exploitation of this mineral resource hastened the country's economic transformation. After 1925, oil sector exports surpassed those of the coffee industry in economic importance. By 1930, for example, 90 percent of its export revenue was derived from oil. The share of oil in the trade account has fluctuated very little historically.[21] Sales of crude oil and refined products accounted for an average of 80 percent of export revenue from 2001 to 2006, and this figure jumped to 93 percent by the third quarter of 2007.[22] Figure 1 shows the contribution of oil export values to total export values from the years 1970 to 2006. Unsurprisingly, the oil sector has also been an important and stable component of total GDP over the years. Approximately 25 percent of total GDP in the early 1950s was attributable to the petroleum industry, and its contribution increased from about 21 percent

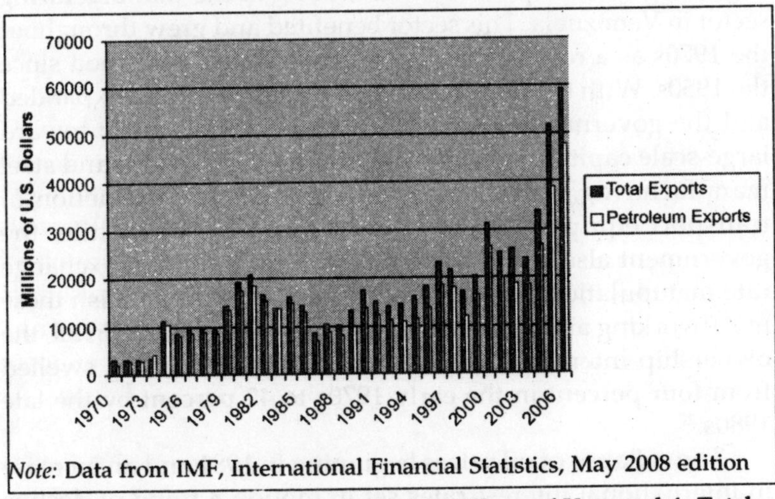

Note: Data from IMF, International Financial Statistics, May 2008 edition

Figure 1: Value of Petroleum Export as a Share of Venezuela's Total Exports: 1970 - 2006

in the early 1990s to about 26 percent in the late 1990s. More recent estimates place the sector's share of GDP at 20 percent.[23]

The rise of the petroleum industry in Venezuela's economy has been complemented by a marked decline of the agricultural sector. Agricultural output made up about one-third of Venezuelan GDP in the 1920s, but this shrank to less than one-tenth by the 1950s.[24] In the 1990s, despite efforts by the government to support the sector with subsidies and low-interest loans, its overall contribution to GDP steadily decreased from roughly 6 percent in 1990 to 4 percent in 1999.[25] This has changed very little in the last nine years, as the agricultural sector presently only accounts for 5 percent of GDP. In regards to the size of the labor force in agriculture, this too has declined sharply. In 1936, 57 percent of the total labor force was in agriculture. By 1960, this share had decreased to 33 percent, and in 1997 the agricultural labor force accounted for only 9 percent of the total labor force. As one might expect, the agricultural sector experienced absolute declines in the number of laborers in the 1970s, which was a decade characterized by high oil prices.[26]

Whilst the agricultural sector languished, the oil booms beginning in 1973 proved to be a boon to the manufacturing sector in Venezuela. This sector benefited and grew throughout the 1970s as a result of government policies established since the 1950s. With the rise in world oil prices, revenues expanded and the government directed its investment strategy toward large-scale capital-intensive industries—such as iron and steel manufacturing, aluminum smelting, and the production of transport equipment and petrochemicals. Meanwhile, the government also relied upon tariffs, import quotas, exchange rate manipulation, and large-scale subsidies to establish these metalworking and other consumer-goods industries. In all, the ownership interest of government in manufacturing swelled from four percent in the early 1970s to 42 percent by the late 1980s.[27]

The collapse of oil prices beginning in 1981 and an increase in international interest rates set in motion a trend of decline from which the Venezuelan economy has been slow to recover.

The windfall from the oil booms of the 1970s instigated a demand-led, temporary boom in growth as a considerable portion of the oil revenues throughout the 1970s was spent on imports. The government relied extensively on external borrowing to finance its current account deficit, but this proved unsustainable once interest rates on this debt spiked in 1979. The country's external debt spiraled dramatically to USD 31 billion in 1982 after the hike in U. S. interest rates in 1979, almost double the level for 1978. The economy contracted sharply, inflation rose, and capital flight accelerated—all of which created pressures on the overvalued bolívar to devalue.[28]

In 1983, a tiered system of exchange controls was imposed to combat this capital flight, with the cheapest rate—for the import of essential goods—set at 7 bolivars to the dollar. This devaluation from 4.3 bolivars to the dollar made debt repayments more difficult. The government soon found itself unable to repay its foreign debts, and the accompanying loss of confidence in the Venezuelan economy caused an enormous increase in capital flight. Investors rapidly divested themselves of Venezuelan securities and shifted their capital to foreign markets. Expansionary policies from 1986 to 1988 led to a temporary rise in growth, but because monetary expansion was used to finance budget deficits, inflation continued to rise and external reserves declined. The government increased interest rates in the late 1980s in order to support the new bolivar exchange rate, attract international capital, and to restrain inflation; however, the high cost of borrowing hurt household and business investment.[29] This condition continued into the late 1980s, as epitomized by Figure 2 and the downward trend in real GDP for much of that decade.

Because the domestic manufacturing sector had been developed under an umbrella of protectionism, the country had failed to establish traded manufacturing that was truly competitive. For example, by 1988, import-substituting domestic industries constituted a major importing block: raw materials for industrial use accounted for 44 percent of total imports; machinery and transportation equipment accounted for another 26 percent and 15 percent of imports, respectively.[30]

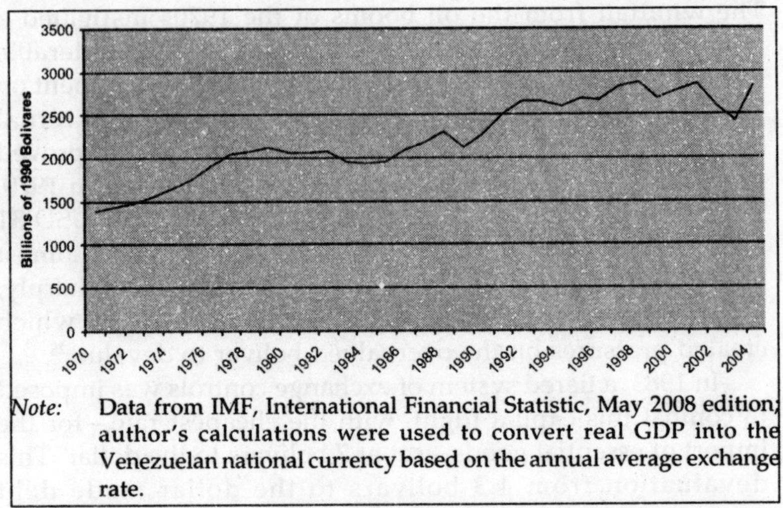

Note: Data from IMF, International Financial Statistic, May 2008 edition; author's calculations were used to convert real GDP into the Venezuelan national currency based on the annual average exchange rate.

Figure 2: Real GDP for Venezuela (in Billions of 1990 Bolivars): 1970 - 2004

Government subsidies and spending had held domestic prices low enough for domestic products to remain competitive with imports in the domestic market. In this way, Venezuela escaped the de-industrialization effect of the Dutch Disease. In fact, after oil prices dropped nearly 50 percent in 1986, the government sought to expand the industrial sector by accelerating a number of industrial diversification programs in specialized fields, including petroleum refining, natural gas, petrochemicals, and mining. It also intensified oil exploration efforts.[31]

Nonetheless, because prices had been artificially controlled through massive borrowing and extra oil revenue, the government's ability to control them was squelched after these resources dried up. This was made clear when prices increased precipitously once structural adjustment was initiated in 1989. The government was forced to scale back its involvement in the manufacturing sector in the 1990s, and there have been striking variations in sector output. For example, manufacturing output grew by 6.8 percent in 1995, contracted by 5.2 percent in 1996, grew by 4.4 percent in 1997, and shrank again in 1998.[32] In all, industrial output as a percentage of GDP declined by 26 percent from 1999 (50 percent of GDP) to 2003 (24 percent of GDP). This compares unfavorably with Latin America as a whole, where average industrial output declined from 36 percent in 1999 to 29 percent in 2003.[33]

Venezuela also lags behind the rest of Latin America in terms of the industrial intensity of its exports. Measured by the share of manufactured exports in total exports and the share of medium- and high-technology products in total exports, Venezuela ranks last among major Latin American economies. This implies that its ability to make more advanced products and move into more dynamic areas of export growth is limited.[34]

The Venezuelan Economy in Recent Years

The Venezuelan economy has rebounded since the 'lost' decade of the 1980s, but it is still susceptible to the whims of the international oil market. Recovery began in 1991 and 1992, as real GDP growth rose to 10.4 percent and 7.3 percent, respectively. This growth was driven in part by the liberalization of the economy, including a privatization program initiated in 1990 and the restructuring of public sector enterprises. More importantly, though, the first Persian Gulf War caused oil prices to increase temporarily, and the petroleum sector expanded as a result.[35] As evidenced in Figure 2, the economy stagnated in 1998 once oil prices fell.

The economy has grown remarkably since 2003, again as a consequence of rising oil prices. Most recently, GDP expanded by 10.3 percent and 8.4 percent in 2006 and 2007, respectively. Furthermore, the current account balance has registered hearty surpluses since 2001—from USD 1,983 million in 2001 to USD 20,001 million in 2007.[36] Venezuela has taken advantage of the current expansion and increased oil revenues to reduce its foreign public debt, which was a chief culprit of the downturn in the 1980s. This debt, as a percentage of GDP, fell from 25.2 percent of GDP in 1998 to approximately 15 percent of GDP in 2006.[37] This decline was not continuous, though, as public foreign debt increased substantially throughout 2002 and 2003 on account of the national strikes during those years.

Nevertheless, in this regard, Venezuela has made great strides in reducing its exposure to international risks like those that caught it off guard in the 1980s.

Upon closer scrutiny of the data, there is cause for concern that Venezuela is once again on the verge of contracting the Dutch disease. While its GDP has increased in recent years, this expansion has been driven by public spending and strong domestic demand. According to *The Economist*, public spending has increased sevenfold since 1999. This increased spending has coincided with considerable budget deficits. In 2007 alone, the budget deficit reached its highest level in eight years, at 1.4 percent of GDP.[38] Private consumption has also soared in Venezuela, increasing by 16.3 percent in 2006 and by 17 percent in 2007. Theory presumes that this increase in consumption ought to be met by rising imports, and this is exactly what one observes in Venezuela. Imports, which hovered between USD eight and 10 billion per year since 1996, reached a record USD 31.3 billion in 2006, equivalent to 54 percent of the country's oil income and 27 percent higher than the import tab for 2005.[39] Figure 3 depicts this recent surge in imports. Despite this surge, though, the current account still registers a surplus because the steady rise in oil prices since 2003 has pushed annual export values to a higher level.

The problem of rising imports has been exacerbated by overvaluation of the exchange rate. The bolivar has been

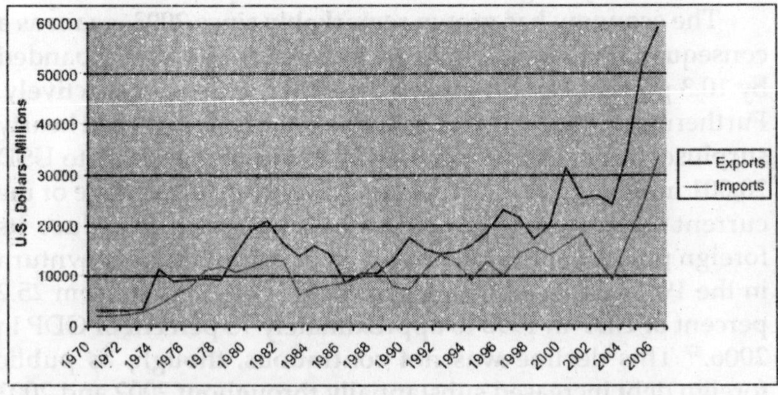

Figure 3: Venezuelan Export and Import Values: 1970 - 2006

pegged to the U.S. dollar at a rate of 2,147/USD since 2005, and it has not been allowed to weaken in line with its market value despite consistent double-digit inflation rates. This overvalued exchange rate continues to encourage strong import growth while adversely affecting the competitiveness of the non-oil export sector. As oil exports' share of GDP has more than doubled from 13.4 percent in 1998 to 32.2 percent in 2006, non-oil exports' share of GDP has declined from 6.1 percent to 3.7 percent in the same time period.[40] Figure 4 shows the evolution of oil and non-oil sector exports in recent times. Obviously, the overvalued exchange rate is something that will have to be remedied if Venezuela wishes to pursue a long-term development strategy that diversifies the economy away from oil. It makes imports artificially cheap and the country's exports more expensive on world markets thus, putting the country's tradable goods at a serious disadvantage in both international and domestic markets.

As yet another symptom of the Dutch Disease that one finds presently in Venezuela, the recent economic expansion has created excess demand of the non-tradable sector. Over the four and a half years from 2003 to the third quarter of 2007,

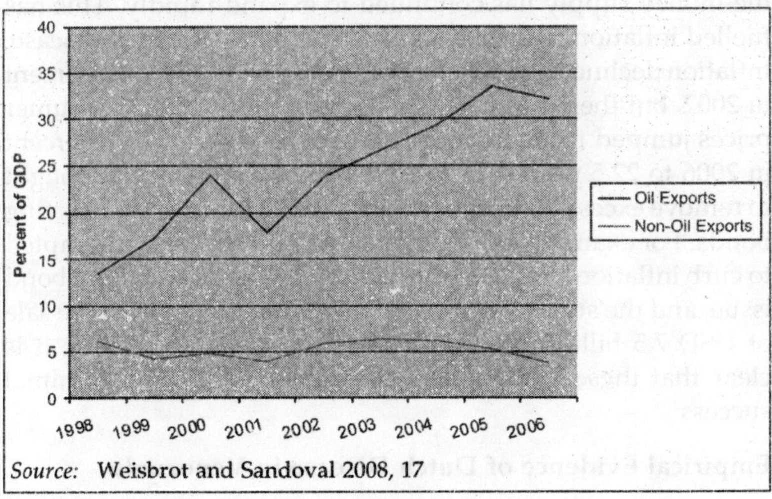

Source: Weisbrot and Sandoval 2008, 17

Figure 4: Venezuelan Oil and Non-Oil Exports as Percent of GDP: 1998 - 2006

the non-tradable sector in Venezuela has been the fastest growing of all. Included among the fastest growing industries within this sector are as follows: finance and insurance (273.4 percent); construction (135.1 percent); trade and repair services (148.1 percent); communications (111.6 percent); and transport and storage (103.6 percent). Comparatively, manufacturing grew by only 93.9 percent in the same time period.[41] Thus, the data indicates that the non-tradable sector has expanded between 2003 and 2007 relative to the other tradable sectors. These findings seem in line with the theoretical prediction that the oil boom is determining a movement of resources towards non-tradables. However, we cannot exclude the possibility that these are in fact long-term trends that are largely independent of the recent oil boom. Given these dynamics, further research will need to track the significance of the resource movement and spending effects in the next few years as consequence of the most recent oil boom.

Despite the massive inflow of foreign exchange from oil exports, the government has pursued an expansionary monetary policy reminiscent of the 1970s. In the context of exchange controls and fiscal dominance over monetary policy, the money supply has continued to expand rapidly. This has fuelled inflation, which is a prime symptom of Dutch disease. Inflation declined steadily from 40 percent in 1998 to 12 percent in 2002, but there has been an upswing since 2006. Consumer prices jumped from an annual rate of increase of 13.7 percent in 2006 to 22.5 percent in 2007.[42] The government has sought to remove excess domestic currency from circulation by issuing bonds. For example, the Central Bank of Venezuela attempted to curb inflation in 2003 by administering a USD 4 billion bond issue, and the state oil company PDVSA followed with the sale of USD 7.5 billion worth of bonds in April 2006.[43] Still, it is clear that these sterilization efforts have had only minimal success.

Empirical Evidence of Dutch Disease in Venezuela

The disappointing economic performance that Venezuela has registered in the past few decades certainly points to strains imposed by the Dutch Disease and immiserizing growth. Economic stagnation, for example, has been a perennial concern. GDP per-capita based on purchasing power parity actually declined in absolute terms over the last fifty years. From 1950 to 1954, GDP per-capita based on purchasing power parity averaged USD 5,600; however, it averaged only USD 5,300 from 2000 to 2004.[44] Moreover, as Figure 2 illustrates, real GDP in 2002 was less than that achieved in 1997. Overall, Figure 2 depicts the fact that Venezuela has witnessed lackluster rates of growth since 1970, and at times has even registered negative growth—particularly in the 1980s.

Zalduendo (2006) provides cursory evidence that the world price of oil has played a significant role in the macroeconomic instability that Venezuela has endured over the last thirty years. While not investigating the presence of Dutch Disease or immiserizing growth in Venezuela specifically, Zalduendo does confirm that the country's real effective exchange rate (REER) is highly correlated with the world price of oil. Figure 3 depicts this correlation, in which 63 percent of the variation in the REER is explained by the variation in the world price of oil. Specifically, increases in world oil prices are associated with the emergence of appreciation pressures on the bolivar, the national currency. Conversely, oil price declines have historically exerted depreciation pressures on the national currency.[45]

One would expect, that Venezuelan exports would decline in the years in which currency appreciation has occurred. This is, in fact, what one gleans when comparing Figure 3 with Figure 1. In the years where the REER appreciates as a result of oil price increases, such as in the years 1983 and 1991, exports also declined relative to the previous year. It should be noted that the steep decline in exports in 2003 is largely attributable to a nation-wide strike that severely impacted production in the oil industry and other important sectors, and it is difficult to separate the impact of this strike from any effect brought about by fluctuations in the REER.

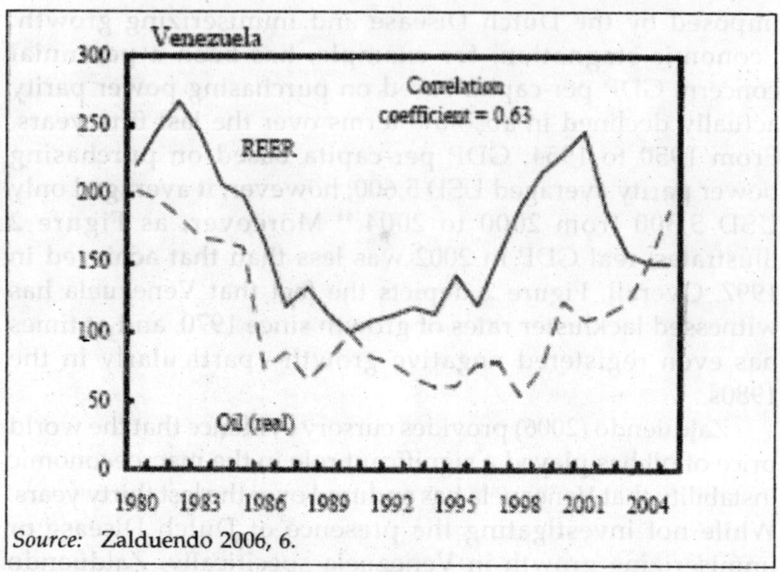

Source: Zalduendo 2006, 6.

Figure 5: Venezuelan Real Effective Exchange Rate and World Oil Prices: 1980–2004

The Dutch Disease in Venezuela: A Quantitative Analysis

This section utilizes a series of regressions in order to investigate more authoritatively whether the symptoms of Dutch disease have been present in Venezuela since the first oil boom of the 1970s as well as to assess the impact of Dutch Disease on economic performance. All data used in the regressions were compiled from the 1999 and May 2008 publications of the IMF's *International Financial Statistics*. The time periods observed in the regressions is between 1970 and 2007. The regressions used in this section are as follows:

Regression of foreign exchange reserves (independent) and the Consumer Price Index (dependent).

Regression of money supply (independent) and the Consumer Price Index (dependent).

Regression of foreign exchange reserves (independent) and Real GDP (dependent).

Regression of export growth (independent) and Real GDP (dependent).

It should be noted that money supply as conceptualized here includes both domestic nominal (M1) money supply plus foreign exchange reserves. As these are reported in two distinct currencies—M1 money supply in Venezuelan bolivars and foreign reserves in U.S. dollars—it was necessary to convert domestic money supply into U.S. dollars by multiplying each data point by the corresponding average annual exchange rate. The same procedure was performed to convert Venezuelan real GDP into U.S. dollars. Finally, the consumer price index (CPI) uses 2000 as the base year.

The tables in the appendix list the results for each regression. The first two tables show that there is a close correlation between foreign exchange reserves and inflation, and money supply and inflation. When regressed separately, foreign exchange reserves explain 79 percent of the variation in the CPI, and money supply explains 86 percent of the variation in the CPI. The low values of the significance F means that we can refute the null hypothesis that money supply and inflation do not contribute to inflation. Furthermore, the t-statistic for each of the regression equations is greater than 2 or less than negative 2, which means that the coefficients are quite significant. Moreover, the p-value is less than .05, which means the observed t-statistics are significant at the 95 percent confidence level. These results allow one to conclude that foreign reserves and money supply can cause inflation, as these variables were largely responsible for the inflation witnessed over the past 37 years.

As the results in Tables 3 and 4 of the appendix illustrate, foreign exchange reserves and export growth do not explain a great deal of the variation in real GDP from 1970 to 2007. Indeed, foreign exchange reserves and export growth explain only 33 percent and 31 percent of the variation in real GDP, respectively. These figures, although acceptable in terms of their t-statistics and significant at the 95 percent level of confidence, suggest that there is only a limited probability of external factors causing economic hardships in Venezuela. On this front, there is only tenuous evidence that Dutch Disease has had an impact on the economy in the time frame studied.

Possible reasons for this finding might be that the significant presence of government in the economy and the large size of the non-tradable sector have limited the extent to which the Venezuelan economy is affected by international disturbances.

CONCLUSION

It is clear from the evidence that Venezuela has been susceptible to the Dutch Disease at various junctures over the past thirty years. Its economic fate continues to be highly dependent on the oil sector and the international price of oil. Also, inappropriate economic policies have undoubtedly exacerbated the effects of Dutch Disease throughout the last thirty years. Quantitative analysis indicates that the symptoms of Dutch Disease, particularly rising inflation on account of foreign exchange reserves and money supply, have been present in the Venezuelan economy. The country should intensify its efforts to combat inflation by amplifying sterilization procedures or by establishing a national trust fund to ensure that large inflows of foreign exchange do not enter the economy. The Chilean government has used such a fund since its copper boom began five years ago, and evidence suggests it has performed quite well. In the short-run, the government should pursue more conservative policies, as expansionary monetary and fiscal policies might once again prove to be unsustainable.

Finally, despite data showing stagnation and real declines in real GDP throughout the 1980s and intermittently since, the quantitative evidence presented here does not allow us to conclude confidently that Venezuela has suffered from an entrenched resource curse. Nonetheless, the country would be well-served by pursuing a long-run strategy of diversifying its export base and using a portion of windfall revenue to invest in strategic sectors.

Appendix: Regression Results for Quantitative Analysis Section

Table 1
Results for Regression 1, Foreign Exchange Reserves and CPI

Regression Statistics						
Multiple R	0.887358034					
R Square	0.787404281					
Adjusted R Square	0.781498844					
Standard Error	42.64008432					
Observations	38					
ANOVA						
	Df	*SS*	*MS*	*F*	*Significance F*	
Regression	1	242427.4908	242427.5	133.3354886	1.16311E-13	
Residual	36	65454.36446	1818.177			
Total	37	307881.8552				
	Coefficients	*Standard Error*	*t Stat*	*P-value*	*Lower 95%*	*Upper 95%*
Intercept	-63.41935492	12.07957378	-5.25013	6.9822E-06	-87.91786586	-38.9208
X Variable 1	0.012913938	0.001118371	11.5471	1.16311E-13	0.010645777	0.015182

Table 2

Results for Regression 2, Money Supply and CPI

Regression Statistics						
Multiple R	0.927743505					
R Square	0.860708011					
Adjusted R Square	0.856838789					
Standard Error	34.51468122					
Observations	38					
ANOVA						
	Df	*SS*	*MS*	*F*	*Significance F*	
Regression	1	264996.3793	264996.4	222.449896	5.52312E-17	
Residual	36	42885.47592	1191.263			
Total	37	307881.8552				
	Coefficients	*Standard Error*	*t Stat*	*P-value*	*Lower 95%*	*Upper 95%*
Intercept	16.43715046	6.057881712	2.71335	0.010154415	4.151196988	28.7231
X Variable 1	1.9733E-06	1.32305E-07	14.91475	5.52312E-17	1.70497E-06	2.24E-06

Table 3
Results for Regression 3, Foreign Exchange Reserves and Real GDP

Regression Statistics						
Multiple R	0.572015					
R Square	0.327202					
Adjusted R Square	0.306814					
Standard Error	163211.1					
Observations	35					
ANOVA						
	Df	*SS*	*MS*	*F*	*Significance F*	
Regression	1	4.28E+11	4.28E+11	16.04887	0.000331	
Residual	33	8.79E+11	2.66E+10			
Total	34	1.31E+12				
	Coefficients	*Standard Error*	*t Stat*	*P-value*	*Lower 95%*	*Upper 95%*
Intercept	417127.8	58778.73	7.096577	3.99E-08	297541.5	536714
X Variable 1	-27.9459	6.975832	-4.0061	0.000331	-42.1383	-13.7535

Table 4
Results for Regression 4, Export Growth and Real GDP

Regression Statistics						
Multiple R	0.557197					
R Square	0.310468					
Adjusted R Square	0.289573					
Standard Error	165228.3					
Observations	35					
ANOVA						
	Df	*SS*	*MS*	*F*	*Significance F*	
Regression	1	4.06E+11	4.06E+11	14.85856	0.000507	
Residual	33	9.01E+11	2.73E+10			
Total	34	1.31E+12				
	Coefficients	*Standard Error*	*t Stat*	*P-value*	*Lower 95%*	*Upper 95%*
Intercept	431128.9	63990	6.737442	1.12E-07	300940.3	561317.5
X Variable 1	-14.4438	3.747088	-3.85468	0.000507	-22.0673	-6.82032

NOTES

1. Kishore Kulkarni, Brijesh Pazhayathodi, and Arvind Kumar Jha. "Dutch Disease Phenomenon in Brazil, Nigeria, Malaysia, and Russia with Lessons for India's Trade Policy" (Unpublished paper, Reserve Bank of India, 2006), 10.
2. Jagdish Bhagwati, "Immiserizing Growth: A Geometrical Note," *The Review of Economic Studies* 25, no.3 (June 1958): 205.
3. W. Max Corden and J. Peter Neary, "Booming Sector and De-Industrialization in a Small Open Economy," *The Economic Journal* 92, no. 368 (December 1982): 826.
4. Kishore Kulkarni, Brijesh Pazhayathodi, and Arvind Kumar Jha. "Dutch Disease Phenomenon in Brazil, Nigeria, Malaysia, and Russia with Lessons for India's Trade Policy" (Unpublished paper, Reserve Bank of India, 2006), 12.
5. Massimiliano Cali and Dirk Willem te Velde. *Is Zambia Contracting Dutch Disease?* (London: Overseas Development Institute, 2007), 2, 9.
6. Kishore Kulkarni, Brijesh Pazhayathodi, and Arvind Kumar Jha. "Dutch Disease Phenomenon in Brazil, Nigeria, Malaysia, and Russia with Lessons for India's Trade Policy" (Unpublished paper, Reserve Bank of India, 2006), 12.
7. W. Max Corden and J. Peter Neary, "Booming Sector and De-Industrialization in a Small Open Economy," *The Economic Journal* 92, no. 368 (December 1982): 841.
8. Massimiliano Cali and Dirk Willem te Velde. *Is Zambia Contracting Dutch Disease?* (London: Overseas Development Institute, 2007), 3.
9. Jeffrey Sachs and Andrew Warner. *Natural Resource Abundance and Economic Growth* (Cambridge: Center for International Development, 1997), 2.
10. *Ibid.*, 5.
11. Nancy Benjamin, S. Devarajan, and R.J. Weiner, "The Dutch Disease in a Developing Country: Oil Reserves in Cameroon," *Journal of Development Economics* 30 (January 1989): 90.
12. Jean-Philippe Stijns, *An Empirical Test of the Dutch Disease Hypothesis Using a Gravity Model of Trade* [paper prepared for the 2003 Congress of the European Economic Association] (Stockholm, Sweden: European Economic Association, May 2003, accessed 2 May 2008); available from http://129.3.20.41/eps/it/papers/0305/0305001.pdf; Internet, 36.
13. *Ibid.*, 34.
14. Angus Deaton, "Commodity Prices and Growth in Africa," *Journal of Economic Perspectives* 13, no.3 (Summer 1999): 24.

15. A. H. Gelb, ed., *Windfall Gains: Blessing or Curse?* (New York: Oxford University Press, 1998), 141.
16. Richard M. Auty, Sustaining Development in Mineral Economies: The Resource Curse Thesis (New York: Routledge, 1993), 71.
17. Jean-Philippe Stijns, *An Empirical Test of the Dutch Disease Hypothesis Using a Gravity Model of Trade* [paper prepared for the 2003 Congress of the European Economic Association] (Stockholm, Sweden: European Economic Association, May 2003, accessed 2 May 2008); available from http://129.3.20.41/eps/it/papers/0305/0305001.pdf; Internet, 11.
18. Norio Usui, "Dutch Disease and Policy Adjustments to the Oil Boom: A Comparative Study of Indonesia and Mexico," *Resources Policy* 23 (December 1997): 160.
19. Graham Davis, "Learning to Love the Dutch Disease: Evidence from the Mineral Economies," *World Development* 23 (October 1995): 1773.
20. *Ibid.*, 1768.
21. Jorge Salazar-Carrillo and Bernadette West, *Oil and Development in Venezuela During the 20th Century* (Westport, CT: Praeger Publishers, 2004), 24.
22. The Economist Online. *Venezuela: Economic Structure.* The Economist Online, 28 April 2008, accessed 5 May 2008. Available online at *http:/ /www.economist.com/countries/Venezuela/profile.cfm?folder=Profile-Economic%20Structure.* Internet.
23. Juan Zalduendo, "Determinants of Venezuela's Equilibrium Real Exchange Rate," (Washington, D.C.: The International Monetary Fund, 2006), 7.
24. All Business. *Venezuela: The Oil Curse*. All Business, 31 October 2005, accessed 18 May 2008. Available online at *http://www.allbusiness.com/legal/international-law-foreign-investment-finance/587502-1.html; Internet.*
25. World Bank. *Venezuela Country Brief, 2000.* World Bank, 29 November 2000, accessed 5 May 2008. Available online at *http://wbln0018.worldbank.org/external/lac/lac.nsf/265a7fff47916d7d852567e4004ce191/5e35ed58ef8e69238525 696700736330?* Open Document; Internet.
26. Rita Butzer, Donald Larson, and Yair Mundlak, "Intersectoral Migration in Venezuela," *Economic Development and Cultural Change* (2002): 233.
27. Encyclopedia of the Nations. *Venezuela.* Encyclopedia of the Nations, 2007, accessed 5 May 2008. Available online at *http://www.nationsencyclopedia.com/economies/Americas/Venezuela.html; Internet.*

28. Richard Gott, "Venezuela's Murdoch" *The New Left Review*, 39 May 2006, accessed 6 May 2008. Available online at *http://www.newleftreview.org/?view=2622*; Internet.
29. Yu Hsing, "Response of Venezuelan Output to Monetary Policy, Deficit Spending, and Currency Depreciation: A VAR Model," *Revista de Economia del Rosario* 2, No. 7 (2004): 90.
30. Herbert Lindow, "Venezuela Begins Reform," *Business America*, 5 June 1989, accessed 18 May 2008. Available online at *http://findarticles.com/p/articles/mi_m1052/is_n11_v110/ai_7647595*; Internet.
31. Richard Gott, "Venezuela's Murdoch" *The New Left Review*, 39 May 2006, accessed 6 May 2008. Available online at *http://www.newleftreview.org/?view=2622*; Internet.
32. Encyclopedia of the Nations. *Venezuela*. Encyclopedia of the Nations, 2007, accessed 5 May 2008. Available online at *http://www.nationsencyclopedia.com/economies/Americas/Venezuela.html*; Internet.
33. All Business. *Venezuela: The Oil Curse*. All Business, 31 October 2005, accessed 18 May 2008. Available online at *http://www.allbusiness.com/legal/international-law-foreign-investment-finance/587502-1.html*; Internet.
34. Oxford Analytica. *Latin America: Region is Losing Ground to Competitors*. Oxford Analytica, 17 November 2006, accessed 18 May 2008. Available online at *http://www.oxan.com/display.aspx?ItemID=DB130098*; Internet.
35. Encyclopedia of the Nations. *Venezuela*. Encyclopedia of the Nations, 2007, accessed 5 May 2008. Available online at *http://www.nationsencyclopedia.com/economies/Americas/Venezuela.html*; Internet.
36. International Monetary Fund, *International Financial Statistics* (Washington, D.C.: International Monetary Fund, May 2008), 299.
37. Mark Weisbrot and Luis Sandoval, "The Venezuelan Economy in the Chavez Years," (Washington, D.C.: Center for Economic and Policy Research, 2008), 17.
38. The Economist Online. *Venezuela: Economic Structure*. The Economist Online, 28 April 2008, accessed 5 May 2008. Available online at *http://www.economist.com/countries/Venezuela/profile.cfm?folder=Profile-Economic%20Structure*. Internet.
39. Humberto Margquez, "Shortages, Speculation Amid Rising Consumption in Venezuela," *Venezuela Analysis*, 16 February 2007, accessed 19 May 2008. Available online at *http://www.venezuelanalysis.com/analysis/2231*; Internet.

40. Mark Weisbrot and Luis Sandoval, "The Venezuelan Economy in the Chavez Years," (Washington, D.C.: Center for Economic and Policy Research, 2008), 19.
41. Mark Weisbrot and Luis Sandoval, "The Venezuelan Economy in the Chavez Years," (Washington, D.C.: Center for Economic and Policy Research, 2008), 8.
42. *Ibid.*, 18.
43. *Ibid.*, 19.
44. Juan Zalduendo, "Determinants of Venezuela's Equilibrium Real Exchange Rate," (Washington, D.C.: The International Monetary Fund, 2006), 7.
45. *Ibid.*, 7.

REFERENCES

All Business. *Venezuela: The Oil Curse*. All Business, 31 October 2005, accessed 18 May 2008. Available online at *http://www.allbusiness.com/legal/international-law-foreign-investment-finance/587502-1.html*; Internet.

Auty, Richard M. *Sustaining Development in Mineral Economies: The Resource Curse Thesis*. New York: Routledge, 1993.

Benjamin, Nancy, S. Devarajan, and R. J. Weiner. "The Dutch Disease in a Developing Country: Oil Reserves in Cameroon." *Journal of Development Economics* 30 (January 1989): 71–92.

Bhagwati, Jagdish. "Immiserizing Growth: A Geometrical Note." *The Review of Economic Studies* 25, no.3 (June 1958): 201-205.

Butzer, Rita, Donald Larson, and Yair Mundlak. "Intersectoral Migration in Venezuela." *Economic Development and Cultural Change* (2002): 227-48.

Cali, Massimiliano, and Dirk Willem te Velde. *Is Zambia Contracting Dutch Disease?* London: Overseas Development Institute, 2007.

Corden, W. Max, and J. Peter Neary. "Booming Sector and De-Industrialization in a Small Open Economy." *The Economic Journal* 92, No. 368 (December 1982): 825-848.

Davis, Graham. "Learning to Love the Dutch Disease: Evidence from the Mineral Economies." *World Development* 23 (October 1995): 1765-79.

Deaton, Angus. "Commodity Prices and Growth in Africa." *Journal of Economic Perspectives* 13, No. 3 (Summer 1999): 23–40.

Encyclopedia of the Nations. *Venezuela*. Encyclopedia of the Nations, 2007, accessed 5 May 2008. Available online at *http://www.nationsencyclopedia.com/economies/Americas/Venezuela.html*; Internet.

Gelb, A. H., ed. *Windfall Gains: Blessing or Curse?*. New York: Oxford University Press, 1988.

Gott, Richard. "Venezuela's Murdoch". *The New Left Review*, 39 May 2006, accessed 6 May 2008. Available online at *http://www.newleftreview.org/?view=2622*; Internet.

Hsing, Yu. "Response of Venezuelan Output to Monetary Policy, Deficit Spending, and Currency Depreciation: A VAR Model." *Revista de Economia del Rosario* 2, No. 7 (2004): 89-99.

International Monetary Fund. *International Financial Statistics*. Washington D.C: International Monetary Fund, 1999 and May 2008.

Kulkarni, Kishore, Brijesh Pazhayathodi, and Arvind Kumar Jha. "Dutch Disease Phenomenon in Brazil, Nigeria, Malaysia, and Russia with Lessons for India's Trade Policy," Unpublished paper, Reserve Bank of India, 2006.

Lindow, Herbert. "Venezuela Begins Reform." *Business America*, 5 June 1989. Accessed 18 May 2008. Available online at *http://findarticles.com/p/articles/mi_m1052/is_n11_v110/ai_7647595*; Internet.

Margquez, Humberto. "Shortages, Speculation Amid Rising Consumption in Venezuela." *Venezuela Analysis*, 16 February 2007, accessed 19 May 2008. Available online at *http://www.venezuelanalysis.com/analysis/2231*; Internet.

Oxford Analytica. *Latin America: Region is Losing Ground to Competitors*. Oxford Analytica, 17 November 2006, accessed 18 May 2008. Available online at *http://www.oxan.com/display.aspx?ItemID=DB130098*; Internet.

Sachs, Jeffrey, and Andrew Warner. *Natural Resource Abundance and Economic Growth*. Cambridge: Center for International Development, 1997.

Salazar-Carrillo, Jorge, and Bernadette West. *Oil and Development in Venezuela During the 20th Century*. Westport, CT: Praeger Publishers, 2004.

Stijns, Jean-Philippe. *An Empirical Test of the Dutch Disease Hypothesis Using a Gravity Model of Trade* [paper prepared for the 2003 Congress of the European Economic Association]. Stockholm, Sweden: European Economic Association, May 2003, accessed 2 May 2008; available from *http://129.3.20.41/eps/it/papers/0305/0305001.pdf*; Internet.

The Economist Online. *Venezuela: Economic Structure*. The Economist Online, 28 April 2008, accessed 5 May 2008. Available online at *http://www.economist.com/countries/Venezuela/profile.cfm?folder=Profile-Economic%20Structure*. Internet.

Usui, Norio. "Dutch Disease and Policy Adjustments to the Oil Boom: A Comparative Study of Indonesia and Mexico." *Resources Policy* 23 (December 1997): 151-162.

Weisbrot, Mark, and Luis Sandoval. *The Venezuelan Economy in the Chavez Years*. Washington, D.C.: Center for Economic and Policy Research, 2008.

World Bank. *Venezuela Country Brief, 2000*. World Bank, 29 November 2000, accessed 5 May 2008. Available online at *http://wbln0018.worldbank.org/external/lac/lac.nsf/265a7fff47916d7d85256 7e4004ce191/5e35ed58ef8e69238525696700736330?*OpenDocument; Internet.

Zalduendo, Juan. "Determinants of Venezuela's Equilibrium Real Exchange Rate." Washington, D.C.: The International Monetary Fund, 2006.

26

INCOME DISTRIBUTION AND ECONOMIC GROWTH: A CASE OF BRAZIL

INTRODUCTION

As inequality applied to income and economic inequality, is a very complex issue economists, sociologists, and political scientists are only a few of the researchers concerned with economic inequality. Is all inequality equal in its effects? Alternatively, do certain types of inequality spur growth while others damage it? Concrete answers to questions regarding the relationship between inequality and economic growth have not been found (see Introduction: Seligson and Passé-Smith, 2003). More specifically, development economists have been trying to understand the reasons why economic inequality is higher in countries that grow fast. Is economic growth the culprit?

These and other related questions have been the focus to study for several prominent economists. Simon Kuznets developed the most famous hypothesis of the relationship between inequality and economic growth. He argued that as a country develops, income inequality initially increases, and only after some time, it declines. In the first section of this paper, we will briefly discuss the social, political, and economic impact of income inequality. The second section is

This Chapter is based on an article co-authored with Ms. Camila Martins-Bekat a review of the literature for and against Kuznets' hypothesis. In section three, we will apply Kuznets' hypothesis to the case of Brazil using time-series data. Suggestions for ameliorating income inequality in Brazil are discussed in the conclusion.

Social Impacts of Income Inequality

Gottschalk and Justino (2006) highlight several important studies regarding the social impact of income inequality and present the argument that high inequality may deteriorate stocks of human capital when associated with high illiteracy and poor health. Ribero and Nunez showed that there is a negative correlation between disability and stature and the ability to earn an income. In other words, an individual's ability to earn money decreases as their nutritional status deteriorates (Gottschalk and Justino, 2006).

The evidence suggests that another social impact of income inequality is the positive relationship between high inequality and forms social and political conflict (Lichbach, 1989 in Gottschalk and Justino, 2006). If the poorest 20% of a society control less than one percent of the national income, their hardships are exasperated. Lack of access to education, healthcare, social security and jobs only fuel the sentiment that the government is not doing its share to alleviate their suffering. Once the tolerance threshold for inequality is reached, society is faced with what Hirschman and Rothschild (1973) called the *Tunnel Effect* (Ray 1998). The implications of Hirschman's tunnel effect hypothesis on economic growth policy are significant. If the tunnel effect is present in a weak society, then an economic policy focused on aggregate growth would not be a prudent choice. Instead, the society should choose a policy that would address growth and distribution simultaneously (1998).

Political Impacts of Income Inequality

Illiterate and poor, the individuals at the lowest ranks of society are often excluded from the political arena either because they cannot afford to vote or due to voter corruption. The latter takes the form of candidates offering small amounts of money to the poor in return for their 'support.' Thus, public policies in high inequality countries regularly exclude the poor (Gottschalk and Justino, 2006). In general, Latin American public policies tend to be the most regressive in the world, which means that the policies in pursuit of fiscal goals do not prioritize the needs of the poor (Weyland, 1996 in Gottschalk and Justino, 2006). The most influential individuals in the political arena are therefore the rich minority. The weight carried by traditional families and businesses transfer to government policies. A result of this is that developing countries with high levels of inequalities often have a low tax rate in proportion to the GDP (2006).

Economic Impacts of Income Inequality

Broadly speaking the economic impact of inequality is widespread and considerable. It affects the demand structure of the lower and middle class. If the lowest class is perpetually at a state of subsistence, lacks access to education, healthcare, social security benefits and has no political influence they will remain in poverty unable to consume a higher percentage of goods and services. According to Murphy *et al.* [(1989) in Gottschalk and Justino, 2006)] "decreases in income inequality imply a wealthier middle class, (enlarged by those coming out of the poorer classes), which are the most significant consumers of manufactured goods."

The saving file is significantly affected at low incomes. According to the Harrod-Domer Model of Economic Growth, the availability of saving is the key to economic growth. A lower the saving file results in less money available for investment therefore yielding a lower rate of growth (see Ray, 1998). The creation of the larger middle class will also increase the saving file. In general, improved opportunities for the poor in the form of reduced income inequality will lead to a higher volume of consumption thereby expanding the internal market, a higher savings rate, and ultimately a better position for economic growth.

SECTION - 1

Literature Review

Simon Kuznets

Simon Kuznets' Inverted-U hypothesis was based on relatively scant cross-sectional data from 1948-1950 from the United Kingdom, and the United States for the developed countries and Puerto Rico, India and Ceylon for the less developed countries. The data indicated that income distribution in these developed countries was somewhat more equal than in these less developed countries (Kuznets, 1955). His findings are represented below.

Table 1
Income Inequalities of the Countries

Country	*Lower 3 quintiles (%)*	*Top quintile (%)*
India	28	55
Ceylon	30	50
Puerto Rico	24	56
United States	34	44
United Kingdom	36	45

* Data from Kuznets, 1955.

Kuznets points out that "Much is to be said for the notion that once the early turbulent phases of industrialization and urbanization had passed, a variety of forces converged to bolster the economic position of the lower-income groups within the urban population" (1955; 17). The forces Kuznets is referring to include a better adaptation and organization of the recent immigrants and an increase in their ability to deal with the hardships of urban life. With time, Kuznets assumes that the lower income class will be able to exert enough political influence to bring about changes in legislation in favor of a more equitable distribution. However, this is not the case in the developing world (see Weyland, 1996). Kuznets also points to the "dislocating effects of the agricultural and industrial revolutions," coupled with rapid population growth in the cities due to a rise in birth rates and a decline in death rates, and concludes that the early phases of economic growth bring about a more unequal size distribution followed by a period of stabilization ending with in a more equal size distribution during later stages of growth after the "new industrial system had shattering effects on long-established pre-industrial economic and social institutions" (1955; 18). This conclusion is what we now call the Kuznets' Inverted-U Hypothesis.

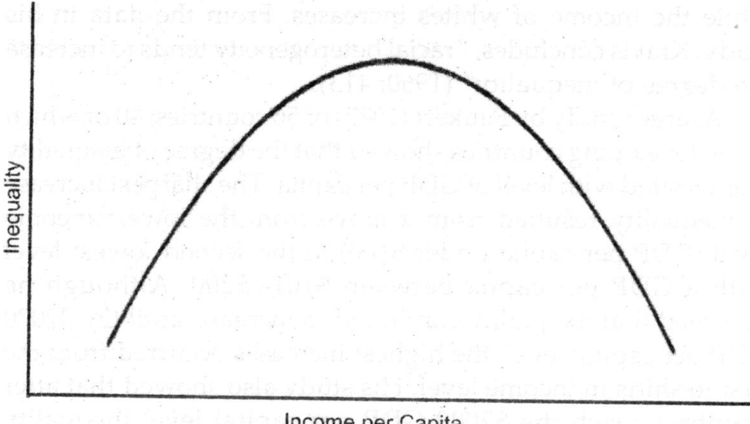

Figure 1: Income Inequality Over Time

Oshima states that "the major determinant of the dispersion of quintile shares between countries is the weight of the farm or rural sector in the total economy" and that other factors have a minimal impact (1962; 442). However, he qualifies this finding by pointing out that the influence of heterogeneous factors such as history, geography, politics, religion, and race on income inequality render the conclusion that developing countries have a higher income inequality than developed countries. Kravis (1960) confirms "Distribution of income tends to be more equal the longer and the more thoroughly the country has been exposed to the processes of economic and social change associated with the idea of industrialization" (1960; 409). The greater initial inequality is the result of a partial integration of the population in new sectors of the economy.

As the population becomes more fully integrated, the economic differentiation between sectors declines.

In the case of Brazil, with its high number of Afro-Brazilian population, studies by Pastore (1982 and 2000) confirm the non-white individuals have a significant disadvantage when it comes to occupational mobility. With only 47.8% of blacks elevating themselves to a higher social status than their parents compared to 55.8% of whites (2000; 89). The implication being that non-whites often remain in the lowest income brackets while the income of whites increases. From the data in his study, Kravis concludes, "racial heterogeneity tends to increase the degree of inequality" (1960; 413).

A larger study by Paukert (1973) of 56 countries, 40 of which were developing countries showed that the degree of inequality is associated with level of GDP per capita. The sharpest increase in inequality resulted from a move from the lowest income level (GDP per capita under $100) to the second lowest level with a GDP per capita between $101- $200. Although he observed that inequality continued to increase until the $2000 GDP per capital level, the highest increases occurred from the first to shifts in income level. His study also showed that after countries reach the $2000 GDP per capital level inequality decreases, confirming Kuznets Inverted U Hypothesis. Ahluwalia (1976) using a different data set also came to the same conclusion.

Problems with Kuznets' Inverted U Hypothesis

A common complaint surrounding Kuznets' work revolves around the availability of data. As Ray (1998) highlights, inequality data from countries that have already completed their inverted-U path is not available and that in conducting a cross-section study it is important to control for inter-country variation. This fact is also supported by Fields (1989) who points out that while Kuznets makes predictions that span several generations, available data was for a period of ten years on average. "There might be evidence of trends, but the variation within those trends may obscure longer-term movements" (169). Pointing out another complication, Fields

(1989) highlights the fact that the Gini curve does not incorporate quality of life nor can it account income generated in the informal sector of a society, which tends to be much larger in developing countries. He tested several hypotheses regarding the relationship between economic growth and inequality. Using time-series data and looking at both the Gini and Lorenz curves, Fields found that inequality increased in just about the same number of countries as it decreased (1989; 171).

Fields also claims that "growth tends to raise inequality in low-income countries and to reduce inequality in high-income countries" (1989; 176). He tested this hypothesis by using inter-temporal data, which he claims is the correct type of data to use. The study reveals that inequality increased nearly as often as it decreased, 48% and 42% respectively (176). Fields concluded that there is no apparent trend for countries to follow the Kuznets Inverted U hypothesis. We now investigate the application of Kuznets Hypothesis in the context of Brazilian economic growth with a special focus on the hyperinflation period of 1989 to 1993 and the stabilization efforts of the 1994 Real Plan.

SECTION - 2

Application of Kuznets' Inverted U to Brazil

It is of no surprise the income distribution in Brazil is among one of the most unequal in the world. Using the Gini Coefficient as the measure of income inequality, in 1989 Brazil ranked second highest in the world (.625) only falling behind Sierra Leone (Ferreira, Leite & Litchfield, 2006). It currently ranks tenth in the world. Only two Latin American countries have a Gini higher than Brazil's: Guatemala and Bolivia (2006). Brazil's level of inequality is more in line with that of Sub-Saharan African countries such as Botswana, Lesotho, South Africa, and Zimbabwe. Pastore (1982 and 2000) has tracked social mobility in Brazil. His findings show that while Brazil has a higher volume of social mobility than Spain, France, the U.S. and Poland, most of the mobility, 62.3%, is accounted by a move from the "inferior-low" (manual rural laborer) status to the "superior-low" (unspecialized manual urban laborer) status and from "superior-low" to "inferior-medium" (semi-qualified urban laborer –such as housekeeper and street vendor) status. The Word Bank Country Study (2004) reveals that in Brazil skin color accounts for 12% of income inequality. This fact can be attributed to the differences in education level, access to healthcare and wages between whites and non-whites. The study also reports that regressive public transfers such as retirement pensions for government employees, inequitable distribution of education and high wage differentials by skill level account for 39%, 29% and 32% of Brazil's excess inequality. However, since 1994, social programs such as *Bolsa Escola,* have contributed to income equalization.

The Numbers

Now we look at the data available to determine whether the relation between Brazil's economic growth from 1980 to 2005 and its inequality follows Kuznets' Inverted U Hypothesis. While the focus of the data is from 1980, it is important to note that during the Brazilian Economic Miracle (late 1960s and early 1970s) when GDP percent growth was at nearly 10% per annum, there is little controversy as to whether Brazil's inequality increased. The Gini coefficient rose from .50 in 1960 to .57 in 1970 and continued to increase until 1976 before declining from 1977 to 1981 (Leite, Ferreira, & Litchfield,

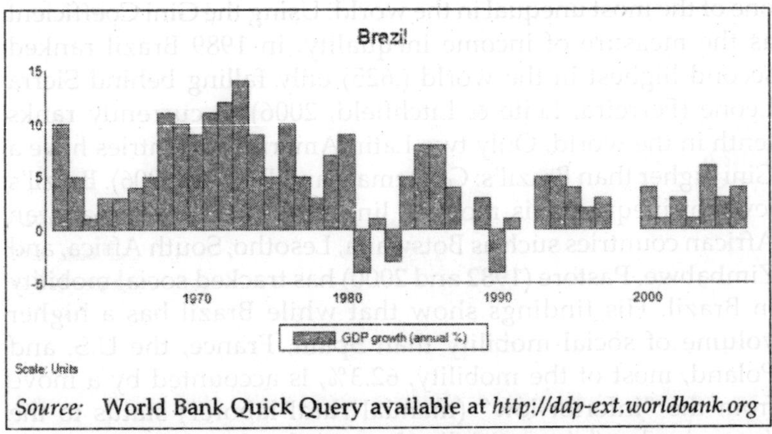

Source: World Bank Quick Query available at *http://ddp-ext.worldbank.org*

Figure 2: Annual GDP Growth 1961-2006 (Percentage)

2006;2). A study conducted by Fishlow (1972) confirms, "The conclusion that inequality has increased over the course of the decade accordingly seems correct, if lamentable" (399).

Table 2
Economic Growth and Gini Coefficient 1980-2006

Year	*GNI per capita (current US$)*	*Gini Coefficient*
1980	2190	.59
1982	2000	.58
1984	1620	.58
1986	1790	.58
1988	2250	.60
1990	2700	.60
1992	2780	.58
1994	3050	.62
1996	4470	.59
1998	4880	.59
2001	3290	.59
2002	3050	.58
2004	3220	.57
2005	3880	.56

Table adapted from Social-Economic Database for Latin America and the Caribbean (SEDLAC) available at *http://www.wider.unu.edu/research/Database/en_GB/income-distribution-links/*, Instituto Brasileiro de Geographia e Estatistica (IBGE) available at *www.ibge.gov.br and World Bank Quick Query available at http://ddp-ext.worldbank.org*

In analyzing the Gini Coefficient over time, we can safely say that in the case of Brazil inequality did increase during the initial stage of development, and that by the end of 1994 to 2005 it did indeed decline. From 1994, when the Gini Coefficient was at its peak (.62) to 2005 when it was at its lowest (.56) there was nearly a 10% decline. From Default Chart, we clearly observe that income inequality did decrease from 1989 to 2005.

Increase in Inequality: The Debt and Inflation Crises

We see from the above table that GNI per capita during the early 1980s follows a downward trend and picks back up

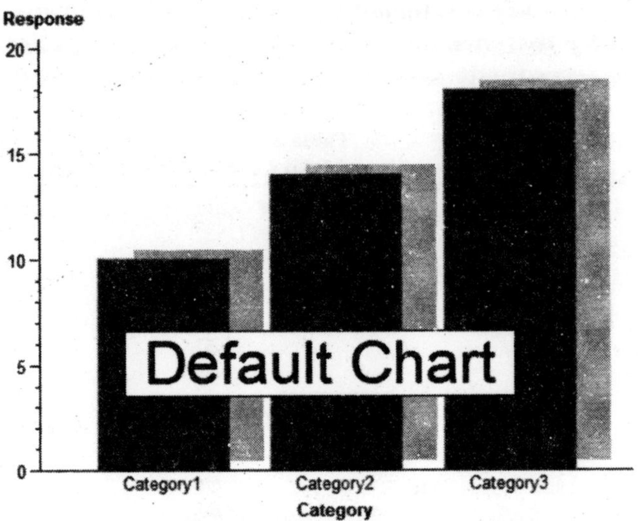

Figure 3: Brazil: Gini Coefficient 1989-2005

toward the end of the decade. This initial decline can be attributed to what economist call the "lost decade" when many of Latin American countries were experiencing a debt and inflation crises. The debt crisis was a result of careless borrowing and irresponsible spending habits during military rule (1964-1985).

An increase in interest rates in 1979 by the U.S. Federal Reserve Bank also increased the interest payments on past loans (most of Brazil's debt was denominated in dollars) (Franko, 1999). In order to cover its debts Brazil simply printed more money resulting in hyperinflation. During the latter part of the 1980s, inflation rates were over 1000% (Font, 2003). As the economy scrambled to maintain afloat, funding for social programs suffered. This, along with the inherent deterioration of incomes due to the debt and inflation crises caused the income inequality to increase during the last three years of the decade (Ferreira, Leite & Litchfield, 2006).

Decrease in Inequality: Stabilization

The decline in inequality that followed from 1994 to 2005 can be attributed to a series of policies and reforms enacted by

President Cardoso. Three previously failed stabilization plans created a great deal of pressure and speculation as to whether Cardoso's plan would be successful. The new currency, the *Real,* introduced in 1994, was pegged one-to-one to the dollar. Cardoso saw high government spending and large fiscal imbalances as the root causes of hyperinflation. To this end, he pursued structural and fiscal adjustments. By 1995 fiscal balance was possible because of budget cuts and new measures taken against tax evasion which is estimated to have cost the Brazilian government anywhere from $25-30 billion a year. Second, overcoming of economic stagnation was accomplished by a trade surplus from exports from 1993-95, increase in hard currency reserves and of course, the decrease in inflation. By 2002, the strong currency, which spurred growth in the import sector, turned the trade surplus into a deficit and the decision to devalue the currency could no longer wait. The success of the *Plano Real* hinged on keeping inflation down and for this Cardoso focused on having sound monetary and fiscal policies. In all, the *Plano Real* worked.

Table 3
Inflation, 1993-2001, In Percent

1993	*1994 (J-J)*	*1994 (J-D)*	*1995*	*1996*	*1997*	*1998*	*1999*	*2000*	*2001*	*2002*[a]
2,564	258.7	16.8	18.8	9.4	6.1	1.0	14.3	7.4	9.3	10.7

Source: Font, M., (2003) Transforming Brazil

a. Annual inflation until September

From 2001 to 2005, Brazil's Gini saw a decline of 4.6% from .593 to .566, one of the fastest rates in the world (Paes de Barros *et al.*, 2007). During this time frame the income proportion of the poorest 20% increased by one-half of a percent. Brazil still has a long way to go.

Ferreira, (200) suggest the following explanation: "the decline in inequality between educational sub-groups which appears to be driven by a persistent reduction in the average returns to schooling in Brazil...income differences between the country's urban and rural areas have fallen dramatically.....

Table 4
Per Capita Income Breakdown By Percentile and Gini Coefficient Between 2001 And 2005

Deciles	*2001*	*2002*	*2003*	*2004*	*2005*	*Variation 2001-2005*
First	.69	.79	.78	.87	.91	.22
Second	2.36	2.55	2.56	2.79	2.87	.51
Third	4.85	5.12	5.17	5.57	5.68	.83
Fourth	8.24	8.55	8.72	9.25	9.40	1.17
Fifth	12.7	13.1	13.3	14.0	14.2	1.52
Sixth	18.5	18.9	19.4	20.2	20.5	1.95
Seventh	26.1	26.5	27.1	28.1	28.4	2.28
Eighth	36.6	37.0	37.7	38.8	39.0	2.44
Ninth	52.8	53.2	54.0	55.0	55.0	2.17
Gini Coefficient	.593	.587	.581	.569	.566	-4.61%

Source: Table adapted from Paes de Barros *et al.*, 2007

[and the] potential decline in racial inequalities" (Ferreira, Leite & Litchfield, 2006; 31).

CONCLUSION

Despite debate over whether Kuznets' hypothesis was founded proper use of available cross-sectional data, the application of the inverted U to the case of Brazil using time-series data reveals that inequality in Brazil does indeed fit an inverted U path. Hence in early days the Brazilian economy experienced the increased inequality of income but in the long term this inequality has subsided. Whether this accelerated downward trend in inequality will persist remains to be seen. However, we can conclude that some governmental policies have been successful. Expansion of income substitution programs such as *Bolsa Escola* and *Bolsa Familia* to create an incentive for poor families to send their kids to school rather than sending them to work menial jobs have seen some positive results. Lastly, continued pension reform for government sector employees can benefit the reduction in income inequality. In general, however, our main observation is that the economic growth by itself is rarely equitable. If it is an objective the government to make it equatable at all, special policy actions have to be adopted.

REFERENCES

Ahluwalia, M. S. (1976), "Income Distribution: some stylized facts," *American Economic Review* 66,128-35.

Paes de Barros, R., *et al.* (2007), A Queda Recente da Desigualdade de Renda no Brasil. Instituto de Pesquisa Economica Aplicada (IPEA). Available at *www.ipea.gov.br*

Ferreira, Francisco H. G., Leite, Phillippe G. and Litchfield, Julie A., "The Rise and Fall of Brazilian Inequality, 1981-2004" (March 1, 2006). World Bank Policy Research Working Paper No. 3867 Available at SSRN: *http://ssrn.com/abstract=922993*

Fishlow, Albert "Brazilian Size Distribution of Income." *American Economic Review* (62).

Fields, G. S., (1989), "Changes in Poverty and Inequality in Developing Countries," *The World Bank Research Observer*, 4(2), 167-185.

Fields, G. S. (1977), "Who Benefits from Economic Development: A Reexamination of the Brazilian Experience," *American Economic Review* 1977.

Font, M. A. (2003), Transforming Brazil. Rowman & Littlefield Publishers: Lanham, Maryland.

Franko, P. (1999), The Puzzle of Latin American Economic Development. Rowman & Littlefield Publishers: Lanham, Maryland.

Kravis, I. (1960), "International Differences in the Distribution of Income," *The Review of Economics and Statistics*, 42(4), 408-416.

Kulkarni, K. (2006), Readings in International Economics: Selected Writings of Prof. Kishore G. Kulkarni. Second Edition, Serials Publications: New Delhi.

Kuznets, S. (1955), "Economic Growth and Income Inequality," *American Economic Review* 45, 1-28.

Gottschalk, R. & Justino, P. (eds.) (2006), Overcoming Inequality in Latin America: Issues and Challenges for the Twenty-first Century. Routledge: New York.

Oshima, H. T. (1962), "The International Comparison of Size Distribution of Family Incomes with a Special Reference to Asia," *Review of Economics and Statistics* 54, 439-445.

Papanek, G. F., and O. Kyn (1986), "The Effect on Income Distribution of Development, the Growth Rate and Economic Strategy," *Journal of Development Economics* 23, 55-65.

Pastore, J. (2000), Mobilidade Social no Brasil. Makron Books do Brasil Editora Ltda: Sao Paulo, Brazil

— —(1982), Inequality and Social Mobility in Brazil. University of Wisconsin Press: Madison, WI.

Paukert, F. (1973), "Income Distribution at Different Levels of Development: A Survey of Evidence," *International Labour Review* 108, 97-125.

Ray, Debraj (1998), Development Economics. Princeton University Press: Princeton, NJ.

Sen, A. K. (1973), *On Economic Inequality.* Oxford: Clarendon Press.

Seligson, M. & Passé-Smith, J., (2003), Development and Underdevelopment: the Political Economy of Global Inequality. Lynne Rienner Publishers Inc.: Boulder, CO.

Shiller, Robert (2007), *Is Inequality Destabilizing?* Economist's View. Retrieved on July 15, 2008 from *http://economistsview.typepad.com/economistsview /2007/02/in_inequality_d.html*

World Bank (2004), World Bank Country Study: Inequality and Economic Development in Brazil. The World Bank: Washington D.

27

EFFECTS OF INDIA'S TRADE POLICY ON RICE PRODUCTION AND EXPORTS

INTRODUCTION

A major food staple, rice is central to the food security of over half the world's population. Primarily cultivated by small farmers, it also serves as a wage commodity for cash crop or non-agricultural sector workers. This duality can lead to conflicting policy objectives, with policy makers intervening to protect farmers from price declines and consumers from price increases (Food & Agriculture Organization of the United Nations, 2003). When the price of rice doubled where in the global economy in the first half of 2008, consumer riots and protests in many developing countries led to increased government intervention.

Food price increases contribute to inflation and disproportionately affect the poor. Mounting concerns about food shortages prompted India's government to engage in several protectionist measures, including prohibiting exports of non-basmati rice in February 2008 (Chandrashekhar, 2008) and imposing export tariffs on basmati rice in April 2008 (Oryza, 2008). Their goal was to increase domestic supplies and lower domestic prices. These actions "triggered a surge in global rice prices" (Mortished, 2008). Prior to export restrictions, India was the third largest rice exporting country,

Co-authored: Nancy Clarkson

after Thailand and Vietnam (USDA, 2008). While high global rice prices existed prior to India's actions, these policies did cause an acceleration of price increases. Given the decrease in world welfare caused by reactionary price increases and resulting shortages, whether India's policies increased national welfare is worthy of review.

Traditional trade models hold that free trade is the best way to maximize economic welfare. However, when the objective is to maximize national welfare, free trade is not necessarily the best policy choice. Section One will outline the theoretical application of the price and welfare effects to a domestic economy of export restrictions and export tariffs under a large country assumption. Partial equilibrium analysis is used to compare consumer and producer welfare in one sector (rice). Economic effects of export restrictions and export tariffs will be reviewed separately, as will the change in dynamics caused by monopoly pricing.

Section Two will apply section one's analysis to evaluate if India's protectionist policies maximized national welfare. Local prices should decrease, which would prove beneficial for Indian consumers yet harm Indian producers, who would benefit from rising international prices. The aggregate welfare will be calculated by adding the gains and losses to consumers, producers, and recipients of government revenue. If positive, the policy has increased national welfare; if negative, it has decreased national welfare. Given India's monopoly power of rice, it is expected trade policies will improve national welfare.

SECTION - 1

Theoretical Trade Policy

This section evaluates the price and welfare effects of export restrictions and export tariffs on a domestic economy. Partial equilibrium is used to compare consumer and producer welfare. Assumptions include: a two country model, a homogenous good that is perfectly substitutable, perfectly competitive markets, and free trade between the two countries. A large country model is used since India's share of rice exports is significant in the world market and world price increases were attributed to their actions. India will be designated the domestic economy; the rest of the world (ROW), the foreign economy; and rice, the good. When referring to export restrictions, non-basmati rice is assumed; export tariffs, basmati rice.

Two definitions are necessary prior to the evaluation of trade policy: consumer welfare and producer welfare. Consumer welfare is measured by consumer surplus and is defined as the satisfaction consumers achieve by paying less for the market price of a good than they would have been willing to pay. Figure 1 denotes how consumer surplus is calculated.

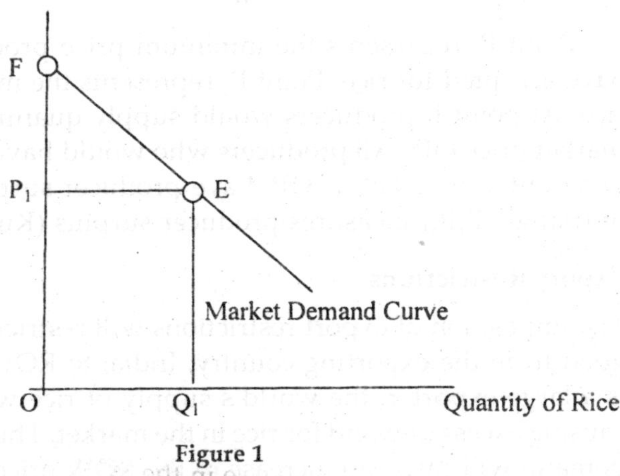

Figure 1

Point OF represents the maximum price that the first consumer would have paid for rice. At point E, consumers would pay the market price OP_1 at quantity OQ_1. All consumers who would have paid a higher price than OP_1 below the demand curve up to point OF have consumer surplus. The area of triangle FP_1E measures consumer surplus (Kulkarni, 2009).

Producer welfare is measured by producer's surplus and is defined as the satisfaction producers receive for having the market price of the good higher than the minimum price they would have accepted for the good. Figure 2 denotes how producer surplus is calculated.

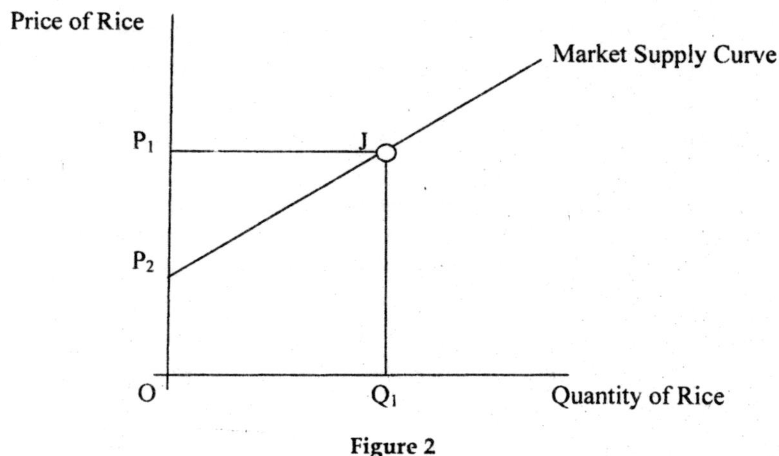

Figure 2

Point P_2 represents the minimum price producers would have accepted for rice. Point P_1 represents the market price of rice. At point J, producers would supply quantity OQ_1 at the market price OP_1. All producers who would have been willing to accept a price below OP_1 have producer surplus. The area of triangle P_1P_2J measures producer surplus (Kulkarni, 2009).

Export Restrictions

The imposition of export restrictions will restrict the flow of a good from the exporting country, India, to ROW. Since India is a large exporter, the world's supply of rice would decline, causing excess demand for rice in the market. This excess ROW demand will cause an increase in the ROW price of rice, since assumptions indicate rice is homogenous and the market is perfectly competitive. As markets adjust, this higher ROW price reduces ROW demand, which increases domestic supply as exports slow. This excess domestic supply will lower domestic prices to their original autarky price, since rice exports are prohibited entirely, which will eventually lower domestic supply while reducing India's export supply to zero (Suranovic, 2007). These effects are demonstrated in Figure 3.

P_1 is the world price prior to India's export restrictions. The blue line represents India's exports, or the difference between the demand and supply curves. If India implements

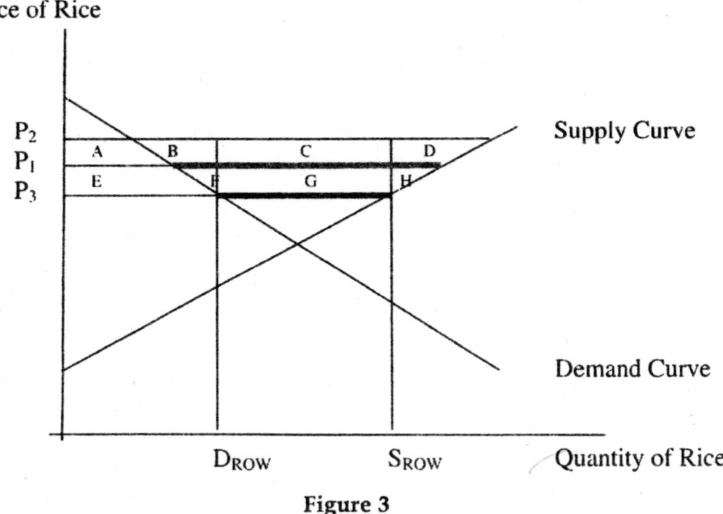

Figure 3

export restrictions equal to the length of the red line, the domestic price will fall until domestic supply is equal to the quota level, at P_3. Excess ROW demand increases ROW price to P_2. If no exports are allowed, excess domestic supply reverts prices to their autarky levels (Suranovic, 2007).

To summarize the domestic welfare effects of restricting rice exports, the quantity of exports declines from the length of the blue line to the length of the red line, or zero with a complete ban. Consumer surplus increases by area E: consumers are better off with lower domestic prices. Producer surplus declines by the total of areas E + F + G + H: producers are worse off with lower domestic prices. There is no government revenue gained since no tax or tariff is applied with a ban[1]. If the loss of producer surplus is less than the gain in consumer surplus, then the government has been successful in raising national welfare (Suranovic, 2007).

Export Tariffs

The imposition of export tariffs has similar pricing effects to export restrictions. Since it will cost more for Indian producers to export the good to ROW and India is under a large country assumption, the ROW price of rice will increase. This higher price will reduce ROW's demand for rice. Decreased ROW demand lowers ROW supply, which shifts the supply of rice back to the domestic market. A higher domestic supply lowers domestic prices, which reduces export supply (Suranovic, 2007). These effects are demonstrated in Figure 4.

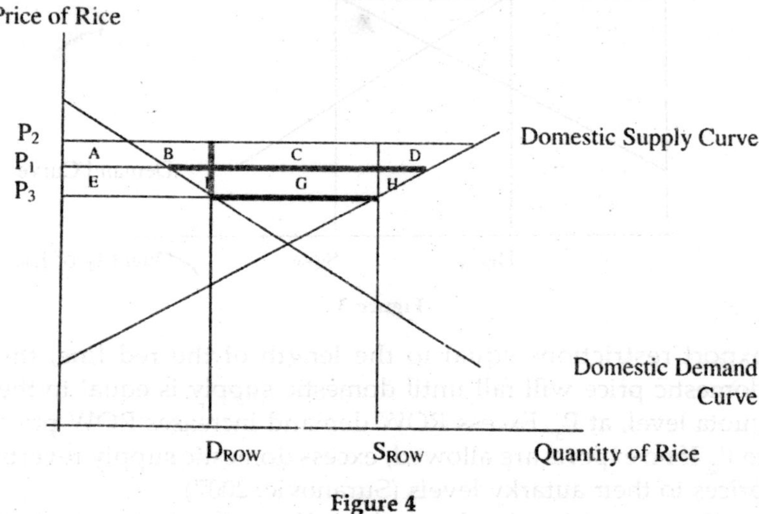

Figure 4

P_1 is the world price prior to India's export tariff. The blue line represents India's exports, or the difference between the demand and supply curves. After the export tariff is applied, ROW price increases to P_2 and domestic price decreases to P_3. Since the export tariff is a specific tax, the tax rate equals P_2 - P_3, which is equal to the length of the green line. The red line represents the reduced export supply resulting from the higher domestic supply lowering domestic prices (Suranovic, 2007).

To summarize the domestic welfare effects of export tariffs, the quantity of exports declines from the length of the blue line to the length of the red line. Consumer surplus increases by area E: consumers are better off with lower domestic prices. Producer surplus declines by the total of areas E + F + G + H: producers are worse off with lower domestic prices. The Indian government gains tax revenue from the export tariff equal to the total of areas C + G. The aggregate welfare effect is found by totaling C - (F + H). If negative, net national welfare has declined due to export tariffs; if positive, net national welfare has improved (Suranovic, 2007).

An increase in net national welfare does not mean everyone is better off; rather, income is redistributed. Government tax revenue gains can be used to offset the redistribution problem by compensating the losers (i.e., producers). This is preferable to export subsidies when prices are already high and domestic supply low, since export subsidies will exacerbate this effect by increasing domestic prices while reducing domestic supply. Consumers that are already worse off from initial price spikes will lose additional welfare. Subsidies collected by the government will be paid to exporters, who are already gaining from high world prices, instead of being redistributed to the losers (i.e., consumers) (Suranovic, 2007).

Thus in theoretical framework, both export restrictions and export tariffs will lower domestic prices and increase domestic supply. Consumers will gain and producers will lose. However, the tax revenue gained from export tariffs can be used to redistribute income from winners to losers. The wisdom of income redistribution depends on the initial welfare of each sector and the size of welfare gains/losses achieved from the protectionist policies. If producers are large, wealthy landowners and consumers consist of rural poor, a temporary income redistribution would help lift net national welfare.

In addition, deviations from the theoretical results can occur when perfect competition does not exist: welfare effects can differ when a country has a domestic monopoly in the production of a good. While not a pure monopoly, India could be said to have monopoly power in trade since the world price is affected when its trade policies are implemented. When domestic monopoly occurs, an export tariff will always lower the domestic price of rice, whereas export restrictions may or may not. Unlike an exporter with export restrictions, the exporter with a tariff has to pay the tax rate, equal to $P_2 - P_3$ in Figure 4, plus the domestic price of the good, P_3. If the domestic price charged by the monopolist is higher than P_3, the domestic price plus tariff will exceed ROW price, P_2. ROW will import less and the increased domestic supply will lower domestic prices until they reach P_3 (Yeh, 1997).

In contrast, after the government prohibits exports, the monopolist will charge P_2, which is higher than the domestic price before the export restrictions, P_1, while producing domestic supply levels. Domestic demand does not change. Under domestic monopoly conditions, export restrictions may not lead to domestic price declines, which would hurt consumers and benefit producers (Yeh, 1997). This effect would be contradictory to the Indian government's goals of reducing domestic prices and increasing domestic supply.

Other variations from the given assumptions are reviewed in Section Two. Given that trade policies have varying welfare effects, the appropriate choice of policy is important.

SECTION - 2

Applied Trade Policy

Faced with rapidly increasing food prices from mid-2007 to mid-2008, many countries adopted policy measures to mitigate the impact of high food prices and increase domestic production. Most measures were adopted in an emergency, short-term context and focused on the reduction or suspension of import tariffs and taxes and support to domestic production with agricultural inputs and credits. Although prices declined through the last half of 2008, rice still remained 54% above the December 2007 average price in December 2008 (Food & Agriculture Organization, 2008) and increased 5% over December in January 2009 due to Thailand's agricultural subsidies and large government purchases intended to increase domestic supplies (Food & Agriculture Organization, 2009).

India responded to the increase in food prices with several protectionist trade policies. In February 2008, it banned exports of non-basmati rice (Chandrashekhar, 2008). In April, it imposed a tax of 8,000 rupees per ton on exports of basmati rice (Oryza, 2008). Minimum export prices were increased throughout the year to increase earnings and slow exports. The ban on exports eventually was eased and limited exports were allowed to neighboring countries by mid-October, although minimum export prices were in place (Food & Agriculture Organization, 2008). India's goals were to reduce prices and increase supplies in the domestic market.

India also increased assistance to producers harmed by these trade policies. It maintained and engaged in limited expansion of fertilizer, irrigation, and power subsidies. In February, the Finance Ministry announced that it was budgeting 600 billion rupees for farm debt relief to cancel or reduce the debt owed by an estimated 40 million small farmers (Timmons, 2008). In September, the government's grain procurement and distribution agency, Food Corporation of India, made record procurements of rice to stabilize prices in the open market, intervene if prices rose, and increase aid to the poor. Farmers benefited from an increase in the minimum support price, which rose nearly 22%, to Rs 695 per quintal (Modi, 2008). Sixty percent of the labor force is employed in agriculture (CIA, 2009).

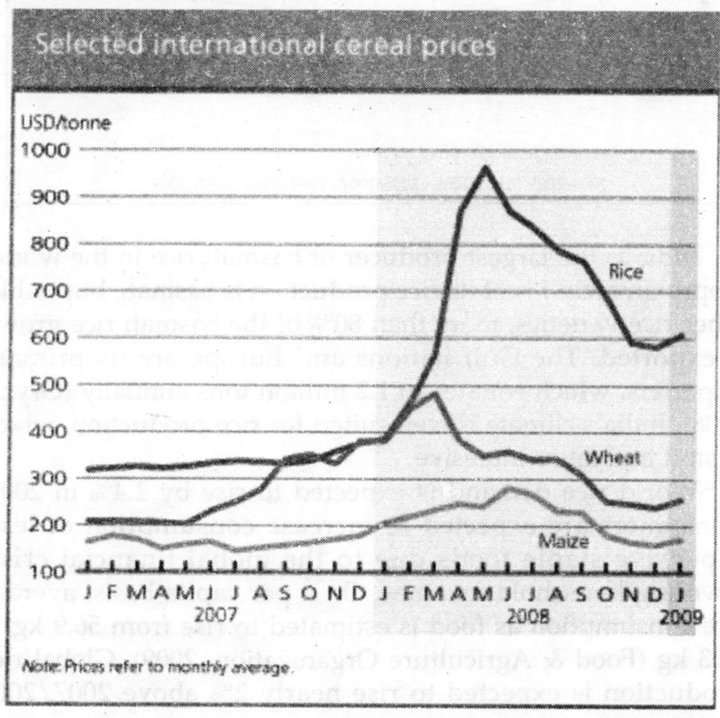

India is the second largest producer of rice, after China, at a projected 97.5 million tons in 2008/2009. Although it consumes, on average, 95% of what it produces, India was still the third largest exporter of rice, after Thailand and Vietnam, with approximately 20% of total rice exports in 2006/2007. After export restrictions, India fell behind Pakistan and the U.S. (see chart below). India's largest trading partners are the U.S. and China (USDA, 2008).

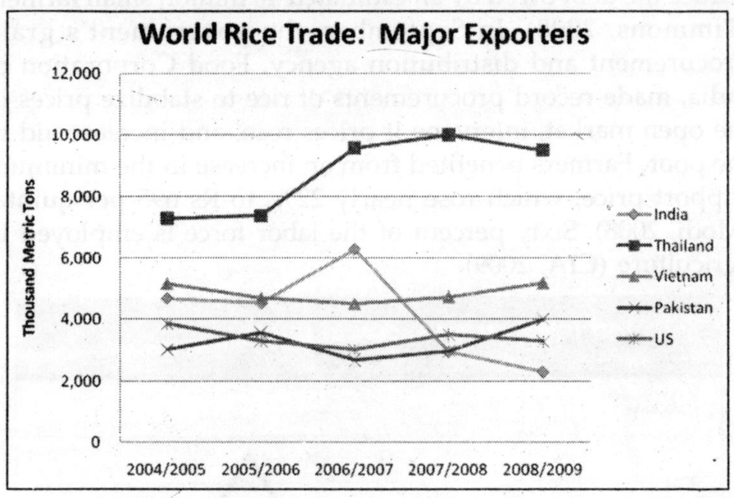

India is the largest producer of basmati rice in the world. Approximately 1% of its rice production is basmati, but unlike other rice varieties, more than 80% of the basmati rice grown is exported. The Gulf nations and Europe are its primary importers, which equates to 1.2 million tons annually (Oryza, 2008). India's climate is well suited for rice production, which is land and labor intensive.

World rice demand is expected to rise by 2.4% in 2009. Consumers are expected to increase consumption of less-expensive staple foods due to the global financial crisis lowering household incomes. On a per capita basis, average rice consumption as food is estimated to rise from 56.9 kg to 57.3 kg (Food & Agriculture Organization, 2009). Global rice production is expected to rise nearly 2% above 2007/2008 production to a record 439.7 million tons. Global rice trade is projected at 29.5 million tons, 1% below 2008 and 8% below a 2007 record (Childs, 2009).

Increases in demand and reductions in trade would drive the world price even higher. A reversal of India's protectionist policies would act to reduce the world price of rice and increase the domestic price as domestic supplies are exported, making domestic consumers worse off while domestic producers gain. Therefore, the national welfare impact that current policies have becomes very important to avoid mis-timing future policy reversals intended to assist domestic farmers. The following section reviews the effects of India's protectionist trade policies.

Domestic Effects of Trade Policies

Overall, India's goals were achieved by lowering prices and increasing supplies by 1.5 million tons in the domestic market, although domestic prices of rice increased throughout 2008 despite protectionist trade policies and a good rice crop. By November 2008, prices were 22 rupees per kg, an increase of 38% year over year (Food & Agriculture Organization, 2008). World prices rose 92% year over year for the same period.

Figures 5-7 apply the theoretical concepts of Section one to outline the effects of India's trade policies in detail.

Quantities are per thousand metric tons and represent India's domestic annual production, less exports, of rice for the time period indicated. The fiscal year ends in June; these

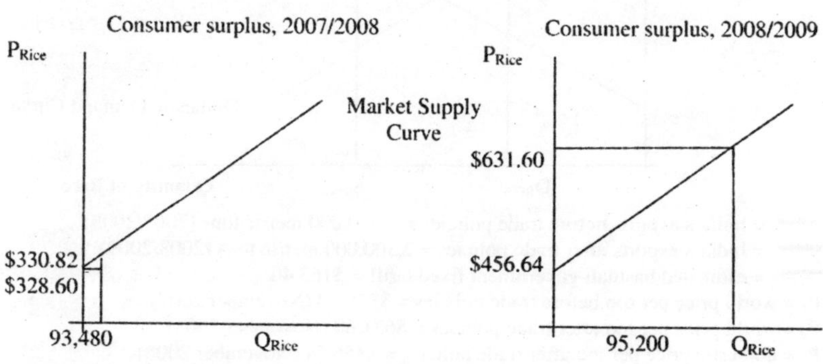

Figure 5

figures were used to obtain annual estimates. In November 2007, consumer surplus was calculated at a negative $103.7 million because the domestic price per ton was slightly below the international market price per ton. In reality, transportation costs would have eliminated this discrepancy. In November 2008, consumer surplus was calculated at $8.33 trillion. This represents a gain in consumer surplus of $8.23 trillion year over year.

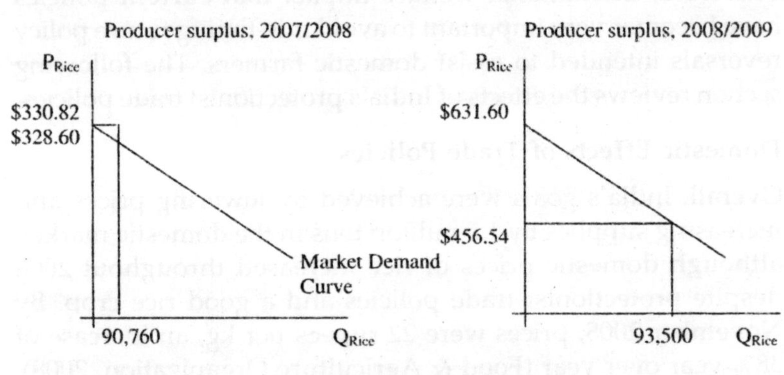

Figure 6

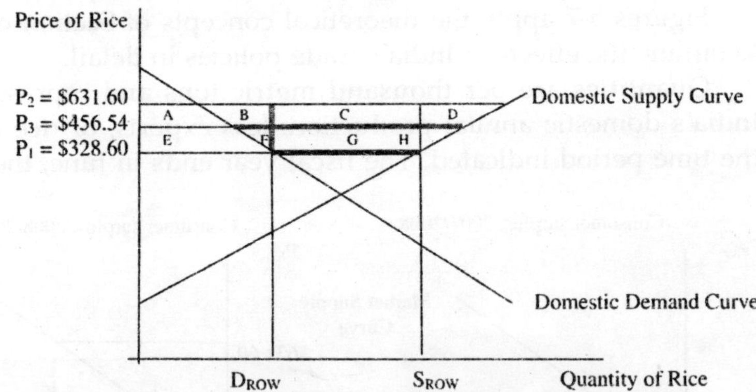

= India's exports before trade policies = 2,950,000 metric tons (2007/2008)
= India's exports after trade policies = 2,300,000 metric tons (2008/2009)
= estimated basmati government fixed tariff = $163.40

P_1 = world price per ton before trade policies = $328.60 (November 2007)
P_2 = world price per ton after trade policies = $631.60 (November 2008)
P_3 = domestic price per ton after trade policies = $456.54 (November 2008)

Data source for Figures 5-7 (USDA, 2008)

Figure 7

Quantities are per thousand metric tons and represent India's domestic annual consumption of rice for the time period indicated. The fiscal year ends in June; these figures were used to obtain annual estimates. In November 2007, producer surplus was calculated at $101 million because the domestic price per ton was slightly below the international market price per ton. In reality, transportation costs would have eliminated this discrepancy. In November 2008, producer surplus was calculated at negative $8.18 trillion. This represents a loss in producer surplus of $8.08 trillion year over year.

Year over year November prices were used to mitigate price effects caused by market over-reaction and speculation immediately after the trade policy announcements. Prices are blended between basmati and non-basmati rice, so P_3 plus the tariff rate will not equal P_2 as the theory suggests. The exchange rate from the first day of the applicable month was used to calculate USD price per ton; these were obtained from the Reserve Bank of India. Prices are not adjusted for inflation, since year over year inflation increases were nominal, and are per metric ton. In addition, the effect of minimum export prices was not calculated. While this certainly had an impact, the data necessary to make a relevant evaluation was not available.

To summarize the effects of protectionist trade policies, India's exports decreased by 650,000 metric tons despite an increase in world demand from 428 million metric tons to 432 million metric tons. Consumer surplus (E) increased by $8.23 trillion. Producer surplus (E + F + G + H) decreased by $8.08 trillion. Amortizing the annual exported basmati rice average of 1.2 million tons over a seven month period, government revenue (C + G) increased by $114.4 million. When adding all gains and losses, national welfare increased by $260 million.

Overall, the policies appear to have been successful in increasing national welfare, although not to the extent that theory would suggest. Although the consumer gain and producer loss appear to cancel each other out, producers were disproportionately affected given their smaller numbers. Assuming 40% of India's labor force is in rice production, this equates to a $27.80 loss per producer compared to a $7.17 gain per consumer. However, this calculation does not take into account the high levels of government support that producers received, including debt reduction and agricultural input subsidies.

The policy actions seem to have limited the full transmission of world price increases to the domestic market, but domestic prices lower than the original world price did not result as the theory would suggest. This could be due to minimum export pricing skewing the price upwards or monopoly power reducing the intended effect of export restrictions, as outlined in Section Two. Since 80% of basmati rice production is exported and very little consumed domestically, the greater domestic price reduction resulting from export tariffs for this single commodity would have had less of an effect on consumer welfare than export restrictions on non-basmati rice and could have caused some price distortion in the analysis (i.e., domestic prices would have trended higher if only non-basmati prices were analyzed). Unfortunately, prices were not broken out by rice variety, so this analysis could not be done. Although basmati prices are higher than non-basmati rice prices, any effect would be small since basmati consists of only 1% of total rice production.

Other factors could contribute to an increase in domestic prices. India typically experiences an average economic growth of 9%, although this slowed in 2008: inflation and the international credit crisis negatively affected demand. The rupee depreciated over 20% in 2008 (Coface, 2009), which would have helped to make rice exports competitive in the world market, had they not been banned. Inflation hit an all-time high of 7.33% in April, but expansionary monetary policy (i.e., interest rate cuts) and the fall in commodity prices slowed this to 3.03% in February. Increasing inflation was caused by high energy and commodity prices (Goyal, 2009). Slowing growth and inflation will negatively impact prices. Currency depreciation will make imports more expensive, which could transfer domestic purchases from higher priced imported grains to domestically produced rice, further reducing supply and increasing prices.

Caveats

An underlying assumption is that rice is a homogenous good that is perfectly substitutable. This assumption does not hold in reality. Unlike other bulk commodities, the international rice market is segmented into a large number of varieties and qualities which are not easily substitutable because of strong consumer preferences. India's higher grade varieties are usually exported, with the domestic market absorbing medium and low grades (Food & Agriculture Organization of the United Nations, 2003). Basmati, a long grain rice known for its favorable fragrance, is grown exclusively in India and Pakistan. These two countries have partnered to gain geographical indication, which will prevent other countries from claiming the right to label or patent their rice as basmati (Kannan, 2008).

While the partial equilibrium approach is useful for isolating the effects of trade policy on national welfare, it assumes that the rice sector has little impact on other sectors in the economy and ignores the effects occurring to other industries as a result of the policy actions (Suranovic, 2007). India's decision to restrict rice exports was in response to increasing world prices for wheat, a major food consumption and import item. High food prices are expected to continue in the medium run as biofuels production increases in response to policies aimed at reducing carbon dioxide emissions and achieving energy security. Although rice typically is not used for biofuels production, wheat is; as grain is diverted for biofuels production and subsequently rises in price, rice consumption will increase. This substitution may present strong trade-offs between energy and food security objectives (Christiaensen, 2008). While a general equilibrium approach would be better suited to analyze these effects, it is outside the scope of this paper.

CONCLUSION

India is a major producer and exporter of rice, a staple commodity vital to the food security and welfare of over half the world's population. Since it consumes 95% of the rice it produces, rice prices are an integral part of national welfare to both consumers and producers, forcing the Indian government to face competing concerns when implementing policies.

The protectionist trade policy actions undertaken in 2008 resulted in an estimated $260 million increase to national welfare. Consumers benefited from lower prices and the loss to producers was offset by government aid, including debt reduction. While its policies appeared to limit the transmission of higher world prices to Indian consumers, India's monopoly power in the production of rice could have limited the full effect of the price decrease. In this regard, export tariffs for all varieties of rice would have been more beneficial in lowering prices and increasing domestic supply than export restrictions.

In reality, the implementation of protectionist trade policies brings other difficulties since world welfare is reduced at the expense of increased national welfare. Trading partners will oppose these policies and look for ways to mitigate their welfare decline or retaliate with protectionist measures of their own. Once India banned all non-basmati rice exports, other large exporting countries followed, including Thailand and Indonesia. While these governments could buy rice supplies and flood their domestic markets, decreasing domestic prices and improving consumer welfare, the impact on the thinly traded rice market was dramatic as world prices rose sharply. Since India imports very little rice, its consumers are not affected by world prices as are those from large importing countries like Indonesia, Iran, and Iraq. Price volatility and shortages in foreign countries from export restrictions led to serious beggar-thy-neighbor effects.

In the long run, export restrictions could have significant consequences for India and rice producers. A limited impact on domestic prices and a negative earnings effect for farmers could encourage smuggling and hoarding, exacerbating the issue. Importing countries could move to self-sufficiency or alternatives to rice, decreasing trade opportunities, growth, and efficiency (Christiaensen, 2008). India's production-oriented aid measures could become fiscally impossible to sustain. Public sector debt is very high, which undermines capital investment through heavy debt service burdens (Coface, 2009). Meeting future rice demand will be a challenge, given the increasing competition for land and water and environmental degradation. While protectionist trade policies have proved beneficial to India in the short run, the effect is not sustainable.

NOTE

1. Export restrictions can result in increased government revenue through quota auctions, but the policy scope reviewed is India's complete ban on non-basmati rice exports.

REFERENCES

Chandrashekhar, G. (2008, 02 12), *Confusion over rice export ban notification.* Retrieved from The Hindu Business Daily: *http://www.blonnet.com/2008/02/13/stories/2008021350471300.htm*

Childs, N. (2009), *Rice Outlook, February.* Washington, D.C.: USDA.

Christiaensen, M. B. (2008), *Rising Food Prices in East Asia: Challenges and Policy Options.* Brussels: World Bank.

CIA. (2009, February 24), *CIA World Factbook.* Retrieved from CIA: *https://www.cia.gov/library/publications/the-world-factbook/geos/in.html*

Coface (2009), *Risk Assessment: India.* Retrieved from *http://www.trading-safely.com/sitecwp/ceen.nsf/vwCRA/96AD8A205EECC63DC125720A0045B4FD?*OpenDocument

Food & Agriculture Organization (2008), *Crop Prospects & Food Situation, December.* Rome: FAO.

Food & Agriculture Organization (2009), *Crop Prospects & Food Situation, February.* Rome: FAO.

Food & Agriculture Organization of the United Nations (2003), *Sustainable Rice Production for Food Security.* Rome: FAO.

Goyal, K. (2009, March 5), *India's Inflation Slows to 3.03%, Lowest Since 2002* . Retrieved from Bloomberg: *http://www.bloomberg.com/apps/news?pid=20601091&sid=aVXvlAV2CFpY&refer=india*

Kulkarni, shouldn't to be included in the bibliography reference word initial graphs?

Kannan, S. (2008, February 15), *India and Pakistan link to protect Basmati.* Retrieved from BBC: *http://news.bbc.co.uk/2/hi/business/7246900.stm*

Modi, A. (2008, September 10), *FCI procurement of rice, wheat touches 50 MT.* Retrieved from Business Standard: *http://www.businessstandard.com/india/news/fci-procurementrice-wheat-touches-50-mt/333894/*

Mortished, C. (2008, March 7), *Already we have riots, hoarding, panic: the sign of things to come?* Retrieved from Times Online: *http://www.timesonline.co.uk/tol/news/environment/article3500975.ece*

Oryza. (2008, April 30), *India Imposes Export Tax On Basmati Rice.* Retrieved from Oryza: *http://oryza.com/Basmati-Rice-Industry/India-Basmati/8419.html*

Oryza. (2008, May 1), *India: Export Tax Hampering Basmati Rice Shipments.* Retrieved from Oryza: *http://oryza.com/Asia-Pacific/India-Market/8426.html*

Suranovic, S. (2007), *International Trade Theory and Policy.* Retrieved from Trade Policy Effects with Perfectly Competitive Markets: *http://internationalecon.com/Trade/Tch90/Tch90.php*

Timmons, H. (2008, February 29), *Indian Budget Aids Farmers with Big Rise in Social Outlay.* Retrieved from International Herald.

Tribune: *http://www.iht.com/articles/2008/02/29/business/rupee.php* USDA. (2008), *Grain: World Markets and Trade, December.* Washington, D.C.: USDA.

Yeh, Y. H. (1997), Export Quotas Vs. Export Tariffs. *Atlantic Economic Journal* , 207-212.

INDEX

B

C

N

O

R

S